Insights to Performance Excellence 2004

Also available from ASQ Quality Press:

From Baldrige to the Bottom Line: A Road Map for Organizational Change and Improvement
David W. Hutton

From Quality to Business Excellence: A Systems Approach to Management
Charles Cobb

The Executive Guide to Improvement and Change
G. Dennis Beecroft, Grace L. Duffy, John W. Moran

Quality into the 21st Century: Perspectives on Quality and Competitiveness for Sustained Performance
International Academy for Quality

Office Kaizen: Transforming Office Operations into a Strategic Competitive Advantage
William Lareau

Creating a Customer-Centered Culture: Leadership in Quality, Innovation, and Speed
Robin L. Lawton

Developing New Services: Incorporating the Voice of the Customer into Strategic Service Development
Caroline Fisher and James Schutta

Customer Centered Six Sigma: Linking Customers, Process improvement, and Financial Results
Earl Naumann and Steven H. Hoisington

Principles and Practices of Organizational Performance Excellence
Thomas J. Cartin

The Change Agent's Guide to Radical Improvement
Ken Miller

The Change Agents' Handbook: A Survival Guide for Quality Improvement Champions
David W. Hutton

*To request a complimentary catalog of ASQ Quality Press publications, call 800-248-1946,
or visit our Web site at http://qualitypress.asq.org.*

Insights to Performance Excellence 2004

An Inside Look at the 2004
Baldrige Award Criteria

Mark L. Blazey

ASQ Quality Press

Milwaukee, Wisconsin

American Society for Quality, Quality Press, Milwaukee 53203
© 2004 by ASQ
All rights reserved. Published 2004
Printed in the United States of America

12 11 10 09 08 07 06 05 04 03   5 4 3 2 1

ISBN 0-87389-623-8

Publisher: William A. Tony
Acquisitions Editor: Annemieke Hytinen
Project Editor: Paul O'Mara
Production Administrator: Randall Benson
Special Marketing Representative: David Luth

ASQ Mission: The American Society for Quality advances individual, organizational, and community excellence worldwide through learning, quality improvement, and knowledge exchange.

Microsoft is a registered trademark of Microsoft Corporation.

Attention bookstores, wholesalers, schools, and corporations: ASQ Quality Press books, videotapes, audiotapes, and software are available at quantity discounts with bulk purchases for business, educational, or instructional use.
For information, please contact ASQ Quality Press at 800-248-1946, or write to ASQ Quality Press, P.O. Box 3005, Milwaukee, WI 53201-3005.

To place orders or to request a free copy of the ASQ Quality Press Publications Catalog, including ASQ membership information, call 800-248-1946. Visit our Web site at http://www.asq.org or http://qualitypress.asq.org.

  Printed on acid-free paper

 Quality Press
600 N. Plankinton Avenue
Milwaukee, Wisconsin 53203
Call toll free 800-248-1946
Fax 414-272-1734
www.asq.org
http://qualitypress.asq.org
http://standardsgroup.asq.org
E-mail: authors@asq.org

This book is dedicated to the memory of my father, Everett,
who taught me the value of continuous improvement,
and to my family members, who provide support for the
continuous search for excellence: my mother, Ann L. Blazey,
who at 76 continues to strive to improve
everything she does; my brothers Scott, Brian, and Brent;
my children Elizabeth and Mark; and most of all,
my lifelong partner and loving wife Karen.

Contents

Foreword ix

Acknowledgments xiii

Preface xiv

Introduction xv

Insights to Performance Excellence 1

Organizational Profile **83**
    P.1 Organizational Description 84
    P.2 Organizational Challenges 86

Category 1—Leadership **89**
    1.1 Organizational Leadership 90
    1.2 Social Responsibility 100

Category 2—Strategic Planning **107**
    2.1 Strategy Development 109
    2.2 Strategy Deployment 118

Category 3—Customer and Market Focus **127**
    3.1 Customer and Market Knowledge 128
    3.2 Customer Relationships and Satisfaction 135

Category 4—Measurement, Analysis, and Knowledge Management **145**
    4.1 Measurement and Analysis of Organizational Performance ... 146
    4.2 Information and Knowledge Management 155

Category 5—Human Resource Focus **163**
    5.1 Work Systems 164
    5.2 Employee Learning and Motivation 174
    5.3 Employee Well-Being and Satisfaction 183

Category 6—Process Management **191**
    6.1 Value Creation Processes 192
    6.2 Support Processes 203

Category 7—Business Results **209**
    7.1 Customer-Focused Results 211
    7.2 Product and Service Results 215
    7.3 Financial and Market Results 219
    7.4 Human Resource Results 223
    7.5 Organizational Effectiveness Results 228
    7.6 Governance and Social Responsibility Results 232

Tips on Preparing a Baldrige Award Application   237

Scoring System   247

Clarifying the Requirements for Basic-, Overall-, and Multiple-Level Scoring   255

Self-Assessments of Organizations and Management Systems   285

The Site Visit   303

Glossary   323

Clarifying Confusing Terms   331

Appendix A: A Global View of Quality   335

Appendix B: Baldrige or ISO 9001   337

Appendix C: Baldrige or Shingo Prize   341

Appendix D: Baldrige or JCAHO   345

Appendix E: Alignment of Baldrige With Six Sigma, Lean Thinking,
*   and Balanced Scorecard*   349

About the Author   357

Index   359

CD-ROM Files

Baldrige Winners and State Award Contact Information

2004 Business

   2004 Business Basic-Overall-Multiple Requirements

   2004 Baldrige Criteria Word and PDF Versions

   Baldrige Application Templates

   ISO 9001 and Baldrige Comparison

   Shingo Prize and Baldrige Comparison

2004 Education

   2004 Education Criteria Word and PDF Versions

   Condensed Insights to Education Excellence

   Middle States Accreditation and Baldrige Comparison

2004 Health Care

   2004 Health Care Criteria Word and PDF Versions

   Condensed Insights to Health Care Excellence

   Baldrige and JCAHO Comparison

Foreword

LEADERSHIP CHALLENGES

A lot of time and energy is put into answering the question, "What drives success in business?" The answer is both deceptively simple and hauntingly complex. It's as much a function of the people and the value the business brings to the marketplace as it is the approaches chosen to deliver them. Success in business is a risky, complex, and challenging human endeavor. It takes more than being able to articulate the lessons learned by the successful—the trick is being able to help others incorporate and leverage those lessons in their own approaches, whether in the private sector, education, healthcare, or government. Dr. Mark Blazey is the leading expert in the application of the Baldrige Criteria to help organizations improve. He provided extremely valuable insight—through his writings and personal consulting—to help us at Xerox develop world-class management systems that led to Xerox Business Services being recognized as a 1997 recipient of the Baldrige Award. This book provides new and valuable insights to help leaders make the changes needed to achieve the highest levels of performance excellence.

Traditionally, success in business has involved the pursuit of functional excellence in fields such as sales (IBM), marketing (Coca-Cola), manufacturing (Ford), capital formation (Morgan Stanley), and the improvement of the human condition (Pearl River School District in New York, School District 15 in Illinois, Baptist Hospital in Florida among others). As important as functional supremacy is today, it is not enough. It is how all the elements of an organization come together and provide value in the marketplace—to customers and other stakeholders—that is the key ingredient to success. Success requires balancing many things at once. It involves understanding how the system works together. What system is used to run the most successful businesses? Can all the executives in the business articulate what that system is? Can each one draw a picture of that system on a single sheet of paper and explain it to 10-year-old children? I once had the CEO of one of the largest transportation companies in North America ask his 35 direct reports to draw a picture of the system they used to run the business on one sheet of paper. He waited five minutes and collected the drawings. As he thumbed through the papers he kept shaking his head in disbelief. No two pieces of paper portrayed the same picture. Think of the message that sends. Here are the 35 senior people in a multibillion-dollar business and they do not have a uniform view of how the business is run or what is most important. This may account, in part, for their poor performance. These executives do not know whether or how they will be able to keep the promises they make to their customers, employees, stockholders, and the communities in which they work and live. Think of the powerful message that could be sent if they all focused on the same themes, pursued the same vision and objectives, and had confidence that the things they asked them to do were indeed the right things for the business to succeed.

Organizations are formed to accomplish a set of objectives to serve people. It's that simple. Whether the organization is for-profit or not-for-profit, small or large, public or private, manufacturing, service, government, healthcare, or education, each must deliver value to stay in business. The main thing that changes from one successful organization to another is the way the score is tallied. Whether the primary indicator of success is profit, children educated, patients cured, miles of roads paved, or the number of overnight packages delivered on time, to be successful each organization must understand and meet the requirements of its many different customers.

Like it or not, to be successful, organizations must identify and serve customers—although they may choose to call them many other names, such as clients, students, patients, families, constituents, communities, voters, rate-payers, passengers, or shoppers, to name a few. The nomenclature changes depending upon the language of the business; but at the end of the day it's the "customers" who make decisions about whether they are going to do business with us. If we can keep the customers we have and attract new ones, it is a sign that the organization is going to thrive. Clearly, without customers, organizations cannot survive.

Strange as it may seem, there are organizations that have not put "delighting customers" at the top of their priority list (or anywhere on the list). Delighted customers are five times more likely to buy from you or recommend you to others than those who are simply satisfied. On the other hand, 80 percent of dissatisfied customers are likely to walk away and not even tell you they were dissatisfied. Moreover, dissatisfied customers are likely to tell at least 20 of their friends, while only five will hear of the startling news associated with "delight." Worst of all, it costs 10 times as much to regain a lost customer as it does to retain a current one. With the large number of Internet-based consumer buying sites in place today, the dissatisfied customer can easily tell thousands about their bad experiences. In the 21st century, it is a more demanding customer-driven economy.

If organizations intend to delight customers, leaders and employees must understand the requirements and expectations of their customers. More than ever before, we need to personalize the customer relationship and build loyalty. Horst Schulze, the former CEO of Ritz-Carlton, a hotel chain that forever altered the nature of customer service, points this out very well when he says, "Customers need a reason to be loyal; give them a reason." While CEO, Schulze took the time to be personally involved in a two-day orientation with all of the staff at the opening of each new Ritz-Carlton hotel. Here was the chief executive making sure that everyone in the business understood the objectives and keys to success. His penetrating but simple questions to staff members up and down the line would focus on who are your customers; what is important to these customers; and how do we make these four or five things that are important to our customers better than anywhere else. To illustrate a typical Ritz-Carlton experience, if a guest has a preference for a hard pillow, a note is entered into the customer database and wherever the guest goes in the Ritz-Carlton chain a hard pillow will be on the bed. In another instance, while cleaning the room in the morning, a housekeeper found a small teddy bear on the floor among the child's dirty clothes. Upon return, the child found the teddy bear sitting at a small table with the Ritz Lion having tea. Now, what do you think went through the minds of the parents and the child?!

To deliver that level of performance consistently, the Ritz-Carlton—or any organization—must put in place a set of processes that focus on customer delight and are capable of delivering consistent results. Again, let's look at the Ritz-Carlton. The person who is recognized as the best at doing a task is the one who documents the process. For three weeks, a new employee follows in the footsteps of an experienced, high-performing employee who volunteers to be a teacher–mentor. At the end of the training period the new person is tested. Passing means the employee begins to work independently; failing means more training and testing. On the job, specific, quantifiable performance goals are set. Goals and timing for "improvement" are then established and progress is reported quarterly. Processes are aimed at things that customers consider important; employees are focused on delivering them at high levels of achievement; and they are constantly engaged in an effort to do it better. This creates an environment of true "continuous improvement." The environment of customer-focused continuous improvement keeps customers coming back and bragging about their delightful experience to their friends. Horst Schulze has figured out that the friends and acquaintances of current customers are the very people that the Ritz is trying to attract.

When key work processes are capable of producing desired results consistently, the outcomes are predictable. That is why a "process" orientation is important. Too many people in non-manufacturing disciplines, such as sales, education, or healthcare, believe that using process discipline to carry out work is an outdated idea and does not apply in their fast-paced world. The recent winners of the Baldrige Award demonstrate clearly that process orientation is critical for success in manufacturing as well as non-manufacturing (such as healthcare and public school systems) and large and small businesses. After talking with hundreds of leaders who are concerned with the level of performance in their organizations, it appears that the fear of discipline and accountability, which a process orientation brings to the workplace, may be one of the real obstacles to change.

Unfortunately, even when organizations begin to execute processes well, their leaders quickly find that excellence and optimum performance continue to elude them. Organizations can fail to satisfy customers when key work processes work as designed—if the design was not tied to customer requirements. "Internally focused" processes have often been driven by the desire to do things more efficiently and effectively from the company's point of view—without regard for customer concerns. The resulting organizational arrogance—the belief that we know better than the customer—is almost certain to bring about customer dissatisfaction and ultimately customer revolt, causing customers to demand change or leave. To be successful, organizations must consistently understand and precisely execute those processes that deliver the four or five characteristics that are critical to customer delight—the vital few. The winners in the highly competitive environment in which we live are the organizations that understand these drivers of customer delight and then design and execute work processes aimed at delivering them better than anyone else.

Many business leaders find it difficult to determine what customers want, fend off the competition, and satisfy workers, all within a budget. That is where the development and execution of "strategy" come into play. Strategy development demands a thorough understanding of the direction in which customers are moving, the direction in which the competition is moving, the direction in which the market is moving; coupling that information with the capabilities and desired direction of the business; and then identifying the few things that are critical to the future success of the business.

Knowing how well all of these factors are working involves having a "dashboard for the business." No one would think of driving a car on a trip or getting on an airplane if the instrument panel were missing. Yet business leaders often make critical decisions with either one-dimensional instruments (financial) or instruments that provide insufficient information about the state of the business (factors measured because they are available but not necessarily important). Relying only on financial instruments is com-

parable to driving the car by only looking in the rearview mirror. The good news is the picture is pretty clear. The bad news is that you will crash sooner or later since you cannot make adjustments in anticipation of problems. Of course, leaders in every organization must be aware of the organization's financial health. That is not enough information, however, to lead the organization effectively through difficult and challenging times. The organization's leaders must also know what is important to customers, how well it is delivering on those things that are important, the reaction of its customers, the direction in which their expectations are moving, and the capability and capacity of its work processes and delivery systems. With this knowledge, leaders are in a much better position to make better decisions about the actions needed to be successful, bring value to the marketplace, and respond to changing circumstances and new opportunities.

While customer focus, strategic planning, and data to support effective decision making are critical components of the successful organization, these factors combined are still not sufficient to ensure success. Every organization must acquire good people, train them, motivate them, and retain them. Today, to be successful, organizations must attract and develop employees who understand that the customers are the most import aspect of the business. Employees must have the competencies to use facts and information to make good decisions, and to continue learning and contribute to their own growth and development. In a world where product and service superiority lasts only a short time, it is the capabilities of the people that will be the source of ongoing excellence and differentiation. No longer are companies simply looking for good employees. Today, more is needed and businesses are looking for employees who are good business people—empowered people making the decisions that move a business forward.

The ability to make this system come together and work harmoniously is the responsibility of leadership. Basically, leadership has two functions:

1. To set the direction very clearly, based on a strategy that brings value to the marketplace; and
2. To establish the environment in which that direction is carried out.

Some leaders find it difficult to establish and articulate a clear vision and role model a set of values. Without a clear direction, the people in an organization are forced to substitute their own ideas about the "right direction." When many do this, the organization finds itself pulled in different directions. Leaders cannot expect people to know what to do if they have not established and continuously reinforced the norms of desired behavior. Leadership is very much about setting and leading by example—role modeling what the company stands for and living the change expected of all.

The best organizations in every sector have demonstrated that all parts of the system must be effectively integrated to optimize performance. It is not possible to achieve excellence by only doing the things that are easy and ignoring the rest of them. The concept of smoothly integrating all the facets of a business into a system is easy to understand but very difficult to execute.

We live in a rapidly changing world where global issues affect our lives in many ways, excellence is expected, and the customer is king. There is enormous opportunity for those prepared to work both hard and smart in the pursuit of excellence. The approaches used to achieve success have proven effective in all types of organizations: sustained results occur from an intense focus on customers; the consistent fulfillment of customer expectations derives from capable work processes that are aligned with a market-driven strategy. The performance of the business is monitored through the continuous acquisition and analysis of information (the dashboard). None of this works without people who are motivated and skilled to consistently execute their work processes. Finally, it is all tied together with leaders whose job it is to set the direction, create the environment for continuous improvement and learning, and lead by role modeling desired behaviors and norms—living the values they expect in others.

With his best-selling series and his personal involvement, Dr. Mark Blazey has been helping leaders and organizations of all types and in all sectors achieve success and develop enviable performance levels. He has helped them develop practical approaches for continuous improvement that serve as the cornerstone for leadership and organizational success. Mark Blazey's personal insight and clear explanations help make complex Baldrige concepts much simpler. That is what makes this book a best-seller. *Insights to Performance Excellence* is a book for beginners as well as experts in the field of organizational development and operational excellence. The book delivers the lessons, provides the insights, and sets the framework for a successful journey to performance excellence.

John Lawrence
Retired Vice President of Quality
Xerox Business Services
1997 Baldrige Winner

Acknowledgments

arry Hertz, Curt Reimann, Barry Diamond-stone, and the dedicated staff of the Malcolm Baldrige National Quality Award office have provided long-standing support and guidance in promoting quality excellence. Karen Davison, John Lawrence, and Paul Grizzell provided substantial editorial and analytical assistance. In addition, John and Paul, respectively, contributed to analyses comparing Baldrige with ISO 9001 and JCAHO requirements.

Several others have helped shape my thinking about performance excellence and refine this book, including Joe Sener, Jeff Calhoun, Kathy Bonner, Rob Marchelonis, Harry Zechman, Olga Striltschuk, Mary Gamble, Angie Germain, Orland Pitts, Ed Hare, April Mitchell, George Bureau, Debra Danziger-Barron, Jim Shipley, Tom Kubiak, Rich Harris, Ginger Baker-Betz, Patricia Billings, Wendy Brennan, Gerald Brown, Beverly Centini, Sheryl Billups, Joe Kilbride, Linda Vincent, Elizabeth Hale, Joan Wills, Steve Hoisington, Liz Menzer, Bundy Trinz, John Gustafson, Brian Lassiter, Jean Bronk, Gary Floss, Mike Reagan, Jack Evans, Arnie Weimerskirch, Don Cates, Marty Mariner, Andy Downs, Jerry Holt, Bill MacLachlan, Doug Green, Paul Kuchuris, Bob Ewy, Jo-Ann Kratz, Sandra Cokley-Pederson, Gary Jones, Bill Smith, Mike Smith, Janice Weinman, Peggy Siegel, Paul Schindler, Steve Uebbing, Lynn Erdle, Jack Evans, Brian Dunster, Robert Frisina, James Miller, Jack Smith, Fred Smith, Dennis Nystrom, Rich Rose, Kathy Malcolm, Harold Stafford, Roberta Early, Judd Prozeller, Dan Thorpe, Ed Bergin, Linda Watson, Nancy Gurney, Diane Rivers, Michael Chapman, Linda Janczak, Judith Cherrington, Laurie Emerson, Patricia Stevens, Charlie Blass, Kelly Gilhooly, Pat Webb, Annemieke Hytinen, and George Raemore. I also greatly appreciate the typing and editorial assistance, background research, and proofreading of Jessica Norris.

The chapter on site visits, the Criteria model and integrated management systems analysis, the management and performance excellence surveys, the performance standard for leadership, the sections concerning the potential adverse consequences of not doing what the Criteria require, and the application preparation files are used with permission of Quantum Performance Group, Inc. The analysis of Six Sigma, Lean and Balanced Scorecard, and JCAHO is used with permission of Paul Grizzell of Performance Leadership Group. The Core Values, Criteria, selected glossary terms, award winners, and background information in this book are drawn from information in the public domain supplied by the Malcolm Baldrige National Quality Award program. Kevin Hendricks and Vinod Singhal provided research results that were used in this book from their extensive study of financial performance. Data from the Economic Evaluation of the Baldrige National Quality Program by Albert Link and John Scott, prepared for NIST in October 2001, and data from Foundation for the Malcolm Baldrige National Quality Award regarding the perception of chief executive officers from more than 300 U.S. organizations are also included in this book.

Mark Blazey

Preface

A substantial portion of my professional life has been spent helping people understand the power and benefits of this integrated management system and become examiners for many performance excellence awards. These people come from all types of organizations and from all levels within those organizations. Participants include CEOs, corporate quality directors, state organization chiefs, small-business owners, heads of hospitals, teachers, professors, medical doctors, and school superintendents, to name a few.

This book was originally developed for them. It was used as a teaching text to guide their decisions and deliberations as they provided feedback to organizations that documented their continuous improvement efforts using Baldrige Award–type management systems. Many examiners who used this text asked me to publish it in a stand-alone format. They wanted to use it to help their own organizations, customers, and suppliers guide and assess their continuous improvement efforts.

These two groups of readers—examiners of quality systems and leaders of high-performing organizations—can gain a competitive edge by understanding not only the parts of a high-performance management system, but how these parts connect and align. My goal for this book is that readers will understand fully what each area of the quality system means for organizations and find the synergy within the seven major parts of the system: leadership; strategic planning; customer and market focus; measurement, analysis, and knowledge management; human resource focus; process management; and business results.

Organization leaders have reported that this book has been valuable as a step-by-step approach to help identify and put in place properly-focused continuous improvement systems. As progress is made, improvement efforts in one area will lead to improvements in other areas. This process is similar to experiences we have all encountered as we carry out home improvement: improve one area, and many other areas needing improvement become apparent. This book will help identify areas that need immediate improvement as well as areas that are less urgent but, nevertheless, vitally linked to organizational and operational excellence.

I am continually looking for feedback about this book and suggestions about how it can be improved. Please contact me via e-mail at authors@asq.org.

Introduction

The Malcolm Baldrige National Quality Award (MBNQA) 2004 Criteria for Performance Excellence and scoring guidelines are powerful assessment instruments that help leaders identify organizational strengths and key opportunities for improvement. The primary task of leaders is then to use the information to achieve higher levels of performance.

Building an effective management system capable of driving performance improvement is an ongoing challenge because of the intricate web of complex relationships among management, labor, customers, stakeholders, partners, and suppliers. The best organizations have a management system that improves its work processes continually. They measure every key facet of business activity and closely monitor organizational performance. Leaders of these organizations set high expectations, value employees and their input, communicate clear directions, and align the work of everyone to optimize performance and achieve organizational goals.

Unfortunately, because of the complexity of modern management systems, the criteria used to examine them are also complex and difficult to understand. *Insights to Performance Excellence 2004* helps performance-excellence examiners and organization-improvement practitioners to clearly understand the 2004 Baldrige performance excellence criteria and the linkages and relationships among the items.

Six types of information are provided in this book for each of the items in categories 1 through 6:

1. The actual language of each item, including notes (presented in the shadow box). [Author's note: The information in these shadow boxes presents the official Baldrige Criteria and serves as the only basis for the examination. The other five types of information presented in this book for each Item (elements 2 through 6) provide the author's interpretation of the official Criteria requirements and should not be used as a basis for establishing additional requirements during an examination or performance review.]

2. A plain English explanation of the requirements of each Item with some suggestions about the rationale for the Item and ways to meet key requirements.

3. A summary of the requirements of each Item in flowchart form. The flowcharts capture the essence of each item and isolate the requirements of each item to help organizations focus on the key points the item is assessing. Note that most boxes in the flowcharts contain an item reference in brackets [ ]. This indicates that the criteria require the action. If there is no item reference in brackets, it means the action is suggested but not required. Occasionally a reference to "[scoring guidelines]" is included in a box. This means that the authority for the requirement comes from the scoring guidelines.

4. The key linkages between each item and the other items. The major or primary linkages are designated using a solid arrow (——▶). The secondary linkages are designated using a dashed arrow (- - -▶).

5. An explanation of some potential adverse consequences that an organization might face if it fails to implement processes required by each Item. (Examiners may find this analysis useful as they prepare relevant feedback concerning opportunities for improvement. However, these generic statements should be customized—based on key factors, core values, or specific circumstances facing the organization being reviewed—before using them to develop feedback comments supporting opportunities for improvements in Categories 1 through 6.)

6. Examples of effective practices that some organizations have developed and followed consistent with the requirements of the Item. These samples present some ideas about how to meet requirements. (Remember, examiners should not convert these sample effective practices into new requirements for organizations they are examining.)

Changes to this 2004 edition include:

- New information from the Baldrige 2004 Criteria for Performance Excellence to help leaders focus on priority opportunities for improvement and better understand the role they must play in refining their management systems and processes.

- The CD-ROM included with this book has been significantly expanded to include analyses of the health care and education criteria. This precludes the need to buy all three books, since all of the most critical information regarding linkages and criteria requirements are included in this volume with its accompanying CD-ROM.

- A review guideline for examiners that highlights processes required at the basic,

overall, and multiple levels of scoring based on the 2004 scoring guidelines.

- Site visit questions have been modified and linked to each Baldrige Area and Subarea to Address.

- A new analysis comparing the Baldrige Criteria with criteria for ISO 9001, JCAHO, and the Shingo Prize.

- Additional definitions to enhance understanding of key words in the Criteria and Scoring Guidelines

Reading *Insights to Performance Excellence 2004* will strengthen your understanding of the Criteria and provide insight on analyzing your organization, improving performance, and applying for the award.

Insights to Performance Excellence

This section provides information for leaders who are transforming their organizations to achieve performance excellence. This section:

- Presents a business case for using the Baldrige Criteria to improve organizational performance

- Describes the core values that drive organizational change to high levels of performance and underlie the Baldrige Criteria

- Provides practical insights and lessons learned—ideas on transition strategies to put high-performance systems in place and promote organizational learning

This section emphasizes themes driven by the 2004 Criteria and Core Values. It also includes suggestions about how to start down the path to systematic organizational improvement, as well as lessons learned from those who chose paths that led nowhere or proved futile despite their best efforts.

BALDRIGE BEGINNINGS AND ONGOING REFINEMENT

During the 1980s, many U.S. businesses suffered losses in the marketplace due to stronger international competition. We found that for nearly 30 years, Japanese business leaders were able to improve the performance of their organizations by following the teachings of W. Edwards Deming and striving to meet the requirements of the Deming Prize Criteria. The story of the Japanese recovery from the devastation of World War II to a dominant global economic power was documented in the CBS documentary *If Japan Can, Why Can't We?*

The documentary explained the strong, positive impact that the prize had on the desire and ability of Japanese business leaders to improve organizational performance. Moreover, it served as a catalyst for the creation of a national quality award for the United States. It was hoped that a similar award would help U.S. business leaders focus on the systems and processes that would lead them to recovery much as the Deming Prize Criteria helped the Japanese.

After nearly five years of work, in 1987, the U.S. Congress created the national quality award named in honor of the secretary of the Department of Commerce, Malcolm Baldrige, who had died a short time earlier in a rodeo accident. The MBNQA or "Baldrige Award" had one key purpose: to help U.S. businesses improve their competitiveness in the global marketplace.

After much debate and discussion, the creators of the award criteria—led by Dr. Curt Reimann of the U.S. Department of Commerce—agreed that the award criteria should not be based on theories of how organizations ought to conduct business in order to win. They had seen too many instances where organizations followed the many piecemeal theories of the management gurus that led nowhere.

On the other hand, some argued that the United States should simply adopt the Deming Prize Criteria, which had been in place for 35 years. After monitoring the performance of earlier Deming Prize winners, however, it became apparent that the practices that enabled many of them to achieve high performance in the past were no longer sufficient to ensure high performance in the present and future. Changes in the marketplace, customer requirements, competition, worker skills and availability, and technology (to name a few) have forced organizations to change the way they manage their business in order to continue to succeed and win.

The designers of the U.S. national award wanted to avoid problems inherent in both approaches.

Accordingly, the principle was adopted that the Criteria must be continually refreshed and be based on the verified management practices of the world's best-performing companies that enabled them to achieve such high levels of performance, productivity, customer satisfaction, and market dominance.

To ensure that the Baldrige Criteria for Performance Excellence continue to be relevant, the U.S. Department of Commerce, National Institute of Standards and Technology (NIST) reviews the drivers of high performance each year. Based on these analyses, the Criteria for the Malcolm Baldrige National Quality Award are validated and refined.

In spite of this ongoing renewal, some critics of the Baldrige Criteria argue that the Baldrige standards are "outdated" and "passé." These critics often ask, "If the Baldrige Criteria are updated each year, why don't they reflect the newest management techniques?" The critics, pointing to the rising success of e-commerce and the dot-coms, seem to prefer to employ unproven theories of what is needed to be successful in today's global market. None of these critics, however, have been able to offer any performance-based evidence to support their opinion. In fact, the collapse of thousands of badly managed dot-coms and other organizations seems to indicate that unproven theories and management fads do no more to build solid performance today than they did in prior decades.

The main reason why the Baldrige Criteria do not require the use of the latest management fads is because a management practice must be a proven driver of high performance before the practice is included as a requirement. Such "proofs" require strong evidence of widespread practice and related performance outcomes.

A new management practice might work well for one organization but not for another. Fact-based evidence must demonstrate that the practice leads to high performance in many types of organizations, including small and large, manufacturing and service, union and nonunion, and public and private.

Because it usually takes two or more years for a "promising practice" to prove its value, the Baldrige Criteria will lag behind the newest, unproven fads. However, the rigor of the Baldrige review is part of the value the Baldrige Criteria add to business excel-

lence. The Criteria help leaders sort out the fads from the proven techniques. The Baldrige Criteria reflect leading-edge, validated management practices essential to achieving optimum performance.

Finally, it is important to mention that the Baldrige Criteria were never intended to limit improvement, innovation, and creativity—in fact, the Criteria require those traits in many Areas to Address. Specifically, the Criteria require leaders to promote innovation throughout the organization [1.1a(2)] and in work and jobs [5.1a(1)]. The Criteria also require, in many areas, that the organization keep certain work processes current with changing business needs, including:

- Listening to customers [3.1a(3)]
- Building relationships with customers [3.2a(4)]
- Determining customer satisfaction [3.2b(4)]
- Performance measurement system [4.1a(3)]
- Data and information availability [4.2a(3)]
- Software and hardware systems [4.2a(3)]
- Value-creation processes [6.1a(6)
- Support processes [6.2a(6)]

The best leaders use the principles described by the Baldrige Criteria as the fundamental way they manage the organization, and then search for methods to refine and enhance their work systems to provide a little more competitive advantage. They experiment with new techniques and are not content to simply follow a "management cookbook." However, they install a solid management system first, then experiment and improve—not the other way around.

Many of these top leaders use the Baldrige principles and management systems to achieve high performance without any public announcements or fanfare. They have never applied for the award and do not intend to do so. They are content to achieve excellence and win in the business world, rather than compete for a prize.

Nearly all business leaders and managers who reject the value of the Criteria out of hand do not understand the principles they contain, even those who claim to have "tried Baldrige." The system that effectively drives top performance in organizations is complex. After all, if it was easy to achieve excellence, everyone would do it. The business landscape is littered with companies that never understood or failed to continue using the validated, leading-edge management practices defined by the Baldrige Criteria. This book is for those leaders who are willing and able to commit to becoming effective leaders and optimizing performance.

THE BUSINESS CASE FOR USING THE BALDRIGE PERFORMANCE EXCELLENCE CRITERIA

All leaders know that change is not easy. They will be asked and perhaps tempted to turn back many times. They may not even be aware of these temptations or of the backsliding that occurs when their peers and subordinates sense their commitment is wavering. Those leaders who are dedicated to achieving high performance appreciate examples of success from organizations that are ahead of them on the journey. These are organizations that have held the course despite nagging doubts, organizational turbulence, and attempts at sabotage.

The following section of the book:

- Summarizes perceptions and predictions about business trends and the value of the MBNQA, based on survey responses of chief executive officers from 308 major U.S. organizations. (This survey was conducted by the Foundation for the Malcolm Baldrige National Quality Award, April 1998.)

- Summarizes research on financial performance of approximately 400 firms that were recognized by local, state, or national awards for quality management practices. (Research results are reported with permission of Dr. Vinod R. Singhal. Research was conducted by Kevin B. Hendricks and Vinod R. Singhal.)

- Describes public- and private-sector organizations that have gained ground and made rapid strides forward on their journeys, having achieved recognition as winners of the MBNQA. It then identifies the core values that have guided these organizations to achieve high levels of performance excellence.

VALUE OF BALDRIGE CRITERIA AND AWARDS

In a report entitled "The Nation's CEOs Look to the Future," 308 CEOs from large, small, and several non-corporate organizations described what they believe lies ahead for business in the United States and the value of the Baldrige Criteria and Award. These trends relate in many ways to the 2004 Criteria and are considered as the Criteria are revised to reflect the current business environment and the most effective management practices for that environment.

The vast majority (67 percent to 79 percent) of the CEOs believe that the Baldrige Criteria and Awards are very or extremely valuable in stimulating improvements in quality and competitiveness in U.S. businesses. Given the trends and business environment they describe in the survey, and how they see U.S. businesses keeping pace, the Criteria provide a valuable competitive advantage.

MAJOR TRENDS

More than 70 percent of the CEOs reported the following trends as major directions that will be likely to affect the business environment significantly in the coming years:

- *Globalization.* This trend, identified as critical by 94 percent of respondents, has implications for all categories, but particularly Strategic Planning, where global competition and alliances must be included in planning, and for Customer and Market Focus, where building and maintaining customer relationships is critical.

- *Improving knowledge management.* This trend, identified as critical by 88 percent of respondents, means that knowledge acquisition management is and will continue to be a significant competitive advantage. How information and data are collected, analyzed, stored, retrieved, disseminated, and used to support decision making will be important to achieving high levels of performance in the future.

- *Cost and cycle-time reduction.* This trend, identified as critical by 79 percent of respondents, is particularly relevant to Process Management. Organizations that effectively manage key product and service design and delivery processes will have a competitive edge in the global marketplace.

- *Improving supply chains globally.* This trend, identified as critical by 78 percent of respondents, is a companion to the trend already described as globalization. As business is increasingly taking place on the global stage, supply chain management needs to improve— either with direct suppliers and partners or beyond to partnerships and alliances. These requirements are particularly important to Process Management.

- *Manufacturing at multiple locations in many countries.* This trend, identified as critical by 76 percent of respondents, again relates to globalization and also to improving supply chain management. To be successful at multiple-country manufacturing, one needs to use a systems approach involving all Categories, from Strategic Planning and Process Management, with a strong focus on Customers and Markets as well as Human Resource activities.

- *Managing the use of more part-time, temporary, and contract workers.* This trend, identified as critical by 71 percent of respondents, reflects the rapidly changing environment within which businesses operate. The "hot" skills and technologies of today become out of date quickly. The product-and-service focus of today is tomorrow's throwaway. Organizations must manage successfully with a more flexible and contingent work force. Yet managers must still manage that work force effectively; workers still need the right skills and knowledge, motivation and incentives, and satisfaction from work. This trend is a major challenge particularly relevant to the Human Resource Focus Category.

OTHER MAJOR TRENDS

More than 51 percent of the CEOs reported the following trends as major directions that will be likely to affect business in the years ahead. These include (from most cited, 69 percent, to least cited, 52 percent):

- Developing new employee relationships based on performance

- Improving human resources management

- Improving the execution of strategic plans

- Developing more appropriate strategic plans

- Measuring and analyzing organizational processes

- Developing a consistent global corporate culture

- Outsourcing of manufacturing

- Creating a learning organization

These directions, together with those listed previously, present a picture of what CEOs predict will be major business trends in the coming decade. The case for using the Baldrige Criteria as a way to manage effectively is validated and strengthened by the specific trends, their close relationship to the Criteria, and also by the next section, in which the same CEOs rate the competencies that major U.S. industries must possess to take advantage of these trends as a competitive advantage. CEOs report a huge gap between current-state competency and future/desired-state competency for many major trends. For example:

- Almost all of the CEOs report globalization as a major trend, but only 18 percent rate major U.S. organization competency as excellent. Seventy percent rated the competency as only fair.

- Improving knowledge management was cited by 88 percent of CEO respondents as a major trend, but only 23 percent see U.S. organization competency as excellent. Fifty-five percent rate the competency level as only fair.

- Competency in cost and cycle-time reduction was rated as excellent by 31 percent and only fair by 52 percent.

These are a sample of competency gaps cited by CEOs in the survey. They reiterate the need to use proven management practices to close these gaps and ensure that U.S. organizations remain or become leaders in the global marketplace to sustain our quality of life.

CEO Skills Needing Improvement

As part of the survey, CEOs were asked to reflect on their own skills and their peer group's skills and to report on which skills were most in need of improvement. The skills cited below were thought by more than 50 percent to need "a great deal" of improvement. They are key to addressing the major business trends reported earlier in this section. The skills include:

- The ability to think globally and execute strategies successfully

- Flexibility in a changing world

- The ability to develop appropriate strategies and rapidly redefine their business

- The understanding of new technologies

Another 40 to 50 percent of CEOs believe that these skills also need to improve "a great deal." Skills needing improvement include the ability to:

- Work well with different stakeholders

- Create a learning organization

- Make the right bets about the future

- Be a visible, articulate, charismatic leader

- Be a strong enough leader to overcome opposition

Stakeholders and Interests That Are Becoming More Important

The majority of CEOs (75 percent or more) think that international customers, consumers, and employees are becoming more important to business success. More than 60 percent believe that suppliers, outside board directors, and institutional shareholders are also becoming more important. Addressing requirements of the Customer and Market Focus Category and Employee Focus Categories is increasing in importance, according to the CEOs surveyed.

Execution of Strategies Is Critical

When asked which required more improvement—the development or execution of appropriate strategies, CEOs selected "execution" by about a three-to-one margin. This means that alignment of work and realistic action plans need to be improved along with accountability. If the organization is pulling in different directions, it is more difficult to accomplish individual unit or division priorities—energies and resources are being drained, execution is flawed, and results are suboptimized.

Expanding Market Size Is Critical

When asked which is more important—to increase market share or expand market size, CEOs selected "expanding market size" by over a four-to-one margin. This will require improved leadership, strategic planning, and customer and market focus, particularly in the global economy. It will also require a more skilled and diverse work force and more effective work processes.

The Competition Ahead

CEOs had various ideas about where the most serious competition to their businesses will come from in the next decade. Only a small number (12 percent) thought the toughest competition would come from other Fortune 500 companies. About 33 percent thought it was most likely to come from U.S. companies not yet on the Fortune 500 list. About 30 percent thought their toughest competitors were most likely to be foreign companies. Some saw start-up, entrepreneurial businesses as being the most serious competition. Comparing services and products to the competition and determining what the competition is doing to satisfy its customers is central to Baldrige-based assessments.

It is interesting, though, that most CEOs did not see the most serious competitors as being the major Fortune 500 companies of today. Perhaps this, more than any other CEO opinion, presents a compelling case for using the Baldrige Criteria—the fast and relentless pace of business change whereby companies on top today are not likely to be on top tomorrow without corresponding changes and improvements in their business.

Research Supports the Business Case

Two researchers were interested in quality award winners and to what extent (if any) quality management impacted financial performance. The research of Dr. Kevin B. Hendricks from the College of William and Mary, School of Business, and Vinod R. Singhal from the Georgia Institute of Technology, Dupree College of Management is the basis for the following piece of evidence that supports the use of the Baldrige Criteria. Their research looked beyond "hype and the popular press" to the real impact of quality management and examined the facts surrounding performance excellence. The research was based on about 600 recipients of various quality awards and similar recognition. The recognition provided to these organizations was based upon similar core values and concepts. Companies were mostly manufacturing firms (75 percent). All were publicly traded companies. Although Hendricks and Singhal did not find that quality management turned "straw into gold," their research added significantly to the business case for using the Criteria as a tool to enhance performance.

Hendricks and Singhal examined the following efficiency or growth measures to determine:

- Percent change in sales

- Stock price performance

- Percent change in total assets

- Percent change in number of employees

- Percent change in return on sales

- Percent change in return on assets

Implementation Costs Do Not Negatively Impact the Bottom Line

The research examined two five-year periods during the quality management implementation cycle. The first period can be called beginning implementation.

This period started six years before and ended one year before the receipt of a first award. During this period, organizations are implementing quality management and incurring associated costs of implementation, such as training, communications, and production and design changes. The researchers found no significant differences in financial measures between these companies (winners) and the control group of companies (nonwinners but similar in other respects) for this period. This is important because of the costs (both direct and indirect) associated with implementing quality management systems. The research suggests that the significant cost savings identified during this period of intensified focus on cycle time, time to market, and other factors pay for the implementation costs.

Improved Financial Results Can Be Expected with Successful Implementation

The study then examined results of companies from one year before winning the award to four years after the award was given. This period can be called mature implementation and it is in this period that one would expect the improved management to bear fruit. This was the case with this research. There were significant differences in financial performance between award winners and controls (nonwinners). For example, the growth in operating income averaged 91 percent for winners contrasted to 43 percent for non–award winners. Award-winning companies reported 69 percent growth in sales compared with 32 percent for the control group. The total assets of the winning companies increased 79 percent compared to 37 percent for the controls. Winners had significantly better results than the control group. The graphs on page 7 represent the study findings. Researchers found that award-winning companies outperformed control firms (non-award-winning companies) at least two-to-one, as Figure 1 indicates.

Hendricks and Singhal also found that there was no significant difference between the companies prior to the period of implementation of these quality principles. Performance of the award-winning firms was significantly better after implementation, suggesting the difference was due to the performance excellence systems that they installed.

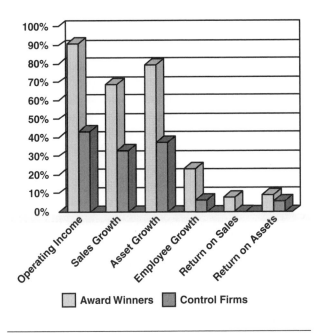

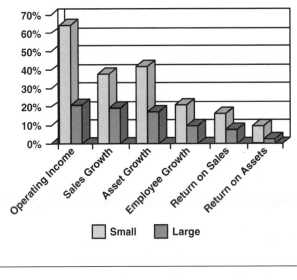

Figure 2 Comparison of large and small award-winning companies.

Figure 1 Comparison of award-winning and control firms.

In addition, Hendricks and Singhal found that small companies did significantly better than large companies in implementing the quality principles. This is depicted in Figure 2. Although large companies may have more resources with which to implement these systems, small companies may have an easier time deploying these systems fully throughout the organization and achieving maximum benefit.

- Although both small (less than $600 million) and large firms benefit, small firms do even better.

- Small winners outperformed the control counterparts by 63 percent, whereas large firms outperformed their controls by 22 percent.

- A similar profile exists for low capital- versus high capital-intensive award winners.

Correlational Study

One of the key management practices that has been a part of the Baldrige Award criteria for many years is the use of business results to analyze and subsequently improve organizational performance. James R. Evans and Eric P. Jack conducted an extensive correlational study to examine 20 hypothesized linkages between various Baldrige-required management practices and organizational results [Evans, James R.

and Eric P. Jack, "Validating Key Results Linkages in the Baldrige Performance Excellence Model." *Quality Management Journal*, 10.2 (April 2003): 7-24]. The first 10 hypotheses in their study represent linkages among the endogenous (internal system) variables as follows [Note: the strikethrough hypotheses (H3, H4, and H10) were not supported by by the data. All other hypotheses were supported.]:

H1: Employee satisfaction has a positive impact on process performance.

H2: Work system improvement has a significant impact on productivity.

~~H3: Work system improvement has a significant impact on employee satisfaction.~~

~~H4: Work system improvement has a significant impact on process performance.~~

H5: Process performance has a significant impact on productivity.

H6: Employee satisfaction has a significant impact on service quality.

H7: Employee satisfaction has a significant impact on product quality.

H8: Process performance has a significant impact on service quality.

H9: Process performance has a significant impact on product quality.

H10: ~~Supplier performance has a significant impact on product quality.~~

The next 10 hypotheses evaluate the direct linkages between the exogenous (external) variables and the exogenous results as follows:

H11: Employee satisfaction has a significant impact on market performance.

H12: Service quality has a significant impact on customer satisfaction.

H13: Product quality has a significant impact on customer satisfaction.

H14: Product quality has a significant impact on financial performance.

H15: Supplier performance has a significant impact on financial performance.

H16: Process performance has a significant impact on financial performance.

H17: Productivity has a significant impact on financial performance.

H18: Customer satisfaction has a significant impact on market performance.

H19: Market performance has a significant impact on financial performance.

H20: Customer satisfaction has a significant impact on financial performance.

The study's empirical results support the overall hypothesis that improving internal management practices leads to improvements in external results (Evans and Jack, p 18):

"Consider the relationships among endogenous variables in the Baldrige results category, such as between employee satisfaction and process performance, and between work system improvement and productivity. Strong correlation among these latent variables suggests the importance of many fundamental management practices that are embedded in the Baldrige requirements, such as a focus on employee well being and motivation, and attention to the design of work systems and their linkage to other categories, such as process management. By strengthening the practices that lead to improved levels of internal performance, the analysis indicates that improved performance of production/delivery processes will likewise occur. Second, high levels of the endogenous variables are correlated with exogenous performance results as measured by market share, customer satisfaction, and financial performance. This provides evidence that improving the performance of endogenous variables will positively impact the most important external business performance measures. Thus, this research provides new evidence of the validity of the Baldrige model and its examination/self-assessment process that seeks to validate strong business results as an outcome of high-performance management practices."

The following is a summary of the study findings:

• Employee satisfaction is driven by process performance and product quality. (This is consistent with observations from many Baldrige Award winners that increased employee satisfaction leads to higher performance.)

• Process performance is correlated significantly with employee satisfaction as a dependent variate, and with product quality and market performance as an independent variate.

• Customer satisfaction is driven by product quality, service quality, and work system improvement. Customer satisfaction is a more significant indicator of satisfaction than customer retention. Customers may indeed be satisfied but still switch allegiance based on other factors. Thus, customer retention is not necessarily a reliable indicator of satisfaction.

• Product quality is driven by employee satisfaction, work system improvement, and process performance. Product quality drives customer satisfaction and financial performance.

• Service quality is correlated significantly only with customer satisfaction. On-time delivery dominates the relationship.

- Work system improvement drives product quality, customer satisfaction, and financial performance.

- Financial performance is driven by productivity, market performance, work system improvement, and product quality. From a practical perspective, this suggests that quality-related initiatives do have a significant impact on financial performance, as many studies have shown (for example, Hendricks and Singhal (1997) and the National Institute of Standards and Technology's continuing study of Baldrige winners). Cost of quality, prevention cost, and warranty cost are the major contributors to productivity and product quality. Return on assets (ROA) and growth in ROA are the major contributors to market performance.

- Productivity is correlated significantly with financial performance. Rework and scrap contribute strongly to the relationship.

- Market performance is correlated significantly with process performance and financial performance.

Quality Management Is a Long-Term Solution

Companies that expect immediate gains from quality management systems are likely to be disappointed. It took years to create the culture you have today; it can take years to change it. Nevertheless, this research, combined with other results, makes a solid business case for using Baldrige-based management Criteria as the way to run the successful business of the future.

High-Performing Organizations

High-performing organizations outrun their competition (or potential competition) by delivering value to stakeholders through an unwavering focus on customers and improved organizational capabilities. Examples of improved capabilities have occurred in all sectors of the economy, not just the private sector. These results range from time and cost savings to customer retention and loyalty.

Many examples of significant improvements from using the Baldrige-based management system

are evident. Consider the performance of the seven 2003 Baldrige Award recipients: Medrad, Boeing Aerospace Support, Caterpillar Financial Services Corp., Stoner Solutions, Community Consolidated School District 15 of Palatine, Illinois, Baptist Hospital, and Saint Luke's Hospital of Kansas City.

Medrad, 2003 manufacturing winner. Medrad develops, manufactures, markets, and services medical devices that enable and enhance imaging of the human body. Medrad's products are sold to hospitals and medical imaging centers worldwide. Medrad's 1194 employees are located in Pennsylvania and 14 other sites around the world, including Africa, Australia, Canada, France, Germany, Japan, Norway, and Singapore.

- Revenue growth exceeded the average growth trend of comparable companies, increasing from $35 million in 1988 to $254 million in 2002, an average annual revenue growth rate of 15 percent.

- Operating income as a percent of revenue increased from 16 percent in 1999 to 20 percent in 2002 and is approaching best in class.

- Results for on-time delivery equaled or exceeded best-in-class levels and ranged from 98 percent to nearly 100 percent for syringes, disposables, injectors, and magnetic resonance coils.

- Medrad ranks third out of 57 nationally for overall satisfaction and second for both quality of products and service and support. The company's key competitor did not finish in the top 10 in any of the performance areas.

- Since 1999, overall employee satisfaction has exceeded the industry best-in-class benchmark. Since 1994, Medrad has outperformed the medical device industry benchmark of 5 OSHA reportable incidents per 100 employees.

- Medrad is committed to providing learning and development opportunities to employees. The company spent $487,000 on tuition reimbursement in 2002 and budgeted $535,000 for 2003, an increase from $325,000 in 1999. Medrad's total training expenditure per employee of

$2,233 in 2002 exceeded the training investment leader benchmark of $1,655.

- Employee empowerment, innovation, and initiative are pervasive in Medrad's culture, as evidenced through the many methods of capturing and capitalizing on diverse ideas and thinking.

- To develop new products or improve existing ones, Medrad used its Integrated Product Development Process to collect ideas from employees, identify customer requirements, prioritize initiatives, and translate initiatives into specifications. In addition, the process proactively addressed regulatory compliance, product safety, and environmental concerns, resulting in risk-mitigation plans that design safety, health, and environmental factors into production and delivery processes.

- Medrad created an environment that fostered legal and ethical behavior. A Code of Conduct defined ethical behavior in all transactions and interactions and was deployed to all employees worldwide as well as to Medrad's suppliers. Code-of-Conduct training was part of the company's employee orientation program, and the training was reinforced through a quarterly Code-of-Conduct Challenge distributed by email to all employees. In addition, Medrad had an anonymous ethics hotline and email address, a Business Ethics Committee, and a Legal Advisory Board.

- Medrad ensured management and fiscal accountability through external audits and monitoring of performance on its five corporate scorecard goals.

- Medrad encouraged employee participation in volunteer community service through its Points of Light community outreach organization. Points of Light organized approximately 20 events each year, including the United Way Day of Caring, during which the company suspended operations for a day to allow employees to participate in volunteer activities. In 2002, 750 employees participated in the Day of Caring, up from 630 in 1998. In recognition of Medrad's

support, the United Way presented the company with the Gold Award in 2001 and the Balto Award in 2002.

Boeing Aerospace Support (AS), 2003 service winner. Boeing AS products and services include aircraft maintenance, modification, and repair; training for aircrews and maintenance staff; and providing spare parts. Boeing AS' primary customer is the Department of Defense. Annual sales were in excess of $4 billion. Boeing AS has 12,303 employees at nine major sites (eight in the United States, one in Australia) and more than 129 secondary and smaller sites.

- For the past four years, Boeing AS earnings grew at an average cumulative growth rate of 17 percent per year.

- New orders improved each year since 1999, exceeding the previous four years, and were significantly higher than competitors' cumulative growth. Annual revenue more than doubled from 1999 to 2003, during a flat market, resulting in a loss of market share by competitors.

- Since 1998, the "exceptional" and "very good" responses from customers regarding Boeing AS performance went up 23 percent. The exceptional responses in 2003 nearly doubled those in 2002 and represented nearly 60 percent of the responses received.

- On-time delivery of maintenance and modification products and services has been at or near 95 percent since 1999. The overall depot quality for the maintenance of C-17s has been at or near 100 percent since 1998, compared to AS' competitor at about 70 percent in 2002 and 90 percent in 2003. AS has provided turnaround times that were steady at three days since 1998, ten times better than the competitor. On-time delivery of significant hardware, aircraft, and kits has been about 99 percent since 2001.

- Contracting Cycle Time, which measures the time elapsed from receiving a request for proposals from customers through modification of the contract, consistently improved from 100 days in 1998 to the 2003 performance level of 23 days.

- Employee-involvement survey scores showed improvement from 150 in 1999 to 170 in 2002, outperforming industry and Boeing data and approaching the best-in-class performance score of 178.

- From 2000 to 2003, AS employees had about one lost workday due to on-the-job injuries per 100 employees. This was under a similar competitor's rate of 3.1.

- Voluntary terminations by employees decreased from 3.5 percent in 2000 to 2.3 percent in 2003, better than the best-in-class level of 5 percent and the industry-average level of 8 percent.

- AS succeeded in creating an organization where collaboration and "shamelessly sharing" information across businesses, sites, and functions was the norm. Employees received a continuous flow of information from a variety of sources including on-line newsletters, cross-functional teams and meetings, and functional and business councils, making AS a role model for rapid adoption of new information.

- AS used an Enterprise Planning Process (EPP) to effectively develop strategic plans. The EPP was comprised of four process elements (Key Data Factors, Strategies, Plans, and Execution) with 10 defined steps. Key participants and responsibilities were defined for senior leaders and Business, Strategic Planning, and Functional Councils. Both the Business and Functional Councils developed action plans with timeframes.

- AS established policies and procedures for corporate governance and ethical behavior in employees. Expectations for ensuring ethical behavior were set during new-employee orientation and annual refresher training. Ninety-five percent of the staff was trained in 1999 and over 98 percent in 2002. A 24-hour ethics line is available to report ethical concerns or to seek advice. Requirements for suppliers were communicated through their contract, personal contact, or on the AS "Doing Business" website. Compliance was monitored through regular AS audits. Employee Survey Ethics Indicators have

shown a positive trend since 1998. AS scored better than the industry average.

- AS received numerous awards for its efforts to protect the environment, including the EPA Clean Air Excellence Award in 2002. Since 1999, AS has received either the gold or silver California Governor's Environmental and Economic Leadership Award and the Kansas Water Environmental Association award.

Caterpillar Financial Services Corporation U.S. (CFSC), 2003 service winner. Located in Nashville, Tennessee and employing 750 people, CFSC is the financial services business unit within Caterpillar, a manufacturer of construction and mining equipment, engines, and industrial turbines. CFSC is the second largest captive-equipment lender in the United States.

- Since 1998, CFSC has increased assets 34 percent and profit 54 percent while industry performance declined 21 percent and 35 percent respectively.

- CFSC contribution to the parent's total earnings improved from 5.6 percent in 1998 to 25.6 percent in 2003.

- The Non-Interest Expense as a Percent of Assets, a key measure of organizational efficiency, has remained below 3 percent from 1998 to present, while the industry top quartile comparison increased from 2.41 percent to 3.99 percent, and the industry average increased from 5.46 percent to 8.73 percent.

- Satisfaction of end users has increased significantly since 1999 and the current levels of performance exceed industry and ACSI (American Customer Satisfaction Index) world-class benchmarks.

- CFSC exceeded customers' expectations 34 percent of the time in 2000 and 2001 and 48 percent in 2002, nearly twice that of its competitors. Only 1 to 2 percent of users were dissatisfied.

- Employee satisfaction with their involvement in the business has improved 15 points to 79 percent since 2001, with the current level of performance significantly better than the industry norm at 51 percent and best-practice benchmark at 68 percent. Trends in the Employee Satisfaction Index improved from 67 percent in 1995 to 89 percent in 2003. Employee satisfaction with the job has ranged between 89 and 92 percent since 2000, which exceeded the 83 percent financial services norm and was consistent with the 91 percent score achieved by best-practice organizations. In 2002, 80 percent of employees rated the organization as a good place to work, up from 67 percent in 2000. The national norm was 55 percent. Likewise, the measurement of Employee Retention has improved four points to 94 percent since 2000, with the 2003 level of performance significantly better than the top quartile comparison.

- CFSC's investment in employee recognition programs improved nearly four times from $84,000 in 1999 to the 2003 level of $263,000. Employee recognition was used to enhance and reinforce workplace initiatives such as Six Sigma. CFSC also recognized employees with quarterly incentive pay.

- Senior leaders made employee development a priority at CFSC based upon employee feedback. The training investment in 2003 was over $2 million.

- Managed Assets per Employee, which reflects the combined impact of process management, Six Sigma, and technology management on the company's overall productivity and efficiency, has improved by more than 10 percent ($2 million) since 1997, with 2003 performance nearly 35 percent better than the average of the financial industry's Top 100.

- CFSC has doubled its Baldrige assessment score since 1993.

- Seventy-nine percent of all Cat users reported that CFSC influenced their decision to buy Cat equipment.

- CFSC supported an environment of innovation. It was one of the first in its industry to launch new technologies, including: FinancExpressSM,

an internet-based financing tool for employees, users, and dealers; AccountExpressSM, a web-based service capability available 24/7 to provide customers with information regarding their accounts; and CustomerExpressSM, a system that improved CFSC's ability to listen to its user and dealer customers and better manage those relationships.

- CFSC used a structured six-step strategic planning process that yielded both a four-year strategic plan and a one-year tactical plan. The process started with an annual retreat where strategic direction was revised by the top senior leaders, followed by a four-month strategy development period; an annual leadership conference where the top 45 leaders and managers developed preliminary division strategies and supported department requirements; a cycle for developing action plans and goals for divisions, support departments, and Six Sigma projects; a plan-review and resource-allocation step; and, the final step of developing unit action plans/goals and individual employee performance and development plans.

- Six Sigma improvement efforts yielded 2002 after-tax savings exceeding $9 million, and 2003 after-tax savings of more than $15 million.

- Since 2000, Employee Perceptions of Ethical Behavior have improved four percentage points to 84 percent, significantly better than the national benchmark. Employee perception of the Truth/Reliability of Leaders improved from 59 percent to 76 percent, with 2003 levels of performance better than industry norms of 52 percent and best-practice norms of 61 percent.

- The Caterpillar Board of Directors was rated by the Institutional Shareholders Services in the top 11 percent nationwide for overall corporate governance, and in the top seven percent within the capital goods industry. The board exceeded national benchmarks for independence. In addition, the organization exceeded requirements of the Sarbanes-Oxley Act requiring all BEC members to certify compliance of financial statements.

Stoner Solutions, 2003 small business winner. Stoner is a small, privately owned manufacturer of more than 300 specialized cleaners, lubricants, and coatings, which include car-care and auto-detailing products, mold-release agents, and specialty cleaners for electronics and other critical components. Products are sold to consumers as well as businesses in aerosol cans and in bulk liquid containers ranging from one to 275 gallons. Stoner is located in Quarryville, PA. With 45 full-time and five part-time employees, it is the smallest business to ever receive a Baldrige Award.

- Stoner's sales have increased 400 percent since 1990, compared to the growth in the U.S. gross domestic product of 63 percent for the same period. Retail sales increased from zero in 1996 to 20 percent of company sales in 2003. Internet sales through the company website *www.moreshine.com* increased 1000 percent from 1999 to 2003. Stoner's 39 percent return on assets exceeded the industry average by 29 percent and its best competitor by 14 percent.

- Since the introduction of "Invisible Glass," Stoner has increased its automotive market share for this glass cleaner product from 5 percent in 2002 to 29 percent in 2003, gaining more than 15,000 retail outlets. Manufacturing productivity has increased 150 percent since 1991 and weekly average output of aerosol can products has increased 33 percent from 1998 to 2003. Stoner sustained consistent profitability that grew along with sales, fueling the company's improvement initiatives and growth.

- Stoner's overall employee morale index increased from 64.6 percent in 2002 to 74.5 percent in 2003, exceeding the benchmark of 60.5 percent. Stoner's overall favorable percentage of satisfied employees increased from 72.8 percent in 2002 to 79.5 percent in 2003, exceeding the benchmark of 64.8 percent.

- Since 2000, Stoner has won three times as many customers as it lost, and, over the past five years, has retained more than 98 percent of its top customers, those accounting for over 60 percent of business. In a national industry survey, Stoner ranked first in satisfaction on four of the five factors most important to its customers—quality, delivery, service, and value. It was in the top quartile for the fifth factor—price.

- Since 2000, Stoner has reduced the amount of toxic chemicals used by 31 percent in an effort to achieve greater environmental compatibility, and increased the use of more environmentally friendly water-based formulations by 74 percent. To reduce cost and increase customer satisfaction, Stoner implemented an Enterprise Resource Planning system. As a result, 100 percent of orders were shipped on the same day they were received and the number of shipping errors was reduced to less than 0.05 percent.

- Stoner's Advisory Board, which included people outside of the company, provided direction and focus to its strategic planning process and advice on priority improvements, helped evaluate risk, assessed leadership effectiveness, and oversaw financial and ethical governance.

- An internal scorecard called "Stoner 60" identifies 60 key measurements and objectives with targets for one, three, and five years, linking future goals, key business milestones, and long-term action plans. All Stoner products carry a 100 percent money back guarantee.

Community Consolidated School District 15, 2003 education winner. District 15 is a kindergarten through eighth-grade school system with 1,898 faculty and staff serving 12,390 students in all or part of seven municipalities in and around Palatine, IL, a western suburb of Chicago. Its student population includes 37.5 percent minority and 32.5 percent low-income. Approximately 32 percent come from non-English-speaking backgrounds; 72 different languages are spoken in the homes of its students. The school system has 14 kindergarten through sixth-grade schools, three junior high schools, and one alternative school. District 15 operates its own transportation, maintenance, technology, and food services departments.

- District 15 provides intensive reading intervention programs. In the 2002–03 school year, 84 percent of second-grade students were reading at or above grade level, up 10 percentage points since 2000–01 and nearly 35 percentage points above the national average.

- The rate at which special education students met goals showed steady improvement since 1998–99, reaching approximately 14 percent in 2002–03, significantly higher than both national and state averages of about 5 percent. For English Language Learners, the rate increased from 8 percent in 1998–99 to approximately 15 percent in 2002–03. In one group of kindergarten students, 18 percent required intervention services when entering school, but this number was reduced to 1 percent by fourth grade. These rates exceeded national and state comparisons.

- Third- and eighth-grade gifted students participating in the 2001–02 World Class Tests for math and problem solving had a higher pass percentage rate than those from the other countries.

- Students demonstrated improvement in meeting or exceeding state standards of learning as assessed through the Illinois Standards Achievement Test, given in grades three, five, and eight for reading and math and in grades four and seven for science. The district equaled or outperformed its comparison district at all levels and in all subjects from 1998–99 through 2001–02. In 2002–03, performance in third grade math exceeded the 90 percent target and approached the state's top 3 percent benchmark. Grade five math, grade seven science, and grade three reading neared the 90 percent target.

- The district increased the number of its teachers who achieved National Board Certification from two in 1994–95 to 48 in 2002–03, the second-highest number in the state. In addition, highly qualified teachers, as defined in the Illinois criteria for meeting the federal "No Child Left Behind" legislation, taught 100 percent of the district's classes.

- Turnover rate for certified staff was 11.7 percent for 2002–03, compared to a national average of 20 percent, and attrition for first-year teachers decreased significantly, from 19.5 percent in 1996–97 to 6.3 percent in 2002–03, well below the 20 percent level of the comparative local

school district. As a result of safety efforts, 97 percent of teachers rated their work environment as safe and secure. The percentage of staff that had accidents decreased from 9.7 percent in 1999–2000 to 3.6 percent in 2002–03 (well below the 7.6 percent figure for the comparative local school district), and the number of workers' compensation claims for the same period decreased from 170 to 73 (compared to 168 for the comparative local school district).

- Parent satisfaction level with school safety and security was at the 93 percent level in 2002–03.

- Over the past three years, the level of student respect has increased an average of 20 percent. Segmentation of data by students' grade level and gender revealed that no significant differences existed in satisfaction levels.

- Among eighth-grade students, enthusiasm for reading increased from about 42 percent in 2001–02 to about 82 percent in 2002–03; enthusiasm for math increased from about 50 percent to about 80 percent; and enthusiasm for science increased from about 42 percent to about 82 percent.

- Since 1996, junior high students with learning disabilities have participated in a weeklong competition at the NASA Space Camp in Huntsville, AL, against non-disabled and gifted students from throughout the nation. During these seven years, the District 15 students finished first in at least one of four competition areas.

- District 15 developed innovative means of assessing performance important to key stakeholders where traditional educational measures were not sufficient. For example, financial performance was determined by calculating the dollar cost per percentage point of performance on state learning standards tests. This allowed a value-creation comparison with other districts in the state. At $111.93, District 15 outperformed three comparison districts that ranged from $118.57 to $122.36. In addition, District 15 maintained a per pupil expenditure rate that was at or above the level of both comparison districts and the state average from 1995–96 to 2001–02. Over the same period, no tax referendum was sought to increase this primary source of funding.

- The district used internal and external audits to ensure its fiscal accountability. Documents submitted for external review (annual budget and annual financial reports) received the highest rating (excellent), and the district received several awards for financial practices.

- To manage its operation by fact, District 15 constructed a system of leading and lagging success measures aligned to the district's six key goals. Data were analyzed and results were then distributed to faculty and staff to make informed decisions and develop innovations in education and support services.

- Processes that support the district's learning-centered processes, including transportation, custodial, central stores, technology infrastructure, and maintenance, were aligned to help achieve student performance targets. Owners of these processes collected student and stakeholder requirement data, and used these data to design, implement, and evaluate processes that improved organizational efficiency and contributed to better student learning results.

Baptist Hospital, 2003 health care winner. Baptist Hospital, a subsidiary of Baptist Health Care, includes two hospitals [Baptist Hospital (BH) of Pensacola, a 492-bed tertiary care and referral hospital and Gulf Breeze Hospital (GBH), a 60-bed medical and surgical hospital], and Baptist Medical Park, an ambulatory care complex that delivers an array of outpatient and diagnostic services. These facilities employ 2252.

- Inpatient and outpatient overall satisfaction for both hospitals was near the 99th percentile of the Press Ganey survey. Ambulatory Surgery overall satisfaction for GBH was near the 99th percentile each quarter since the second quarter of 2000 and for BH was above the 95th percentile since the first quarter of 1997. The overall satisfaction of home health care for services provided by BH has been close to the 99th percentile since the first quarter of 1999. The Emergency

Room for GBH was in the 99th percentile as was LifeFlight, which served all three locations.

- For the past several years, patient surveys of staff sensitivity, attitude, and concern, and overall cheerfulness of hospital staff all have been near the 99th percentile for both hospitals.

- The employee turnover rate at BH improved from 27 percent in 1997 to 13.9 percent in 2003 and at GBH improved from 31 percent in 1997 to 14 percent in 2003. These levels for both hospitals were more favorable than the northwest Florida and national averages and were at the best-in-class levels.

- Baptist Healthcare Corporation, BHI's parent organization, was ranked 15th among the 100 Best Companies to Work for in America in Fortune magazine's 2003 annual survey. BHI staff report positive morale rose from 47 percent in 1996 to 84 percent in 2001. Its best competitor reported positive morale for about 70 percent of staff.

- A Customer Value Analysis Survey, which gathered information on how BHI compares to its competitors, demonstrated that all responses—including nine care/service questions, two emotional questions, one location/environment question, two nurse questions, and one physician question—rated BHI more favorable than its two competitors. In addition, BHI ranked higher than its two competitors in loyalty, 54 percent vs. 45 percent.

- BHI developed a comprehensive tool called CARE (Clinical Accountability Report of Excellence) that used an index scoring method to capture more than 50 departmental and hospital-wide results. One indicator was the hospital-wide medication event rate, which measured adverse reactions to medication, including medication errors. In fiscal year 2000, 2.5 events occurred per 10,000 doses dispensed, while only 1.5 events occurred per 10,000 doses dispensed in fiscal year 2002. These results were at levels more favorable than the Voluntary Hospitals of America (VHA) benchmark of 18. (VHA is a private, for-profit cooperative that serves not-for-profit health care organizations nationwide.)

- Another CARE indicator measured the rate at which patients developed pressure ulcers. This indicator sustained improvements from 7.2 percent in fiscal year 1998 to 3.5 percent (BHI's target) in fiscal year 2002. The results were more favorable than the benchmark of 7 percent.

- Diverse thinking was captured through the Bright Ideas program, FOCUS-PDCA (a performance improvement process) teams, around-the-clock employee forums, and peer interviewing using behavior-based questions. The number of ideas generated increased from 1,400 in 1998 to 6,800 in 2003 and the number of ideas implemented increased from 370 in 1998 to 5,000 in 2003.

- BHI was governed by an independent Board of Directors, and surveys indicated an improving trend in the overall rating of the Board's effectiveness by its members from a 60 percent "strongly approve" rating in 1999 to 78 percent in 2003. A similar trend was seen in the self-evaluation of board effectiveness, from 69 percent in 1999 to 81 percent in 2001.

- Health screenings and physicals provided by BHI to the community were increasing. For example, through the HeartFirst program, heart risk screenings increased from 1,100 in fiscal year 2000 to more than 2,400 in fiscal year 2003. BHI's new Women's Heart Advantage program was established to improve awareness of heart disease among women, provide education on healthy lifestyles, and provide women with easy access to cardiac testing and treatment. BHI's goal was to provide 2,500 screenings to women in 2003.

- BHI used surveys and Customer Value Analysis to determine patient requirements and loyalty attributes. Information was collected and analyzed using a customer-relationship-management database to identify the key requirements for each customer group and as input into strategic planning, service design, and the performance improvement process.

- BHI's Hospital Information System (HIS) was used to gather, connect, and integrate data from clinical systems, employees, patients, financial systems, decision-support systems, and physicians. The HIS system was accessed through mobile terminals, through the Medical Information Data Access System (MIDAS) system for physicians, and through kiosks located throughout the organization.

- Baptist University, which included operational and clinical programs, was used as the primary source for training. All employees were required to receive 60 hours of learning per year. All leaders and employees met in a "daily line-up" to communicate important operational information and reinforce values. BHI's return on learning tracking and investment research led to its being named as a "Top 50" learning organization by Training magazine in 2003.

- BHI defined "integrity" as one of its core values. In support of this core value, BHI created a Corporate Compliance Department and instituted a Code of Conduct to affirm the day-to-day practice of complete and consistent understanding of all standards, including BHC's Standards of Conduct.

- HealthSource, BHI's 24-hour medical call center, was a key tool for identifying market opportunities and customer requirements and for identifying potential patients. HealthSource has fielded over 100,000 calls annually since 2000.

- BHI provided 6.7 percent of its total revenue to indigent patients compared to 5.2 percent and 4 percent for its competitors. In fiscal year 2002, 2,700 prescriptions valued at more than $550,000 were provided to hospital patients too poor to pay, and another $250,000 worth of prescriptions were provided to over 1,100 low-income outpatients through its various programs for the uninsured. BHI had 26,000 visits from 16,000 indigent patients through its outpatient clinic.

- Senior leaders served as role models and were held accountable for organizational performance excellence through a "No Excuses" policy. BHI's culture provided "open-door" access to everyone, including access to the president to discuss work design and improvement opportunities.

Saint Luke's Hospital of Kansas City, 2003 health care winner. Founded in 1882, Saint Luke's Hospital (SLH) is the largest hospital in the Kansas City, MO metropolitan area, with 3,186 employees and 500 physicians. Affiliated with the Diocese of West Missouri of the Protestant Episcopal Church, it is a not-for-profit comprehensive teaching and referral health care organization that provides 24-hour coverage in every health care discipline. Other facilities include the Mid America Heart Institute, the Mid-America Brain and Stroke Institute, an ambulatory surgery center, an outpatient care center, and a nursing college.

- In 2002, a consumer education organization ranked SLH 35th in the nation out of 4,500 hospitals evaluated. SLH received an overall score of 7669 compared to a national average of 5418. Consumer's Checkbook rating for SLH physicians was 86 percent compared to a national average of 33 percent.

- SLH utilized a broad-based Medical Staff Clinical Indicator Index to track 58 critical measures of clinical quality, such as readmitted patients, returns to intensive care unit, and returns to the operating room. The index denoted the number of indicators that fell outside of statistically allowed tolerances. In 2002, 95.3 percent of the 58 indicators were in control. The percent rate of Returns Following Ambulatory Procedures was significantly better for SLH at 14.2 percent compared to 39.18 percent for national teaching hospitals with more than 18,000 discharges per year.

- The annual independent National Research Corporation (NRC) study of regional providers showed that patients believed that SLH delivered the best quality health care and had the best doctors and the best nurses of the 21 facilities in the market area. This top position has been sustained since 1997. Additionally, the study found that patients believed that SLH delivered the best cardiac, neurology, and orthopedic care and has ranked among the top four in obstetrical care since 2001.

- In 2002, SLH participated in measuring and comparing its performance in the areas of Acute Myocardial Infarction treatment and Surgical Infection with 10 best peer hospitals through the Voluntary Hospitals of America. SLH was best-in-class in surgical infection and second out of the 10 in Acute Myocardial Infarction.

- SLH demonstrated improving financial performance over a four-year period as represented by improvements in total margin and operating margin. SLH outperformed the Council of Teaching Hospitals (COTH) top quartile and ranked in the top 5 percent of hospitals nationwide in total margin. SLH showed financial improvements over a four-year period in the areas of Days Cash On Hand, from 215.9 days to 359.9 days, and Net Revenue per Case Mix Index (CMI) Adjusted Discharge from $10,000 to $14,500. Sustained financial improvements in these areas resulted in SLH exceeding hospitals with similar bond ratings and achieving an A1 Standard and Poor's rating and an A+ bond rating from Moody's.

- SLH's performance results for Employee Retention showed continual improvement over the previous four years. Organizational employee retention consistently exceeded the Saratoga Institute's median for the previous five years and approached 90 percent.

- SLH designed and redesigned clinical pathways for high-volume, high-cost diagnoses. (Clinical pathways are treatment protocol designed to standardize care and reduce variation.) A team approach was used in the design process to review the best practices found in the medical literature and then restructure and redesign clinical care.

- SLH translated its understanding of how patients want to be treated and involved and established a clear set of 12 Customer Contact Requirements. Requirements included "Address patients/guests by last name unless otherwise told," and "Address all complaints within 24 hours or less."

- SLH aligned its operations from top to bottom, using the Strategic Planning Process (SPP), the

Balanced Scorecard (BSC), the Process Scorecards, the Performance Management Process, and the Performance Improvement Model. In 2002 and 2003, nearly 90 percent of departments had action plans supporting the SPP.

- SLH had a human resource planning system responsive to both current and changing health care needs. The system included a "Work force Planning and Assessment Tool," a detailed staffing analysis for all departments supporting patient care, and human resource action Plans that were created based upon the strategic plan.

- SLH identified Centers of Excellence within its clinical products and services, and focused its resources on them. These centers were recognized regionally and nationally. They represented a partnership with the hospital's physicians and provided an opportunity to further the hospital's commitment to research.

- SLH had a community education program as one strategy to impact the health of its communities. The level of financial commitment to community education steadily increased from $9.6 million in 1999 to $12.7 million in 2002. During this same period the satisfaction of the community with educational services stayed constant, at more than 97 percent.

- Senior management was accountable to the Board for SLH's performance. The Board reviewed the BSC, independent, and external audits and evaluated the CEO based on their findings.

- SLH won recognition from numerous local, state, and national awards programs for clinical excellence, patient and employee satisfaction, and overall quality.

The performance of earlier winners is just as strong.

Motorola, Commercial, Government, and Industrial Solutions Sector (CGISS), a 2002 manufacturing winner, produces and provides integrated communications and information solutions to fire and police, military, public service, and business enterprise organizations. Since 1999, CGISS has improved cash flow as a percent of revenue (more than 20 percent versus an average of five percent for telecom organizations), gross margin, and return on assets (seven percent versus a negative average for telecom organizations). Between 1999 and 2001, overall satisfaction and repurchase/recommend satisfaction levels exceeded 88 percent, and customer service satisfaction levels went from 85 percent to 99 percent. Perceived quality ratings are more than 21 percent higher than the closest competitor. The cost of poor quality averaged 2.5 percent of sales from 1999 to 2002. Defect rate is only 52 parts per million. An already short manufacturing cycle time (book to bill) decreased from 3.25 days in 1999 to 2.4 days in 2002 and sales per employee increased 32 percent during the same period.

Branch-Smith Printing Division (BSPD), a 2002 small business winner. With sales of more than $10 million, BSPD provides a wide range of printing services. BSPD's sales growth rate has outperformed the industry each year since 1998 and held that gain in 2002, even when the industry declined. Its market share in its primary area almost tripled in 2002. In 2001, BSPD's 35 percent gross profit level exceeded that of industry leaders for both book and magazine segments.

BSPD's commitment to its customers was evidenced by its systematic customer complaint process, customer satisfaction surveys, regular meetings with key customers, and a unique database to identify and meet the specific needs of customers. From 1998 to 2002, the division was rated at least 8.7 out of a possible 10 and exceeded competitors' ratings, which ranged from 7.6 to 8.1 during that time period. Results for recordable accidents fell from 16 per 100 employees in 1996 to an annualized rate of 2.7 in 2002, with levels below the industry average. In addition, the division reduced the voluntary turnover rate of employees, from a high of 43.7 percent in 1996 to 7.75 percent in 2002. From 1999 through 2001, BSPD's rate was comparable to the average for Fortune magazine's top 15 best companies to work for in America. The impact of the division's investments and improvements on employee productivity was demonstrated in the results of value-added sales per employee, which increased 33 percent over five years.

Sisters of Saint Mary (SSM) Health Care, a 2002 health care winner, is a not-for-profit Catholic health system providing primary, secondary, and tertiary health care services. The system owns, manages, and is affiliated with 21 acute care hospitals and three nursing homes in four states: Missouri, Illinois, Wisconsin, and Oklahoma. Nearly 22,200 employees work together to provide emergency, medical/surgical, oncology, mental health, obstetric, cardiology, orthopedic, pediatric, and rehabilitative care. SSMHC generates approximately $1.7 billion annually. For the fourth consecutive year, SSMHC has maintained an investment grade rating in the "AA Credit Rating" category (by Standard & Poor's and Fitch). This rating is attained by fewer than one percent of U.S. hospitals. SSMHC encourages employees at all levels of the organization to participate on teams involved in identifying opportunities for community outreach. In 2002, SSMHC provided in excess of 29 percent of the previous year's operating margin to provide care to communities that are economically, physically, and socially disadvantaged. SSMHC tailors employee benefits to provide flexibility. SSMHC's turnover rate for all employees has improved from 21 percent in 1999 to 13 percent as of August 2002. Minorities in professional and managerial positions increased from under eight percent in 1997 to 9.2 percent in 2001, considerably better than the industry benchmark of two percent.

Clarke American Checks, a 2001 manufacturing winner, provides personalized checks, checkbooks, checking account and bill-paying accessories, and financial forms throughout the United States. Its market share increased 50 percent since 1996. In the same period, revenue increased both in actual dollars and percentage growth—from $300 million in 1995 to $462 million in 2000. Revenue growth has improved from 4.2 percent in 1996 to 16 percent in 2000, compared to the average industry growth of less than one percent. Revenue generated by customer service operations increased 279 percent from 1997 to 2000; revenue from e-commerce solutions has increased 1077 percent since January 2000; and direct response marketing revenue has increased more than 768 percent from 1995 to 2000. Customer satisfaction with business products reached 98 percent for September 2001, outperforming the banking industry average of 90 per-

cent. Manufacturing cycle time (in-plant production time) has improved by more than 44 percent since 1995. Check manufacturing units per hour have improved over 150 percent since 1991. Internal errors have decreased 55 percent since 1995 and met Industry Week magazine's average for Best Plants. The STAR (suggestions, teams, actions, results) program encourages associates to capture, implement, and share process improvements. Clarke American has implemented six STAR ideas per associate for 2001, which exceeds the average level reported by the Employee Involvement Association. STAR ideas implementation rates have increased from less than 20 percent in 1995 to 70 percent, or more than 20,000 ideas implemented for 2001. The company's Team Excellence program is responsible for more than $15 million in cost reductions and $103 million in revenue growth from 1996-2000.

Chugach School District (CSD), a 2001 education winner, has 214 students from preschool to age 21, scattered throughout 22,000 square miles of south-central Alaska, with 30 faculty and staff. CSD delivers education instruction 24 hours a day, seven days a week in the workplace, community, home, and school. Results on the California Achievement Tests improved in all content areas from 1995 to 1999. Average national percentile scores increased in reading from 28th to 71st, in language arts from 26th to 72nd, in math from 54th to 78th, and in spelling from 22nd to 65th. In addition, the percentage of students in the top quartile increased in reading from 17 to 56, in language arts from 25 to 33, and in math from 42 to 79. The percentage of CSD students who take college entrance exams has increased from zero percent to 70 percent since 1998. Every CSD student has an individual learning plan developed jointly with students, teachers, and parents to enable students to learn at their own pace. CSD's percentage of state funds that are used for instruction has increased steadily from 51 percent in 1995 to 82 percent in 2001. CSD reduced the faculty turnover rate from an average of 55 percent prior to 1994 to an average of 12 percent during 1995–2000.

The Pearl River School District (PRSD), a 2001 education winner, located 20 miles north of New York City, has three elementary schools, one middle school, and one high school. The district has about 330 employees and approximately 2460 students. The percentage of students graduating with a Regents diploma increased from 63 percent in 1996 to 86 percent in 2001, while the graduation percentage of students in other schools with similar socio-economic profiles decreased to 58 percent. PRSD achieved a 90 percent passing rate in 2001. Helping students to prepare for college, PRSD improved advanced placement (AP) course performance from 34 percent of the students achieving a "three" or better in 1997 to 76 percent in 2001, while dramatically increasing the percentage of students taking the AP courses. PRSD has increased its market share (percentage of all students eligible to attend PRSD who actually enroll in the district) from 71 percent in 1990 to 90 percent in 2000. PRSD reduced non-instructional expenditures an average of 21 percent during the period 1994 to 2001. Instructional expenditures increased 43 percent during this same period. PRSD earned top scores on national surveys: student satisfaction increased from 70 percent in 1998 to 92 percent in 2001; parent satisfaction increased from 62 percent in 1996 to 96 percent in 2001; and staff and faculty satisfaction increased from 89 percent to 98 percent for staff and from 86 percent to 96 percent for faculty.

The University of Wisconsin-Stout Campus, a 2001 education winner, has about 1200 faculty and staff members and about 7700 students. UW-Stout offers 27 undergraduate and 16 graduate degrees through three academic colleges: Technology, Engineering, and Management; Human Development; and Arts and Sciences, as well as a variety of outreach programs. More than 90 percent of graduate program alumni and nearly 90 percent of undergraduate alumni say they would attend the university again. Employer ratings of graduates have consistently scored 99 to 100 percent of Stout graduates as "prepared for work." The percent of budget allocated to instruction has increased from 55 percent in 1997 to almost 60 percent in 2001, outperforming the UW system comprehensive university average.

Pal's Sudden Service, a 2001 small business winner, is a privately owned quick-service restaurant company with 17 locations in Tennessee and Virginia. Pal's has about 465 employees, 95 percent of whom are in direct production and service roles. Pal's com-

petes directly with national fast-food chains and offers hamburgers, hot dogs, chipped ham, chicken, crispy fried potato strips, and beverages, as well as breakfast items. Pal's 2001 market share of nearly 19 percent is up from 10 percent in 1994. Pal's profit leads the primary competitor by three percent. Customer satisfaction for quality in 2001 was 95.8 percent versus 84.1 percent for its best competitors. Pal's order handout speed has improved by more than 30 percent since 1995, decreasing from 31 seconds to 20 seconds, while competitors' time, increased from 73 seconds to 76 seconds. Pal's level of customer complaints over the last seven years is less than one-fourth of the level of the best/primary competitor and is continuing to trend downward. Pal's has reduced front-line employee turnover from 200 percent in 1995 to 127 percent in 2000, and it continues to decline. The best competitor's turnover rate is more than 300 percent. On-the-job injury/accident claims have declined 75 percent since 1992.

Dana Corporation—Spicer Driveshaft Division, a 2000 manufacturing winner, is North America's largest independent manufacturer and marketer of driveshafts for light, medium, heavy duty, and off-highway vehicles. From 1997 to 1999, sales increased by nearly 10 percent; economic value added increased from $15 million to $35 million. Internal defect rates decreased more than 75 percent from 1996 to 2000. Customer satisfaction rates are the best in the industry and complaints are less than three per million units shipped. Finally, employee satisfaction and turnover are better than the best competitor.

KARLEE Company, a 2000 manufacturing winner, is a contract manufacturer of precision sheet metal and machined components for the telecommunications, semiconductor, and medical equipment industries. KARLEE is a woman-owned business located in Garland, Texas, with 550 team members. For the past six years, sales growth rate has averaged more than 25 percent per year. In 2000, KARLEE went from an assembly lead time of two to three weeks to less than two days. Overall customer satisfaction ratings have improved 32.2 percent, while production volumes have more than tripled. Team member satisfaction results since 1995 have been higher than its competitors.

Los Alamos National Bank, a 2000 small business winner, is an independent community bank that provides a full range of financial services to the consumer, commercial, and government markets in New Mexico. Because of streamlined procedures, LANB approves home equity loans in two days or fewer, while its competitors take from one to six weeks. Eighty percent of the bank's customers are "very satisfied" with the service they received, considerably higher than the levels achieved by its primary competitors (52 percent to 40 percent) and the national average for banks (55 percent). Customer loyalty is more than five times the national average. The bank's net income increased by more than 60 percent over the last five years. Assets per employee increased from $5 million in 1995 to $7 million in 2000—$1.2 million higher than the best competitor and nearly $4 million higher than the national average. Employee turnover has been cut from 34 percent to 17 percent with an employee profit-sharing plan.

Operations Management International (OMI), a 2000 service winner, operates and maintains wastewater and water treatment facilities in 29 states and worldwide. Total revenue increased from about $80 million in 1996 to about $145 million in 2000, an average annual growth rate of 15 percent, while top competitor revenues dropped by 4.5 percent. OMI has never failed to meet expectations and has exceeded expectations for 88 percent of its industrial clients. Accident rates among employees are half of the national average. OMI doubled its work force over the past two years and reduced turnover by one-third.

BI, 1999 service winner, is a training organization

STMicroelectronics, a 1999 manufacturing winner, designs, develops, manufactures, and markets semiconductor-integrated circuits

The Ritz-Carlton Hotel Company, (now part of Marriott International), a 1999 and 1992 service winner, manages 36 luxury hotels worldwide; it is the only service company to receive the Baldrige Award twice

Sunny Fresh Foods, a 1999 small business winner. is the first food manufacturer to receive the Baldrige Award

Boeing Airlift and Tanker, 1998 manufacturing winner

Texas Nameplate Company, 1998 small business winner

Solar Turbines, 1998 manufacturing winner

M Dental Products Division, 1997 manufacturing winner

Merrill Lynch Credit Corporation, 1997 service winner

Solectron Corporation, 1997 and 1991 manufacturing winner

Xerox Business Services, 1997 service winner

ADAC Laboratories of California, 1996 manufacturing winner

Custom Research, 1996 small business winner

Dana Commercial Credit Corporation, 1996 service winner

Trident Precision Manufacturing, 1996 small business winner

Armstrong World Industries, Building Products Operations, 1995 manufacturing winner

Corning, Telecommunications Products Division, 1995 manufacturing winner

AT&T Consumer Communications Services (now Consumer Markets Division), 1994 service winner

Verizon Information Services (formerly GTE Directories Corporation, 1994 service winner

Wainwright Industries, a 1994 Baldrige winner, cut the time for making one of its principal extruded products from 8.75 days to 15 minutes, and reduced defect rates tenfold

Ames Rubber, 1993 small business winner

Eastman Chemical Company, 1993 manufacturing winner

AT&T Network Systems Group, Transmissions System Business Unit, 1992 manufacturing winner

AT&T Universal Card Services (now part of Citigroup), 1992 service winner

Granite Rock Company, 1992 small business winner

Texas Instruments, Defense Systems and Electronics Group, 1992 manufacturing winner

Marlow Industries, 1991 small business winner

Zytec Corporation (now part of Artesyn Technologies), 1991 manufacturing winner

Cadillac Motor Car Company, 1990 manufacturing winner

Federal Express Corporation, 1990 service winner

IBM Rochester, 1990 manufacturing winner

Wallace Company, 1990 small business winner

Milliken and Company, 1989 manufacturing winner

Xerox Corporation, Business Products and Systems, 1989 manufacturing winner

Globe Metallurgical, 1988 small business winner

Motorola, 1988 manufacturing winner

Westinghouse Electric Corporation, Commercial Nuclear Fuel Division, 1988 manufacturing winner

• Since the Baldrige Program began until 2003, there have been 919 applicants for the Malcolm Baldrige National Quality Award. These applicants have received vigorous evaluations by the Board of Examiners using the Criteria for Performance Excellence.

• Through 2003, 58 Award recipients have been selected across five categories: 24 manufacturing companies, 13 service companies, 14 small businesses, 4 education organizations, and three health care organizations.

• As of June 2003, there were 52 active state and local quality award programs in 43 states. All 52 programs are modeled to some degree after the Baldrige National Quality Program, and their award criteria are based on the Criteria for Performance Excellence.

• From 1996 to 2002, 20 of the 27 Baldrige Award recipients were previous winners in state award programs.

• Since 1991, there have been more than 7000 applications for state and local quality awards.

• In its 16 years of existence, the Baldrige Program has trained more than 2000 Examiners. Since 1991, the state and local programs have trained more than 21,000 Examiners.

• The same processes that drive high levels of productivity and performance excellence in the private sector also produce spectacular gains in the government sector. Many U.S. government organizations have also implemented the Baldrige Criteria and produced savings, improvements, and efficiency similar to that found in the private sector. Between 1990 and 2000, the U.S. Congress has adopted more than $136 billion in savings. Improved processes for government procurement have saved more than $12 million alone. More than 1,200 work teams inside of various government agencies have improved work processes and reduced costs to save approximately $37 billion.

Economic Impact of the Baldrige National Quality Program

In October 2001, Albert N. Link, Department of Economics, University of North Carolina at Greensboro, and John T. Scott, Department of Economics at Dartmouth College reported on a study they completed that examined the economic impact of the Baldrige National Quality Program. Specifically, their study examined the net private benefits associated with the Baldrige National Quality Program to the U.S. private and public sector and the relationship between economy-wide net benefits and the social costs associated with operating the program.

Based on information collected from a mail survey of the U.S. organizational members of the American Society for Quality (ASQ), the conservative estimate of the value (in constant 2000 dollars) of the net private benefits associated with the Baldrige National Quality Program is $2.17 billion. Conservatively, Link and Scott estimate the value (in constant 2000 dollars) of social benefits associated with the Baldrige National Quality Program to be $24.65 billion. Based on information provided by the Baldrige National Quality Program, the value (in constant 2000 dollars) of social costs associated with the program to date is $119 million. Therefore, from an evaluative perspective for the economy as a whole, the benefit-to-cost ratio characterizing the Baldrige National Quality Program is conservatively 207 to 1.

The Worldwide Use of the Baldrige Criteria

As indicated, the performance of U.S. companies using the Baldrige principles has steadily increased since the launch of the Baldrige Award in 1987. U.S. companies began to recapture market share lost to international competition. When the reason for the increased success of U.S. companies became appar- ent, other countries throughout the world began to create their own national quality awards based on the Baldrige Criteria. Although the U.S. Congress did not intend the Criteria to benefit companies through- out the world, that is precisely what has happened. After all, the Criteria are not secret. Millions of copies of the Criteria are distributed freely through the World Wide Web. Many books have been written about the Criteria and its impact on business perfor- mance.

According to the U.S. Department of Commerce, more than 50 countries throughout the world have adopted the Criteria as a basis for their own quality awards in an effort to improve the competitiveness of businesses in their own countries.

THE INTEGRATED MANAGEMENT SYSTEM

Ingredients to Optimum Performance

Clearly, in today's highly competitive economy, past success means nothing. Desire, without disciplined and appropriate action, also means nothing. However, it is just as clear that implementing a disciplined approach to performance excellence based on the Baldrige Criteria produces winning levels of performance. The key to the success of the Baldrige Criteria has been the identification of the key drivers of high performance. The National Quality Award Office within the National Institute of Standards and Technology (NIST) ensures that each element of the Baldrige Criteria is necessary, and that together they are sufficient to achieve the highest levels of performance. Many management practices of the past have proven to be "necessary" ingredients of high performance. However, taken piecemeal, these practices by themselves have not been sufficient to achieve optimum performance.

Achieving winning levels of performance requires that each component of the organization's management system be optimized. In many ways, optimizing the performance of an organization's management system is like making an award-winning cake. Too much or too little of any key ingredient suboptimizes the system. For example, a cake may require eggs, flour, sugar, butter, and cocoa. A cake also requires a specific level of heat for a certain time in an oven. Too little or too much of any ingredient, including oven temperature, and the system (in this case the cake) fails to achieve desired results. The same principle applies in an organization. A successful organization requires a strong customer focus, skilled workers, efficient work processes, fact-based decision making, clear direction, and continuous improvement. Organizations that do not focus on all of these elements find that their performance suffers. Focusing on only a few of the required ingredients, such as reengineering to improve work processes or training to improve worker skills, is necessary but not sufficient by itself to drive high levels of performance.

The following figures depict the elements necessary and sufficient to achieve high levels of perfor-

Integrated Management System

Figure 3   Get results, produce value.

mance in any organization or part of an organization. The elements apply to any managed enterprise, large or small, regardless of size, sector, product, or service.

Get Results, Produce Value. (Figure 3) In the first place, in order for an organization, team, or individual to stay in business (or keep a job) for any length of time, it must produce desired results. The work results must be valued. History has demonstrated that people, organizations, or even governments that failed to deliver value eventually went away or were overturned. Value can be measured in a variety of ways, including fitness for use, return on assets, profitability, reliability, and durability, to name a few.

Customers. (Figure 4) Understand and meet their requirements. In addition, we have learned that it makes no difference if the producer of the goods or services believes they are valuable if the customer or user of the goods or services believes they are not. The customer is the only entity that can legitimately judge the value of the goods or services its suppliers produce. It is the customers who finally must decide whether the organization, team, or government continues to stay in business. Imagine that you go to a restaurant, order seafood, and find that it tastes awful. Upon complaining about the bad tasting meal, you are not impressed with the chef's claim that "only the finest ingredients were used." It also does not help if the chef claims that he likes the taste of the fish. It still tastes bad to you, and unless the chef is willing to make an adjustment, you are not going to be satisfied and are unlikely to return. If enough customers find

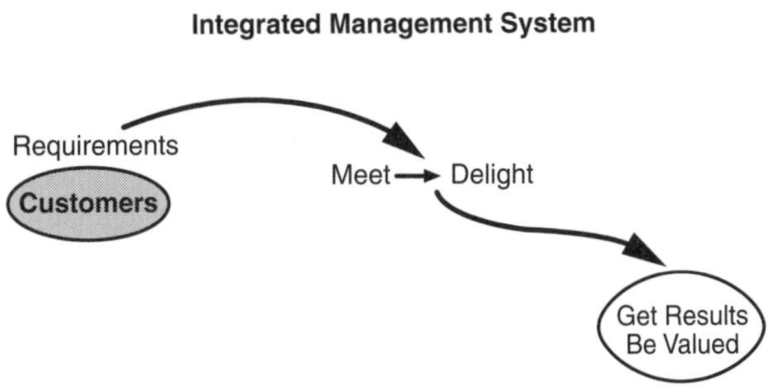

Integrated Management System

Requirements

Customers

Meet → Delight

Get Results
Be Valued

Figure 4 Customer requirements.

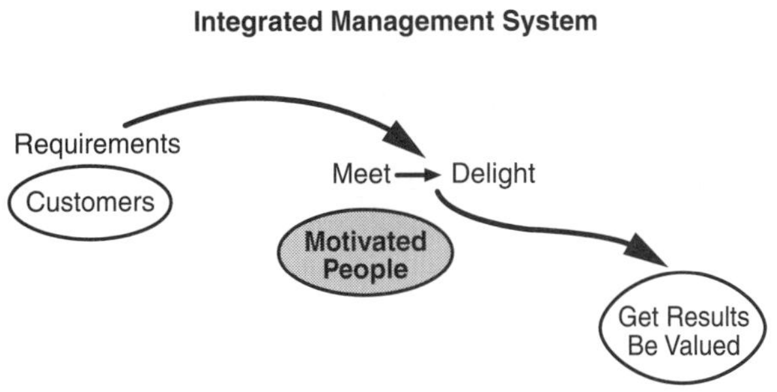

Integrated Management System

Requirements

Customers

Meet → Delight

Motivated
People

Get Results
Be Valued

Figure 5 Motivated people.

the food or service offensive and do not return, the restaurant goes out of business.

Accordingly, it is very important for the organization to clearly understand the requirements of its customers and obtain feedback from the customers after they have had an opportunity to experience its products or services. The failure to understand the requirements of the customers may cause the organization to deliver the wrong thing, creating customer dissatisfaction, delay, or lower value. Every time our organizations fail to understand and meet customer requirements, value suffers. In order to consistently produce value, therefore, organizations must accurately determine the requirements of its customers and consistently meet or exceed those requirements. This creates the initial value chain that provides the competitive advantage for any organization or part of an organization.

To ensure that the customer is satisfied and likely to return (or recommend your service or product to others), it is important to determine if the customer received appropriate value. If the customer is dissatisfied, you have an opportunity to correct the problem and still maintain customer loyalty. In any case, it is important to remember that it is the customer and not the marketing, engineering, or manufacturing departments or the service provider that ultimately judges value received and determines satisfaction.

Motivated People. (Figure 5) Motivated people are key to the next part of the management system to ensure optimum performance and value. In any orga-

nization or part of an organization, people do the work that produces customer value. As described previously, if the work is not focused on customer requirements, customers may be dissatisfied. In order to satisfy customers, work may have to be redone, adding cost and suboptimizing value. In order to optimize output and value, people doing the work must have the willingness and desire to work. Disgruntled, disaffected, unwilling workers hurt productivity.

However, "motivated people" means more than simply possessing the willingness to work. People must also possess the knowledge and skills to carry out their jobs effectively. In leading-edge technologies such as microelectronics engineering, the half-life of useful knowledge is 11 months. That means that one-half of the relevant knowledge of a microelectronics engineer becomes obsolete within 11 months. In 1989 the half-life was 18 months, approximately 50 percent greater. As new knowledge is created at an accelerating rate, it is more critical than ever to have effective training systems in place to ensure workers stay current and can effectively apply the new knowledge.

In addition, in order to optimize output, people must be free from bureaucratic barriers and arbitrary restrictions that inhibit work. Every minute that work is delayed while waiting for an unnecessary approval adds cost but not value. Every minute that work has to be redone because of sloppy performance of a coworker adds cost but not value. Every minute that work has to be redone because of inadequate knowledge or ability adds cost but not value.

Remember that one person cannot produce optimum levels of performance. However, one person can prevent optimum levels of performance, and may not be aware that he or she is doing so. The question that should concern management is, "In your organization, how many people are disgruntled, discouraged, underskilled, or prevented from working effectively so that they suboptimize the organization's performance?"

Efficient Processes. (Figure 6) Even the most highly skilled, knowledgeable, and willing workers will fail to optimize value if asked to do stupid things. Over time, even the most efficient processes can become suboptimum and inefficient. Business process reengineering has been seen by some as a panacea for organizational optimization. Business process reengineering allows organizations to redesign and quickly eliminate much of the bureaucratic silliness and inefficiency that grows up over time. However, how long does it take for the newly reengineered process to lose efficiency? Even new processes must be evaluated periodically and improved or they eventually become suboptimal and obsolete. Ensuring that processes are optimal requires ongoing evaluation and refinement.

Every process in the organization has the potential for increasing or decreasing the value provided to customers. Obviously, core business processes are perhaps the most important. However, frequently the core processes of an organization are disrupted because of failed support processes. For example, production can come to a halt if key material from the procurement office is not available on time. Production can also be disrupted if key workers that were supposed to be provided by the personnel office are not available.

Any time an organization engages in rework, value for the customer is suboptimized. To make matters worse, if the need to engage in rework is not discovered until the product or service is complete, the cost of correction is higher, driving value lower. It is important, therefore, to uncover potential problems as early as possible, rather than wait for the end result to determine if the product or service is satisfactory. In order to uncover potential problems early we must be able to predict the outcomes of our work processes. This requires "in-process" measures. Through the use of these measures, organizations can determine if the product or service is likely to meet expectations. Consider the two examples that follow:

- Example one: A customer comes to the "Wait-And-See" coffee shop and orders a cup of coffee. The coffee is poured and delivered to the customer. The customer promptly takes a sip and informs the server that the coffee is too cold, too bitter, too weak, and has a harsh aroma. Furthermore, the customer complains that it took too long for the coffee to be served. The server, in an effort to satisfy the customer, discards the original coffee, brews a fresh pot, and delivers a new cup of coffee to the customer at no additional charge. This problem happens frequently. The "Wait-And-See" coffee shop has been forced to raise the price of coffee in order to stay in business and has noticed that fewer customers are willing to pay the higher price. Many customers have stopped coming to this coffee shop entirely. The customers that continue to buy coffee from this shop are subsidizing the sloppy performance and poor quality.

- Example two: In order to increase the likelihood that its customers will like the coffee it serves, the "In-Process-Measure" coffee shop has asked its customers key questions about the quality of coffee and service that they expect. The "In-Process-Measure" coffee shop has determined through testing and surveys that its customers like coffee served hot (between 76 and 82 degrees Celsius); not too bitter or acidic (pH >

Integrated Management System

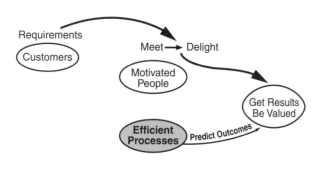

Figure 6 Efficient processes.

7.4); strong, but not too strong (75 grams of super-fine grind per liter of filtered water); with a fresh aroma (is served within five minutes of brewing). By checking these measures, this coffee shop knows that nearly all customers will be satisfied with the quality and service it delivers. Since its customers like the coffee within the limits described previously, no rework is required, no coffee is discarded, the price is lower, the value is higher, the store is profitable, and it is taking customers from the "Wait-And-See" coffee shop down the street.

Data and Dashboard to Monitor Progress. (Figure 7) Data and information help the organization and its employees make better decisions about their work. This enables them to spot problems more quickly and take actions to improve performance and correct or minimize non-value-added costs. Without appropriate measures, organizations and their employees must rely on intuition. They must wait for customers to respond or guess at their likely satisfaction/dissatisfaction.

One of the problems in basing decisions on intuition or best guess is that it produces highly variable outcomes. The guess of one employee is not likely to be consistent with the guess of another. Appropriate data, therefore, are critical to increase decision-making consistency and accuracy. In order for data to be used correctly to support decision making, organizations must develop a system to manage, collect, analyze, and display the results.

If the data that drive decision making are not accurate or reliable, effective decision making suffers. More mistakes are made, costs increase, and value is suboptimized. Furthermore, in the absence of relevant data and supporting analyses, leaders are generally unwilling to allow subordinates to substitute their intuition for that of the leader. As a result, decisions tend to get pulled to higher and higher levels in an organization, further suboptimizing the contribution of employees who are generally closest to and know the most about the work they do. Failure to fully utilize the talents of workers, as discussed previously, further reduces efficiency and morale, and suboptimizes value production.

The system described in Figure 7, which includes customers, motivated people, efficient processes, and a dashboard to monitor progress leading to desired results and value, applies to any managed enterprise. It applies to whole corporations as well as departments, divisions, teams, and individual work.

The system applies to schools, classrooms, government agencies, and health care organizations. In each case, in order to produce optimal value, the requirements of customers must be understood and met. People must be motivated, possess the skill and knowledge needed to do their work, and be free from distractions in order to optimize their performance. The organization must develop efficient work processes and monitor effectiveness of work to make adjustments in an effort to maximize value.

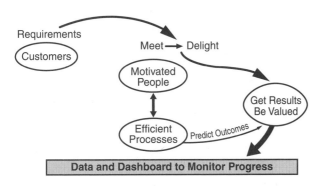

Figure 7 Information and data dashboard.

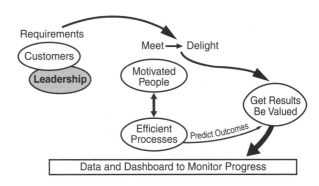

Figure 8 Leadership.

Leadership. (Figure 8) What makes an organization unique is the direction that top leaders set for it. Leaders must understand the requirements of customers and the marketplace in deciding what direction is necessary to achieve success. However, it is not enough simply to understand customer requirements. Leaders must also understand organizational capabilities and the needs and capabilities of employees, partners, and suppliers of critical goods and services.

Strategy. (Figure 9) Effective leaders use the process of strategy development to determine the most appropriate direction for the organization and identify the actions that must be taken to be successful in the future. Leaders use this strategy to identify the people and the processes that must be put in place to produce desired results and be valued by customers.

If leaders are not clear about the strategy and direction that must be taken to be successful, they force subordinates to substitute their own ideas about the proper direction and actions. This creates chaos within an organization. People come to work and want to be successful. Without direction from the top, they will still work hard but often at cross-purposes. Unless everyone is pulling in the same direction, processes, products, and services will not be optimized and value will be reduced.

Leaders cannot eliminate a single part of this management system and still expect to produce optimum value. Each part is necessary. Furthermore, studies repeatedly demonstrate that when these processes are integrated and used to run the business, they are sufficient to achieve high levels of performance. Imagine what might happen if one or more of the pieces of the integrated management system described previously were missing. The following table provides some suggestions.

Integrated Management System

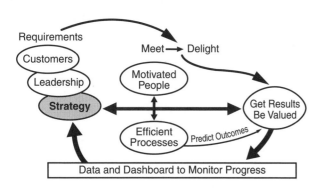

Figure 9   Strategy development and execution.

MISSING ELEMENT	ADVERSE CONSEQUENCE LEADING TO SUBOPTIMUM PERFORMANCE
Systems to understand customer requirements.	Designing, building, and delivering an unsatisfactory product or service. Adds delay. Increases cost due to rework.
Poor employee skills Minimal initiative or self-direction.	Limited expansion opportunities. Unable to keep up with changing technology. Requires close monitoring. Difficulty in finding better ways to carry out work. Ultimately reduces morale, motivation, and performance.
Data about customer satisfaction, key process performance, and overall organizational performance do not exist or are incomplete.	Makes it difficult to engage employees in decision making about their work. Forces decisions to be made at higher levels on the basis of intuition or guesswork. Reduces decision accuracy and increases incorrect decisions. Makes it difficult to allocate resources appropriately or determine the best use of limited resources.
Leaders do not clearly set direction, performance expectations, vision, or values.	Causes subordinates to invent their own ideas and substitute them for a common set of performance expectations, vision, and values. Creates significant inefficiencies as people throughout the organization begin the work at cross-purposes, suboptimizing organizational performance.
Plans do not contain measurable objectives and a time line for accomplishing each objective.	Leaders, managers, and employees do not know what level of performance is expected at any given time, making it difficult or impossible to effectively monitor progress. Accountability is not present.
Leaders do not make it clear that customers are the key to success.	If managers and employees do not focus on customers, then they become internally focused. Managers, engineers, or marketers drive the business, not customers. Customers and their requirements lose importance.
Top leaders do not encourage employees to develop and use their full potential.	Employee empowerment and well-being become optional. Some managers encourage employee participation, innovation, and creativity; most do not. The organization risks losing its best employees to competitors.
Customer comments and complaints are not encouraged. If a complaint is received it is not resolved promptly. The root cause of complaints is not identified.	Failure to capture customer comments and complaints, identify the root causes of the complaint, and work to prevent the problem from happening again makes it difficult to learn about problems quickly and dooms the organization to repeat its failures. Failure to resolve complaints promptly increases customer dissatisfaction and reduces loyalty.
Poor two-way communication exists between leaders and the organization.	Unclear top-down communication makes it difficult to ensure alignment and focus throughout the organization, reducing teamwork and increasing bureaucratic stagnation. Poor upward communication maintains organizational fragmentation and prevents problems and barriers to effective work from being discussed and resolved.

THE CORE VALUES TO ACHIEVE PERFORMANCE EXCELLENCE

The Criteria are built upon a set of interrelated Core Values and Concepts, which are embedded beliefs and behaviors found in high-performing organizations. They are the foundation for integrating key business requirements within a results-oriented framework that create a basis for action and feedback.

The 2004 Core Values and Concepts follow. The text in the box presents the exact wording of the Baldrige core values and concepts.

Visionary Leadership

Every system, strategy, and method for achieving excellence must be guided by visionary leadership.

- Effective leaders convey a strong sense of urgency to counter the natural resistance to change that can prevent the organization from taking the steps that these Core Values for success demand.

- Such leaders serve as enthusiastic role models, reinforcing and communicating the Core Values by their words and actions.

- Words alone are not enough.

Visionary Leadership

Your organization's senior leaders should set directions and create a customer focus, clear and visible values, and high expectations. The directions, values, and expectations should balance the needs of all your stakeholders. Your leaders should ensure the creation of strategies, systems, and methods for achieving excellence, stimulating innovation, and building knowledge and capabilities. The values and strategies should help guide all activities and decisions of your organization. Senior leaders should inspire and motivate your entire work force and should encourage all employees to contribute, to develop and learn, to be innovative, and to be creative. Senior leaders

Continued

---

should be responsible to your organization's governance body for their actions and performance. The governance body should be responsible ultimately to all your stakeholders for the ethics, vision, actions, and performance of your organization and its senior leaders.

Senior leaders should serve as role models through their ethical behavior and their personal involvement in planning, communications, coaching, development of future leaders, review of organizational performance, and employee recognition. As role models, they can reinforce ethics, values, and expectations while building leadership, commitment, and initiative throughout your organization.

Customer-Driven Excellence

This value demonstrates a passion for making the organization customer-driven. Without this, little else matters. Customers are the final judges of how well the organization did its job, and what they say counts. It is their perception of the service and product that will determine whether they remain loyal or constantly seek better providers.

- The organization must focus on systematically listening to customers and acting quickly on what they say.

- The organization must build positive relationships with its customers through focusing on accessibility and management of complaints.

- Dissatisfied customers must be heeded most closely, for they often deliver the most valuable information.

- If only satisfied and loyal customers (those who continue to do business with us no matter what) are paid attention, the organization will be led astray. The most successful organizations keep an eye on customers who are not satisfied and work to understand their preferences and meet their demands.

Customer-Driven Excellence

Quality and performance are judged by an organization's customers. Thus, your organization must take into account all product and service features and characteristics and all modes of customer access that contribute value to your customers. Such behavior leads to customer acquisition, satisfaction, preference, referral, retention and loyalty, and business expansion. Customer-driven excellence has both current and future components: understanding today's customer desires and anticipating future customer desires and marketplace potential.

Value and satisfaction may be influenced by many factors throughout your customers' overall purchase, ownership, and service experiences. These factors include your organization's relationships with customers, which help to build trust, confidence, and loyalty.

Customer-driven excellence means much more than reducing defects and errors, merely meeting specifications, or reducing complaints. Nevertheless, reducing defects and errors and eliminating causes of dissatisfaction contribute to your customers' view of your organization and thus also are important parts of customer-driven excellence. In addition, your organization's success in recovering from defects and mistakes ("making things right for your customer") is crucial to retaining customers and building customer relationships.

Customer-driven organizations address not only the product and service characteristics that meet basic customer requirements but also those features and characteristics that differentiate products and services from competing offerings. Such differentiation may be based upon new or modified offerings, combinations of product and service offerings, customization of offerings, multiple access mechanisms, rapid response, or special relationships.

Customer-driven excellence is thus a strategic concept. It is directed toward customer retention and loyalty, market share gain, and growth. It demands constant sensitivity to changing and

Continued

emerging customer and market requirements and to the factors that drive customer satisfaction and loyalty. It demands listening to your customers. It demands anticipating changes in the marketplace.

Therefore, customer-driven excellence demands awareness of developments in technology and competitors' offerings, as well as rapid and flexible response to customer and market changes

Organizational and Personal Learning

The most potent value is organizational and personal learning. High-performing organizations are learning organizations—they evaluate and improve everything they do. They strive to get better at getting better.

- A culture of continuous improvement is essential to maintaining and sustaining true competitive advantage.

- Without systematic improvement and ongoing learning, organizations will ultimately face extinction.

- With systematic, continuous, organizational improvement, time becomes a powerful ally. As time passes, the organization grows stronger and smarter.

- Leaders embed this value by linking rewards, recognition, and incentives for employees, supervisors, and managers at all levels to innovation, improvement, and learning. Otherwise, people do not think continuous change is important.

Organizational and Personal Learning

Achieving the highest levels of business performance requires a well-executed approach to organizational and personal learning. Organizational learning includes both continuous improvement of existing approaches and adaptation to change, leading to new goals and/or approaches. Learning needs to be embedded in the way your organization operates. This means that learning (1) is a regular part of daily work; 2) is practiced at personal, work unit, and organizational levels; (3) results in solving problems at their source ("root cause"); (4) is focused on building and sharing knowledge throughout your organization; and (5) is driven by opportunities to effect significant, meaningful change. Sources for learning include employees' ideas, research and development (R&D), customers' input, best practice sharing, and benchmarking.

Organizational learning can result in (1) enhancing value to customers through new and improved products and services; (2) developing new business opportunities; (3) reducing errors, defects, waste, and related costs; (4) improving responsiveness and cycle time performance; (5) increasing productivity and effectiveness in the use of all resources throughout your organization; and (6) enhancing your organization's performance in fulfilling its societal responsibilities and its service to your community as a good citizen.

Employees' success depends increasingly on having opportunities for personal learning and practicing new skills. Organizations invest in employees' personal learning through education, training, and other opportunities for continuing growth. Such opportunities might include job rotation and increased pay for demonstrated knowledge and skills. On-the-job training offers a cost-effective way to train and to better link training to your organizational needs and priorities. Education and training programs may benefit from advanced technologies, such as computer- and Internet-based learning and satellite broadcasts.

Continued

Personal learning can result in (1) more satisfied and versatile employees who stay with your organization, (2) organizational cross-functional learning, (3) building the knowledge assets of your organization, and (4) an improved environment for innovation.

Thus, learning is directed not only toward better products and services but also toward being more responsive, adaptive, innovative, and efficient—giving your organization marketplace sustainability and performance advantages and giving your employees satisfaction and motivation to excel.

Valuing Employees and Partners

Organizations must invest in their people to ensure they have the skills for today and to do what is necessary to succeed in the future. This core value has broadened from employee participation and development to valuing employees and partners. In high-performing organizations, the people who do the work of the organization should make most of the decisions about how the work is done. A significant barrier exists, however, that limits employee decision making—access to data and poor data-based decision-making skills.

- As mentioned previously, leaders are unwilling to let subordinates make decisions based on intuition—they reserve that type of decision for themselves.

- Therefore, access to data and developing skills to manage by fact are prerequisites for optimizing employee contributions to the organization's success.

- Organizations cannot effectively push decision making down to the level where most of the work is done unless those doing the work have access to the necessary data and are skilled at making fact-based decisions.

Valuing Employees and Partners

An organization's success depends increasingly on the diverse knowledge, skills, creativity, and motivation of all its employees and partners.

Valuing employees means committing to their satisfaction, development, and well-being. Increasingly, this involves more flexible, high-performance work practices tailored to employees with diverse workplace and home life needs. Major challenges in the area of valuing employees include (1) demonstrating your leaders' commitment to your employees' success, (2) recognition that goes beyond the regular compensation system, (3) development and progression within your organization, (4) sharing your organization's knowledge so your employees can better serve your customers and contribute to achieving your strategic objectives, and (5) creating an environment that encourages risk taking and innovation.

Organizations need to build internal and external partnerships to better accomplish overall goals. Internal partnerships might include labor-management cooperation, such as agreements with unions. Partnerships with employees might entail employee development, cross-training, or new work organizations, such as high-performance work teams. Internal partnerships also might involve creating network relationships among your work units to improve flexibility, responsiveness, and knowledge sharing.

External partnerships might be with customers, suppliers, and education organizations. Strategic partnerships or alliances are increasingly important kinds of external partnerships. Such partnerships might offer entry into new markets or a basis for new products or services. Also, partnerships might permit the blending of your organization's core competencies or leadership capabilities with the complementary strengths and capabilities of partners.

Successful internal and external partnerships develop longer term objectives, thereby creating a basis for mutual investments and respect.

Continued

Partners should address the key requirements for success, means for regular communication, approaches to evaluating progress, and means for adapting to changing conditions. In some cases, joint education and training could offer a cost-effective method for employee development.

Agility

Agility is a value usually driven by customer requirements and the desire to improve operating efficiency and lower costs.

- Except for a few pleasurable experiences, everyone wants things faster.

- Organizations that develop the capacity to respond faster by eliminating activities and tasks that do not add value find that productivity increases, costs go down, and customers are more loyal.

- Analyzing and improving work processes enables organizations to perform better, faster, and cheaper.

- To improve work processes, organizations must focus on improving design quality and preventing problems. The cost of preventing problems and building quality into products and services is significantly less than the cost of taking corrective action later.

- It is critical to capture learning from other design projects.

- Use information concerning customer preference, competitors' products, cost and pricing, marketplace profiles, and research and development (R&D) to optimize the process from the start, and avoid delay and rework.

- Public responsibility issues and factors, including environmental demands, must be included at the design stage.

Agility

Success in globally competitive markets demands agility—a capacity for rapid change and flexibility. E-business requires and enables more rapid, flexible, and customized responses. Businesses face ever-shorter cycles for the introduction of new/improved products and services, as well as for faster and more flexible response to customers. Major improvements in response time often require simplification of work units and processes and/or the ability for rapid changeover from one process to another. Cross-trained and empowered employees are vital assets in such a demanding environment.

A major success factor in meeting competitive challenges is the design-to-introduction (product or service initiation) or innovation cycle time. To meet the demands of rapidly changing global markets, organizations need to carry out stage-to-stage integration (such as concurrent engineering) of activities from research or concept to commercialization.

All aspects of time performance now are more critical, and cycle time has become a key process measure. Other important benefits can be derived from this focus on time; time improvements often drive simultaneous improvements in organization, quality, cost, and productivity.

Focus on the Future

To remain competitive, every organization must be guided by a common set of measurable goals and a focus on the future.

- These measurable goals, which emerge from the strategic planning process, serve to align the work of everyone in the organization.

- Measurable goals allow everyone to know where they are going and when they deviate from their path.

- Without measurable goals, everyone still works hard, but they tend to focus on the things they believe are important, not the direction set by top leaders. As a result, they can easily go in different directions—suboptimizing the success of the organization.

- Focusing on the future requires the organization's leaders to consider new, even revolutionary, ideas. Strategic objectives should reflect this future focus.

Focus on the Future

In today's competitive environment, a focus on the future requires understanding the short and longer-term factors that affect your business and marketplace. Pursuit of sustainable growth and market leadership requires a strong future orientation and a willingness to make long-term commitments to key stakeholders—your customers, employees, suppliers and partners, stockholders, the public, and your community. Your organization's planning should anticipate many factors, such as customers' expectations, new business and partnering opportunities, employee development and hiring needs, the increasingly global marketplace, technological developments, the evolving e-business environment, new customer and market segments, evolving regulatory requirements, community and societal expectations, and strategic moves by competitors. Strategic objectives and resource allocations need to accommodate these influences. A focus on the future includes developing employees and suppliers, doing effective succession planning, creating opportunities for innovation, and anticipating public responsibilities.

Managing for Innovation

The accelerating rate of change today demands ever-increasing innovation. Such innovation cannot be random. It must be focused on factors that are essential to organizational success. To be focused, innovation must be managed. Innovation should focus on changing products, services, and processes to create more value for the organization's stakeholders, employees, and customers. The winners in the highly competitive race to innovate will be the organizations that uncover new paradigms of breakthrough performance. To begin to optimize this breakthrough capacity, everyone in the organization needs to be involved. The more brain power, the better. Requirements for innovation should be a part of every employee and managerial performance plan and appraisal. Just like continuous improvement, innovation must be embedded in the culture and fabric of daily work. The best organizations are not satisfied to just "improve" or "innovate." The best organizations work hard at increasing the speed at which they improve and innovate. Anything less allows competitors to overtake them. Anything less allows customer expectations to exceed the speed of change, causing the customers to look elsewhere.

Managing for Innovation

Innovation means making meaningful change to improve an organization's products, services, and processes and to create new value for the organization's stakeholders. Innovation should lead your organization to new dimensions of performance. Innovation is no longer strictly the purview of research and development departments; innovation is important for all aspects of your business and all processes. Organizations should be led and managed so that innovation becomes part of the learning culture and is integrated into daily work.

Innovation builds on the accumulated knowledge of your organization and its employees. Therefore, the ability to capitalize on this knowledge is critical to managing for innovation.

Management by Fact

Management by fact is the cornerstone value for effective planning, operational decision making at all levels, employee involvement and empowerment, and leadership.

- People make decisions every day. However, without data, the basis for decision making is usually intuition—gut feel. Although intuition can be valuable at times, it introduces too much variation in the decision-making process. Intuition is not consistent person-to-person or time-to-time. It is also difficult to explain the rationale for decisions based on intuition. That makes communication more difficult within the organization. Finally, if the decision must be made on the basis of intuition, it is usually the boss' intuition that drives the decision. Because of this phenomenon, issues are pulled to ever-higher levels for resolution. As a result, excessive reliance on intuition minimizes employee empowerment.

- Most drivers decide when to fill their fuel tanks based on data from the fuel gage and get very uncomfortable if the gage is broken. Yet people routinely make decisions of enormous consequence about customers, strategies, goals, and employees with little or no data. This is a recipe for disaster, not one designed to ensure optimization.

Management by Fact

Organizations depend on the measurement and analysis of performance. Such measurements should derive from business needs and strategy, and they should provide critical data and information about key processes, outputs, and results. Many types of data and information are needed for performance management. Performance measurement should include customer, product, and service performance; comparisons of operational, market, and competitive performance; and supplier, employee, and cost and financial perfor-

Continued

mance. Data should be segmented by, for example, markets, product lines, and employee groups to facilitate analysis.

Analysis refers to extracting larger meaning from data and information to support evaluation, decision making, and improvement. Analysis entails using data to determine trends, projections, and cause and effect that might not otherwise be evident. Analysis supports a variety of purposes, such as planning, reviewing your overall performance, improving operations, change management, and comparing your performance with competitors' or with "best practices" benchmarks.

A major consideration in performance improvement and change management involves the selection and use of performance measures or indicators. *The measures or indicators you select should best represent the factors that lead to improved customer, operational, and financial performance. A comprehensive set of measures or indicators tied to customer and/or organizational performance requirements represents a clear basis for aligning all processes with your organization's goals.* Through the analysis of data from your tracking processes, your measures or indicators themselves may be evaluated and changed to better support your goals.

Social Responsibility

Every high-performing organization practices good public responsibility and citizenship.

- Organizations must determine and anticipate any adverse effects to the public of their products, services, and operations. Failure to do so can undermine public trust and distract workers, and also adversely affect the bottom line. This is true of both private and public organizations.

- During the last few years we have seen several examples of companies that have been seriously hurt by failing to practice good citizenship or protect the interests of the public from risks they created. Enron and Arthur-Anderson are well-known examples. Even when unintended, failure to protect stakeholder interests can cripple companies. Consider Dow-Corning and the silicone breast implants, banks sued because they failed to provide adequate security for automatic teller machines (cash machines), or Exxon for the massive oil spill in the Pacific.

- Safety and legal requirements need to be met beyond mere compliance. The best organizations stay ahead of minimum requirements and actually lead efforts to raise the bar. In this manner, when regulatory agencies increase requirements, the best organizations are not caught off guard and may even be able to place their competitors at a disadvantage.

Social Responsibility

An organization's leaders should stress responsibilities to the public, ethical behavior, and the need to practice good citizenship. Leaders should be role models for your organization in focusing on business ethics and protection of public health, safety, and the environment. Protection of health, safety, and the environment includes your organization's operations, as well as the life cycles of your products and services. Also, organizations should emphasize resource conservation and waste reduction at the source. Planning should anticipate adverse impacts from production, distribution, transportation, use, and disposal of your products. Effective planning should prevent problems, provide for a forthright response if problems occur, and make available information and support needed to maintain public awareness, safety, and confidence.

For many organizations, the product design stage is critical from the point of view of public responsibility. Design decisions impact your production processes and often the content of municipal and industrial waste. Effective design strategies should anticipate growing environmental concerns and responsibilities.

Continued

Organizations should not only meet all local, state, and federal laws and regulatory requirements, but they should treat these and related requirements as opportunities for improvement "beyond mere compliance." Organizations should stress ethical behavior in all stakeholder transactions and interactions. Highly ethical conduct should be a requirement of and should be monitored by the organization's governance body.

Practicing good citizenship refers to leadership and support—within the limits of an organization's resources—of publicly important purposes. Such purposes might include improving education and health care in your community, environmental excellence, resource conservation, community service, improving industry and business practices, and sharing nonproprietary information. Leadership as a corporate citizen also entails influencing other organizations, private and public, to partner for these purposes. For example, your organization might lead or participate in efforts to help define the obligations of your industry to its communities. Managing social responsibility requires the use of appropriate measures and leadership responsibility for those measures.

Focus on Results and Creating Value

A results focus and an emphasis on creating value helps organizations communicate requirements, monitor actual performance, make adjustments in priorities, and reallocate resources. Without a results focus, organizations can become fixated on internal, self-directed processes and lose sight of the important factors for success—such as customers and their requirements.

Focus on Results and Creating Value

An organization's performance measurements need to focus on key results. Results should be used to create and balance value for your key stakeholders—customers, employees, stockholders, suppliers and partners, the public, and the community. By creating value for your key stakeholders, your organization builds loyalty and contributes to growing the economy. To meet the sometimes conflicting and changing aims that balancing value implies, organizational strategy should explicitly include key stakeholder requirements. This will help ensure that plans and actions meet differing stakeholder needs and avoid adverse impacts on any stakeholders. The use of a balanced composite of leading and lagging performance measures offers an effective means to communicate short- and longer-term priorities, monitor actual performance, and provide a clear basis for improving results.

Systems Perspective

Taken together, the Baldrige Criteria promote a systems perspective and define the processes required to achieve optimum organizational performance. As with any system, no part can be ignored and the whole still be expected to perform at peak levels. When part of a well-functioning system begins to underperform or work in a manner that is inconsistent with system requirements, the performance of the whole system suffers.

The same is true of a management system. If leaders are ambiguous, if plans are not clear, if work processes are not consistent, if people are not able to do the work they are asked to do, and if it is difficult to keep track of progress and make appropriate adjustments, it will be impossible for the organization to achieve maximum levels of performance. For most of the 20th century, a long list of "management gurus" has suggested a variety of quick and simple remedies to enhance organizational performance. By itself, each quick fix has failed. Hopefully we have learned that no single solution is sufficient to optimize performance in a complex system. Leaders who approach management from a systems perspective are more likely to optimize organizational performance than leaders who continue to take a piecemeal approach to organizational management. There is no magic potion for excellent management to achieve high performance.

There are always better ways to do things. The challenge is to find them, but we are not likely to find them alone. We must create an environment—a work climate where better ways will be sought out, recognized, and put in place by everyone.

Systems Perspective

The Baldrige Criteria provide a systems perspective for managing your organization and its key processes to achieve results—performance excellence. The seven Baldrige Categories and the Core Values form the building blocks and the integrating mechanism for the system. However, successful management of overall performance requires organization-specific synthesis, alignment, and integration. Synthesis means looking at your organization as a whole and builds upon key business requirements, including your strategic objectives and action plans. Alignment means using the key linkages among requirements given in the Baldrige Categories to ensure consistency of plans, processes, measures, and actions. Integration builds on alignment so that the individual components of your performance management system operate in a fully interconnected manner

These concepts are depicted in the Baldrige framework on page 5. A systems perspective includes your senior leaders' focus on strategic directions and on your customers. It means that your senior leaders monitor, respond to, and manage performance based on your business results. A systems perspective also includes using your measures, indicators, and organizational knowledge to build your key strategies. It means linking these strategies with your key processes and aligning your resources to improve overall performance and satisfy customers. Thus, a systems perspective means managing your whole organization, as well as its components, to achieve success.

PRACTICAL INSIGHTS

Connections and Linkages

A popular children's activity, connect the dots, helps them understand that, when properly connected, apparently random dots create a meaningful picture. In many ways, the seven Categories, 19 Items, and 32 Areas to Address in the Baldrige Criteria are like the dots that must be connected to reveal a meaningful picture. With no tools to connect the dots, human resource activities are not related to strategic planning; measurement, analysis, and knowledge management are isolated from process management; and overall improvement efforts are disjointed, fragmented, and do not yield robust results. This book describes the linkages among and between each item. The exciting part about having them identified is that you can look for these linkages in your own organization and, if they don't exist, start building them.

Transition Strategies

Putting high-performance management systems in place is a major commitment that will not happen quickly. At the beginning, you will need a transition strategy to get you across the bridge from management by opinion or intuition to more data-driven management. The next part of this section describes one approach that has worked for many organizations in various sectors: creating a performance improvement council.

Performance Improvement Council

Identify a top-level executive leadership group of six to 10 members. Each additional member will seem to double the complexity of issues and render decision making much more cumbersome. The executive leadership group could send a message to the entire organization by naming the group "the performance improvement council"—reinforcing the importance of continuous performance improvement to the future success of the organization.

The performance improvement council should be the primary policy-making body for the organization. It should spawn other performance improvement councils at lower levels to share practices and policies with every employee in the organization as well as to involve customers and suppliers. The structure permeates the organization as members of the performance improvement council become area leaders for major improvement efforts and sponsors for several process or continuous improvement task teams throughout the organization. The council structure, networked and cascaded fully, can effectively align the work and optimize performance at all levels and across all functions.

Council Membership

Selecting members for the performance improvement council should be done carefully. Each member should be essential for the success of the operation, and together they must be sufficient for success. The most important member is the senior leader of the organization or work unit. This person must participate actively, demonstrating the kind of leadership that all should emulate. Of particular importance is a commitment to consensus building as the modus operandi for the council. This tool, a core of performance improvement programs, is often overlooked by leadership. Other council members selected should have leadership responsibility for broad areas of the organization such as human resources, operations planning, customers, and data systems.

Performance Improvement Council Learning and Planning

The performance improvement council should be extremely knowledgeable about high-performance management systems. If not, as is often the case, performance improvement council members should be among the first in the organization to learn about continuous improvement tools and processes.

To be effective, every member of the council (and every member in the organization) must understand the Baldrige Criteria, because the Criteria describe the components of the entire management system. Participation in examiner training has proved to be the best way to understand the complexities of the system needed to achieve performance excellence. Any additional training beyond this should be carried out in the context of planning—that is, learn tools and use them to plan the performance improvement implementation, practices, and policies.

The performance improvement council should:

- Develop a business plan that integrates continuous improvement and strategic performance improvement.

- Create the web (communication plan and infrastructure) to transmit performance improvement policies throughout the organization.

- Define the roles of employees, including new recognition and reward structures, to cause needed behavioral changes.

- Develop a master training and development plan. Involve team representatives in planning so they can learn skills close to when they are needed. Define what is provided to whom, and when and how success will be measured.

- Launch improvement projects that will produce both short- and long-term successes. Improvement projects should be clearly defined by the performance improvement council and driven by the strategic plan. Typical improvement projects include important human resource processes such as career development, performance measurement, and diversity, as well as improving operational products and services in the line areas.

- Develop a plan to communicate the progress and successes of the organization. Through this approach, the need for performance improvement processes is consistently communicated to all employees. Barriers to optimum performance are weakened and eliminated.

- Create champions to promote performance excellence through the Categories of the Baldrige Criteria.

Category Champions

This section describes the responsibilities of category champions. The people in the administrative or leadership cabinet should each be the champion of a category.

Organizational Leadership Champion

The *organizational leadership champion* is a senior executive who, in addition to other executive duties, works to coordinate and enhance leadership effectiveness and alignment throughout the organization. It is both a strategic and an operational activity.

From the strategic side, the champion should focus on ensuring that all senior leaders:

- Understand what is expected of them as leaders of organizational change.

- Ensure that effective governance systems are in place to protect the interests of all stakeholder groups and maintain organizational integrity and ethical behavior.

- Consistently speak with one voice as a senior leadership team.

- Serve as role models of performance excellence for managers and employees at all levels of the organization.

- Set clear strategy and directions to enhance future opportunities for the organization.

- Develop future leaders (succession planning) throughout the organization.

- Create measurable performance expectations and monitor performance to achieve the key improvements and strategic objectives of the organization. This means that necessary data and analyses must be coordinated to ensure appropriate information is available for the champion and the entire senior leadership team.

From the operational side, the champion should work to identify and eliminate both individual and system deficiencies, territorial conflicts, and knowledge shortfalls that limit leaders' ability to meet expectations and goals consistently.

The champion should be the focal point in the organization to ensure all parts of the organization have systematic processes in place so they fully understand leadership and management requirements.

A process should exist to monitor ongoing initiatives to ensure leaders effectively set and communicate organizational values to employees:

- They must demonstrate that they focus on delivering value to customers and other stakeholders.

- They must aggressively reinforce an environment that promotes empowerment and innova-

tion throughout the work force. This may involve reviewing policies, systems, work processes, and the use of resources—ensuring sufficient data are available to assist in manager and employee decision making.

- They should review (conduct independent audits) ethical and legal behavior of all leaders and managers and hold them accountable for their actions.

The champion should coordinate the activities involving the review of organizational performance and capabilities:

- Define key performance measures.

- Install systems to review organizational success, performance, and progress relative to goals.

- Use performance review findings to identify priorities for improvement. Communicate those priorities to all units that have responsibilities for making the improvements, including suppliers.

- Systematically use performance review findings, together with employee feedback, to assess and improve senior leadership (including the chief executive) effectiveness and the effectiveness of managers throughout the leadership system.

Finally, the champion must work as part of the senior leadership team to help coordinate all facets of the management system to drive high performance. This involves teaching the team about the requirements of effective and consistent leadership at all levels and its impact on organizational performance. The senior leader of the organization usually serves as the organizational leadership champion and leads this council.

Strategic-Planning Champion

The *strategic-planning champion* is a senior executive who, in addition to other executive duties, works to coordinate and enhance strategic planning and action-plan alignment throughout the organization. It is both a strategic and an operational activity.

From the strategic side, the champion should ensure that the focus of strategy development is on sustained competitive leadership, which usually depends on achieving revenue growth, as well as consistently improving operational effectiveness. The strategic-planning champion should help the senior leadership team acquire a view of the future and provide clear strategic guidance to the organization through goals, objectives, action plans, and measures.

From the operational side, the champion should work to ensure sufficient data are available regarding:

- The organization's operational and human resource strengths and weaknesses

- External risks and threats that may arise from competitors, supplier weaknesses, regulatory changes, economic conditions, and financial, ethical, and societal risks

- The competitive environment and other challenges that might affect future direction

The champion should be the focal point in the organization to ensure all parts of the organization have systematic processes in place so they fully understand the implications of strategy on their daily work.

The champion should ensure that strategy is customer- and market-focused and is actually used to guide ongoing decision making and resource allocation at all levels of the organization:

- A process should exist at each level of the organization to convert strategy into actions, which are aligned to achieve goals necessary for business success.

- Every employee should understand their role in carrying out actions to achieve the organization's goals.

The champion should coordinate the activities involving strategy development and deployment to:

- Acquire and use various types of forecasts, projections, scenarios, or other techniques to understand the plausible range of future options.

- Determine how the projected performance of competitors is likely to compare with the projected performance of the organization in the same time frame in order to set goals to ensure competitive advantage.

- Define the expected path along which growth and performance are likely to take each for strategic objective. Time lines of projected future performance should match the frequency of organizational performance reviews.

- Determine what capabilities must be developed within the organization to achieve strategic. goals and coordinate with other members of the senior leadership team and category champions to ensure those capabilities are in place.

- Determine what changes in services or products might be needed as a part of strategic positioning and direction.

- Ensure a system is in place to develop action plans that address strategic goals and objectives. Ensure those action plans are understood throughout the organization, as appropriate.

- Ensure a system is in place to identify the human resource requirements necessary to achieve strategic goals and objectives. This may include training, support services for employees, reorganization, and new recruitment, to name a few.

- Ensure a system is in place to allocate resources throughout the organization sufficient to accomplish the action plans.

- Coordinate with the leadership system during performance reviews to help ensure that priorities for improvement and innovation at different levels throughout the organization are aligned with strategy and action plans.

- Ensure the process for strategic planning, plan deployment, the development of action plans, and the alignment of resources to support actions is systematically evaluated and improved each cycle. Also evaluate and improve the effectiveness of determining the projected performance of competitors for use in goal setting.

Finally, the champion must work as contributing member of the senior leadership team to help coordinate all facets of the management system to drive high performance. This involves teaching the team about the requirements of strategic planning and its impact on organizational performance.

Customer-Value Champion

The *customer-value champion* is a senior executive who, in addition to other executive duties, will coordinate and enhance customer satisfaction, relations, and loyalty throughout the organization. It is both a strategic and an operational activity.

From the strategic side, the champion should focus on ensuring that the drivers of customer satisfaction, customer retention, and related market share (which are key factors in competitiveness, profitability, and business success) are considered fully in the strategic planning process. This means that necessary data and analyses must be coordinated to ensure appropriate information is available for the executive planning councils.

From the operational side, the champion should work to identify and eliminate system deficiencies, territorial conflicts, and knowledge shortfalls that limit the organization's ability to meet customer satisfaction, retention, and loyalty goals consistently.

The champion should be the focal point in the organization to ensure all parts of the organization have systematic processes in place so they fully understand key customer, market, and operational requirements as input to customer satisfaction and market goals.

A process should exist to monitor ongoing initiatives to ensure they are aligned with the customer aspects of the strategic direction. This may involve:

• Reviewing policies, systems, work processes, the use of resources, and the availability of employees who are knowledgeable and focus on customer relations and loyalty

• Ensuring sufficient data are available to assist in decision making about customer issues

• Ensuring that strategies and actions relating to customer issues are aligned at all levels of reorganization from the executives to the work unit or individual job level

The champion should coordinate the activities involving understanding customer requirements as well as managing the interaction with customers, including how the organization determines customer satisfaction and satisfaction relative to competitors. (Satisfaction relative to competitors and the factors that lead to customer preference are of increasing importance to managing in a competitive environment.)

• The champion should also examine the means by which customers have access to seek information, assistance, or comment and complain.

• The champion should coordinate the definition of customer contact requirements (sometimes called customer service standards) and the deployment of those requirements to all points and people in the organization that have contact with customers.

• The champion should ensure that systems exist to respond quickly and resolve complaints promptly to recover customer confidence that might be otherwise lost.

• The champion should ensure that employees responsible for the design and delivery of products and services receive information about customer complaints so they may eliminate the causes of these complaints.

• The champion should work with appropriate line managers to help set priorities for improvement projects based on the potential impact of the cost of complaints and the impact of customer dissatisfaction and attrition on the organization.

• The champion should be charged with coordinating activities to build loyalty and positive referral, as well as evaluating and improving customer relationship–building processes throughout the organization.

Finally, the champion must work as contributing member of the senior leadership team to help coordinate all facets of the management system to drive high performance. This involves teaching the team about the requirements of customer and market focus and its impact on organizational performance.

Measurement, Analysis, and Knowledge-Management Champion

The *measurement, analysis, and knowledge-management champion* is an executive-level person who, in addition to other executive duties, will coordinate and enhance information, analysis, and knowledge management systems throughout the organization to ensure that they meet the decision-making needs of managers, employees, customers, and suppliers. It is both a strategic and an operational activity.

From the strategic side, information and analyses and the resulting knowledge can provide a competitive advantage. The champion should focus on ensuring, to the extent possible, that timely and accurate information and analyses are available to enhance knowledge acquisition and the development and delivery of new and existing products and services to meet ongoing and emerging customer needs.

From the operational side, the champion should work to ensure that information and analyses are available throughout the organization to aid in decision making at all levels. This means coordinating with all other champions to ensure data are available for day-to-day review and decision making at all levels for their areas of responsibility.

The measurement, analysis, and knowledge-management champion has responsibility for the information infrastructure as well as ensuring the appropriate use of data for decision making. The champion should coordinate activities throughout the organization involving data collection, accuracy, analysis, retrieval, and use for decision making. The champion should ensure:

- Complete data are available and aligned to strategic goals, objectives, and action plans to ensure performance against these goals, objectives, and action plans can be effectively monitored.

- Systems are in place to collect and use comparative data and information to support strategy development, goal setting, and performance improvement.

- Data and information throughout the organization are accurate and reliable to enhance fact-based decision making.

- Data and information are used to support a better understanding of the cost and financial impacts of various improvement options.

- Appropriate correlations and performance projections are available to support planning.

- The performance measurement system is evaluated and improved to ensure it meets business needs.

- Data analysis supports the senior executives' organizational performance review and organizational planning.

- Data analysis addresses the overall health of the organization.

- Information, data, and supporting analyses are available to workgroup and functional-level operations to support decision making at those levels.

- Data analysis supports daily decisions regarding operations throughout the organization to ensure actions align with plans.

- Information management systems, including hardware and software, are easy to use, reliable, and regularly updated to keep them current with changing decision-making needs. Data in these systems are correct (accurate), consistent (reliable), complete (integrity), free from tampering or inappropriate disclosure (secure and confidential), and available when needed (timely).

Finally, the champion must work as part of an organizationwide council to help coordinate all facets of the management system to drive high performance.

Human Resource-Focus Champion

The *human resource-focus champion* is an executive-level person who, in addition to other executive duties, will coordinate and enhance systems to enable employees to develop and utilize their full potential, consistent with the organization's strategic objectives. This includes building and maintaining a work environment conducive to full employee participation and growth. It is both a strategic and an operational activity.

From the strategic side, the human resource constraints of the organization must be considered in the development of strategy, and subsequently eliminated to ensure the work force is capable of achieving the strategies necessary for business success.

From the operational side, the champion should ensure that the work climate enhances employee satisfaction and well-being and that work is organized and jobs are designed to enable employees to achieve higher levels of performance.

The human resource-focus champion has responsibility for ensuring that employees' (including managers and supervisors at all levels, permanent, temporary, and part-time personnel, and contract employees and volunteers supervised by the organization) needs are met to enable them to contribute fully to the organization's goals and objectives. The champion should ensure:

- Work and jobs are structured to promote cooperation, collaboration, individual initiative, innovation, and flexibility.

- An effective system exists to provide accurate feedback about employee performance and to enhance their performance. This includes systems to identify skill gaps and recruit or reassign employees to close those gaps, as well as ensuring that fair work practices are followed within the organization. This may also include evaluating managers and enhancing their ability to provide accurate feedback and effective coaching to improve employee performance.

- Compensation, recognition, and rewards are aligned to support high-performance objectives of the organization (contained in strategic plans and reported in the balanced scorecard or business results report card).

- Education and training support business objectives and build employee knowledge, skills, and capabilities to enhance employee career progression and performance. This includes ensuring employees understand tools and techniques of performance measurement, performance improvement, quality control methods, and benchmarking. This also includes ensuring that managers and supervisors reinforce knowledge and skills on the job.

- The work environment is safe, with measurable performance measures and targets for each key factor affecting employee safety.

- Factors that affect employee well-being, satisfaction, and motivation are routinely measured and actions are taken promptly to improve conditions that adversely affect morale, motivation, productivity, and other related business results.

Finally, the champion must work as part of an organization-wide council to help coordinate all facets of the management system to drive high performance.

Process Management Champion

The *process management champion* is an executive-level person who, in addition to other executive duties, will coordinate and enhance all aspects of the organization's systems to manage and improve work processes to meet the organization's strategic objectives. This includes activities and processes to create value for customers and other stakeholders and involves customer-focused design, product and service delivery, and internal support services. It is both a strategic and operational activity.

From the strategic side, rapid and accurate design, development, and delivery of products and services create a competitive advantage in the marketplace.

From the operational side, the champion should work to ensure all key work processes are examined and optimized to achieve higher levels of performance, reduce cycle time and costs, and subsequently add to organizational profitability.

The process management champion has responsibility for creating a process management orientation within the organization. Since all work is a process, the process management champion must ensure that the process owners (including other champions) systematically examine, improve, and execute their processes consistently. The champion should ensure:

- Systematic continuous improvement activities are embedded in all processes, which lead to ongoing refinements.

- Initial and ongoing customer requirements are incorporated into all product and service designs, production and delivery systems, and processes. This includes core production processes as well as key business (such as research and development, asset management, technology acquisition, and supply chain management) and internal support processes (such as finance and accounting, facilities management, administration, procurement, and personnel).

- Design, production, and delivery processes are structured and analyzed to reduce cycle time; increase the use of learning from past projects or other parts of the organization; reduce costs; increase the use of new technology and other effectiveness or efficiency factors;

and ensure all products and services meet performance requirements.

Finally, the champion must work as part of an organization-wide council to help coordinate all facets of the management system to drive high performance.

Results Champion

The *results champion* is an executive-level person who, in addition to other executive duties, will coordinate the display of the organization's business results. This champion has substantially different work than the champions for Categories 1 through 6. No actions leading to or resulting from the performance outcome data are championed by the business results champion. Those actions are driven by the Category 1 through 6 champions because they have responsibility for taking action to implement and deploy procedures necessary to produce the business results. For example, the analysis and knowledge management champion (Category 4) is responsible for collecting data that reflect all areas of strategic importance leading to business results. The analysis and knowledge management champion is also responsible for ensuring data accuracy and reliability.

The results champion is responsible, however, for ensuring that the organization is able to display all business results required by Category 7 to provide evidence of the organization's performance and improvement in key business areas and facilitate monitoring by leaders. These include customer satisfaction, product and service performance, financial and marketplace performance, human resource results, and operational performance.

Results must be displayed by appropriate segment and group, such as different customer groups, market segments, employee groups, or supplier groups. Appropriate comparison data must be included in the business-results display to judge the relative "goodness" or "strength" of the results achieved. These results are used by senior leaders to monitor organizational performance.

Finally, the results champion must work as part of an organization-wide council to help coordinate all facets of the management system to drive high per-

formance. For example, if the organization is not collecting data necessary for inclusion in the business results report card, the results champion coordinates work with the other champions on the council to ensure those data are available, used for decision making, and included in appropriate reports.

The Critical Skills

A uniform message, set of skills or core competencies, and constancy of purpose are critical to success. Core training should provide all employees with the knowledge and skills on which to build a learning organization that continually gets better. Such training typically includes team building, leadership skills, consensus building, communications, and effective meeting management. These are necessary for effective teams to become involved in solving critical problems.

Another important core skill involves using a common process to define customer requirements accurately, determining the ability to meet those requirements, measure success, and determine the extent to which customers—internal and external—are satisfied. When a problem arises, employees must be able to define the problem correctly, isolate the root causes, generate and select the best solution to eliminate the root causes, and implement the best solution.

It is also important to be able to understand data and make decisions based on facts, not merely intuition or feelings. Therefore, familiarity with tools to analyze work processes and performance data is important. With these tools, work processes can be analyzed and vastly improved. Reducing unnecessary steps in work processes, increasing process consistency, reducing variability, and reducing cycle time are powerful ways to improve quality and reduce cost simultaneously.

Courses in techniques to acquire comparison and benchmarking data, work-process improvement and reengineering, supplier partnerships and certification, role modeling for leaders, strategic planning, team building, and customer satisfaction and loyalty will help managers and employees increase their effectiveness.

LESSONS LEARNED

General Lessons

Twenty years ago the fierce global competition that inspired the quality movement in the United States was felt primarily by major manufacturers. Today, all sectors are under intense pressure to "be the best or be history." The demand for performance excellence reaches all corners of the economy, from manufacturing and service industries to professional services, education, health care, public utilities, and government. All of these segments have contributed valuable lessons to the quality movement and have played an important part in our recovery from the economic slump of the 1970s caused by poor service and products. Relying on the Baldrige model, I will share some of the insights and lessons learned from leaders of high-performing organizations.

Desire and History Are Not Enough

It is important to point out a fact that is perhaps obvious to most: *In order to optimize organizational performance, organizations must actually use the principles contained in the Baldrige Criteria.* It is not enough to think about them. It is not enough to have used them in the past and no longer continue to do so. It is not enough to use a part but not all of the Criteria. To leave out any part suboptimizes the performance of the organization.

The recent experience of Xerox provides a useful example. Xerox won the Baldrige Award in 1989. They demonstrated significant performance improvement through the 1980s and continued to grow substantially through the 1990s. They used the Baldrige Criteria as the way they ran their business, not just a list of additional activities they would do if they felt like it. They were absolutely customer focused. They made decisions based on data, and fully engaged and involved their entire work force. They continuously evaluated and improved their effectiveness in every aspect of their work. In fact, one business unit, Xerox Business Services (XBS), which makes copies of and manages documents, won the Baldrige Award again in 1997. The performance of XBS was similar to Xerox as a whole. In 1989, XBS, with a few hundred employees, generated approximately $300 million in annual revenue. They worked so efficiently and satisfied customers so well that their market grew from $300 million in 1989 to approximately $2 billion in 1997 and to approximately $6 billion in 2000.

However, the new Xerox CEO, Richard Thoman (a transplant from IBM who replaced Paul Allaire), did not use the Baldrige Criteria to provide the leadership needed to maintain the customer focus and bring the company into the emerging digital market. Within a year and a half Xerox performance began to suffer. Its stock price plummeted, losing approximately 80 percent of its value. The Xerox board of directors, after firing Thoman and rehiring the previous CEO, has been struggling to rebuild the processes and systems that led Xerox to high levels of performance excellence in the past. However, it may take the company years to recover.

The Xerox story points out an important lesson. While using the Baldrige Criteria can help an organization reach high levels of performance, organizations cannot expect to sustain those levels of performance without continuing to use the Criteria as the way they run the business. High-performing athletes of all types know this lesson well. To continue to win, they cannot rest on the success of the past. To continue to win, world-class athletes must continue to follow the discipline of training, diet, and effective coaching, and take advantage of technological advances in equipment. The same is true in any competitive environment.

A Tale of Two Leaders

It was a time of turbulence; it was a time of peace. It was a time of growth and streamlining. It was the happiest of times; it was also the most painful of times. Most of all it was a time that demanded change—although it was more comfortable to consider it a time for the status quo.

The following tales are of two leaders. One is consistent and persistent in communicating the direction and message that will bring about excellent results and high performance. Another is uncertain and vague. He does not wish to push his people into anything, let alone the significant commitment related to using the Baldrige Criteria as the way to run the business. After all, the business is still profitable and healthy. Why rock the boat? You may know these people or someone who reminds you of them. If so, you will understand the reason for this section.

There is no lonelier, more challenging, yet critical and rewarding job than that of the leader. I work with many, many leaders who listen to advice carefully. They really want to know the best approaches to optimize their organizations. Yet what they do with the advice and counsel is always interesting and unpredictable. This section is intended to help those leaders go resolutely down the right path.

Neither leader exists in real life, but both leader profiles are based on actual events and observations of different people in leadership positions.

Tale One

John was the CEO of a *Fortune 500* manufacturing company that was slowly but surely losing market share. Shareholders and employees were happy because profits and growth, although slower, were still hearty. However, their business that once enjoyed a near monopoly position was rapidly facing more and more competition. Customers who had to beg and plead for limited products and service over the years were happily turning to competitors that were trying in earnest to meet their needs and even delight them. In such an environment, aggressive, customer-focused companies were winning the hearts, minds, and pocketbooks of John's customers. After working with a consulting firm or two and studying the work of W. Edwards Deming, John decided that performance excellence was urgently needed to keep the company in business more than five years.

The First Message to the Leadership Team

John called an urgent meeting of his senior team. Many members of this team had been there since the company began its 20-year growth spurt and had been good soldiers in times of runaway growth and profit. John was wondering how many members of the senior staff would welcome the message he was about to send. The meeting was scheduled the next week for five days at the corporate headquarters. Short of an emergency illness, attendance was required.

During the next few days, John received 20 phone calls from secretaries who informed John their bosses could not attend because of other priority commitments. Priorities were quickly realigned when they were informed that attendance was not optional.

The week-long meeting began with training—the kind of training in which the group was required to participate, listen, and discuss the content. The training was presented by an outside firm with frequent discussions of company-wide application and emphasis presented by John. At the end of three days, John took over the meeting and asked for input on how best to apply these principles to the organization at all levels. The leadership group voiced resistance to change, some more than others. They basically voiced concern that "this performance excellence stuff with all of its requirements for empowerment and data" would get in the way of their doing business and was not needed.

John clarified the objectives of the group by walking to the white board and writing: "This new program, performance excellence, is in the way of doing business effectively." The senior staff pretty much agreed.

John responded by placing a large "X" through the word "in." The statement now read, "Performance excellence is the way of doing business effectively." John notified the attendees, "I will negotiate an exit package with anyone who does not understand the implications of this message, and who does not want to be part of this new way of doing business." John learned that day that to institute meaningful change, it may be necessary to fire someone he liked. He also realized that to ignore the challenges and lack of commitment would be seen by everyone as tacit approval and send the message that the new way of doing business was "optional."

The Next Steps

John focused on two next steps: 1) making sure his top team role-modeled behavior that would facilitate the needed changes; and 2) planning and implementing a company-wide training requirement to communicate the new skills and performance expectations. John started to change his behavior and the behavior of his top staff, feeling that "walking the talk" would signal the importance of new behaviors more than any speech or videotaped presentation. The next top staff meeting was called within a week to plan the design and rollout of training corporate-wide, including all foreign and domestic sites. The top staff had very little interest in training, feeling largely that this was a human resource function and should be delegated to that department.

Based on the advice of external advisors, John informed the staff that it was now their job to plan, design, and execute this training. A "core design team" was formed with senior leaders and expert content and course design specialists to design the training within one month and present it to the senior corporate leaders.

In spite of prior agreements to manage their meetings effectively, to be on time, not interrupt, and follow the agenda, most continued to ignore the rules. Behaviors of the top leadership group at this meeting included the usual set of interruptions, "I told you so's," and everyone talking at the same time. John, whose goal was to create a listening and learning environment, challenged the group to "ante up." He asked that all top leaders bring 50 $20 bills to the meeting. John introduced new meeting ground rules. They were simple. Interruptions, put downs, blocking behaviors, and talking over someone else, were violations of meeting ground rules. On the other hand, building on ideas, clarifying ideas, supporting, and disagreeing respectfully were good meeting behaviors. Every violation was worth a $20 bill. Good meeting behaviors were rewarded, although they did not materialize until several meetings had been completed.

At first, it seemed that the pot would win big time—no one took John seriously. After about the third meeting, with penalties piling up, leadership group participants' behavior actually changed. Other meeting management skills were slowly introduced, such as time-frame limits and action planning. Then John was confident his team could role-model this behavior to others. He ordered that, "This is the way we treat each other at all meetings, including staff meetings, communication forums, and all company business meetings." A core value and new behavior of courtesy and professionalism became deployed company-wide through the senior management team.

Training and the Change Process
Each five-day, high-performance management course was identical, ensuring that a uniform message and set of skills were communicated. Each course was eventually taught by two instructors, a shop supervisor and a manager, so that management and the work force would both be involved. John personally taught the top leadership team the entire five-day course, assisted by a member of the design team, and this tale spread across the organization like wildfire. It became the thing to be invited to take part in this instruction

because their leader had done it. The core skills became part of the fabric of the organization—the way to conduct business. They included fact-based decisions, a focus on customers, and using and improving processes. Also included was a way to solve problems continually with a well-defined process at the level the problem was occurring.

The focus had shifted from status quo to a thirst for improvement. Improvement began to bring rewards whereas the status quo was disdained. A comprehensive business evaluation was conducted and improvement targets were identified. Clear assignments with reasonable but aggressive goals were cascaded to all levels of the organization. Performance planning, goals, compensation, and recognition were aligned to support the overall business strategy, especially the need to focus better on satisfying internal and external customers. Managers who did not work to meet these new goals, who did not role-model the behaviors necessary to achieve high performance, were reassigned to jobs that did not require their management skills. New role models emerged to lead the organization at all levels. Within three years the company regained market share, improved profitability, expanded its employee base, and became, once again, one of the world's most admired companies.

Tale Two

Victor was the CEO of a West Coast manufacturing company that also was a proud member of the *Fortune 500*. Company performance had been uneven over the past few years. Profits were low this year relative to previous years, but the company still met financial targets. Product demands were high and the outlook was fairly good for the next quarter. The industry as a whole was fairly evenly matched as far as management problems. Trends for return on investment were also uneven, and other indicators such as sales volume and net profit were up and down. Investors were not happy, especially when other companies consistently outperformed them. Victor thought it was time to do something different. Victor consulted several valuable and trusted advisors and then decided that high-performance excellence might be worth considering.

The First Message to the Leadership Team
Victor scheduled a series of weekly dinner meetings over the next month (January) and engaged several

top consultants to talk to the group about the business case for using high-performance management. He invited 50 top-level managers from across the country to attend. Most top leaders attended the meetings, enjoyed the dinners, and Victor attended most but not all of them. The sessions were interesting—the top leaders found the meetings were a great forum for politicking, posturing, wining and dining, and trying to sharpshoot the consultant. Victor asked his top leaders to come together for a half day in the spring to discuss the content and direction of the high-performance initiative, being convinced intellectually by the dinner discussions that this was the right direction for the company. At the half-day meeting, it was obvious that about half of the group agreed with the CEO and about half were uncertain or downright resistant, particularly one very senior vice president. Victor left the team with this message, "Let me take your comments under advisement and think about them as we go forward." Later, at the consultant's suggestion, he conducted an organizational assessment to identify problems that might be contributory to the uneven, up-and-down performance. The assessment uncovered several serious problems that required change, yet the senior leaders continued to resist.

The Next Steps
Victor finally hired one of the external advisors who had withstood the test of several dinner meetings and the challenges of his threatened senior management team. Victor asked the advisor to speak to the top leaders of the entire company about what a great group they were and how important the performance excellence initiative was going to be for the company. The advisor closed by telling them that only the best go after high performance; if they did not, their competitors would. During the following discussion sessions, Victor's chief operating officer (COO) announced to the group that he was far from convinced and stated he was not going to change the way he did business. That comment went unchallenged by Victor or anyone else in the company. Frustration continued to build.

In an effort to regain momentum, Victor wanted to create a change team. He asked each division to send a person to "facilitate" the initiative and receive appropriate training in managing change. The people selected were far from the best each division could offer since no selection criteria had been provided

and many thought this was a waste of time and talent. The division leaders supplied people who were expendable. The people who formed the facilitator group, for their part, were very enthusiastic but not particularly respected or credible. They were given absolutely no relief from any regular duties so they were stretched very thin. Also, the division heads were not supportive in any way of their participation, so they were almost punished for participating on this team. As the facilitators worked to please the demands of the CEO, there was no clear charter or mission as to what they were actually supposed to accomplish—no way to assess their performance or keep track of progress.

The power struggle intensified between the COO (who thought this was not the way to go and would have none of it) and the CEO. The CEO and the top management team arranged to travel to a leadership conference where they could hear presentations from high-performance organizations that had used the performance excellence techniques successfully. The CEO made it a priority to plan only morning presentations so everyone could play tennis or golf together each afternoon. Tennis and golf, not the need for better management systems, was the main topic of discussion at the evening dinners. A good time was had by all, but no consensus around change developed or was even discussed.

Training and the Change Process
Still, Victor wanted the facilitators to continue their work to assist change. The internal facilitators were placed in charge of conducting training for the entire organization. After the initial training was designed, a date was set to present a half-day version to the senior staff. Although the training designed for employees and lower-level managers was a four-day course, the senior staff did not feel they needed the same intense training or skills as the work force. However, Victor made it a high priority for his direct reports to attend. At the last minute, Victor had to attend a function related to the board of directors and did not attend the training.

The training was, to put it mildly, a disaster. The executives, prompted by the snide comments of the COO, never gave it a chance. They concluded that the training was not effective and should not be rolled out to the employees. In the face of compelling opposition, Victor quietly diverted his attention elsewhere.

Leadership Style Summary

It is probably obvious what is the current state of John's high-performance "way to run the business" versus the high-performance "initiative" at Victor's company. Perhaps you could spot some of the problems each type of leader addressed and solutions they supported.

Using symbols and language to manage the change to high performance is tricky and usually demands that some external person be involved who can provide good sound advice, based on experience and expertise, to the CEO. Using power constructively is absolutely critical, since failure of the top leader to use all forms of power and influence available will intensify conflict and power struggles that act as a de facto barrier to change.

Motivating people to act constructively, and not feel threatened, is another challenge. Providing a clear focus on the future state while rewarding behavior that facilitates the transition will work to ensure the change actually happens. Victor's vision was unclear. He did not act as a leader. He ensured his facilitators would never succeed by never championing their work in any way. The next time Victor gets a new idea, these people (if they are still employees) will take a nosedive rather than be at the forefront of the initiative.

John never lost his vision or influence as CEO. He ensured his management team was supportive by first defining and clarifying organizational values, direction, and expectations; encouraging them to climb on board; and ensuring they acquired the skills and support to spread the approaches throughout the company.

Leadership Lessons

Based on the CEO research cited earlier, coupled with the relentless pace of change in all sectors and increasingly global competition, there are several strong messages leaders need to understand. Then they must be willing to take the necessary steps to change. This will require an assessment of current management systems and a willingness to drive the necessary adjustment. Once the assessment is complete and priorities are agreed upon, line up plans and resources and support

the change wholeheartedly. Focus on the marketplace for your cues to change. Ask, for example:

- Is your competition growing weaker?

- Is the economy more stable and secure?

- Are the demands of all of your customers declining?

- Do you have all of the resources you need to meet your future goals?

- Do you believe your employees will be willing or able to continue working at the pace you have set for them? Will they do more?

If the answer is no to any of these questions, read on. Assess management systems and launch improvements. This will require your organization to assess its management against the Baldrige Criteria. After the assessment is complete, identify the vital few next steps, assign responsibility, make improvements, and reevaluate.

Great Leaders Are Great Communicators Who Lead by Example

One characteristic of a high-performance organization is outstanding performance results. How does an organization achieve such results? How does it become world-class? We have found unanimous agreement on the critical and fundamental role of leadership. There is not one example of an organization or unit within an organization that achieves superior levels of performance without the personal and active involvement of its top leadership. Similarly, in all cases where an organization has not been able to achieve or sustain high performance, the cause can be traced to leadership failures.

Top leaders in high-performing organizations create a powerful vision that focuses and energizes the work force. They drive change and innovation. Everyone is pulling together toward the same goals. An inspired vision, combined with appropriately aligned recognition and reward, is the catalyst that builds trust and launches initiatives to overcome the organizational *status quo.*

Great leaders also communicate clear objectives. They assign accountability, ensure that employees have the tools and skills required, and create a work climate where individual initiative and the transfer of learning thrives. They reward teamwork and data-driven improvement. While practicing what they preach they serve as role models for continuous improvement, consensus building, and fact-based decision making; they push authority and accountability to the lowest possible levels.

One lesson from great leaders is to refrain from the use of the word "quality." Unfortunately, the use of the word quality can create an unintended barrier of mistrust and negativism that leaders must overcome before even starting on the road to performance excellence. Too often, when skilled, hard-working, dedicated employees are told by leaders, "We must improve quality," they conclude that their leaders believe they have not been working hard enough. The work force hears an unintended message, "We have to do this because we are not good." They frequently retort with, "We already do quality work!" Registered professionals (engineers, chemists, psychologists, physicians, teachers, to name a few) often exacerbate the communication problem by arguing that they, not customers, are the best ones in a position to know and define "quality." These messages confuse the work force.

Instead, we advise leaders to create a work climate that enables employees to develop and use their full potential, to improve continually the way they work—to seek higher performance levels and reduce activities that do not add value or optimize performance.

Most employees readily agree that there is always room for improvement—all have seen work that does not add value.

The use of the word "quality" can also open leadership to challenges as to what definition of quality the organization should use. This leads to our second lesson learned. Leaders will have to overcome two organizational tendencies—to reject any management model or approach "not invented here" and to think that there are many equally valid models. Quality differs from a decision tree or problem-solving model where there are many acceptable alternatives. The Baldrige model—and the many national, state, and organization assessment systems based on it—is accepted as the standard for defining performance excellence in organizations worldwide. Its criteria provide validated, leading-edge practices for managing an organization to achieve peak performance.

Fifteen years of extraordinary business results shown by Baldrige Award winners and numerous state-level, Baldrige Award–based winners have helped convince those willing to learn and listen.

To be effective, leaders must understand the Baldrige model and communicate to the work force and leadership system their intention to use that model for assessment and improvement. Without clear leadership commitment to achieving the requirements of the comprehensive Baldrige model, resources may be spent chasing fads, special projects, and isolated strategies such as activity-based costing, management by objective, reengineering, project management, quality circles, balanced scorecards, six sigma, lean thinking, and ISO 9000 certification, to name a few. Many of these initiatives have produced good results, but unless leaders focus on the entire system, performance is not optimized.

Without clear leadership there will be many "hikers" walking around but no marked trails for them to follow. Once leaders understand the entire system and realize that it is their responsibility to share the knowledge and mark the trails clearly, performance optimization is attainable. This brings us to our third leadership lesson learned.

A significant portion of senior leaders' time—as much as 60 to 80 percent—should be spent in visible Baldrige-related leadership activities such as goal setting, planning, reviewing performance, recognizing and rewarding high performance, and spending time understanding and communicating with customers and suppliers, not micromanaging subordinates' work. In setting goals, planning, and reviewing performance, senior leaders must look at the inside from the outside. Looking at the organization through the critical eyes of external customers, suppliers, and other stakeholders is a vital perspective.

A key role of the effective senior leader is to focus the organization on satisfying customers through an effective leadership system. Leaders must champion change. They must role-model the tools of consensus building and decision making as the organization focuses on its vision, mission, and strategic direction to keep customers loyal.

Falling back on command-and-control behavior is likely to be self-defeating. The leadership system will suffer from crossed wires and mixed messages. Proclamations such as, "I want this mission rolled out by the end of the second quarter" fall into the self-defeating, major-mistake category. Leaders must be clear and resolute as well as encouraging and nurturing. Using the consensus approach to focus the organization on its mission and vision will take longer. This is similar to taking more time during the product-design phase to ensure that problems are prevented later. The additional time is necessary for organizational learning, support, and buy-in, particularly around two areas—integrating global marketplace realities and better understanding the competitive environment. The resulting vision will have more depth and focus. The leadership system will be stronger as more leaders and managers understand and agree on the course of action. Ultimately, the deployment of the vision and focus will take less time because of the greater buy-in and support created during the process.

Listen

Successful leaders know the power in listening to their people—those they rely on to achieve their goals. One vital link to the pulse of the organization is employee feedback. To determine whether what you have said has been understood, ask for feedback and then listen carefully. To know whether what you have outlined as a plan makes sense or has gaping faults, ask for feedback and then listen. Your leadership system cannot improve without your listening and acting on employee feedback, and your goals and action plans cannot be improved without it. In fact, the 2004 Baldrige Criteria [Item 1.1c(4), Note 3] suggest that leaders use employee feedback in assessing and improving their leadership effectiveness and the effectiveness of managers at all levels.

Manage and Drive Change

Business leaders can count on relentless, rapid change being part of the business world. The rate of change confronting business today is far greater than that driven by the Industrial Revolution. Skills born out of the Industrial Revolution carried our parents through a 40-year work life. Human knowledge now doubles every five to seven years, instead of the 40 years it took in the mid- to late-twentieth century. Today, our children are told to expect five career (not job) changes during their work life.

There are several lessons for leaders today. Change may not occur on the schedule they set for it. It is often faster or too uneven to predict at all. Also, change driven by leaders is often resisted by their most successful followers—they have difficulty seeing the need to change. Take, for example, a school district that scheduled a quality improvement workshop for its middle school faculty. The day before the training, the district leadership received a letter protesting the workshop on the grounds it was not needed. The letter was signed by the 20 best teachers in the school. To the credit of the school district leadership, they held the workshop anyway, and the truly outstanding teachers saw the value in continuous improvement once they began to listen.

Leaders who hold the values of high performance will need to drive change to make the necessary improvements. Change will not happen naturally. It is rarely driven by those at the bottom (except for revolutionaries). Embracing the concepts of organizational (not just individual) learning will facilitate change in the organization. Leaders will need organizational learning as an ally as they manage change and drive it through the organization.

Strategic Planning Lessons

Deploy through People Not Paper

Strategic planning helps identify the things an organization must consider as it plans its future. The resulting strategic plan may also include elements of a quality plan, business plan, tactical plan, operational plan, financial plan, facilities plan, environmental, health, and safety plan, and human resources plan, to name a few. Each subplan seeks to identify the specific things to do in order to be successful in the future and achieve the overall strategy. Easily enough said, but attempts to get agreement on exactly what is strategic planning will result in an interesting variety of ideas. Therefore, the planning process should begin by ensuring that all contributors agree on terminology. Otherwise the strategic plan may be incomplete—a marketing plan, a budget plan, or a financial business plan, depending on who is leading the team.

Developing separate plans for each aspect of business success is counterproductive. This approach almost guarantees a nonintegrated and short-lived systematic performance improvement effort. Therefore, leaders should concentrate on the few critical improvement goals in the strategic plan necessary for organizational success, such as improving customer loyalty and reducing errors or cycle time. The well-developed strategic plan also:

- Documents the financial and market impact of achieving these few goals

- Details actions to support the goals

- Discusses the competitive environment that drives the goals

- Specifies, in measurable terms, the expected performance milestones that must be met to achieve the goals. The milestones (or timelines) match the review cycle (that is, if leaders review progress quarterly, then the plan should list quarterly milestones.

The most critical lesson learned when it comes to strategic plans is that there can be no rest until every person in the organization understands their role in the plan and how their contribution will be measured. The goals, actions, measures, and milestones need not be complex. For every unit, they can be presented as a one-page electronic scorecard, to which senior leaders refer each month during performance reviews. Everyone at all levels should be able to use their own one-page scorecard to deploy the plan, define actions needed, and monitor actual progress against expected progress.

Customer and Market Focus Lessons

Customers Expect Solutions to Problems They Don't Know They Have

The high-performing organization systematically determines its customers' short- and long-term service and product requirements. It does this based on information from former as well as current and potential customers. It builds relationships with customers and continuously obtains information, using it to improve its service and products and better understand customer preferences. The smart organization prioritizes the drivers of satisfaction and loyalty of its customers, compares itself to its competitors, and continuously strives to improve customer satisfaction and loyalty levels.

As the organization becomes more systematic and effective in determining customer needs, it learns that there is high variation in customer needs. The more sophisticated the measurement system, the

more variation will become apparent. It is particularly important that organizations focus on this vital process and make it a top priority that their customers have access to people to make known their requirements and their preferences. How else can modern organizations ensure they are building relationships with their customers? After all, few of us have storefront windows on Main Street where our customers come and chat regularly.

One specific lesson learned comes from voice mail—a big step forward in convenience and efficiency can be a big step backward in customer relationship building if used poorly. For example, a major international financial institution put its highest priority customers on a new voice-mail system. Customers were never informed about the system and one day called their special line to find rock music and a multi-tiered voice-menu system instead of their personal financial account manager. These preferred customers were furious. This is a good example of a step in the wrong direction—customers were never asked about their requirements and preferences, and the organization lost accounts and created many frustrated customers.

Another important first lesson is to segment customers according to their needs and preferences and do what is necessary to build strong, positive relationships with them. More and more customers are looking for service providers to define their unique needs for them and respond to those unique needs. In short, customers are expecting solutions to problems that they, the customers, have not yet realized.

Organizations that make it easy for customers to complain are in a good position to hear about problems early so that they can fix them and plan ahead to prevent them. If organizations handle customer complaints effectively at the first point of contact, customer loyalty and satisfaction will increase. When organizations do not make it easy for customers to complain, when finally given the chance to provide feedback, they will not bother to complain; they simply will no longer do business with these organizations.

As the customer-focused organization matures, it will likely evolve around customer types. This evolution leads to restructuring that is guided by shared organizational values. The speed with which this restructuring occurs varies according to marketplace conditions and the organization's ability to change. Today we see more restructuring that eliminates parochial, regional centers in favor of creating customer service groups that meet customer requirements around the world using up-to-date technologies.

The next lesson has to do with educating the organization's leadership in the fundamentals of customer loyalty and customer satisfaction research models before beginning to collect customer satisfaction data. Failure to do this may affect the usefulness of the data as a strategic tool. At the very least, it will make the development of data collection instruments a long, misunderstood effort, creating rework and unnecessary cost.

Do not expect everyone in your organization to welcome customer feedback—many fear accountability. Time and time again, the organizations most resistant to surveying customers, conducting focus groups, and making it easy for customers to complain are the same organizations that do not have everyday contact-handling systems, response-time standards, or trained and empowered front-line employees to serve customers and deal with their concerns promptly. Front-line employees who do not have sufficient decision-making authority and are not ready to acknowledge customer concerns are not capable of assuming responsibility to solve customer problems.

No single customer feedback tool is sufficient by itself. A mail-based survey does not take the place of personal interviews. Focus groups do not replace surveys. The high-performance organization uses multiple listening posts and trains front-line employees to collect customer feedback and improve those listening posts. In the high-performance organization, for example, even an accounts-receivable system is viewed as a listening post.

Do not lose sight of the fact that the best customer feedback method, whether it be a survey, focus group, or one-on-one interview, is only a tool:

- Make sure the data gathered are actionable.

- Aggregate the data from all sources to permit complete analyses.

- Use the data to improve strategic planning and work processes.

Finally, be aware that customers are not interested in your problems. They merely want products or services delivered as promised. They become loyal when consistent value is provided that sets you above all others. Merely meeting their basic expectations brands you as marginal. To be valued you must consistently delight and exceed the customers' expectations.

Measurement, Analysis, and Knowledge Management Lessons

Data-Driven Management and Avoiding Contephobia

The high-performance organization collects, manages, and analyzes data and information to drive excellence and improve its overall performance. Said another way, information is used to drive actions and build accountability. Using data and information as strategic weapons, effective leaders compare their organization constantly to competitors, similar service providers, and world-class organizations.

While people tend to think of data and measurement as objective and hard, there is often a softer by-product of measurement. That by-product is the basic human emotion of fear. This perspective on data and measurement leads to the first lesson learned about information and analysis. Human fear must be recognized and managed in order to practice data-driven management.

This fear can be found in two types of people. The first are those who have a simple fear of numbers—those who hated mathematics in school and probably stretch their quantitative capabilities to balance their checkbook. These individuals are lost in numerical data discussions. When asked to measure or when presented with data, they can become fearful, resistant, or even angry. These reactions can undermine improvement efforts.

The second type of individual, who may be comfortable with numbers, realizes that numbers can impose higher levels of accountability. The fear of accountability, contephobia (from 14th-century Latin "to count," modified by the French "to account"), is based on the fear of real performance failure that numbers might reveal or, more often, an overall fear of the unknown that will drive important decisions. Power structures can and do shift when decisions are data driven.

Fearful individuals can undermine effective data-driven management systems. In managing this fear, leaders must believe and communicate through their behavior that a number is not inherently right or wrong. It is important for leaders at all levels to demonstrate that system and process improvement, not individuals, is the focus of performance improvement.

A mature, high-performance organization will collect data on competitors and similar providers and benchmark itself against world-class leaders. Some individuals may not be capable of seeing the benefit of using this process performance information. This type of data is known as benchmarking data. The focus is on identifying, learning from, and adopting best practices or methods from similar processes, regardless of industry or product similarity. Adopting the best practices of other organizations has driven quantum leap improvements and provided great opportunities for breakthrough improvements.

Lesson number two, therefore, is that an organization that has difficulty comparing itself with dissimilar organizations is not ready to benchmark and is not likely to be able to optimize its own performance as a result.

The third lesson in this area relates to not being a DRIP. This refers to a tendency to collect so much data (which contributes to contephobia) that the organization becomes data rich and information poor. This is wrong. Avoid wasting capital resources by asking this question: "Will these data help make improvements for our customers, key financials, employees, or top result areas?" If the answer is no, do not waste time collecting, analyzing, and trying to use the data. Ideally, data should not be collected unless it supports decision making.

Human Resource Lessons

Human Resources (Broad Concept Not the Internal Department)

Personnel departments have been renamed in many organizations to "human resources." This name change is intended to draw attention to the fact that people are valuable resources of the organization, not just dispensable commodities to be hired, commanded, and fired. Now, however, the leap made by successful organizations is that human resources need to be part of every strategic and operational decision of the organization. This focus goes far beyond the department of human resources. In high-performing organizations, employees are treated like any valuable asset of the organization—investment and development are critical to optimize the asset. In many respects employees can be perceived as internal customers, and a vital part of the chain that eventually serves an external customer.

One of the valuable lessons learned in this regard is not to let an out-of-date or territorial "personnel or human resources department" use archaic rules to stop your performance improvement program. Although many human resources professionals are among the brave pioneers in high-performance organizations, others have tried to keep compensation and promotions tied to "seat time" and tenure rather than performance. This outdated approach will definitely stop progress in its tracks or slow it significantly.

The Big Challenge Is Trust

The high-performing organization values its employees and demonstrates this by enabling employees to develop and realize their full potential while providing them incentives to do so. The organization that is focused on human resource excellence maintains a climate that builds trust. Trust is essential for employee participation, engagement, personal and professional growth, and high organizational performance.

The first human resource lesson is perhaps the most critical one. That is, revise—overhaul, if necessary—recognition, compensation, promotion, and feedback systems to align with and support high-performance work systems and strategic objectives. If leaders personally demonstrate all the correct leadership behaviors, yet continue to recognize and reward "fire-fighting" performance, offer pay and bonuses tied only to traditional bottom-line results, and promote individuals who do not represent high-performance role models—their organization-wide improvement effort will be short lived. The leadership system with all its webs and intricate circuits will short out due to mixed signals.

Promotion, compensation, recognition, and reward must be tied to the achievement of key high-performance results, including customer satisfaction, innovation, performance improvement, and other business results. The promotion/compensation/recognition tool is a powerful lever to assist in aligning, or misaligning, the work of the organization.

Developing and Maintaining Skills

A second human resource lesson learned relates to training and development. Training is not a panacea or a goal in itself. The organization's direction and goals must support training, and training must support organization priorities. Its human resources are the competitive edge of a high-performing organization. Training must be part of an overall business strategy. If not, money and resources are probably better spent on a memorable holiday party.

Timing is critical. Broad-based work force skill training should not come first. Many organizations rush out and train their entire work force only to find themselves having to retrain months or years later. Key participants should be involved in planning skill training so that they develop important skills just in time to use them in their assignments.

Continuous skill development requires management support to reinforce the use of new skills on the job. Training must be offered when an application exists to use and reinforce the skill. Otherwise, most of what is learned will be forgotten. The effectiveness of training must be assessed based on the impact on the job, not merely the likability of the instructor or the clarity of course materials.

Leadership development at all levels of the organization needs to be built into employee development. New technology has increased training flexibility so that all knowledge does not have to be transferred in a classroom setting. Consider many options when planning how best to update skills. After initial skill building occurs, high-performing organizations emphasize organizational learning where employees take charge of their own learning, using traditional classroom instruction as only one avenue for skill upgrading.

Transferring learning to other parts of the organization or projects is a valuable organizational learning strategy and reinforcement technique.

Employee Satisfaction

Empowered, satisfied employees enhance organizational productivity, customer satisfaction, and financial success.

Employee surveys are often used to measure and improve employee satisfaction. Surveys are especially useful to identify key issues that should be discussed in open employee forums. Such forums are truly useful if they clarify perceptions, provide more in-depth understanding of employee concerns, and open the communication channels with leaders. Organizations have success in improving employee-satisfaction by conducting routine employee satisfaction surveys, meeting with employees to plan improvements, and tying improvements in satisfaction ratings to managers' compensation.

Two final human resource-excellence lessons have to do with engaging and involving employees in decisions about their work. Involving employees in decision making without the right skills or a sense of direction produces chaos, not high performance.

- First, leaders who empower employees before communicating and testing that a sense of direction has been fully understood and that the necessary skills are in place will find that they are managing chaos.

- Second, not everyone wants to be empowered, and to do so may represent a barrier to high performance. While there may be individuals who truly seek to avoid responsibility for making improvements, claiming "that's management's job," these individuals do not last long in a high-performing organization. They begin to stick out like a lone bird in the winter. Team members who want the organization to thrive and survive do not permit such people to influence (or even remain on) their team.

The bigger reason for individuals failing to "take the empowerment and run with it" is management's mixed messages. In short, management must convince employees that they (managers) really believe that employees know their own processes and, with proper training and support, are best suited to make decisions about their work. Consistent leadership is required to help employees overcome legitimate, long-standing fear of traditional management practices used so often in the past to control and punish.

Remember, aligning compensation and reward systems to reinforce performance plans and core values is one of the most critical means to enhance organizational performance; however, getting employees to believe their leaders really trust them to make decisions and improve their own processes is difficult.

Process Management Lessons

Listen to Process Owners and Keep Them Involved

Process management involves the continuous improvement of processes required to meet customer requirements and deliver quality products and services. Virtually every high-performance organization identifies key processes and manages them to ensure that customer requirements are met consistently and performance is improved continuously.

The first lesson learned has to do with the visibility of processes. Many processes are highly visible, such as serving a meal or purchasing. However, when processes are hard to observe as so many are in the service sector (for example, service design or customer response), they are hard to improve. The simple exercise of drawing a process flow diagram with people involved in a process can be a struggle, but also a valuable source of information that can help identify improvement opportunities. With no vantage point from which to see work as a process, many people never think of themselves as engaged in a process. Some even deny it. The fact that all work—visible and invisible—is part of a process must be understood throughout the organization before employees can begin to consistently execute and improve key processes.

Once this is understood, a second process management lesson comes to light. Process owners are the best ones, but not the only ones, to improve their processes. They should be part of process improvement teams, but outsiders should be involved as well. Effective process improvement teams are often made up of carefully selected cross-discipline, cross-functional, multilevel people who bring detailed inner knowledge and fresh insight to the examination of a process. Do not lose sight of the process owner—the person with expert knowledge of the process who should be accountable for long-term improvement to it. In a misguided effort to ensure that all of its process improvement teams were cross-functional and multilevel, one organization enlisted volunteers to join process improvement teams. Using this democratic process, a marketing process improvement team ended up with no credible marketing expertise among its members. Instead, a group of frustrated support and technical staff members, who knew nothing about marketing, wasted time and money mapping and redesigning a process doomed to fail.

The third process management lesson learned involves an issue mentioned earlier. When focusing too closely on internal process data, there is a tendency to lose sight of external requirements. Organizations often succeed at making their processes better, faster, and (maybe) cheaper for them, but not necessarily to the benefit of their customers. When analyzing work processes, someone must stubbornly play the role of advocate for the customers' perspective. Ensure that process changes will help make improvements for customers, key financials, employees, or top result areas. Avoid wasting resources on process improvements that do not appropriately benefit customers, employees, or the key performance objectives of your organization.

A fourth lesson involves design processes, an important but often neglected part of process management. The best organizations have learned that improvements made early in the process, beginning with design, save more time and resources than those made farther "downstream." To identify how design processes can be improved it is necessary to include ongoing evaluation and improvement cycles.

Results Lessons

The Right Activities Lead to Desired Results

Results fall into six equally important categories:

1. Customer-focused, such as customer satisfaction

2. Customer-perceived value product and service quality

3. Financial and market

4. Human resource

5. Organizational effectiveness, such as key design, production, delivery and support performance, regulatory/legal compliance, ethics, and fiscal accountability

6. The extent that strategic objectives were achieved

Systems must exist to make sure that the data from customer satisfaction and dissatisfaction are used at all levels to plan and make improvements. Remember that when customers are asked their opinion, an expectation is created in their minds that the information will be used to make improvements that benefit them.

Some organizations have found it beneficial to have their customers analyze some of their business results with the idea of learning from them as well as building and strengthening relationships. This may or may not be appropriate for your organization, but many successful ones have shared results with key customer groups at a level appropriate for their specific organization.

Product and service quality results provide useful information on key measures of the product or service itself. This information allows an organization to predict whether customers are likely to be satisfied—usually without asking them. For example, one of the nation's most successful and fastest-growing coffee shops knows from its customers that a good cup of coffee is hot, has a good taste, is not too bitter, and has a rich aroma. The measures for these product characteristics are temperature, pH (acidity), and the time lapsed between brewing and serving. With these measures, they can predict whether their customers are likely to be satisfied with the coffee before they serve it. One important lesson in this area is to select measures that correlate with, and predict, customer preference, satisfaction, and loyalty.

Financial and market performance is a key to survival. Organizations that make improvements that do not ultimately improve financial performance are wasting resources and growing weaker financially. This is true for both private-sector (for-profit) and public-sector (not-for-profit, education, government) organizations. It is important to avoid overreliance on financial results. Financial results are the lagging indicators of organization performance. Leaders who focus primarily on financials often overlook or cannot respond quickly to changing business needs. Focusing on finances to run the business—to the exclusion of leading indicators such as operational performance and employee satisfaction—is like driving your car by looking only in the rear-view mirror. You cannot avoid potholes and turns in the road.

Human resource performance results provide early alert to problems that may threaten success. Absenteeism, turnover, accidents, low morale, grievances, and poor skills or ineffective training suboptimize organizational effectiveness. By monitoring performance in these areas, leaders can adjust quickly and prevent minor problems from overwhelming the organization.

Organizational effectiveness and operational and service results pertain to measures of internal effectiveness that may not be of immediate interest to customers, such as cycle time (how long it takes to brew a pot of coffee), waste (how many pots you have to pour out because the coffee sat too long), and payroll accuracy (which may upset the affected workers). Ultimately, improving internal work process efficiency can result in reduced cost, rework, waste, scrap, and other factors that affect the bottom line, whether profit-driven or budget-driven. As a result, customers are indirectly affected. To stay in business, to remain competitive, or to meet increased performance demands with fewer resources, the organization will be required to improve processes that enhance operational and support service results.

Regulatory, legal compliance, and citizenship, including behaving ethically as an organization and as individuals, has proven critical to long-term organizational survival. Just think of Enron and the problems that poor ethics and inadequate governance has cause the entire U.S. economy.

LEADERSHIP SUMMARY: SEVEN MUST-DO PRACTICES

Keys to Optimizing Performance

There is no evidence of an organization optimizing performance and achieving Baldrige recognition without enhancing the entire management system, from leadership and planning to customers, people, and processes. Although all of these processes are critical in the long term, it is the responsibility of top leaders to set the direction, values, and expectations that drive change and create a sense of urgency. Leader actions absolutely determine the speed and success of the effort to optimize organizational performance. If leaders fail to take the following actions, the transformation to a high-performing organization will be seriously delayed and most likely not take place at all.

1. *Role-model effective leadership practices.* Like it or not, leader example drives the actions of others far better than words. Rhetoric without appropriate action is virtually worthless. Do not expect anyone else to do the things you will not. The concept of "do as I say, not as I do" has never worked to guide or change behavior.

- If you do not aggressively drive performance excellence in word and deed, others will think it is optional.

- If you do not have time to innovate, no one else will think innovation is important.

- If you do not empower the employees with whom you work, other managers will follow your lead (and fail to empower and engage their employees).

- If you do not seek improvement ideas from others, people will stop thinking of ways to improve.

- If you do not hold managers accountable for empowering their subordinates, they will believe empowerment is optional.

- If you do not seek data to help make better decisions, others will "shoot from the hip" as well

- If you do not learn new things, you may not keep up with important changes affecting

your business and others will not see the value in learning.

Develop a list of attributes you want to role-model in addition to those listed. Check how you are perceived on these leadership attributes from peer, subordinate, and employee feedback. Change where you are role-modeling the wrong things.

2. *Favor actions based on fact rather than intuition.* The lack of facts and data forces leaders to default to intuition as the basis for decision making. Many great leaders have relied on intuition when facts were unavailable. However, no great leader relied only on intuition, or even mostly on intuition. The best leaders make consistently good decisions, which require reliable facts and data.

We rarely have access to all of the information we want prior to making decisions. However, we will surely not have enough fact-based information unless we prepare in advance. To make consistently better decisions, the best leaders drive fact-based diagnoses of organizational performance that focus on closing the gaps in areas critical to success. This information is readily available and easy to understand.

3. *Learn constantly.* Great leaders recognize that current knowledge limits their capabilities and success. You may think you have all of the knowledge and skills you need, but how do you know what you do not know? Do not expect your subordinates to learn for you because they suffer from the same limits. Considering the pace of change and the speed with which human knowledge is doubling, unless you aggressively pursue new knowledge, you will most certainly become obsolete and less effective faster.

Identify and list the things you must learn to become a better leader. Ask your subordinates to give you feedback to help you complete the list. Set learning goals and time lines to monitor the pace of new learning.

4. *Share knowledge.* Enhance the impact of your new knowledge by sharing it with others. By teaching others and answering their questions, your understanding of the knowledge becomes stronger and you can apply it faster and easier. It is also a good way to role-model the value of learning. Set a schedule to teach others about performance excel-

lence systems and processes at least two to four times each year, and stick to it.

5. *Require other leaders in your organization to do the same.* The performance of individuals drives the performance of the organization. If your performance is suboptimal because you lack certain knowledge, skills, and abilities, the same is certainly true for your subordinates and their employees. After they see the value you place in role-modeling effective practices, learning, and coaching, make it clear you expect them to do the same. It is critical to clearly set this expectation for learning, as well as set clear, measurable expectations for work after they complete the training.

Discuss your concerns and expectations, and answer their questions. You will have to do this very often at first. Be consistent. Those who resist change look for loopholes and ways to avoid change. Do not create loopholes for them. Permit no excuses for those who refuse to learn. Champion the requirements leading to optimum organizational performance.

6. *Align expectations, measures, rewards, and recognition.* The system you have put in place is perfectly suited to produce the results you are currently getting. If you want to change the outcomes you must change the people and processes that produce them. Training is only a part of the change process.

- Express all new expectations for both individual and group performance in measurable terms.

- Measure progress regularly and give prompt feedback.

- Visibly reward and recognize the desired behavior.

- Find other work for those who cannot or will not do the things needed for driving high performance. By rewarding those who achieve desired results and removing those who do not, you make it clear that performance excellence is crucial to success—it is not optional. If you keep a manager in place who has not taken the necessary steps to improve, you must realize that the subordinates of that manager will conclude that such performance must be acceptable.

To enhance desired business results, ensure that goals, strategic objectives, actions, measures, analysis, reward, and recognition are completely aligned. Remember, "What gets measured gets done. What gets rewarded gets done first." If achieving strategic objectives is truly critical to our future success, be sure to assign actions, measure and monitor progress, and reward desired behavior and outcomes.

7. *Use training as a tool to develop skills and inform—not as a substitute for personal leadership action.* Employees desire and expect important information to come from their leaders. Do not simply tell employees to do something new and different and expect it will be done. You must check understanding, measure and monitor progress, and provide appropriate incentives to actually get the desired behavior.

- Sending subordinate managers and employees to training and expecting the trainer to give the new management directions will rarely produce the desired results. It usually produces high skepticism and hostility, and reinforces the idea that leaders are not serious and committed to the new program or change—otherwise they would introduce it themselves. It also makes the trainer and the curriculum the target of criticism and blame:

  - "This class is a waste of time."

  - "The trainer should tell us what to do when we get back to the office."

  - "I do not know why I am here."

  - "Just how serious is management about these changes/programs? Have they taken this training?"

  - "What resources is management going to commit to this effort?"

Before anyone is sent to training, participants need to understand and *be able to describe* why they are there and what they are expected to get out of the training. These expectations should be set by the leaders who send the participants, not the trainers. Leaders could ask trainers to "pretest" the class to determine the extent to which participants understand why they are there. Those who are not prepared should be sent back. It should be the job of the sending managers to provide the proper foundation and preparation for their subordinate employees prior to training.

If you do not do the seven listed activities listed, you are by your actions telling your employees and subordinate managers that performance excellence is optional—something to do when they have nothing else to do. In that event, you and your organization will most certainly fail to achieve the desired change and improvement.

LEADING THE CHANGE TO HIGH PERFORMANCE

Changing organizational culture is not easy and requires dedicated and unwavering consistency in support of the "new way" or "desired way" of behaving and believing. The following actions are usually critical to change culture in an organization:

- *Establish clear goals and a clear direction.* Explain clearly what will be required and how the new requirements are different from the old. If you do not know what new behaviors are required, find out. Talk to leaders who have successfully engineered this kind of improvement in the past. Leaders who are not clear invite confusion and inaction.

- *Show unwavering commitment.* Leaders are pivotal to the success of the enterprise—employees watch them closely. Don't blink in the face of setbacks—quitting is easy and doing so will make employees more cynical and demoralized. When leadership commitment and support are seen as tentative, employees and other subordinates will perceive the changes as "optional," take-or-leave suggestions. Considering the profound ability most people have to resist change, this creates more support for doing nothing.

- *Prove you will change.* If leaders do not "walk the talk," and demonstrate their eagerness to operate differently, others once again conclude that the leaders are not serious and the new requirements are optional.

- *Keep the energy level high and focused on both process improvements and better performance outcomes.* Select improvements that are easy as well as difficult. Small successes are needed to keep the energy and support for performance excellence high. Larger improvement projects take longer to carry out but usually bring greater benefit. Celebrate process improvements as well as better performance outcomes.

- *Encourage people to challenge the status quo when doing so is consistent with enhancing customer value and organizational goals.* Do not tolerate system craziness—break old bureaucratic rules and policies that prevent or inhibit work toward goals. Free your people from bureaucratic silliness and you will find great energy and support from employees.

- *Change rewards to make them consistent with goals and objectives.* Make following the new culture and achieving goals worthwhile by rewarding desired behaviors and making the continued use of the old ones unpleasant. All employees must understand that the rewards are issued for behaving in a certain way and for achieving desired results. Rewards, including compensation and incentives, should not be considered an entitlement of employment. It is important to test the effectiveness of rewards and recognition. Remember, just because you value a reward does not mean that employees will do the same.

- *Measure progress.* What gets measured gets done. When leaders use measurements to track progress, people think they are serious about tracking and improving. If you do not bother measuring, employee productivity is usually lower. In addition, measurements help identify those who should be rewarded and those who should not. Finally, keep measurements simple and efficient. Do not allow the process of measurement to divert energy and focus. Stop collecting data that no longer supports effective decision making.

- *Communicate, communicate, communicate.* Communication cannot replace an inspiring vision and sound goals, but poor communication can scuttle them. People must understand the logic and rationale behind the vision and goals. Leaders must tell them what's coming, how they will be affected, and what's expected of them. Remember to take every opportunity to communicate your desires—once is not enough. The opponents of change will work nonstop to undermine the new goal, vision, and culture; communicate consistently to overcome this resistance. Also remember that even motivated and supportive people forget; remind them often of the vision and new expectations. Leaders who do not communicate effectively invite the rumor mill to fill in the blank spaces. Bad news, bad rumors, and outright lies frequently fill the communication gap leaders might inadvertently leave.

- *Involve everyone.* People who do not actively support change oppose it, perhaps reflexively. Insist on full involvement and define a role for everyone. Find ways to make everyone accountable for transforming the culture and improving performance. Remember that if a manager fails to support the changes needed to improve performance, it is probably a good idea to encourage that person to find other work—preferably with a competitor.

- *Start fast, then go faster.* Slow progress, which the opponents of change like to see, creates a self-fulfilling prophecy—that the proposed changes will not be effective. However, speed creates a sense of urgency that helps overcome organizational inertia, achieve stunning results, and defeat the gloom and pessimism of naysayers.

Remember to remain steadfast in support, walk the talk, involve everyone, communicate, achieve quick results, measure, and reward progress.

Improve Performance, Efficiency, and Timeliness

What Does It Mean?

- Includes but is not limited to process identification, analysis, and ongoing improvement. We must define and measure process cycle time and defects and reduce them consistently.

What Is the Manager's Responsibility?

- Set an example—ask for data/measurements on cycle time and defects.

- Make time available.

- Make training available.

- Ensure that records discipline exists.

- Charter teams.

- Set low goals, get low performance.

- If you do not tell employees what you expect, do not be surprised if they do not get where you want them to go.

Create a Participative, Cooperative Workplace

What Does It Mean?

- Includes but is not limited to setting boundary conditions and relevant goals, then moving decisions to the lowest possible level, using work teams for planning and process improvement, and creating a "family-friendly" work environment. Leaders motivate people, provide training for managers and employees, encourage the development of self-directed work teams, delegate authority and decision making downward, empower people to focus on achieving mission and vision, value diversity, provide open communication in all directions, and measure and improve employee well-being, motivation, and satisfaction.

What Is the Manager's Responsibility?

- Coach and counsel, rather than control.

- Encourage participation with the goal of achieving better decision quality—make better use of human resources.

- Create and build a highly motivated and satisfied work force.

Planning Action

- Based on vision and results from the previous year, every organization clarifies direction through planning and the deployment of the plan to guide daily action.

- Leaders are responsible for:

  - Identifying improvement opportunities in their units and identifying the key actions needed to achieve the improvements

  - Identifying who will lead the improvements and chartering teams to do so

- All managers have responsibility for identifying unit and individual performance objectives to achieve desired performance levels and targets at all levels of the organization.

Taking Action

• All leaders have a responsibility for communicating the mission, vision, goals, and improvement targets to all employees.

• It is very important that leaders and employees understand and agree fully with the planned objectives. The plan deployment process cascades from top management to all locations and levels of the organization. Top managers do not micromanage the process. This means that the top leaders determine the objective or target and an action officer determines the means. This then sets the target for the next level to determine means. Figure 10 provides one example of this effect.

Personal Management Effectiveness—The Use of Upward Evaluations

Formal upward evaluations have been used for more than 50 years to help assess job performance. As organizations become committed to improving labor relations and manager effectiveness, upward evaluation has become a widely used tool that more and more leaders value.

Three reasons why upward feedback is beneficial include:

1. *Validity.* Subordinates interact regularly with their managers and have a unique vantage from which to assess manager style.

2. *Reliability.* Numerous subordinates provide the best chance for reliable data.

3. *Involvement and morale.* Asking people to comment on the effectiveness and style of their managers boosts morale and sends a clear message that the organization is serious about increasing employee involvement.

Before managers can effectively change the way they manage, they should gather facts about their current style. They need to know what aspects of their style are considered strong and should not be changed. The starting point for improving management style, therefore, is an honest assessment of each

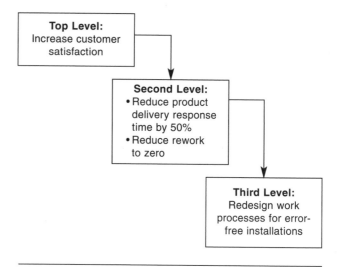

Figure 10 Deploying strategic objectives.

manager's current behavior by subordinates, peers, and supervisors.

The Feedback Process

1. Leaders solicit feedback on how they perform against specific behaviors that are characteristic of an effective manager.

2. They use this information to plan personal improvement strategies.

3. They share the results of the survey with their employees and discuss improvement actions.

4. They make improvements as planned and start the process again next year.

Figure 11 maps the process.

This process enables employees to help their manager understand how he or she is perceived, as well as identify areas of strength on which the manager can build. However, some important procedures should be in place to prevent improper use of the tool:

• Feedback should always be used and interpreted in the spirit of continuous personal improvement. Personally identifiable results should go only to the manager who was rated and should not be used as a basis for performance ratings, promotion, assignments, or pay adjustments (unless, of course, the manager refuses to work to improve).

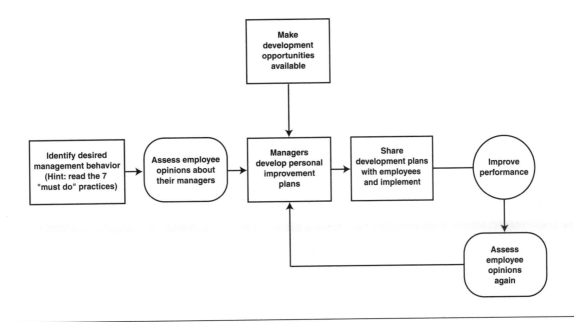

Figure 11 Improving leadership effectiveness.

- Anonymity for those completing questionnaires should be carefully protected. No one other than the employee should see the actual completed questionnaire. To further protect anonymity, questionnaires should not be summarized and reported to the manager in cases where fewer than three to five employees completed the questionnaire.

- Personally identifiable results should be provided only to the manager named on the questionnaire. When the managers receive the results, they review their own ratings to determine their strengths and opportunities for improvement. Then they take steps to improve.

The Management Effectiveness Survey (Figures 12 and 13) can provide information that might help leaders and managers at all levels determine areas to address to strengthen their personal effectiveness. It represents one set of questions to examine leadership communication, openness, and effectiveness.

Certainly other questions may be asked as circumstances change. In fact, in order to determine if any survey is asking the correct questions, the survey itself should be evaluated. This can be done by using open-ended questions and asking the employees to identify other issues that are of concern to them and should be included in the survey. Also, ask if some of the questions are not relevant or important and should be eliminated; then adjust the survey accordingly.

In addition to aggregating scores from employees, it is also useful to compare the perceptions of managers with the perception of the leader or manager who is the target of the assessment. Many times, employees identify a specific weakness that the leader believes is much stronger. These differences, together with key areas where both parties agree that a weakness exists, could be targeted for specific improvement. By aggregating the assessment data for all managers and making the overall results available to individuals, they can determine how their stage of development compares with other managers in the office.

MANAGEMENT EFFECTIVENESS SURVEY

The following questionnaire lists some key indicators to help you assess your manager's style in several key areas. Enter 1 for strongly disagree, 2 for disagree, 3 for agree, and 4 for strongly agree. If you cannot answer a question leave it blank.

General

1. My manager keeps me well informed about what's going on in the office. 1 2 3 4
2. My manager clearly and accurately explains the reasons for decisions that affect my work. 1 2 3 4
3. I am satisfied with my involvement in decisions that affect my work. 1 2 3 4
4. My manager delegates the right amount of responsibility to me and does not micromanage. 1 2 3 4
5. My manager gives me honest feedback on my performance. 1 2 3 4
6. I have confidence in my manager's decisions. 1 2 3 4
7. My manager has the knowledge he/she needs to be effective. 1 2 3 4
8. I can depend on my manager to honor the commitments he/she makes to me. 1 2 3 4
9. My manager treats people fairly and with dignity and respect. 1 2 3 4
10. My manager is straightforward and honest with me. 1 2 3 4
11. My manager is committed to resolving the concerns that may be identified in this survey and has made improvements based on past surveys (if applicable). 1 2 3 4
12. My manager strongly supports doing the right thing for the customer and all other stakeholders. 1 2 3 4
13. The communication process in my unit is effective. I always understand what is being communicated. (Unit refers to the level in the office your manager heads.) 1 2 3 4
14. In my unit, there is an environment of openness and trust. 1 2 3 4
15. I feel free to speak up when I disagree with a decision. 1 2 3 4
16. I feel I can elevate issues to higher-level managers without fear of reprisal. 1 2 3 4
17. The people I work with cooperate to get the job done. 1 2 3 4
18. In my unit, we are simplifying the way we do our work. 1 2 3 4
19. We have an effective process for preparing people to fill open positions. 1 2 3 4
20. All employees have fair advancement opportunities based on skills and abilities. Diversity of ideas is valued. 1 2 3 4

Effective Management Practices

My manager frequently...
21. provides me with honest feedback on my performance. 1 2 3 4
22. encourages me to monitor my own efforts. 1 2 3 4
23. encourages me to make suggestions to improve work processes. 1 2 3 4
24. ensures I have the knowledge, information, facts, and analysis I need to do my job. 1 2 3 4
25. defines his/her requirements of me in clear, measurable terms. 1 2 3 4
26. acts as a positive role model for performance excellence. 1 2 3 4
27. ensures that organizational goals, strategic objectives, and related actions are understood at all levels. 1 2 3 4
28. favors facts before making decisions affecting our customers, employees, partners, and organization. 1 2 3 4
29. identifies and removes barriers to alleviate work-related problems. 1 2 3 4
30. encourages people in our unit to work as a team. 1 2 3 4
31. informs us regularly about the state of the business. 1 2 3 4
32. encourages me to ask questions and creates an environment of openness and trust. 1 2 3 4
33. behaves in ways that demonstrate respect for others. 1 2 3 4
34. ensures regularly scheduled reviews of progress toward goals. 1 2 3 4
35. monitors my progress and compares it against goals. 1 2 3 4
36. ensures that rewards and recognition are fairly applied and closely tied to strategic goals, objectives, and required action plans. 1 2 3 4
37. sets objectives based on strategic objectives and customer requirements. 1 2 3 4
38. runs effective meetings. 1 2 3 4
39. uses a disciplined, fact-based process to make business and operational decisions and solve problems. 1 2 3 4
40. treats performance excellence as a basic operating principle. 1 2 3 4

Please list on the back of this form additional questions that the survey should ask about your manager. Also tell us which questions already on the survey are not very important and should be removed. In this way we can improve the effectiveness of the survey and better identify areas most needing improvement.

Figure 12 Sample Management Effectiveness Survey.

SAMPLE SCORED SURVEY
10 employees completed the instrument

General

	#	1	2	3	4	Mean
1. My manager keeps me well informed about [The manager's self score (circle) is different than the employee's. Possible failure to recognize a problem.]	10	3	5	→	(1)	2.0
2. My manager clearly and accurately explains [...] affect my work.	10		2	5	3	3.1
3. I am satisfied with my involvement in decisions that affect my work.	10		5	5		2.5
4. My manager delegates the right amount of responsibility to me and does not micromanage.	10	2	3	3	2	2.5
5. My manager gives me honest feedback on my performance.	10	4	2	3	1	2.1
6. I have confidence in my manager's decisions. [Relatively strong]	10		5	5		2.5
7. My manager has the knowledge he/she needs [...]	10		5	5		2.5
8. I can depend on my manager to honor the com[...] he/she makes to me.	10			2	8	3.8
9. My manager treats people fairly and with dignity and respect.	10		3	3	4	3.1
10. My manager is straightforward and honest with me. [Relatively weak]	10	2	7	1		1.9
11. My manager is committed to resolving the concerns th[...] identified in this survey and has made improvements based on past surveys (if applicable).	10	3	4	2	1	1.9
12. My manager strongly supports doing the right thing for the customer and all other stakeholders.	10			6	4	3.4
13. The communication process in my unit is effective. I always understand what is being communicated. (Unit refers to the level in the office your manager heads.)						0
14. In my unit, there is an environment of openness and trust.						0
15. I feel free to speak up when I disagree with a decision.						0
16. I feel I can elevate issues to higher-level managers without fear of reprisal.						0
17. The people I work with cooperate to get the job done.						0
18. In my unit, we are simplifying the way we do our work.						0
19. We have an effective process for preparing people to fill open positions.						0
20. All employees have fair advancement opportunities based on skills and abilities. Diversity of ideas is valued.						0

Effective Management Practices

My manager frequently . . .

	Mean
21. provides me with honest feedback on my performance.	0
22. encourages me to monitor my own efforts.	0
23. encourages me to make suggestions to improve work processes.	0
24. ensures I have the knowledge, information, facts, and analysis I need to do my job.	0
25. defines his/her requirements of me in clear, measurable terms.	0
26. acts as a positive role model for performance excellence.	0
27. ensures that organizational goals, strategic objectives, and related actions are understood at all levels	0
28. favors facts before making decisions affecting our customers, employees, partners, and organization.	0
29. identifies and removes barriers to alleviate work-related problems.	0
30. encourages people in our unit to work as a team.	0
31. informs us regularly about the state of the business.	0
32. encourages me to ask questions and creates an environment of openness and trust.	0
33. behaves in ways that demonstrate respect for others.	0
34. ensures regularly scheduled reviews of progress toward goals.	0
35. monitors my progress and compares it against goals.	0
36. ensures that rewards and recognition are fairly applied and closely tied to strategic goals, objectives, and required action plans.	0
37. sets work goals based on strategic objectives and customer requirements.	0
38. runs effective meetings.	0
39. uses a disciplined, fact-based process to make business and operational decisions and solve problems.	0
40. treats performance excellence as a basic operating principle.	0

Figure 13 Sample Management Effectiveness Survey partially scored.

Create Performance Excellence Standards for Managers—A Key Job Element

Virtually every organization has the ability to determine what performance requirements are critical for the success of employees and managers. These critical performance requirements are usually included as a key element in performance plans and appraisals. By declaring that performance excellence is critical to the success of the organization, a specific key performance requirement can be included in the performance plan (sometimes these are called personal commitment plans, personal improvement plans, or personal management objectives, to name a few) and evaluation of managers and leaders. Using this approach, every manager and supervisor begins to take performance excellence more seriously.

- Using the following performance standards as an example, in order for a manager to receive a rating at a particular level, that manager must have accomplished all of the activities described for that rating level. If all are not met, the rating goes to the lowest level at which all are met.

- The writer of the performance appraisal must cite measurable examples in the performance appraisal for actions listed under the rating level.

- Supervising reviewers must verify that these actions have indeed been taken. Under this system, managers are strongly encouraged to keep accurate records of activities that might exemplify compliance with these standards.

Overall Performance Standard for Leadership

The individual visibly demonstrates adherence to the high personal standards and characteristics of leaders in a high-performing organization.
The individual:

- Understands the business processes of the unit.

- Is customer-focused and customer-driven.

- Demonstrates a firm commitment to the principles of customer satisfaction. Understands their requirements and consistently works to meet and exceed them.

- Understands and personally uses performance excellence principles and tools for decision making and planning:

  - Favors the use of data and facts to drive decisions and ensures that employees and subordinate managers do the same.

  - Ensures that organizational goals are converted to appropriate actions to align work within the organizational unit.

  - Measures and monitors progress toward achieving the goals within the organizational unit.

- Demonstrates a firm commitment to the principles of employee empowerment, well-being, and satisfaction:

  - Promotes flexibility and individual initiative.

  - Encourages and supports the personal and professional development of self and employees.

  - Supports effective training and reinforces the use of new skills on the job.

  - Ensures compensation is aligned to support business strategies and actions.

  - Rewards and recognizes employees who incorporate the principles of performance excellence in their day-to-day work.

  - Fosters an atmosphere of open, honest communication and knowledge sharing among employees and business units throughout the organization.

- Rigorously drives the systematic, continuous improvement of all work processes, including personal self-improvement as an effective leader.

- Achieves consistently improving performance outcomes in customer satisfaction, employee well-being, motivation, and satisfaction, operational excellence, and financial (cost/budget) performance.

Rating No. 1: Performance is unsatisfactory. The individual frequently fails to meet the performance standard for leadership.

- Does not fully understand the business processes of the unit.

- Consistently disregards the needs of customers.

- Does not understand and has not taken steps to implement performance excellence (may even work against the changes needed).

  – Intuition, not data or facts, tends to dominate decision making.

  – Organizational goals and actions are not aligned to actions within the unit.

  – May measure and monitor some performance outcomes (such as budget tracking), but most measures are not aligned to organizational goals.

- Does not effectively promote employee well-being, motivation, and morale.

  – Tends to micromanage—does not delegate decision-making authority to the lower levels except as directly instructed to do so.

  – Rarely listens to employees or cares what they think.

  – Does not consistently promote flexibility and individual initiative.

  – Does not consistently encourage and support the personal and professional development of self and employees.

  – May send employees to training but does not consistently reinforce the use of new skills on the job.

  – Has not taken effective steps to ensure that compensation and other rewards or recognition are aligned to support business strategies and actions.

  – Reward and recognition are not aligned to support organizational goals or the principles of performance excellence or customer satisfaction.

- Does not communicate effectively or foster an atmosphere of knowledge-sharing among employees and business units.

- Does not regularly assess or improve work processes, including their personal effectiveness as a leader.

- Does not achieve consistently improving performance outcomes in customer satisfaction, employee well-being, motivation, and satisfaction, operational excellence, and financial (cost/budget) performance.

Rating No. 2: Performance is minimally acceptable. Individual occasionally fails to meet the performance standard for leadership. Performs higher than indicated by level one but less than level three.

Rating No. 3: Performance is acceptable. Individual basically meets the performance standard for leadership.

- Is considered to be a capable leader.

- Understands the key business processes of the unit.

- Is customer-driven and promotes customer-focused values throughout the unit.

  – Demonstrates a commitment to the principles of customer satisfaction.

  – Develops systems to understand customer requirements, strengthen customer relationships, resolve customer problems and prevent them from happening again, and obtain information about customer satisfaction and dissatisfaction.

- Personally uses many performance excellence principles and tools for decision making and planning.

- Visibly supports performance excellence within the organization. Usually uses data and facts to drive decisions and ensures that many employees and subordinate managers do the same.

- Ensures that key organizational goals are converted to appropriate actions to align most work within the organizational unit. Most goals and actions have defined measures of progress and time lines for achieving desired results.

- Demonstrates some commitment to the principles of employee empowerment, well-being, and satisfaction. Is well-regarded by employees for:

- Involving the work force in identifying improvement opportunities and developing improvement plans.

- Valuing employee input on work-related matters.

- Promoting flexibility and individual initiative and ensuring that many subordinate managers do the same.

- Encouraging and supporting the personal and professional development of self and employees.

- Supporting effective training and reinforcing the use of new skills on the job.

- Ensuring compensation is aligned to support business strategies and actions.

- Rewarding and recognizing employees who incorporate the principles of performance excellence in their day-to-day work.

• Fosters an atmosphere of open, honest communication and knowledge-sharing among employees and business units throughout the organization.

• Visibly drives continuous improvement of many work processes, including their personal effectiveness as a leader.

• Achieves consistently improving performance outcomes in customer satisfaction, employee well-being, motivation, and satisfaction, operational excellence, and financial (cost/budget) performance.

• The levels of performance outcomes are better than average when compared with organizations providing similar programs, products, or services.

Rating No. 4: Individual occasionally exceeds the performance standard for leadership. Performs higher than indicated by level three but less than level five. Performance is very good.

Rating No. 5: Individual consistently exceeds the performance standard for leadership. *Is considered a role model for leadership.* Performance is superior.

• Understands the business processes of the unit in great detail.

• Is customer-driven and actively promotes customer-focused values throughout the unit.

- Demonstrates a firm commitment to the principles of customer satisfaction.

- Develops effective systems to understand customer requirements, strengthen loyalty and customer relationships, resolve customer problems immediately and prevent them from happening again, and obtain timely information about customer satisfaction and dissatisfaction.

- Advocates the needs of customers through the collection and use of information on customer satisfaction, dissatisfaction, and product performance.

• Personally uses performance excellence principles and tools for decision making and planning.

- Serves as a performance excellence champion within the organization and as a resource within the work unit, providing guidance, counsel, and instruction in performance excellence tools, processes, and principles.

- Is a role model for using data and facts to drive decisions and ensures that employees and subordinate managers do the same.

- Ensures that all organizational goals are converted to appropriate actions to align work within the organizational unit.

- Each goal and action has defined measures of progress and time lines for achieving desired results.

• Demonstrates a firm commitment to the principles of employee empowerment, well-being, and satisfaction. Is highly regarded by employees for:

- Involving the work force in setting standards of performance, identifying improvement opportunities, and developing improvement plans.

– Seeking and valuing employee input on work-related matters.

– Promoting flexibility and individual initiative and ensuring that subordinate managers do the same.

– Encouraging and supporting the personal and professional development of self and employees.

– Supporting effective training and reinforcing the use of new skills on the job.

– Ensuring compensation is aligned to support business strategies and actions.

– Rewarding and recognizing employees who incorporate the principles of performance excellence in their day-to-day work.

• Fosters an atmosphere of open, honest communication and knowledge sharing among employees and business units throughout the organization.

– Checks the effectiveness of nearly all communication and makes changes to improve.

• Rigorously drives the systematic, continuous improvement of all work processes, including personal self-improvement as an effective leader.

– Develops personal action plan and always incorporates results of 360-degree feedback to continuously improve personal leadership effectiveness and ensures subordinate managers do the same.

• Achieves consistently improving performance outcomes in customer satisfaction; employee well-being, motivation, and satisfaction; operational excellence; and financial (cost/budget) performance.

– The levels of performance outcomes are among the highest in the organization and are also high when compared with organizations providing similar programs, products, or services.

The following tables display the performance excellence ratings side by side to make it easier to see the progression from poor (1) to excellent (5).

Performance Excellence Standards Table

Level 1	Level 2	Level 3	Level 4	Level 5
Performance is unsatisfactory: Individual frequently fails to meet the performance standard for leadership. Is considered a poor leader.	**Better than level 1 and some of level 3.**	**Performance is acceptable: Individual basically meets the performance standard for leadership. Is considered to be a capable leader.**	**All of level 3 and some of level 5.**	**Performance is superior: Individual consistently exceeds the performance standard for leadership. Is considered a role model for leadership.**
• Does not fully understand the key business processes of the unit.		• Understands the key business processes of the unit.		• Understands the business processes of the unit in great detail.

• Consistently disregards the needs of customers.		• Is customer-driven and promotes customer-focused values throughout the unit.
		  – Demonstrates a commitment to the principles of customer satisfaction.
		  – Develops systems to understand customer requirements, strengthen customer relationships, resolve customer problems and prevent them from happening again, and obtain information about customer satisfaction and dissatisfaction.
				• Is customer-driven and actively promotes customer-focused values throughout the unit.
				  – Demonstrates a firm commitment to the principles of customer satisfaction.
				  – Develops effective systems to understand customer requirements, strengthen loyalty and customer relationships, resolve customer problems immediately and prevent them from happening again, and obtain timely information about customer satisfaction and dissatisfaction.
				  – Advocates the needs of customers through the collection and use of information on customer satisfaction, dissatisfaction, and product performance.

Performance Excellence Standards Table

Level 1	Level 2	Level 3	Level 4	Level 5
Performance is unsatisfactory: Individual frequently fails to meet the performance standard for leadership. Is considered a poor leader.	**Better than level 1 and some of level 3.**	**Performance is acceptable: Individual basically meets the performance standard for leadership. Is considered to be a capable leader.**	**All of level 3 and some of level 5.**	**Performance is superior: Individual consistently exceeds the performance standard for leadership. Is considered a role model for leadership.**
• Does not understand and has not taken steps to implement performance excellence (may even work against the changes needed). – Intuition, not data or facts, tends to dominate decision making. – Organizational goals and actions are not aligned to actions within the unit. – May measure and monitor some performance outcomes (such as budget tracking) but most measures are not aligned to organizational goals. • Does not understand and has not taken steps to implement performance excellence (may even work against the changes needed).		• Personally uses many performance excellence principles and tools for decision making and planning. – Visibly supports performance excellence within the organization. – Usually uses data and facts to drive decisions and ensures that many employees and subordinate managers do the same. – Ensures that key organizational goals are converted to appropriate actions to align most work within the organizational unit. – Most goals and actions have defined measures of progress and time lines for achieving desired results.		• Personally uses nearly all performance excellence principles and tools for decision making and planning. – Serves as a performance excellence champion within the organization and as a resource within the work unit, providing guidance, counsel, and instruction in performance excellence tools, processes, and principles. – Is a role model for using data and facts to drive decisions and ensures that employees and subordinate managers do the same. – Ensures that all organizational goals are converted to appropriate actions to align nearly all work within the organizational unit. – Each goal and action has defined measures of progress and time lines for achieving desired results.

Performance Excellence Standards Table

Level 1	Level 2	Level 3	Level 4	Level 5
Performance is unsatisfactory: Individual frequently fails to meet the performance standard for leadership. Is considered a poor leader.	Better than level 1 and some of level 3.	**Performance is acceptable: Individual basically meets the performance standard for leadership. Is considered to be a capable leader.**	All of level 3 and some of level 5.	**Performance is superior: Individual consistently exceeds the performance standard for leadership. Is considered a role model for leadership.**
• Does not effectively promote employee well-being, motivation, and morale. – Tends to micromanage; does not delegate decision-making authority to the lower levels except as directly instructed to do so. – Rarely listens to employees or cares what they think. – Does not consistently promote flexibility and individual initiative. – Does not consistently encourage and support the personal and professional development of self and employees. – May send employees to training but does not consistently reinforce the use of new skills on the job. – Has not taken effective steps to ensure compensation and other rewards or recognition are aligned to support business strategies and actions. – Reward and recognition are not aligned to support organizational goals or the principles of performance excellence or customer satisfaction.		• Demonstrates some commitment to the principles of employee empowerment, well-being, and satisfaction. Is well regarded by employees for: – Involving the work force in identifying improvement opportunities and developing improvement plans. – Valuing employee input on work-related matters. – Promoting flexibility and individual initiative and ensuring that many subordinate managers do the same. – Encouraging and supporting the personal and professional development of self and employees. – Supporting effective training and reinforcing the use of new skills on the job. – Ensuring compensation is aligned to support business strategies and actions. – Rewarding and recognizing employees who incorporate the principles of performance excellence in their day-to-day work.		• Demonstrates a firm commitment to the principles of employee empowerment, well-being, and satisfaction. Is highly regarded by employees for: – Involving the work force in setting standards of performance, identifying improvement opportunities, and developing improvement plans. – Seeking and valuing employee input on work-related matters. – Promoting flexibility and individual initiative and ensuring that nearly all subordinate managers do the same. – Encouraging and supporting the personal and professional development of self and employees. – Supporting effective training and reinforcing the use of new skills on the job. – Ensuring compensation is aligned to support business strategies and actions. – Rewarding and recognizing employees who incorporate the principles of performance excellence in their day-to-day work.

Performance Excellence Standards Table

Level 1	Level 2	Level 3	Level 4	Level 5
Performance is unsatisfactory: Individual frequently fails to meet the performance standard for leadership. Is considered a poor leader.	**Better than level 1 and some of level 3.**	**Performance is acceptable: Individual basically meets the performance standard for leadership. Is considered to be a capable leader.**	**All of level 3 and some of level 5.**	**Performance is superior: Individual consistently exceeds the performance standard for leadership. Is considered a role model for leadership.**
• Does not communicate effectively or foster an atmosphere of knowledge-sharing among employees and business units.		• Fosters an atmosphere of open, honest communication and knowledge-sharing among employees and business units throughout the organization.		• Fosters an atmosphere of open, honest communication and knowledge-sharing among employees and business units throughout the organization. – Checks the effectiveness of nearly all communication and makes changes to improve.
• Does not regularly assess or improve work processes, including his or her personal effectiveness as a leader.		• Visibly drives continuous improvement of many work processes, including his or her personal effectiveness as a leader.		• Rigorously drives the systematic, continuous improvement of all work processes, including his or her personal effectiveness as a leader. – Develops personal action plan and always incorporates results of 360-degree feedback to continuously improve his/her leadership effectiveness and ensures subordinate managers do the same.
• Does not achieve consistently improving performance outcomes in customer satisfaction, employee well-being, motivation, and satisfaction, operational excellence, and financial (cost/budget) performance.		• Achieves consistently improving performance outcomes in customer satisfaction, employee well-being, motivation, and satisfaction, operational excellence, and financial (cost/budget) performance. – The levels of performance outcomes are better than average when compared with organizations providing similar programs, products, or services.		• Achieves consistently improving performance outcomes in customer satisfaction, employee well-being, motivation, and satisfaction, operational excellence, and financial (cost/budget) performance. – The levels of performance outcomes are among the highest in the organization and are also high when compared with organizations providing similar programs, products, or services.

Lessons Learned Conclusions

Successful leaders will create a customer focus and a context for action at all levels of the organization. Effective leaders will distribute authority and decision making to all levels of the organization. Nearly instantaneous, two-way communication will permit clear strategies, measurable objectives, and priorities to be identified and deployed organization-wide. Problems will be identified and resolved with similar speed. Success in this environment will demand different skills of employees and managers. Unless all managers and employees understand where the organization is going and what must be done to beat the competition, it will be difficult for them to make effective decisions consistent with overall direction and strategy. If employees at all levels are not involved in decision making, organizational effectiveness is reduced—making it more difficult to win in a highly competitive market.

In closing this section, I would like to suggest that the scenario previously described is already happening today among the world's best-performing organizations.

- These organizations have effective leadership at all levels, with a clear strategy focused on maximizing customer value. Middle-level managers support, rather than block, the values and direction of the top leaders.

- They have developed ways to challenge themselves and improve their own processes when doing so promotes customer value and improves operating effectiveness.

- They engage workers fully and promote organizational and personal learning at all levels. They ensure that knowledge is shared within the organization to avoid duplication of effort.

- They have created effective data systems to enhance decision making at all levels.

- They have developed and aligned reward, recognition, compensation, and incentives to support the desired customer-focused behavior among all leaders, managers, and employees.

- They have found ways to design effective work processes and ensure that those processes are improved continuously.

- They closely monitor their performance and the performance of their principal competitors. They use this information to adjust their work and continue to improve.

These organizations are among the best in the world at what they do and they will continue to win, as long as they continue to apply the current principles of performance excellence.

AWARD CRITERIA FRAMEWORK

Organizations must position themselves to respond well to the environment within which they compete. They must understand and manage threats and vulnerabilities as well as capitalize on their strengths and opportunities, including the vulnerabilities of competitors. These factors guide strategy development, support operational decisions, and align measures and actions—all of which must be done well for the organization to succeed. Consistent with this overarching purpose, the Award Criteria contain the following basic elements: Driver Triad, Work Core, Brain Center, and Business Outcomes (Figure 14).

The Driver Triad

The Driver Triad (Figure 15) consists of the categories of Leadership, Strategic Planning, and Customer and Market Focus. Leaders use these processes to set direction and goals, monitor progress, make resource decisions, and take corrective action when progress does not proceed according to plan. The processes that make up the Driver Triad require leaders to set direction and expectations for the organization to meet customer and market requirements, and fully empower employees (Category 1), provide the vehicle for determining the short- and long-term strategies for success as well as communicating and

aligning the organization's work (Category 2), and produce information about critical customer requirements and levels of satisfaction, and strengthen customer relations and loyalty (Category 3).

The Work Core

The Work Core (Figure 16) describes the processes through which the primary work of the organization takes place and consists of Human Resource Focus (Category 5) and Process Management (Category 6). These Categories recognize that the people of an organization are responsible for doing the work. To achieve peak performance, these people must possess the right skills and must be allowed to work in an environment that promotes initiative and self-direction. The work processes provide the structure for continuous learning and improvement to optimize performance.

Business Results

The processes defined by the Driver Triad, Work Core, and Brain Center produce the Business Results

Figure 15 Driver Triad.

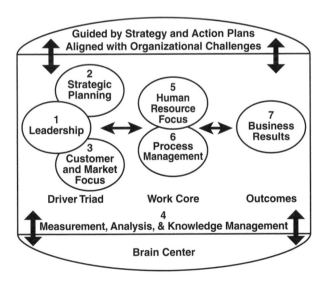

Figure 14 Performance excellence framework.

Figure 16 Work Core.

(Category 7). Business Results (Figure 17) reflect the organization's actual performance and serve as the basis for leaders to monitor progress against goals and make adjustments to increase performance. These Business Results include customer focus, financial and market performance, human resource performance, and internal operating effectiveness.

Brain Center

The foundation for the entire management system is Measurement, Analysis, and Knowledge Management (Category 4). These processes (Figure 18) capture, store, analyze, and retrieve information and data critical to the effective management of the organization and to a fact-based system for improving organization performance and competitiveness. Rapid access to reliable data and information systems are especially critical to enhance effective decision making in an increasingly complex, fast-paced, global competitive environment.

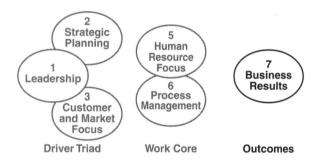

Figure 17 Outcomes.

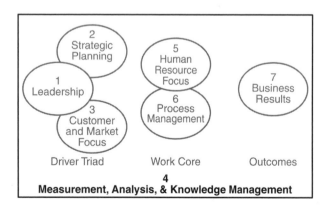

Figure 18 Measurement, Analysis, and Knowledge Management.

Measurement, Analysis, and Knowledge Management is also called the Brain Center of an effective management system (Figure 19).

Organizations develop effective strategic plans to help set the direction necessary to achieve future success. Unfortunately, these plans are not always communicated and used to drive actions. The planning process and the resulting strategy are virtually worthless if the organization does not use the plan and strategy to guide decision making at all levels of the organization (Figure 20).

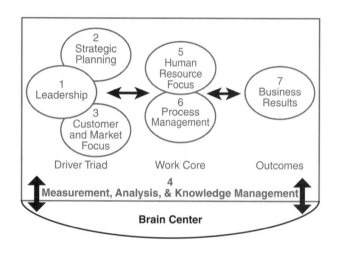

Figure 19 Brain Center.

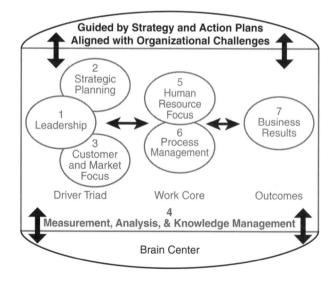

Figure 20 Guide decision making.

When decisions are not guided by strategy, managers and other employees tend to substitute their own ideas for the correct direction. This frequently causes teams, individuals, and whole business units to work at cross-purposes, suboptimizing performance and making it more difficult for the organization to achieve desired results.

Taken together, these processes define the essential ingredients of a complex, integrated management system designed to promote and deliver performance excellence. If any part of the system is missing, the performance results suffer. If fully implemented, these processes are sufficient to enable organizations to achieve winning performance.

Award Criteria Organization

Categories

The seven Criteria Categories are subdivided into Items and Areas to Address. Figure 21 demonstrates the organization of Category 1.

Items

There are 19 Items, each focusing on a major requirement.

Areas to Address

Items consist of one or more Areas to Address (Areas). Information is submitted by applicants in response to the specific requirements of these Areas. There are 32 Areas to Address.

Subparts

There are 81 subparts in the 2004 Criteria. Areas consist of one or more subparts, where numbers are shown in parentheses. A response should be made to each subpart.

Notes

If a note indicates the process "should" include something, examiners will interpret it as a requirement. If a note indicates that the process "might" include something, examiners will not treat the list as a requirement—only as an example. There are 56 notes.

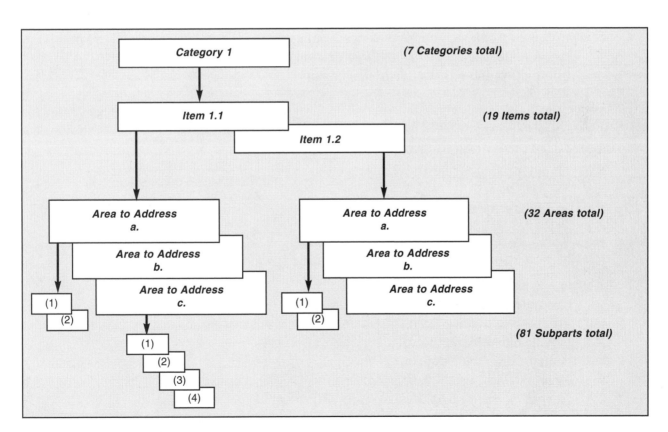

Figure 21 Organization of Category 1.

BALDRIGE AWARD CATEGORIES AND POINT VALUES

Examination Categories/Items	Maximum Points
Preface **Organizational Profile**	**(0 points)**
P.1 Organizational Description	0
P.2 Organizational Challenges	0
1 **Leadership**	**(120 points)**
1.1 Organizational Leadership	70
1.2 Social Responsibility	50
2 **Strategic Planning**	**(85 points)**
2.1 Strategy Development	40
2.2 Strategy Deployment	45
3 **Customer and Market Focus**	**(85 points)**
3.1 Customer and Market Knowledge	40
3.2 Customer Relationships and Satisfaction	45
4 **Measurement, Analysis, and Knowledge Management**	**(90 points)**
4.1 Measurement and Analysis of Organizational Performance	45
4.2 Information and Knowledge Management	45
5 **Human Resource Focus**	**(85 points)**
5.1 Work Systems	35
5.2 Employee Learning and Motivation	25
5.3 Employee Well-Being and Satisfaction	25
6 **Process Management**	**(85 points)**
6.1 Value Creation Processes	50
6.2 Support Processes	35
7 **Business Results**	**(450 points)**
7.1 Customer-Focused Results	75
7.2 Product and Service Results	75
7.3 Financial and Market Results	75
7.4 Human Resource Results	75
7.5 Organizational Effectiveness Results	75
7.6 Governance and Social Responsibility Results	75
Total Points	**1000**

KEY CHARACTERISTICS— 2004 PERFORMANCE EXCELLENCE CRITERIA

The Criteria focus on business results and the processes required to achieve them. Business results are a composite of the following:

- Customer-focused results

- Product and service results

- Financial and market results

- Human resource results

- Organizational effectiveness results, including key internal operational performance measures

- Governance and social responsibility results

The use of this composite of indicators is intended to ensure that strategies are balanced—that they do not inappropriately trade off among important stakeholders, objectives, or short- and longer-term goals.

These results areas cover overall organization performance, including financial performance. The results areas also recognize the importance of suppliers and of community and national well-being.

The Criteria *do not* prescribe that your organization should or should not have any particular functions such, as departments for quality, planning, or personnel. The Criteria do not prescribe how your organization should be structured or how different units in your organization should be managed. These factors differ among organizations, and they are likely to change within an organization over time as needs and strategies evolve. The Criteria are non-prescriptive for the following reasons:

- The focus is on results, not on procedures, tools, or organizational structure. Organizations are encouraged to develop and demonstrate creative, adaptive, and flexible approaches for meeting basic requirements. Non-prescriptive requirements are intended to foster incremental and major ("breakthrough") improvements, as well as basic change.

- The selection of tools, techniques, systems, and organizational structure usually depends on factors such as business type and size, organizational relationships, your organization's stage of development, and employee capabilities and responsibilities.

- A focus on common requirements, rather than on common procedures, fosters better understanding, communication, sharing, and alignment, while supporting innovation and diversity in approaches.

The Criteria support a systems approach to organization-wide goal alignment. The systems approach to goal alignment is embedded in the integrated structure of the Criteria and the results-oriented, cause–effect linkages among the Criteria parts.

The measures in the Criteria tie directly to customer value and to overall performance that relate to key internal and external requirements of the organization. Measures serve both as a communications tool and a basis for deploying performance requirements. Such alignment ensures consistency of purpose while at the same time supports speed, innovation, and decentralized decision making.

Learning Cycles and Continuous Improvement

In high-performing organizations, action-oriented learning takes place through feedback between processes and results facilitated by learning or continuous improvement cycles. The learning cycles have four clearly defined and well-established stages (Figure 22).

1. Plan—planning, including design of processes, selection of measures, and deployment of requirements

2. Do—execute plans

3. Study/Check—assess progress, taking into account internal and external results

4. Act—revise plans based on assessment findings, learning, new inputs, and new requirements

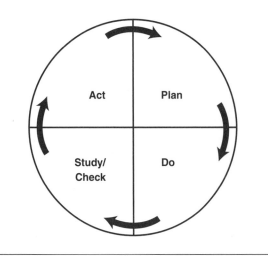

Figure 22 Continuous improvement cycle.

Goal-Based Diagnosis

The Criteria and the Scoring Guidelines are the two elements that combine to make the diagnostic tool, which is part of a developmental assessment. A developmental assessment, unlike a compliance review, seeks to determine how advanced an organization is and then identify the vital few processes that need to be developed to move to the next higher level. The basic systems must be in place before they can be refined and enhanced. In a compliance review, on the other hand, all conditions or requirements must be met or the organization is "out of compliance" and may not be certified or registered. By design, compliance reviews audit against a set of minimum standards. A developmental review, such as that provided through the Baldrige Criteria, identifies continuous improvement opportunities to help the organization achieve best-in-class performance—to excel and win.

This diagnostic assessment is a useful management tool that goes beyond most performance reviews and is applicable to a wide range of strategies and management systems.

Changes from the 2003 Criteria

The Criteria for Performance Excellence have evolved significantly over time to help businesses address a dynamic marketplace, focus on strategy-driven performance, and most recently address national concerns about governance and ethics. The Criteria have continually progressed toward an integrated systems perspective of overall organizational performance management.

Each year, the decision whether to revise the Criteria must balance two important considerations. On one hand, there is a need for Criteria that are at the leading edge of validated management practice to help users address the increasingly complex challenges they face; on the other hand, there is a desire to stabilize the Criteria to allow users continuity in their applications. Recognizing the significant challenges associated with the changes made to Categories 1 (Leadership), 4 (Measurement, Analysis, and Knowledge Management), 6 (Process Management), and 7 (Business Results) in the 2003 Criteria, and the challenges provided by the added focus on "running the business" today and "changing the business" to prepare for the future, the decision was made to make no revisions to the Criteria or to the Item Notes for 2004.

The most significant changes in the Criteria booklet for 2004 are summarized as follows:

- The Scoring System description and the Scoring Guidelines table have been rewritten and redesigned.

- The Category and Item Descriptions section has been expanded to include the Organizational Profile.

- An Index of Key Terms has been added to the Criteria booklet.

- "Ethical Behavior," "Learning," and "Segment" have been added to the Glossary of Key Terms.

Minor wording improvements have been made in other sections of the Criteria booklet, with the exception of the actual Criteria Items and Item Notes.

Organizational Profile

*The **Organizational Profile** is a snapshot of your organization, the key influences on how you operate, and the key challenges you face.*

IMPORTANCE OF THE ORGANIZATIONAL PROFILE

The Organizational Profile is critically important because:

- It is the most appropriate starting point for self-assessment and for writing an application.

- It helps you identify potential gaps in key information and focus on key performance requirements and business results.

- It is used by the examiners and judges in all stages of application review, including the site visit, to understand your organization and what you consider important. It sets the context for the assessment.

- It may be used by itself for an initial self-assessment. If you identify topics for which conflicting, little, or no information is available, it is possible that your assessment need go no further and you can use these topics for action planning.

Page Limit

For Baldrige Award applicants, the Organizational Profile is limited to five pages. These are not counted in the overall 50-page limit for the application. Typing and format instructions for the Organizational Profile are the same as for the application. These instructions are given in the Baldrige Award Application Forms booklet, a copy of which appears on the compact disk enclosed with this book.

P.1 ORGANIZATIONAL DESCRIPTION

Describe your organization's business environment and your key relationships with customers, suppliers, and other partners.

Within your response, include answers to the following questions:

a. Organizational Environment

(1) What are your organization's main products and services? What are the delivery mechanisms used to provide your products and services to your customers?

(2) What is your organizational culture? What are your stated purpose, vision, mission, and values?

(3) What is your employee profile? What are their educational levels? What are your organization's workforce and job diversity, organized bargaining units, use of contract employees, and special health and safety requirements?

(4) What are your major technologies, equipment, and facilities?

(5) What is the regulatory environment under which your organization operates? What are the applicable occupational health and safety regulations; accreditation, certification, or registration requirements; and environmental, financial, and product regulations?

b. Organizational Relationships

(1) What is your organization structure and governance system? What are the reporting relationships among your board of directors, senior leaders, and your parent organization, as appropriate?

(2) What are your key customer groups and market segments, as appropriate? What are their key requirements and expectations for your products and services? What are the differences in these requirements and expectations among customer groups and market segments?

(3) What role do suppliers and distributors play in your value creation processes? What are your most important types of suppliers and distributors? What are your most important supply chain requirements?

(4) What are your key supplier and customer partnering relationships and communication mechanisms?

Notes:

N1. Product and service delivery to your customers (P.1a[1]) might be direct, or through dealers, distributors, or channel partners.

N2. Market segments (P.1b[2]) might be based on product lines or features, geography, distribution channels, business volume, or other factors that allow your organization to define related market characteristics.

N3. Customer group and market segment requirements (P.1b[2]) might include on-time delivery, low defect levels, ongoing price reductions, electronic communication, and after-sales service.

N4. Communication mechanisms (P.1b[4]) should be two-way and might be in person, electronic, by telephone, and/or written. For many organizations, these mechanisms might be changing as marketplace requirements change.

P.1 Organizational Description Item Linkages

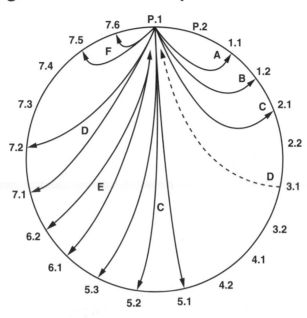

NATURE OF RELATIONSHIP	
A	The organizational structure and governance system described in P.1b(1) sets the context for the review of the management systems for proper governance and ethical behavior [1.1a(2)].
B	The regulatory environment described in P.1a(5) sets the context for the review of the management systems for public responsibility [1.2a(1)].
C	Employee educational levels, diversity, and other characteristics [P.1a(3)] may affect the determination of human resource strengths and weaknesses as a part of the strategic planning process [2.1a(2)]. Employee characteristics such as educational levels, work force and job diversity, the existence of bargaining units, the use of contract employees, and other special requirements help set the context for determining the requirements for knowledge and skill sharing across work units, jobs, and locations [5.1a(3)], determining appropriate training needs by employee segment [5.2a(3)], and tailoring benefits, services, and satisfaction assessment methods for employees according to various types of categories [5.3b(1, 2, and 3].
D	The customer and market groups reported in P.1b(2) were determined using the processes described in 3.1a(1 and 2). The information in P.1b(2) helps examiners identify the kind of results, broken out by customer and market segment, that should be reported in Items 7.1 and 7.2.
E	The information in P.1a(1) derives from the delivery processes described in 6.1a and helps set the context for the examiner review of those processes [6.1a(3)].
F	The regulatory requirements descried in P.1a(5), and the key suppliers and dealers/distributors listed in P.1b(3) create an expectation that related performance results will be reported in 7.6 and 7.5 respectively.

P.2 ORGANIZATIONAL CHALLENGES

Describe your organization's competitive environment, your key strategic challenges, and your system for performance improvement.

Within your response, include answers to the following questions:

a. Competitive Environment

(1) What is your competitive position? What is your relative size and growth in your industry or markets served? What are the numbers and types of competitors for your organization?

(2) What are the principal factors that determine your success relative to your competitors? What are any key changes taking place that affect your competitive situation?

(3) What are your key available sources of comparative and competitive data from within your industry? What are your key available sources of comparative data for analogous processes outside your industry? What limitations, if any, are there in your ability to obtain these data?

b. Strategic Challenges

What are your key business, operational, and human resource strategic challenges?

c. Performance Improvement System

(1) What is the overall approach you use to maintain an organizational focus on performance improvement and to guide systematic evaluation and improvement of key processes?

(2) What is your overall approach to organizational learning and sharing your knowledge assets within the organization?

Notes:

N1. Factors (P.2a[2]) might include differentiators such as price leadership, design services, e-services, geographic proximity, and warranty and product options.

N2. Challenges (P.2b) might include electronic communication with businesses and end-use consumers, reduced cycle times for product introduction, mergers and acquisitions, global marketing and competition, customer retention, staff retention, and value chain integration.

N3. Performance improvement (P.2c) is an assessment dimension used in the Scoring System to evaluate the maturity of organizational approaches and deployment (see pages 55–58). This question is intended to help you and the Baldrige Examiners set a context for your approach to performance improvement.

N4. Overall approaches to process improvement (P.2c[1]) might include implementing a Lean Enterprise System, Six Sigma methodology, use of ISO 9000:2000 standards, or other process improvement tools.

P.2 Organizational Challenges Item Linkages

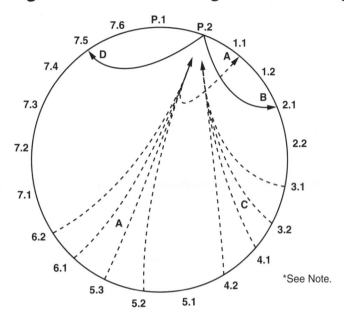

	NATURE OF RELATIONSHIP
A	Leaders [1.1a(2)] are responsible for creating an environment that drives organizational learning, which in turn contributes to the overall focus on performance improvement [P.2c(1)]. The overall approaches to systematic evaluation and improvement, organizational learning, and knowledge sharing identified in P.2c should be consistent with overall requirements for improvement specifically required in Items 1.1c(4) leadership effectiveness; 3.1a(3) improving customer requirements definition; 3.2a(4) improving customer relationships and customer access; 3.2b(4) improving processes to determine customer satisfaction; 4.1a supporting innovation and keeping up with rapid or unexpected organizational or external changes; 4.2a(3) keeping data availability (including software and hardware) current, especially in a volatile work environment; 5.2a(6) improving training and education effectiveness; 5.3a(1) improving work force health, safety, and well-being; 6.1a(6) improving the value creation processes; and 6.2a(6) improving support services.
B	The competitive environment defined in P.2a should be examined as part of the strategy development process [2.1a(2)]. In addition, the strategic challenges identified in P.2b should be addressed by the strategic objectives in 2.1b(1).
C	Information about competitors, which is needed to create the description for P.2a, uses processes discussed in Items 3.1a(1), 3.2b(3), and 4.1a(2).
D	Progress in achieving strategic challenges, as described in P.2b, should be reported in Item 7.5a(3).

*Note: To make the circle diagrams less cluttered, all of the links described in paragraph A will not be repeated on the other diagrams.

1 Leadership—120 Points

*The **Leadership** Category examines how your organization's senior leaders address values, directions, and performance expectations, as well as a focus on customers and other stakeholders, empowerment, innovation, and learning. Also examined are your organization's governance and how your organization addresses its public and community responsibilities.*

The leadership system must promote organizational core values, set performance expectations, and promote an organization-wide focus on stakeholders, customers, employee empowerment, learning, and innovation. The Leadership Category looks at how senior leaders guide the organization in setting directions and seeking future opportunities. Senior leaders must communicate clear values and performance expectations that address the needs of all stakeholders. The category also looks at the how the organization practices effective governance, meets its responsibilities to the public, and practices good citizenship.

The category contains two Items:

Organizational Leadership

- Communicating and reinforcing clear values, performance expectations, and a focus on creating value for customers and other stakeholders

- Reinforcing an environment for empowerment and innovation and employee and organizational learning

- Providing effective governance that holds management accountable for the organization's actions, provides for fiscal accountability, and protects stockholder and stakeholder interests

- Reviewing organizational performance and capabilities, competitiveness, and progress relative to goals, and setting priorities for improvement

- Evaluating and improving the effectiveness of senior leadership and management throughout the organization, including employee input in the process

Social Responsibility

- For regulatory and other legal requirements in areas such as safety, environmental protection, and waste management; anticipating public concerns and addressing risks to the public

- For ensuring ethical business practices

- For strengthening and supporting key communities

1.1 ORGANIZATIONAL LEADERSHIP (70 PTS.)
PROCESS

Describe how senior leaders guide your organization. Describe your organization's governance system. Describe how senior leaders review organizational performance.

Within your response, include answers to the following questions:

a. Senior Leadership Direction

(1) How do senior leaders set and deploy organizational values, short- and longer-term directions, and performance expectations? How do senior leaders include a focus on creating and balancing value for customers and other stakeholders in their performance expectations? How do senior leaders communicate organizational values, directions, and expectations through your leadership system, to all employees, and to key suppliers and partners? How do senior leaders ensure two-way communication on these topics?

(2) How do senior leaders create an environment for empowerment, innovation, and organizational agility? How do they create an environment for organizational and employee learning? How do they create an environment that fosters and requires legal and ethical behavior?

b. Organizational Governance

How does your organization address the following key factors in your governance system?

- Management accountability for the organization's actions

- Fiscal accountability

- Independence in internal and external audits

- Protection of stockholder and stakeholder interests, as appropriate

c. Organizational Performance Review

(1) How do senior leaders review organizational performance and capabilities? How do they use these reviews to assess organizational success, competitive performance, and progress relative to short- and longer-term goals? How do they use these reviews to assess your organizational ability to address changing organizational needs?

(2) What are the key performance measures regularly reviewed by your senior leaders? What are your key recent performance review findings?

(3) How do senior leaders translate organizational performance review findings into priorities for continuous and breakthrough improvement of key business results and into opportunities for innovation? How are these priorities and opportunities deployed throughout your organization? When appropriate, how are they deployed to your suppliers and partners to ensure organizational alignment?

(4) How do you evaluate the performance of your senior leaders, including the chief executive? How do you evaluate the performance of members of the board of directors, as appropriate? How do senior leaders use organizational performance review findings to improve both their own leadership effectiveness and that of your board and leadership system, as appropriate?

Continued

> **Notes:** *Continued*
>
> N1. Organizational directions [1.1a(1)] relate to creating the vision for the organization and to setting the context for strategic objectives and action plans described in Items 2.1 and 2.2.
>
> N2. Senior leaders' organizational performance reviews (1.1c) should be informed by organizational performance analyses described in 4.1b and guided by strategic objectives and action plans described in Items 2.1 and 2.2. Senior leaders' organizational performance reviews also might be informed by internal or external Baldrige assessments.
>
> N3. Leadership performance evaluation (1.1c[4]) might be supported by peer reviews, formal performance management reviews (5.1b), and formal and/or informal employee and other stakeholder feedback and surveys.
>
> N4. Your organizational performance results should be reported in Items 7.1–7.6.

There are three distinctly different aspects to the requirements of Item 1.1. First, 1.1a describes "sending" or outgoing actions of leaders. Through their outward focus they push values, create expectations, and align the work of the organization. Second, 1.1b addresses how the governance or oversight processes ensure fiscal accountability and the protection of stakeholder and stockholder interests. Third, 1.1c requires leaders to receive, rather than send, information. Here they must monitor progress and use these incoming data to determine where resources and priorities must be aligned to ensure appropriate progress is achieved.

The "sending" part of this Item [1.1a] looks at how senior leaders create and sustain values that promote high performance throughout the organization. In promoting high performance, senior leaders set and deploy values, short- and longer-term directions, and performance expectations and balance the expectations of customers and other stakeholders. Leaders develop and implement systems to ensure values are understood and consistently followed. An organization's failure to achieve high levels of performance can almost always be traced to a failure in leadership.

- To consistently promote high performance, leaders must clearly set direction and make sure everyone in the organization understands his or her responsibilities. Success requires a strong future orientation and a commitment to improvement, innovation, and the disciplined

change that is needed to carry it out. This requires creating an environment for empowerment, learning, innovation, and organizational agility, as well as the means for rapid and effective application of knowledge.

- Leaders also ensure that organizational values actually guide the behavior of managers and employees throughout the organization or the values are meaningless. To enhance performance excellence the "right" values must be adopted. These values must include a focus on customers and other stakeholders. Since various customer and stakeholder groups often have conflicting interests, leaders must strike a balance that optimizes the interests of all groups. The failure to ensure a customer focus usually causes the organization and its employees to focus internally. The lack of a customer focus forces workers to default to their own ideas of what customers really "need." This increases the risk of becoming arrogant and not caring about the requirements of customers. It also increases the potential for creating and delivering products and services that no customer wants or values. That, in turn, increases rework, scrap, waste, and added cost/lower value.

- Senior leaders must ensure two-way communication with subordinate leaders and other employees, key suppliers, and partners regarding organizational values, directions, and expectations. This two-way communication also provides an opportunity for senior leaders to receive feedback from others about their effectiveness as leaders. It replaces, to some extent, the requirement in previous versions of the Criteria that leaders seek feedback from employees through formal or informal means. Two-way communication should help foster this type of feedback. Accordingly, it is recommended that part of the communication with employees involve formal and informal employee and peer feedback of leader effectiveness, such as using a 360-degree feedback survey or an upward evaluation. This information could be structured to help evaluate the effectiveness of leaders at all levels, including the board of directors, as required in Item 1.1c(4).

- Leaders must create an environment for empowerment and agility, as well as the means for rapid and effective application of knowledge.

The new for 2003 organizational governance requirement [1.1b] is intended to address the need for a responsible, informed, and accountable governance body that can protect the interests of key stakeholders, including stockholders. It should have independence in review and audit functions. It should also have a performance evaluation function that monitors organizational and CEO performance. The governance structure should ensure that all leaders and managers are held accountable for the organization's actions.

The "receiving" part of this Item [1.1c] looks at how senior leaders review organizational performance in a disciplined, fact-based manner, what key performance measures they regularly review, and how review findings are used to drive improvement and innovation. This organizational review should cover all areas of performance, and provide a complete and accurate picture of the "state of health" of the organization. This includes not only how well the organization is currently performing but also how well it is moving to secure future success.

- Key performance measures should focus on and reflect the key drivers of success leaders regularly review. These measures should relate to the strategic objectives necessary for success.

- Leaders should use these reviews to drive improvement and change. These reviews should provide a reliable means to guide the improvement and change needed to achieve the organization's key objectives, success factors, and measures.

- Leaders must create a consistent process to translate the review findings into an action agenda, sufficiently specific for deployment throughout the organization and to suppliers/partners—people who need to take action to improve.

- In addition, the organization must evaluate the effectiveness of senior leaders, board members, and the entire leadership system. To ensure the evaluation is accurate, employees should provide feedback to the leaders and managers at all levels, which may be accomplished, in part, by the two-way communication required in Item 1.1a(1) and using tools such as 360-degree reviews and upward evaluations.

- Finally, leaders and managers at all levels should take action, based on the feedback, to improve their effectiveness. It is critical that leaders, managers, and supervisors at all levels and in all parts of the organization effectively drive and reinforce the principles of performance excellence through words and actions. Remember, nearly every failure to achieve and sustain excellence can be traced to a failure on the part of leaders and managers. Jack Welch, former CEO of General Electric, in his last letter to stockholders emphasized the importance of rewarding and nurturing the top 20 percent of employees, and getting rid of the bottom 10 percent. The same is true of managers who do not or will not aggressively and effectively lead the effort to enhance performance excellence.

1.1 Organizational Leadership

How senior leaders guide the organization in setting direction and developing and sustaining an effective leadership system throughout the organization

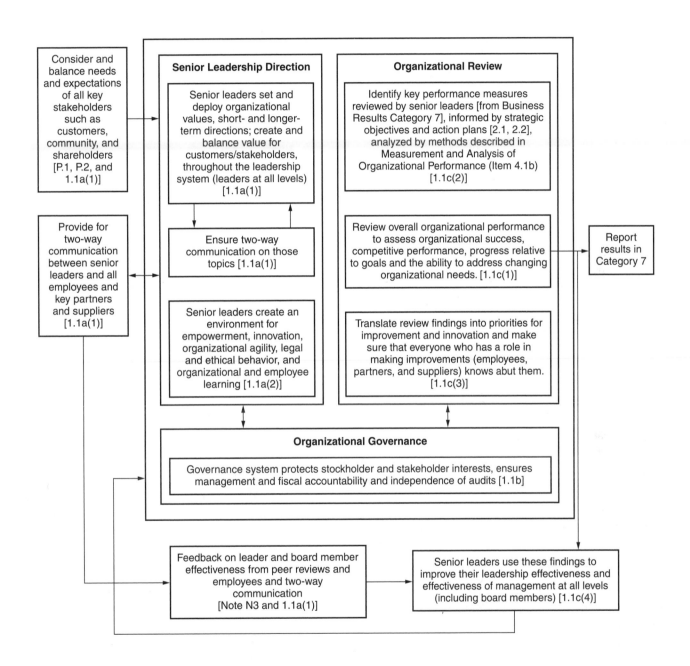

Consider and balance needs and expectations of all key stakeholders such as customers, community, and shareholders [P.1, P.2, and 1.1a(1)]

Provide for two-way communication between senior leaders and all employees and key partners and suppliers [1.1a(1)]

Senior Leadership Direction

Senior leaders set and deploy organizational values, short- and longer-term directions; create and balance value for customers/stakeholders, throughout the leadership system (leaders at all levels) [1.1a(1)]

Ensure two-way communication on those topics [1.1a(1)]

Senior leaders create an environment for empowerment, innovation, organizational agility, legal and ethical behavior, and organizational and employee learning [1.1a(2)]

Organizational Review

Identify key performance measures reviewed by senior leaders [from Business Results Category 7], informed by strategic objectives and action plans [2.1, 2.2], analyzed by methods described in Measurement and Analysis of Organizational Performance (Item 4.1b) [1.1c(2)]

Review overall organizational performance to assess organizational success, competitive performance, progress relative to goals and the ability to address changing organizational needs. [1.1c(1)]

Translate review findings into priorities for improvement and innovation and make sure that everyone who has a role in making improvements (employees, partners, and suppliers) knows abut them. [1.1c(3)]

Report results in Category 7

Organizational Governance

Governance system protects stockholder and stakeholder interests, ensures management and fiscal accountability and independence of audits [1.1b]

Feedback on leader and board member effectiveness from peer reviews and employees and two-way communication [Note N3 and 1.1a(1)]

Senior leaders use these findings to improve their leadership effectiveness and effectiveness of management at all levels (including board members) [1.1c(4)]

1.1 Leadership Item Linkages

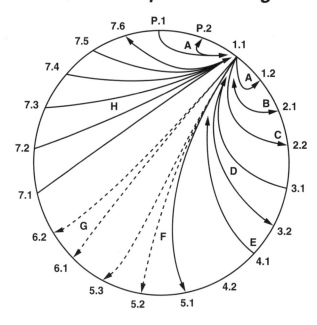

	NATURE OF RELATIONSHIP
A	Leaders [1.1], in support of organizational values, role-model and support ethical behavior [1.2b] and corporate responsibility [1.2a] and practice good citizenship [1.2c]. The organizational structure and governance system described in P.1b(1) sets the context for the review of the management systems for proper governance [1.1b] and ethical behavior [1.1a(2) and 1.2b]. Leaders [1.1a(2)] are responsible for creating an environment that drives organizational learning, which in turn contributes to the overall focus on performance improvement [P.2c].
B	To effectively set organizational direction and expectations, leaders [1.1a(1)] participate in the strategic planning process [2.1]. As part of this effort, leaders [1.1a(1)] ensure that strategic objectives balance the needs of key stakeholders [2.1b(2)]. Leaders also use the time lines for achieving strategic objectives [2.1b(1)] as a basis for defining and monitoring expected progress closely [1.1c(1)], which means the time lines in 2.1b(1)] should define the expected levels of future performance that the leaders use during the performance reviews [1.1c(1)] to determine if the organization is making appropriate progress against desired goals.
C	Leaders [1.1a(1)] ensure that plans are clearly communicated and understood (deployed) at all levels throughout the organization and used to align work [2.2a(1)]. Leaders [1.1a] also approve the overall goals set forth in the plan based, in part, on information about the expected levels of competitor performance [2.2b].
D	Leaders [1.1a(1)] use information from customers about requirements and preferences [3.1a(2)] and satisfaction/dissatisfaction [3.2b] to set direction and create opportunity for the organization. Leaders [1.1] also have a responsibility for creating and driving customer-focused value to meet customer requirements and expectations throughout the organization [3.2a].

Continued

	NATURE OF RELATIONSHIP *Continued*
E	Leaders [1.1c(1)] use analyses of data [4.1b(1, 2)] to monitor organizational performance and understand relationships among performance, employee satisfaction, customers, markets, and financial success. These analyses are also used for decision making at all levels to set priorities for action and allocate resources for maximum advantage [1.1c(3)]. They are also responsible for using comparative data [from 4.1a(2)] to set meaningful goals to achieve organizational success.
F	Leaders [1.1a(2)] create an environment for employee empowerment, innovation, and learning throughout the entire organization through the design of work and jobs [5.1a(1)]. They ensure that the compensation and recognition system [5.1b] encourages employees at all levels to achieve performance excellence in areas most critical to the organization. Leaders [1.1a(2)] are also responsible for creating an environment that supports appropriate skill development of all employees through training and development systems and reinforcing learning on the job [5.2a], as well as creating effective systems to enhance employee satisfaction, well-being, and motivation [5.3b].
G	Leaders [1.1] are responsible for creating an environment that supports high performance, including monitoring processes for value creation [6.1] and support services [6.2] processes. Leaders must ensure that design, production/delivery, support, and supplier performance processes are aligned and consistently evaluated and refined.
H	Senior leaders [1.1c] use performance results data [from Category 7] for many activities, including monitoring organizational performance [1.1c(1)]; deploying priority improvement areas to focus work and ensure alignment [1.1c(3)]; strategic planning [2.1a]; setting goals and priorities [2.1b(1)]; reinforcing or rewarding employee performance [5.1b]; and for improving their effectiveness and the effectiveness of leaders at all levels [1.1c(4)]. In addition, key results of leadership behavior, such as results related to ethical behavior [1.1a(2)] and fiscal accountability [1.1b], are reported in Governance and Social Responsibilities Results [7.6a(1 and 2)].

	IF YOU DON'T DO WHAT THE CRITERIA REQUIRE . . .
Item Reference	**Possible Adverse Consequences**
1.1a(1)	If senior leaders fail to make performance expectations clear (especially defining them in measurable terms), it may create uncertainty among managers and employees throughout the organization about what they must accomplish, and the direction they must follow. This may cause managers to substitute their own ideas, objectives, and directions, which may not be in alignment with those of top leadership. The lack of alignment may also contribute to redundancy and wasted resources. As a consequence, some parts of the organization may work at cross-purposes with other parts of the organization.
1.1a(1)	If senior leaders do not create an environment that focuses on creating value for customers and other stakeholders, employees and managers within the organization may become internally focused and risk negatively impacting the customer value on which the organization was built. An internal focus may contribute to a climate where employees are not primarily interested in listening to customer requirements or concerns. This may produce a high level of organizational arrogance where employees believe they know what the customers want better than the customer. This type of behavior can antagonize customers and produce high levels of customer dissatisfaction. In a related area, if senior leaders do not create an environment that focuses on balancing value for customers and other stakeholders—especially when different customer groups have competing interests—it may erode customer confidence in one group and eventually cause a loss of customers. For example, end users of a product want inexpensive, reliable products, while stockholders want profits and stock price to increase. Excessive focus on one group over the other makes it difficult to maximize value and keep both end users and stockholders loyal.
1.1a(2)	If senior leaders do not create an environment that promotes employee empowerment, they risk not leveraging the high power of a formidable asset—their people. As a consequence, leaders may be effectively sending a message that employees do not have the skills or ability to make decisions on their own—that micromanagement is the preferred approach within the organization. This kind of environment tends to migrate decision making to higher and higher levels in the organization, creating excessive delay and working against organizational agility. Unnecessary levels of review and approval may also tend to minimize innovation and creativity throughout the organization. Taken together, these problems are likely to add cost but not value—making it increasingly difficult to be successful in a highly competitive industry.
1.1b	The adverse consequences of corrupt or incompetent organizational governance can be sudden and spectacular. One need only consider the impact of poor governance on Enron and similar companies whose businesses failed suddenly, hurting thousands of stakeholders, and tearing the economic fabric of the national and world economy. With increased stakeholder scrutiny and decreased trust, organizations that do not have visible and effective processes in place to ensure fiscal and management accountability and protect stockholder and employee interests may not be able to overcome the climate of distrust that permeates the corporate sector today. Their stock prices and consumer confidence may remain flat. Intrusive government oversight may increase, which diverts leadership attention and company resources away from value-adding outcomes needed to beat competitors and satisfy customers and other stakeholders.

Continued

	IF YOU DON'T DO WHAT THE CRITERIA REQUIRE . . . *Continued*
Item Reference	**Possible Adverse Consequences**
1.1c(1)	If senior leaders do not have a systematic, fact-based process in place that enables them to review organizational performance and assess progress toward goals, it may send a message throughout the organization that performance outcomes are really not that important. If results are not important to top leaders, they may not be considered important to lower levels within the organization and employees at all levels may not contribute optimum effort to achieve these (unimportant) results.
1.1c(2)	If key performance measures that are used to review organizational performance have not been defined or are not consistent with organizational strategic priorities [Item 2.1b(1)] and related actions [Item 2.2a(1)], people in the organization may not be focusing their work in areas essential to organizational success, further suboptimizing organizational performance and value to the customer. The wrong performance measures may prevent senior leaders from monitoring the things that are most critical to organizational success and making appropriate adjustments when needed.
1.1c(3)	Even if senior leaders have an effective process to review organizational performance [Item 1.1c(1)], but do not effectively use these review findings to identify priorities for improvement and areas that should be targets of innovation, they may not be providing appropriate focus and alignment throughout the organization and to affected suppliers and partners. This may make it difficult for workers, managers, partners, and suppliers to make the changes needed to correct problems or comply with the new priorities for improvement, contributing to wasted resources and performance failures. The long-standing failure to identify priorities for improvement or targets of innovation may contribute to the perception that the status quo is acceptable and continuous improvement is not important. This may further contribute to organizational stagnation and may make it difficult to keep pace with competitors and increasing customer requirements.
1.1c(4)	Even a new employee can tell the difference between an effective leader and an incompetent one. Unfortunately, an incompetent leader is frequently blind to this fact. (Where do you think Scott Adams gets his material for the "Dilbert" cartoon?) The combination of organizational performance outcomes and employee (subordinate) feedback can provide critical information to help leaders throughout the leadership system identify personal strengths and opportunities for improvement. Without this information, leaders may not be able to focus effectively on areas where improvement would be essential not only to personal growth and development but also to better organizational results. Leaders who do not receive accurate feedback about their strengths and weaknesses may not be able to keep pace with changing business needs and directions, as they are challenged to work smarter by customers, competitors, and the demands of stockholders and other stakeholders. They may not be able to lead their organization to winning levels of performance excellence.

1.1 ORGANIZATIONAL LEADERSHIP—SAMPLE EFFECTIVE PRACTICES

Perhaps most critical is that senior leaders demonstrate absolute, unwavering commitment to performance excellence—even aligning reward and recognition to provide incentives and disincentives. The best senior leaders do not tolerate a lack of aggressive commitment and urgent action from subordinate managers at any level. They send a clear message to employees that the effort is serious.

A. Senior Leadership Direction

- All senior leaders are personally involved in performance improvement.

- Senior leaders spend a significant portion of their time on performance improvement activities.

- Senior leaders carry out many visible activities (for example, goal-setting, planning, and recognition and reward of performance and process improvement).

- Senior leaders regularly communicate performance excellence values to managers and ensure that managers demonstrate those values in their work.

- Senior leaders participate on performance improvement teams and use quality tools and practices.

- Senior leaders mentor managers and ensure that promotion criteria reflect organizational values, especially customer satisfaction.

- Senior leaders study and learn about the improvement practices of other organizations.

- Senior leaders clearly and consistently articulate values (customer focus, customer satisfaction, role model leadership, continuous improvement, work force involvement, and performance optimization) throughout the organization.

- Senior leaders ensure that organizational values are used to provide direction to all employees in the organization to help achieve the mission, vision, and performance goals.

- Senior leaders use effective and innovative approaches to reach out to all employees to spread the organization's values and align its work to support organizational goals.

- Senior leaders effectively surface problems and encourage employee risk-taking.

- Roles and responsibilities of managers are clearly defined, understood by them, and used to evaluate and improve their performance.

- Managers serve as role models (walk the talk) in leading quality and systematic performance improvement.

- Job definitions with quality indices are clearly delineated for each level of the organization, objectively measured, and presented in a logical and organized structure.

- Many different communication strategies are used to reinforce quality values. Leaders at all levels make two-way communication easy through personal methods such as voice mail, e-mail, town hall meetings, and face-to-face meetings. They also use anonymous methods such as 360-degree surveys to ensure feedback is honest and complete.

- Leader behavior (not merely words) clearly communicates what is expected of the organization and its employees.

- Systems and procedures are deployed that encourage cooperation and a cross-functional approach to management, team activities, and problem solving.

- Leaders monitor employee acceptance and adoption of vision and values using annual surveys, employee focus groups, and e-mail questions.

- A systematic process is in place for evaluating and improving the integration or alignment of quality values throughout the organization.

B. Organizational Governance

- Independence of the board of directors is ensured by requiring that a substantial percentage of directors come from outside the organization.

- Fiscal accountability is assured by a variety of processes including independent audits and separation of consultants from auditing functions. Audit and consulting services are not provided by the same or affiliated companies.

- Stockholders approve the election slates for the board of directors and even place names on the slate.

- Board term limits enable rotating membership to ensure a fresh and objective voice is present on the board.

- Board audit committees contain at least one financial expert who is independent of the company.

- The full board of directors reviews financial statements quarterly after the CEO and CFO certify accuracy.

- Eliminate or minimize directors with competing interests, such as key suppliers or interlocking directors.

- Dissent, debate, and open criticism are encouraged among board members.

- CEOs promote candor and meaningful discussion at board meetings by sharing relevant information with directors before meetings to permit careful analysis before the deliberation begins.

- Board members formally assess their peers in writing and ask poorly performing members to resign.

- A climate of trust and candor exists among board members. No secret group wields power to make back-room decisions.

C. Organizational Performance Review

- Reviews against measurable performance standards are held frequently.

- Actions are taken to assist units that are not meeting goals or performing to plan.

- Senior leaders systematically and routinely check the effectiveness of their leadership activities (for example, seeking feedback at least annually from employees and peers using an upward or 360-degree evaluation), and take steps to improve.

- Leaders at all levels determine how well they carried out their activities (what went right or wrong and how they could be done better).

- There is evidence of adopting changes to improve leader effectiveness.

- Customer, performance, and financial data drive priorities for organizational improvement and innovation.

- Senior leaders base their business decisions on reliable data and facts pertaining to customers, operational processes, and employee performance and satisfaction.

- Senior leaders hold regular meetings to review performance data and communicate problems, successes, and effective approaches to improve work.

- Senior leaders conduct monthly reviews of organizational performance. This requires that subordinates conduct biweekly reviews, and workers and work teams provide daily performance updates. Corrective actions are developed to improve performance that deviates from planned performance.

1.2 SOCIAL RESPONSIBILITY (50 PTS.)
PROCESS

Describe how your organization addresses its responsibilities to the public, ensures ethical behavior, and practices good citizenship.

Within your response, include answers to the following questions:

a. Responsibilities to the Public

(1) How do you address the impacts on society of your products, services, and operations? What are your key compliance processes, measures, and goals for achieving and surpassing regulatory and legal requirements, as appropriate? What are your key processes, measures, and goals for addressing risks associated with your products, services, and operations?

(2) How do you anticipate public concerns with current and future products, services, and operations? How do you prepare for these concerns in a proactive manner?

b. Ethical Behavior

How do you ensure ethical behavior in all stakeholder transactions and interactions? What are your key processes and measures or indicators for monitoring ethical behavior throughout your organization, with key partners, and in your governance structure?

c. Support of Key Communities

How does your organization actively support and strengthen your key communities? How do you identify key communities and determine areas of emphasis for organizational involvement and support? What are your key communities? How do your senior leaders and your employees contribute to improving these communities?

Notes:

N1. Societal responsibilities in areas critical to your business also should be addressed in Strategy Development (Item 2.1) and in Process Management (Category 6). Key results, such as results of regulatory and legal compliance or environmental improvements through use of "green" technology or other means, should be reported as Governance and Social Responsibility Results (in Item 7.6).

N2. Measures or indicators of ethical behavior (1.2b) might include the percentage of independent board members, measures of relationships with stockholder and nonstockholder constituencies, and results of ethics reviews and audits.

N3. Areas of community support appropriate for inclusion in 1.2c might include your efforts to strengthen local community services, education, and health; the environment; and practices of trade, business, or professional associations.

N4. The health and safety of employees are not addressed in Item 1.2; you should address these employee factors in Item 5.3.

This Item [1.2] looks at how the organization fulfills its public responsibilities and encourages, supports, and practices good citizenship.

The first part of this Item [1.2a] looks at how the organization addresses current and future impacts on society in a proactive manner. The impacts and practices are expected to cover all relevant and important areas—products, services, and operations.

- An integral part of performance management and improvement is proactively addressing legal and regulatory requirements and risk factors. Addressing these areas requires establishing appropriate measures and/or indicators that senior leaders track in their overall performance review. The organization should be sensitive to issues of public concern, whether or not these issues are currently embodied in law. The failure to address these areas can expose the organization to future problems when it least expects them. Problems can range from a sudden decline in consumer confidence to extensive and costly litigation. In this regard, it is important to anticipate potential problems the public may have with both current and future products. Sometimes a well-intended product or service could create adverse public consequences.

- For example, consider the use of automatic teller machines (ATMs) or cash machines as they are called today. When these machines were first introduced, many in the industry believed that the public would never accept the machines as a surrogate for a human being. For the most part, these machines were considered an eyesore and were installed in out-of-the-way places, usually at the back of the bank building. The extraordinary success of these devices, however, resulted in hundreds of millions of people conducting cash transactions outside the relative safety of the bank building. This gave rise to more robberies, abductions, and even murder. By failing to consider the potential adverse consequence of these cash machines located in out-of-the-way places, banks were exposed to increased litigation and costs associated with relocating or providing appropriate security enclosures for the machines in an effort to reduce public risk.

- Good public responsibility implies going beyond minimum compliance with laws and regulations. Top-performing organizations frequently serve as role models of responsibility and provide leadership in areas key to business success. For example, a manufacturing company might go beyond the requirements of the environmental protection regulations and develop innovative and award-winning systems to protect the environment and reduce pollution. This has a double benefit. Not only do they develop good relations with regulators (and occasionally receive the "benefit of the doubt"), but when regulators increase requirements, the high-performing organizations are already in compliance, usually way ahead of competitors who only met minimum requirements.

- Good citizenship opportunities are available to organizations of all sizes. These opportunities include encouraging and supporting employees' community service.

- Ensuring ethical business practices are followed by all employees lessens the organization's risk of adverse public reaction as well as criminal prosecution. Programs to ensure ethical business practices typically seek to prevent activities that might be perceived as criminal or near criminal. Examples of unethical business practices might include falsifying expense reports or quality control data, accepting lavish gifts from a contractor, or seeking kickbacks.

The second part of this Item [1.2b] looks at how the organization, its senior leaders, and its employees ensure ethical business practices are followed in all stakeholder transactions and interactions. Standards of ethical behavior should be defined (preferably in measurable terms) and everyone in the organization should understand and follow the standards. The organization must systematically monitor ethical behavior throughout the organization and with key suppliers, partners, and within the governance structure. Failing to follow the standards of ethical behavior should have prompt and serious consequences for every governing board member, leader, manager, employee, supplier, and partner.

The third part of this Item [1.2c] looks at how the organization, its senior leaders, and its employees identify, support, and strengthen key communities as part of good citizenship practices:

- Good citizenship practices typically vary according to the size, complexity, and location of the organization. Larger organizations are generally expected to have a more comprehensive approach to citizenship than small organizations.

- Examples of organizational community involvement include: influencing the adoption of higher standards in education by communicating employability requirements to schools and school boards; partnering with other businesses and health care providers to improve health in the local community by providing education and volunteer services to address public health issues; and partnering to influence trade and business associations to engage in beneficial, cooperative activities, such as sharing best practices to improve overall U.S. global competitiveness and the environment.

- In addition to activities directly carried out by the organization, opportunities to practice good citizenship include employee community service that is encouraged and supported by the organization. Frequently, the organization's leaders actively participate on community boards and actively support their work. Usually, organizations—like people—support causes and issues that they value. Top-performing organizations are not content to simply donate money, people, and products/services to these causes without examining the impact of this support. Just as senior leaders examine the other parts of their business, they also evaluate and refine the effectiveness of community support, consistent with business strategies and objectives.

1.2 Social Responsibility

How the organization addresses public responsibilities, ensures ethical behavior, and practices good citizenship

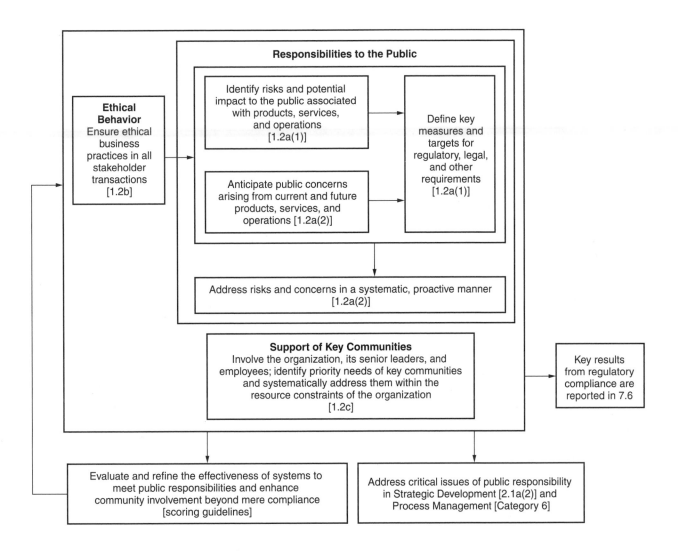

1.2 Social Responsibility Item Linkages

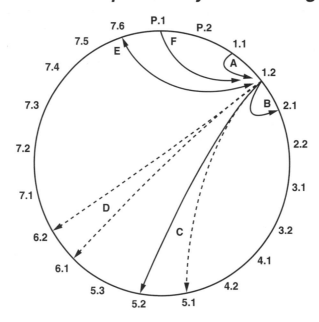

	NATURE OF RELATIONSHIP
A	Leaders, in support of organizational values [1.1a(1)], have a responsibility for setting policies and ensuring that practices and products of the organization and its employees do not adversely impact society or violate ethical standards, regulations, or law [1.2a and b]. They are also responsible to be personally involved and to ensure that the organization and its employees strengthen key communities in areas such as local community services, education, health, the environment, and business, professional, and trade associations, [1.2c].
B	Public health and safety concerns, environmental protection, and waste management issues [1.2a] are important factors to consider in strategy development [2.1a(2)].
C	Training [5.2] is provided to ensure all employees understand organization ethical business practices [1.2b] as well as the importance of strengthening key communities [1.2c]. In addition, recruitment and hiring and the design of work systems should capitalize on the ideas, culture, and thinking of key communities and their impact on the organization [5.1c(2)].
D	Managers at all levels have responsibility for ensuring that work practices of the organization [6.1 and 6.2] are consistent with the organization's standards of ethics and public responsibility [1.2a and b].
E	Key results, such as results of regulatory and legal compliance [1.2a], anticipating public concerns [1.2a(2)], ethical behavior [1.2b], and support to key communities [1.2c], are reported in Governance and Social Responsibilities Results [7.6a(2, 3, and 4)]. In addition, these results are monitored to determine if process changes are needed. (Results in areas of employee safety and well-being are reported in 7.4, based on processes described in Item 5.3, Employee Well-Being and Satisfaction, and are not a part of the requirements in 1.2.)
F	The regulatory environment described in P.1a(5) sets the context for the review of the management systems for public responsibility citizenship [1.2a(1)].

IF YOU DON'T DO WHAT THE CRITERIA REQUIRE . . .	
Item Reference	**Possible Adverse Consequences**
1.2a(1)	Organizations that fail to consider the impact on the public of their products, services, and operations may be seriously impaired in the future if it is determined that these products or services cause harm. (The problem may be so serious that it could cause the organization to go out of business relatively quickly, as in the case of Dow-Corning and the silicone breast implants.) In the short term, organizations that fail to comply with regulatory and legal requirements may find themselves facing costly sanctions or be inhibited from conducting business. The failure to consider risks associated with products, services, and operations may contribute to costly corrective action or litigation. For example, banks throughout the world have been forced to pay damages to users of automatic teller machines (ATMs) because of the failure to provide adequate security, which resulted in abductions, robbery, and murders.
1.2a(2)	Organizations that fail to anticipate and consider potential concerns that the public may have with current and future products, services, and operations may be faced with costly redesign or redirection. When an organization appears to treat the public and the community within which it works with impunity and disregards their concerns, it becomes extremely difficult to recover trust and confidence. When the organization finds it needs public support to carry out its work or expand its operations, it may find it difficult to secure that support from the public.
1.2b	Organizations that do not ensure ethical business practices in all transactions and interactions with stakeholders (public, customers, stockholders, employees, suppliers, and so on) run the risk of violating the public trust. Accordingly, these organizations may face serious adverse consequences when their misdeeds are discovered. (One only needs to consider the difference between Enron and Tylenol. Both companies faced disasters that threatened their existence. Tylenol responded ethically and is still thriving.) Moreover, if the unethical practices of leaders are considered an acceptable business standard in the organization and repeated by others, they can contribute to numerous unpredictable problems that divert human and financial resources to correct.
1.2c	Organizations that fail to act as good corporate citizens and support the local community may find it difficult to get support in return, especially for projects or initiatives that require local approval. For example, local communities typically provide the bulk of support for services as well as new workers. Organizations that fail to support local education or trade and professional associations may find themselves faced with a shortage of skilled workers in key areas and important services they need to conduct business.

1.2 SOCIAL RESPONSIBILITY— SAMPLE EFFECTIVE PRACTICES

A. Responsibilities to the Public

- The organization's principal business activities include systems to analyze, anticipate, and minimize public hazards or risk.

- Indicators for risk areas are identified and monitored.

- Improvement strategies are used consistently, target performance levels are set, and progress is reviewed regularly and tied to recognition and reward.

- The organization considers the impact that its operations, products, and services might have on society and considers those impacts in planning.

- The effectiveness of systems to meet or exceed regulatory or legal requirements is systematically evaluated and improved.

B. Ethical Behavior

- A formal system to train all employees about ethical business requirements is in place.

- A process is in place to test the understanding of ethical principles for all people who must follow the principles. This may include employees, governing board members, suppliers, and partners.

- An audit process is in place to communicate and ensure ethical requirements, and practices are deployed to all levels of the organization and to key partners, suppliers, and members of the board of directors (governance group).

- The effectiveness of systems to meet or exceed ethical requirements is systematically evaluated and improved.

C. Support of Key Communities

- Senior leaders and employees at various levels in the organization are involved in professional organizations, committees, task forces, or other community activities.

- Organizational resources are allocated to support involvement in community activities outside the organization. The effectiveness of these allocations is examined to determine if expectations are met and resources are used wisely.

- Employees participate in local, state, or national quality award programs and receive recognition from the organization.

- Employees participate in a variety of professional quality and business improvement associations.

- The effectiveness of processes to support and strengthen key communities is systematically measured, evaluated, and improved.

2 Strategic Planning—85 Points

*The **Strategic Planning** Category examines how your organization develops strategic objectives and action plans. Also examined are how your chosen strategic objectives and action plans are deployed and how progress is measured.*

The Strategic Planning Category looks at the organization's process for strategic and action planning, and deployment of plans to make sure everyone is working to achieve those plans. Customer-driven quality and operational performance excellence are key strategic issues that need to be integral parts of the organization's overall planning.

- Customer-driven quality is a strategic view of quality. The focus is on the drivers of customer satisfaction, customer retention, new markets, and market share—key factors in competitiveness, profitability, and business success.

- Operational performance improvement contributes to short- and longer-term productivity growth and cost/price competitiveness. Building operational capability—including speed, responsiveness, and flexibility—represents an investment in strengthening the organization's competitive position now and into the future.

Over the years, much debate and discussion have taken place around planning. Professors in our colleges and universities spend a great deal of time trying to differentiate strategic planning, long-term planning, short-term planning, tactical planning, operational planning, quality planning, business planning, and human resource planning, to name a few. A much simpler view, however, might serve us better. For our purposes, the following captures the essence of planning:

- Strategic planning is simply an effort to identify the things we must do to be successful in the future.

- Once we have determined what we must do to be successful (the plan), we must take steps to execute that plan (the actions).

Accordingly, the key role of strategic planning is to provide a basis for aligning the organization's work processes with its strategic directions, thereby ensuring people and processes in different parts of the organization are not working at cross-purposes. To the extent that alignment does not occur, the organization's effectiveness and competitiveness is reduced.

The Strategic Planning Category looks at how the organization:

- Understands the key customer, market, and operational requirements as input to setting strategic directions. This helps to ensure that ongoing process improvements are aligned with the organization's strategic directions.

- Optimizes the use of resources and ensures bridging between short- and longer-term requirements that may entail capital expenditures, supplier development, new human resource recruitment strategies, reengineering key processes, and other factors affecting business success.

- Ensures that deployment will be effective—that there are mechanisms to transmit requirements and achieve alignment on three basic levels: 1) the organization/executive level; 2) the key process level; and 3) the work unit/individual job level.

The requirements for the Strategic Planning Category are intended to encourage strategic thinking and acting—to develop a basis for achieving and maintaining a competitive position. These requirements do not demand formalized plans, planning systems, departments, or specific planning cycles. They also do not imply that all improvements could or should be planned in advance. They do, however, require plans and the alignment of actions to those plans at all levels of the organization. An effective improvement system combines improvements of many types and degrees of involvement. An effective system to improve performance and competitive advantage requires fact-based strategic guidance, particularly when improvement alternatives compete for limited resources. In most cases, priority setting depends heavily upon a cost rationale. However, an organization might also have to deal with critical requirements, such as public responsibilities, that are not driven by cost considerations alone.

Strategic planning consists of the planning process, the identification of goals and actions necessary to achieve success, and the deployment of those actions to align the work of the organization.

Strategy Development

- Customers: market requirements and evolving expectations and opportunities

- Competitive environment and capabilities relative to competitors: industry and market

- Technologies and other innovations that might affect products and services and future business operations

- Internal strengths and weaknesses, including human resource capabilities and needs, resource availability, and operational capabilities and needs

- Financial, societal, ethical, regulatory, and other potential risks that may affect business success risks

- Opportunities to redirect resources to higher-priority products, services or business areas

- Changes in economic conditions (local, national, or global) that might affect the business

- Unique organizational factors such as supplier and supply chain, capabilities, and needs

- Develop clear strategic objectives with timetables that help leaders determine where the organization should be at given points in time so they can effectively monitor progress

Strategy Deployment

- Translate strategy into action plans and related human resource plans

- Align and deploy action plan requirements, performance measures, and resources throughout the organization to ensure changes or improvements are sustained

- Define measures for tracking progress on action plans and ensure actions are aligned throughout the organization

- Project expected performance results, including assumptions of competitor performance increases

2.1 STRATEGY DEVELOPMENT (40 PTS.)
PROCESS

Describe how your organization establishes its strategic objectives, including how it enhances its competitive position, overall performance, and future success.

Within your response, include answers to the following questions:

a. Strategy Development Process

(1) What is your overall strategic planning process? What are the key steps? Who are the key participants? What are your short- and longer-term planning time horizons? How are these timing horizons set? How does your strategic planning process address these timing horizons?

(2) How do you ensure that strategic planning addresses the key factors listed below? How do you collect and analyze relevant data and information to address these factors as they relate to your strategic planning:

- Your customer and market needs, expectations, and opportunities

- Your competitive environment and your capabilities relative to competitors

- Technological and other key innovations or changes that might affect your products and services and how you operate

- Your strengths and weaknesses, including human and other resources

- Your opportunities to redirect resources to higher priority products, services, or areas.

- Financial, societal and ethical, regulatory, and other potential risks

- Changes in the national or global economy

- Factors unique to your organization, including partner and supply chain needs, strengths, and weaknesses

b. Strategic Objectives

(1) What are your key strategic objectives and your timetable for accomplishing them? What are your most important goals for these strategic objectives?

(2) How do your strategic objectives address the challenges identified in response to P.2 in your Organizational Profile? How do you ensure that your strategic objectives balance short- and longer-term challenges and opportunities? How do you ensure that your strategic objectives balance the needs of all key stakeholders?

Notes:

N1. "Strategy development" refers to your organization's approach (formal or informal) to preparing for the future. Strategy development might utilize various types of forecasts, projections, options, scenarios, and/or other approaches to envisioning the future for purposes of decision making and resource allocation.

N2. "Strategy" should be interpreted broadly. Strategy might be built around or lead to any or all of the following: new products, services, and markets; revenue growth via various approaches, including acquisitions; and new partnerships and alliances. Strategy might be directed toward becoming a preferred supplier, a local supplier in each of your major customers' markets, a low-cost producer, a market innovator, or a high-end or customized product or service provider.

Continued

Notes: *Continued*

N3. Strategies to address key challenges [2.1b(2)] might include rapid response, customization, lean or virtual manufacturing, rapid innovation, ISO 9000:2000 registration, Web-based supplier and customer relationship management, and product and service quality. Responses to Item 2.1 should focus on your specific challenges—those most important to your business success and to strengthening your organization's overall performance.

N4. Item 2.1 addresses your overall organizational strategy, which might include changes in services, products, and product lines. However, the Item does not address product and service design; you should address these factors in Item 6.1, as appropriate.

This Item [2.1] looks at how the organization sets strategic directions and develops strategic objectives, with the aim of strengthening overall performance and competitiveness.

The first part of this Item [2.1a(1)] asks the organization to describe its strategic planning process and identify the key participants, key steps, and planning-time horizons. This helps examiners understand the steps and data used in the planning process. It is usually a good idea to provide a flowchart of the planning process. This helps examiners understand how the planning process works without wasting valuable space in the application.

The organization must consider the key factors that affect its future success. These factors cover external and internal influences on the organization. Each factor must be addressed and outlined to show how relevant data and information are gathered and analyzed. Although the organization is not limited to the number of factors it considers important in planning, the eight factors identified in Item 2.1a(2) must be addressed unless a valid rationale can be offered as to why the factor is not appropriate. Together, these eight factors will cover the most important variables for any organization's future success.

- The planning process should examine all the key influences, risks, challenges, and other factors that might affect the organization's future opportunities and directions—taking as long-term a view as possible. This approach is intended to provide a thorough and realistic context for the development of a customer- and market-focused strategy to guide ongoing decision making, resource allocation, and overall management.

- This planning process should cover all types of businesses, competitive situations, strategic issues, planning approaches, and plans. The requirement calls for a future-oriented basis for action but does not specifically require formalized planning, planning departments, planning cycles, or a specified way of visualizing the future. Even if the organization is seeking to create an entirely new business situation, it is still necessary to set and to test the objectives that define and guide critical actions and performance.

- This Item also focuses on identifying the factors and actions the organization must take to achieve a leadership position in a competitive market. This usually requires ongoing revenue growth and improvements in operational effectiveness. Achieving and sustaining a leadership position in a competitive market requires a view of the future that includes not only the markets or segments in which the organization competes, but also how it competes. How it competes presents many options and requires understanding of the organization's and competitors' strengths and weaknesses. No specific time horizon for planning is required by the Criteria; the thrust of this Item is finding ways to create and ensure sustained competitive leadership.

To maintain competitive leadership, an increasingly important part of strategic planning requires processes to project the competitive environment accurately. Such projections help detect and reduce competitive threats, shorten reaction time, and identify opportunities. Depending on the size and type of business, maturity of markets, pace of change, and competitive parameters (such as price or innovation rate), organizations might use a variety of modeling, scenario, or other techniques and judgments to project the competitive environment.

The second part of this Item [2.1b] asks for a summary of the organization's key strategic objectives and the timetable for accomplishing them. It also asks how these objectives address the challenges outlined in the Organizational Profile.

- The purpose of the timetable is to provide a basis for projecting the path that improvement is likely to take. This allows the leaders who monitor progress to determine when performance is deviating from plan and when adjustments should be made to get back on track. Consider Figure 23. The performance goal four years into the future is to achieve a level of performance of 100. Currently the organization is at 20. At the end of year one, the organi-

zation achieved a performance level of 40, represented by the circle symbol. It appears that that level of performance is on track toward the goal of 100. However, the path from the current state to the future state is rarely a straight line. Unless the expected trajectory is known (or at least estimated), it is not possible to evaluate the progress accurately. Without timetables or trajectories, leaders are forced to default to best guess or intuition as a basis for comparing actual, measurable progress against expected progress.

In Figure 24, the planned trajectory is represented by the triangle symbols. When compared with the current level of performance (circle symbol), it is clear that there is a performance shortfall of approximately 30.

In Figure 25, the planned trajectory is represented by the square symbols. When compared with the current level of performance (the circle symbol), it is clear that the performance is ahead of schedule.

There are several possible decisions that leaders could make based on this information. It might mean that the original estimates/goals were low and should be reset. It might also mean that the process did not need all of the resources it had available. These

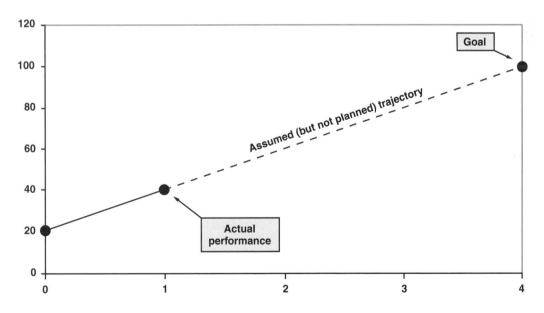

Figure 23 Assumed trajectory.

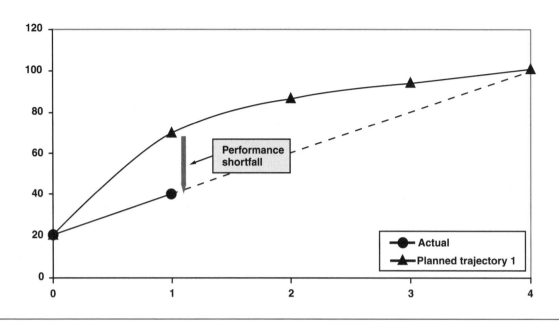

Figure 24 Planned trajectory 1—performance shortfall.

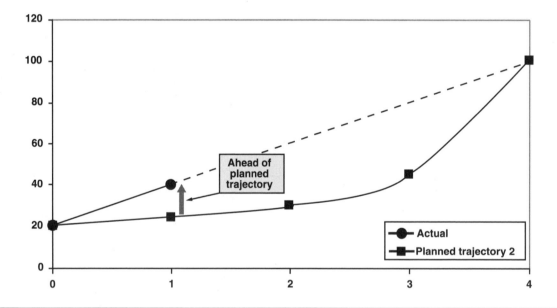

Figure 25 Planned trajectory 2—ahead of plan.

resources may be better used in areas where performance is not ahead of schedule.

In any case, without knowing the expected path toward a goal, leaders are forced to guess whether the level of progress is appropriate.

- Finally, the last part of this Item requires the organization to evaluate the options it considered

in the strategic planning process to ensure it responded fully to the six factors identified in Item 2.1a(2) that were most important to business success. This last step helps the organization "close the loop" to make sure that the factors influencing organization success were adequately analyzed and support key strategic objectives.

2.1 Strategy Development

How the organization establishes strategic objectives, including how it enhances its competitive position, overall performance, and future success

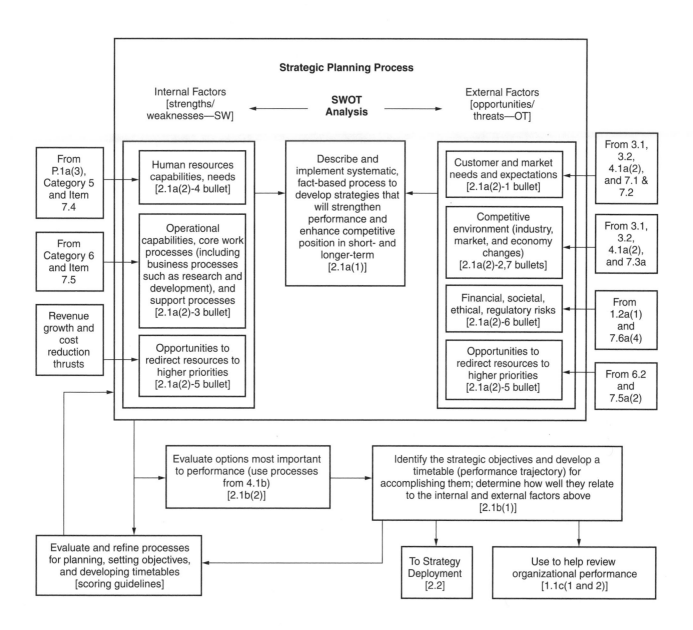

2.1 Strategy Development Item Linkages

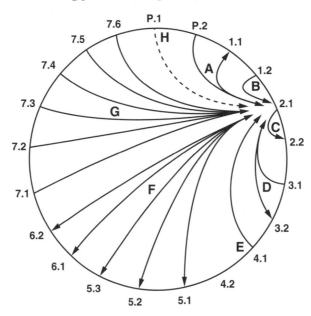

	NATURE OF RELATIONSHIP
A	The planning process [2.1] includes senior leaders—as part of their responsibilities for setting direction, expectations, and ensuring a strong focus on customers and employee empowerment [1.1a], and the protection of stakeholder interests [1.1b]. In addition, the time lines or expected performance trajectories [2.1b(1)] provide a basis for leaders to determine if progress is on track when they monitor progress [1.1c(1)]. The competitive environment [partly defined in P.2a] is also examined as part of the strategy development process [2.1a(2)]. In addition, before the planning cycle is complete, leaders must ensure that the strategic objectives [2.1b(2)] address the challenges identified in the Organizational Profile [P.2b].
B	Public health, environmental, waste management, and related concerns [1.2a] as well as the need to promote ethical behavior in all transactions [1.2b], are considered, as appropriate, in the strategy development process [2.1a(2)].
C	The planning process [2.1a] produces a set of strategic objectives [2.1b(1)] that must be converted into action plans that are deployed to the work force [2.2a].
D	The planning process [2.1] includes information on current and potential customer requirements and preferences and the projected competitive environment [3.1], as well as intelligence obtained from customer-contact people (complaints and comments) [3.2a] and customer satisfaction data [3.2b].
E	Key organizational and competitive comparison data [4.1a(2)] and analytical data, including various forecasts and projections [4.1b], are used for planning [2.1a(2)] and setting objectives [2.1b].

Continued

	NATURE OF RELATIONSHIP *Continued*
F	Information on human resource capabilities [Category 5] and work process capabilities [Category 6] is considered in the strategic planning process as part of the determination of internal strengths and weaknesses and to help determine if resources should be redirected to higher priority products, services, or areas [2.1a(2)]. Employee educational levels, diversity, and other characteristics [P.1a(3)] may affect the determination of human resource strengths and weaknesses as a part of the strategic planning process [2.1a(2)]. *To avoid cluttering diagrams in Categories 5 and 6, these linkage arrows will not be repeated there.*
G	Customer-focused [7.1], product and service quality [7.2], financial and market [7.3], human resource [7.4], organization effectiveness [7.5], and governance and social responsibility [7.6] results are used in the planning process [2.1a(2)] to set strategic objectives [2.1b(1)]. In addition, results in 7.5a(3) must specifically report on progress toward achieving the strategic objectives and are used in subsequent planning.
H	Employee educational levels, diversity, and other characteristics [P.1a(3)] relate to human resource strengths and weaknesses and are considered during the strategic planning process [2.1a(2)].

IF YOU DON'T DO WHAT THE CRITERIA REQUIRE . . .	
Item Reference	**Possible Adverse Consequences**
2.1a(1)	Without clearly defined short- and longer-term planning horizons, it may be difficult to properly align the analysis and collection of market and industry forecast data to support effective planning. The shorter the planning horizon, the easier it is to be accurate in forecasting. However, the planning horizon must be at least as long as the time it takes the organization to design, develop, and deliver new products and services required by customers and markets. For example, if the design–delivery cycle is seven years (as it was in the U.S. automobile industry), then to be effective an organization must be able to forecast or anticipate customer and market requirements seven years out—which is difficult to do accurately. Alternatively, the organization should reduce its design–delivery cycle time to less than 24 months (as did the Japanese automobile industry), reduce the required planning horizon, and be able to more accurately anticipate customer and market requirements.
2.1a(2)	The failure to address the eight key factors (customers and market needs; competitive environment; technological and other key innovations or changes that might affect operations; internal strengths and weaknesses; opportunities to redirect resources to higher priority areas or services; external risks such as financial, societal, ethical, and regulatory; changes in the economy; and partner and supply chain strengths and weaknesses) usually results in a flawed strategic plan—a plan that has overlooked an element critical to future success. For example, an organization may fail to achieve strategic objectives if it assumed (incorrectly) that a key supplier would be able to deliver critical components at a certain time. Likewise, a strategic plan that does not adequately account for the arrival of competitive offerings or new technologies in the marketplace can be faced with major hurdles (consider the impact of the quartz watch on the traditional Swiss watch industry). Failing to consider or incorrectly forecast these eight elements may result in a strategic plan that cannot be achieved.
2.1b(1)	Knowing whether the strategy is unfolding as expected is critical to the successful performance of the organization and the leadership. The failure to develop a timetable with clearly defined targets for accomplishing strategic objectives that are consistent with the performance review frequency makes it extremely difficult for leaders to monitor organizational performance effectively [as required by Item 1.1c(1)]. Without defined milestones, leaders must guess whether the rate of progress is appropriate or not. Without clear time lines or trajectories for growth, leaders frequently assume the path between current state and desired state (goals) is linear. Data indicate that the actual path is almost never linear; so the assumptions of linearity that leaders make in the absence of clear time lines and trajectories are usually incorrect.
2.1b(2)	Strategy development is an ongoing, dynamic process. It is often a difficult process that takes a considerable amount of time to complete initially and then requires continual attention to address a rapidly changing marketplace. However, if leaders fail to ensure that planning has fully addressed organizational changes and ensure that the strategic objectives effectively balance the needs of all key stakeholders, the plan may be ineffective and the time it took to develop the plan may be wasted.

2.1 STRATEGY DEVELOPMENT—SAMPLE EFFECTIVE PRACTICES

A. Strategy Development Process

- Business goals, strategies, and issues are addressed and reported in measurable terms. Strategic objectives consider future requirements needed to achieve organizational leadership after considering the performance levels that other organizations are likely to achieve in the same planning time frame.

- Web-based or e-commerce initiatives are considered as part of developing new business or new markets.

- The planning and objective-setting process encourages input (but not necessarily decision making) from a variety of people at all levels throughout the organization.

- Data on customer requirements, key markets, benchmarks, supplier and partner, human resource, and organizational capabilities (internal and external factors) are used to develop business plans.

- Plans and the planning process itself are evaluated each cycle for accuracy and completeness—more often if needed to keep pace with changing business requirements.

- Opportunities for improvement in the planning process are identified systematically and carried out in each planning cycle.

- Refinements in the process of planning, plan deployment, and receiving input from work units have been made. Improvements in plan cycle time, plan resources, and planning accuracy are documented.

B. Strategic Objectives

- Strategic objectives are identified and a timetable (or planned growth trajectory) for accomplishing the objectives is set. The timelines match the senior leaders' review cycle. For example, if leaders review progress against goals quarterly, the timelines identify the expected level of performance by quarters.

- Options to obtain best performance for the strategic objectives are systematically evaluated against the internal and external factors used in the strategy development process.

- The process of setting timelines or trajectories and the accuracy of the projections are analyzed and refined.

- Best practices from other providers, competitors, or outside benchmarks are identified and used to provide better estimates of trajectories.

2.2 STRATEGY DEPLOYMENT (45 PTS.)
PROCESS

Describe how your organization converts its strategic objectives into action plans. Summarize your organization's action plans and related key performance measures or indicators. Project your organization's future performance on these key performance measures or indicators.

Within your response, include answers to the following questions:

a. Action Plan Development and Deployment

(1) How do you develop and deploy action plans to achieve your key strategic objectives? How do you allocate resources to ensure accomplishment of your action plans? How do you ensure that the key changes resulting from action plans can be sustained?

(2) What are your key short- and longer-term action plans? What are the key changes, if any, in your products and services, your customers and markets, and in how you will operate?

(3) What are your key human resource plans that derive from your short- and longer-term strategic objectives and action plans?

(4) What are your key performance measures or indicators for tracking progress on your action plans? How do you ensure that your overall action plan measurement system reinforces organizational alignment? How do you ensure that the measurement system covers all key deployment areas and stakeholders?

b. Performance Projection

For the key performance measures or indicators identified in 2.2a(4), what are your performance projections for both your short- and longer-term planning time horizons? How does your projected performance compare with competitors' projected performance? How does it compare with key benchmarks, goals, and past performance, as appropriate?

Notes:

N1. Strategy and action plan development and deployment are closely linked to other Items in the Criteria. Examples of key linkages are:

- Item 1.1 for how your senior leaders set and communicate directions

- Category 3 for gathering customer and market knowledge as input to your strategy and action plans and for deploying action plans

- Category 4 for information, analysis, and knowledge management to support your key information needs, to support your development of strategy, to provide an effective basis for your performance measurements, and to track progress relative to your strategic objectives and action plans

- Category 5 for your work system needs; employee education, training, and development needs; and related human resource factors resulting from action plans

- Category 6 for process requirements resulting from your action plans

- Item 7.5 for specific accomplishments relative to your organizational strategy and action plans

N2. Measures and indicators of projected performance (2.2b) might include changes resulting from new business ventures; business acquisitions or mergers; new value creation; market entry and shifts; and significant anticipated innovations in products, services, and technology.

The first part of this Item [2.2a] looks at how the organization translates its strategic objectives (which were identified in item 2.1b) into action plans to accomplish the objectives and to enable assessment of progress relative to action plans. Overall, the intent of this item is to ensure that strategies are deployed at all levels throughout the organization to align work for goal achievement.

The first part of this Item [2.2a] calls for information on how action plans are developed and deployed. This includes spelling out key performance requirements and measures, as well as allocating resources and aligning work throughout the organization. Leaders must develop action plans that address the key strategic objectives (which were developed using the processes in Item 2.1). Organizations must summarize key short- and longer-term action plans. Particular attention is given to products/services, customers/markets, how the organization operates, and key human resource plans that will enable accomplishment of strategic objectives and action plans.

The organization should provide the key measures/indicators used in tracking progress relative to the action plans. The organization should also use these measures or indicators to achieve organizational alignment and coverage of all key work units and stakeholders.

Consistently accomplishing action plans and making necessary course corrections or adjustments requires resources and performance measures, as well as the alignment of work unit and supplier/partner plans. Alignment and consistency are intended to provide a basis for setting and communicating priorities for ongoing improvement activities—part of the daily work of all units. Also required are the key measures and/or indicators used in tracking progress relative to the action plans, how they are communicated, and how strategic objectives, action plans, and performance are aligned. Action plans include human resource plans that support the overall strategy.

Without effective alignment, routine work and acts of improvement can be random and serve to suboptimize organizational performance. In Figure 26, the arrows represent the well-intended work carried out by employees of organizations who lack a clear set of expectations and direction. Each person, manager, and work unit works diligently to achieve goals they believe are important. Each is pulling hard—but not necessarily in ways that ensure performance excellence. This encourages the creation of "fiefdoms" or "silos" within organizations.

With a clear, well-communicated strategic plan, it is easier to know when daily work is out of alignment. The large arrow in Figure 27 represents the strategic plan pointing the direction the organization must take to be successful and achieve its mission and vision. The strategic plan and accompanying measures make it possible to analyze work and business practices to know when they are not aligned and to help employees, including leaders, to know when adjustments are required.

A well-deployed and understood strategic plan helps everyone in the organization distinguish between random acts of improvement and aligned improvement. Random acts of improvement give a false sense of accomplishment and rarely produce optimum benefits for the organization. For example, a decision to improve a business process that is not aligned with the strategic plan (as the small bold arrow in Figure 28 represents) usually results in a

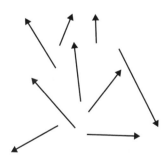

Figure 26   Nonaligned work.

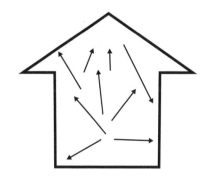

Figure 27   Strategic direction.

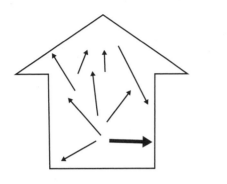

Figure 28   Random improvement.

wasteful expenditure of time, money, and human resources—improvement without benefiting customers or enhancing operating effectiveness.

On the other hand, by working systematically to strengthen processes that are aligned with the strategic plan, the organization moves closer to achieving success, as Figure 29 indicates.

Ultimately, all processes and procedures of an organization should be aligned to maximize the achievement of strategic plans, as Figure 30 demonstrates.

Critical action plan resource requirements include human resource plans that support the overall strategy. Examples of possible human resource plan elements are:

- Redesign of work organization and/or jobs to increase employee empowerment and decision making

- Initiatives to promote greater labor-management cooperation, such as union partnerships

- Initiatives to foster knowledge sharing and organizational learning

- Modification of compensation and recognition systems to recognize team, organizational, stock market, customer, or other performance attributes

- Education and training initiatives, such as developmental programs for future leaders, partnerships with universities to help ensure the availability of future employees, and/or establishment of technology-based training capabilities

Finally, the second part of this Item [2.2b] asks the organization to provide a projection of key performance measures and/or indicators, including key performance targets and/or goals for both short- and longer-term planning time horizons. This projected performance is the basis for comparing past performance and performance relative to competitors and benchmarks, as appropriate.

- Projections and comparisons in this Area are intended to help the organization's leaders improve their ability to understand and track dynamic, competitive performance factors. Through this tracking process, they should be better prepared to take into account rate of improvement and change relative to competitors and relative to their own targets or stretch goals. Such tracking serves as a key diagnostic management tool.

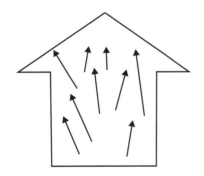

Figure 29   Moving toward alignment.

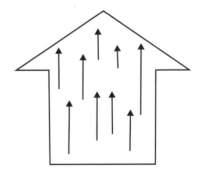

Figure 30   Systematic alignment.

- In addition to improvement relative to past performance and to competitors, projected performance also might include changes resulting from new business ventures, entry into new markets, e-commerce initiatives, product/service innovations, or other strategic thrusts. Without this comparison information, it is possible to set goals that, even if attained, may not result in competitive advantage. More than one high-performing company has been surprised by a competitor that set and achieved more aggressive goals. Consider the example represented by Figure 31. Imagine that you are ahead of your competition and committed to a 10 percent increase in profit over your base year. After eight years you are twice as profitable. To your surprise, you find that your competitor has increased 20 percent each year. You have achieved your goal, but your competitor has beaten you, making slightly more. After 10 years, the competitor has a significant lead. It is not good enough to achieve your goals unless your goals place you in a competitive position.

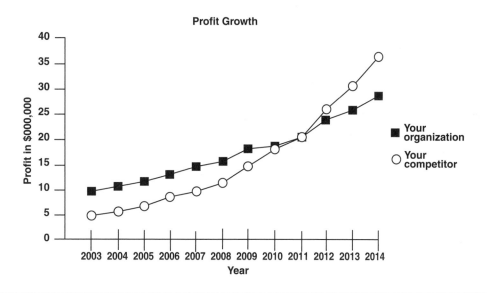

Figure 31   Projecting competitor's future performance.

2.2 Strategy Deployment

Summary of strategy, action plans, and related key performance measures and indicators and performance projections; how they are developed, communicated, and deployed

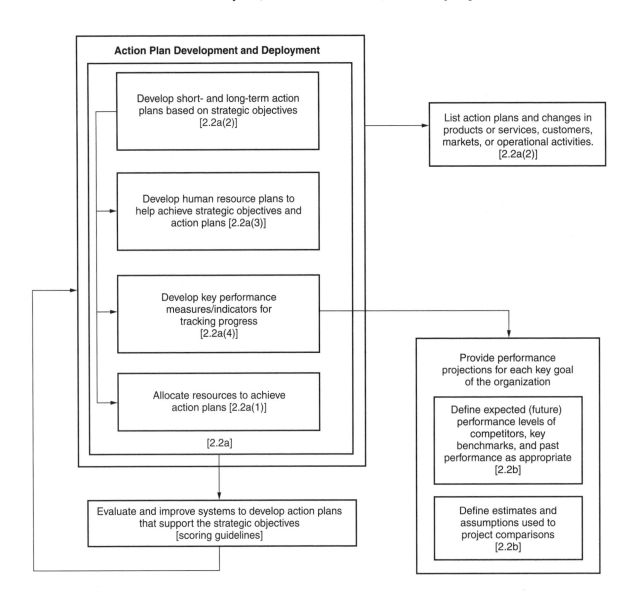

2.2 Strategy Deployment Item Linkages

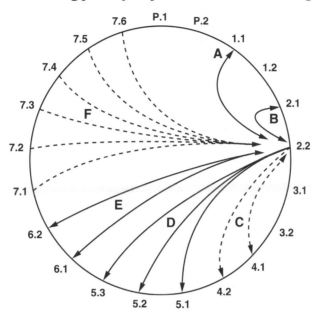

	NATURE OF RELATIONSHIP
A	The leadership team [1.1a(1)] ensures that action plans are aligned throughout the organization with strategic objectives, and that resources are allocated to ensure the actions are accomplished [2.2a(1)].
B	The planning process [2.1] develops the strategic objectives that are converted into action plans to support these objectives [2.2a(1)].
C	The action plans [2.2a(1)] and related performance measures [2.2a(4)] define part of the data that need to be collected to monitor alignment [4.1a] and analyzed to support decision making [4.1b], help define requirements for data availability and hardware and software reliability [4.2b]. Benchmarking comparison data [4.1a(2)] and analytical processes [4.1b(1)] are used to project future performance of competitors [2.2b].
D	Measures, objectives, action plans, and human resource plans [2.2a] are used to align and develop human resources [5.1, 5.2, 5.3]. It is particularly important that action plans and measures [2.2a] are aligned with and supported by employee feedback and related recognition and reward [5.1b].
E	Measures, objectives, and action plans [2.2a] are used to drive and align actions to achieve improved performance [6.1, 6.2].
F	Results data [Category 7] are used to help determine performance projections for short- and longer-term goal setting [2.2b]. In addition, specific accomplishments related to organizational strategy and actions must be reported in Item 7.5a(3). *To avoid clutter and make the diagrams more readable, these relationships will not be repeated on the Category 7 linkage diagrams.*

	IF YOU DON'T DO WHAT THE CRITERIA REQUIRE . . .
Item Reference	**Possible Adverse Consequences**
2.2a(1)	The failure to develop action plans to carry out strategic objectives and employ them at all levels of the organization usually means that work may not be aligned to achieve the strategy. Instead, there is a tendency for managers and other employees to focus their work on things they believe are important. This can result in significant resources being spent on activities that do not contribute to the objectives the organization's leaders have determined are critical for its future success. In addition, the failure to allocate resources appropriately to accomplish action plans frequently means that some plans are not accomplished because of insufficient resources, while other plans are accomplished inefficiently because of too many resources. In both cases, the value to the customer and the organization is suboptimized.
2.2a(2)	The inability to articulate and communicate key short- and longer-term action plans usually means those plans do not exist, or they are only expressed as vague generalities. Unclear plans make it more difficult to help employees at all levels of the organization understand what work they must do to help the organization achieve future success. Again, without clear direction from the top, employees will still work hard, but their work may be unfocused as they follow their own ideas for appropriate action—everyone is not pulling in the same direction.
2.2a(3)	By definition, "plans" describe activities or actions that have not yet taken place. Many times, in order to execute plans, employees must possess skills, knowledge, or abilities that they do not currently possess. Without appropriate plans to develop, acquire, or motivate the human resources necessary to carry out desired actions, the organization may not be able to achieve its strategic objectives. Its employees may not have the knowledge, skills, or abilities to carry out the actions required for success in the future.
2.2a(4)	Without appropriate measures or indicators it is difficult for leaders, managers, and employees throughout the organization to determine if they are making appropriate progress. It is also more difficult for leaders to communicate expectations accurately. Unclear expectations increase the likelihood that employees will not understand what they are required to do to achieve strategic objectives. Consider the adage, "what gets measured gets done." Without appropriate measures it is difficult to focus everyone on doing the right things.
2.2b	In the best-performing organizations, strategic goals are designed to enable the organization to win in highly competitive situations. If an organization desires to achieve a leadership position, it must understand where the competition is likely to be in the future before it sets its goals. Unless the organization's leaders understand the likely future performance levels of key competitors (in the same planning horizon), they may set an aggressive goal, achieve that goal, and still lose—finding themselves behind the competition.

2.2 STRATEGY DEPLOYMENT— SAMPLE EFFECTIVE PRACTICES

A. Action Plan Development and Deployment

- Plans are in place to optimize operational performance and improve customer focus using tools such as reengineering, streamlining work processes, and reducing cycle time.

- Actions have been defined in measurable terms, which align with strategic objectives and enable the organization to sustain established leadership positions for major products and services for key customers or markets.

- Strategies to achieve key organizational results (operational performance requirements) are defined.

- Planned performance and productivity levels are defined in measurable terms for key features of products and services.

- Planned actions are challenging, realistic, achievable, and understood by employees throughout the organization. Every employee understands their role in achieving strategic and operational goals and objectives.

- Resources are available and committed to achieve the plans (no unfunded mandates). Capital projects are funded according to business improvement plans.

- Plans are absolutely used to guide operational performance improvements. Plans drive budget and action, not the other way around.

- Incremental (short-term) strategies to achieve long-term plans are defined in measurable terms and time lines are in place to help monitor progress.

- Business plans, short- and long-term goals, and performance measures are understood and used to drive actions throughout the organization.

- Every individual in the organization, at all levels, understands how their work contributes to achieving organizational goals and plans.

- Plans are followed to ensure that resources are deployed and redeployed as needed to support goals.

- Human resource plans support strategic plans and goals. Plans show how the work force will be developed to enable the organization to achieve its strategic goals.

- Key issues of training and development, hiring, retention, employee participation, involvement, empowerment, and recognition and reward are addressed as a part of the human resource plan. Appropriate measures and targets for each are defined.

- Innovative strategies may involve one or more of the following:

  - Redesigning work to increase employee responsibility.

  - Improving labor–management relations. (That is, prior to contract negotiations, train both sides in effective negotiation skills so people focus on the merits of issues, not on positions. A goal, for example, is to improve relations and shorten negotiation time by 50 percent.)

  - Forming partnerships with education institutions to develop employees and ensure a supply of well-prepared future employees.

  - Developing gain-sharing or equity-building compensation systems for all employees to increase motivation and productivity.

  - Broadening employee responsibilities; creating self-directed or high-performance work teams.

- Key performance measures (for example, employee satisfaction or work climate surveys) have been identified to gather data to manage progress. (Note: Improvement results associated with these measures should be reported in 7.4.)

- The effectiveness of human resource planning and alignment with strategic plans is evaluated systematically.

- Data are used to evaluate and improve performance and participation for all types of employees (for example, absenteeism, turnover, grievances, accidents, recognition and reward, and training participation).

- Routine, two-way communication about performance of employees occurs.

- The process to develop action plans to support strategic objectives is systematically evaluated.

B. Performance Projection

- Projections of two- to five-year changes in performance levels are developed and used to collect data (measure) and track progress.

- Data from competitors, key benchmarks, and/or past performance form a valid basis for comparison. The organization has valid strategies and goals in place to meet or exceed the planned levels of performance for these competitors and benchmarks.

- Plans include expected future levels of competitor or comparison performance and are used to set and validate the organization's own plans and goals.

- Future plans and projections of performance consider new acquisition, optimum but secure growth, reducing costs through operational excellence processes, and anticipated research and development of innovations internally or among competitors. The accuracy of these projections is mapped and analyzed. Techniques to improve accuracy are developed and implemented.

3 Customer and Market Focus—85 Points

*The **Customer and Market Focus** Category examines how your organization determines requirements, expectations, and preferences of customers and markets. Also examined is how your organization builds relationships with customers and determines the key factors that lead to customer acquisition, satisfaction, loyalty, and retention, and to business expansion.*

This Category addresses how the organization seeks to understand the voices of customers and of the marketplace. The Category stresses relationships as an important part of an overall listening, learning, and performance excellence strategy. Customer satisfaction and dissatisfaction results provide vital information for understanding customers and the marketplace. In many cases, such results and trends provide the most meaningful information, not only on customers' views but also on their marketplace behaviors—repeat business and positive referrals.

Customer and Market Focus contains two Items that focus on understanding customer and market requirements, and building relationships and determining satisfaction.

Customer and Market Knowledge

- Determining market or customer segments
- Determining customer information validity
- Determining important product or service features
- Using complaint information and data from potential and former customers

Customer Relationships and Satisfaction

- Making customer contact and feedback easy and useful
- Handling complaints effectively and responsively
- Ensuring complaint data are used to eliminate causes of complaints
- Building customer relationships and loyalty
- Systematically determining customer satisfaction and the satisfaction of competitor's customers

3.1 CUSTOMER AND MARKET KNOWLEDGE (40 PTS.)
PROCESS

Describe how your organization determines requirements, expectations, and preferences of customers and markets to ensure the continuing relevance of your products and services and to develop new opportunities.

Within your response, include answers to the following questions:

a. Customer and Market Knowledge

(1) How do you determine or target customers, customer groups, and market segments? How do you include customers of competitors and other potential customers and markets in this determination?

(2) How do you listen and learn to determine key customer requirements and expectations (including product and service features) and their relative importance to customers' purchasing decisions? How do determination methods vary for different customers or customer groups? How do you use relevant information from current and former customers, including marketing and sales information, customer loyalty and retention data, win/loss analysis, and complaints? How do you use this information for purposes of product and service planning, marketing, process improvements, and other business development?

(3) How do you keep your listening and learning methods current with business needs and directions?

Notes:

N1 Your responses to this Item should include the customer groups and market segments identified in P.1b(2).

N2. If your products and services are sold to or delivered to end-use customers via other businesses such as retail stores or dealers, customer groups [3.1a(1)] should include both the end users and these intermediate businesses.

N3. "Product and service features" [3.1a(2)] refers to all the important characteristics of products and services and to their performance throughout their full life cycle and the full "consumption chain." This includes all customers' purchase experiences and other interactions with your organization that influence purchase decisions. The focus should be on features that affect customer preference and repeat business—for example, those features that differentiate your products and services from competing offerings. Those features might include price, reliability, value, delivery, requirements for hazardous materials use and disposal, customer or technical support, and the sales relationship. Key product and service features and purchasing decisions [3.1a(2)] might take into account how transactions occur and factors such as confidentiality and security.

N4. Listening and learning [3.1a(2)] might include gathering and integrating surveys, focus group findings, and Web-based and other data and information that bear upon customers' purchasing decisions. Keeping your listening and learning methods current with business needs and directions [3.1a(3)] also might include use of newer technology, such as Web-based data gathering.

This Item [3.1] looks at the organization's key processes for gaining knowledge about its current and future customers and markets, in order to offer relevant products and services, understand emerging customer requirements and expectations, and keep pace with changing markets and marketplaces. Processes required by Item 3.1 permit the organization to gather intelligence about its customers and competition. It is a critical starting place for determining direction and strategic planning.

This information is intended to support marketing, business development, and planning. In a rapidly changing competitive environment, many factors may affect customer preference and loyalty and the interface with customers in the marketplace, making it necessary to listen and learn on a continuous basis. To be effective, such listening and learning strategies need to have a close connection with the organization's overall business strategy. For example, if the organization customizes its products and services, the listening and learning strategy needs to be backed by a capable information system—one that rapidly accumulates information about customers and makes this information available where needed throughout the organization or elsewhere within the overall value chain.

The organization must have a process for determining or segmenting key customer groups and markets. To ensure that a complete and accurate picture of customer requirements and concerns is obtained, organizations should consider the requirements of potential customers, including competitors' customers. (Note: A potential customer is a customer the organization wants but is currently being served by a competitor.) The organization should show how these determinations include relevant information from current and former customers. In addition, the organization should tailor its listening and learning techniques to different customer groups and market segments. A relationship or listening strategy might work with some customers, but not with others.

- Information sought should be sensitive to specific product and service requirements and their relative importance or value to the different customer groups. This determination should be supported by use of information and data, such as complaints and gains and losses of customers.

- In addition to defining customer requirements, organizations must determine key requirements and drivers of purchase decisions and key product/service features. In other words, the organization must be able to prioritize key customer requirements and drivers of purchase decisions. These priorities are likely to be different for different customer groups and market segments. Knowledge of customer groups and market segments allows the organization to tailor listening and learning strategies and marketplace offerings, to support marketing strategies, and to develop new business.

- In a rapidly changing competitive environment, many factors may affect customer preference and loyalty. This makes it necessary to listen and learn on a continuous basis. In effective organizations, listening and learning need to be closely linked with the overall business strategy and strategy planning process.

- E-commerce is changing the competitive arena rapidly. This may significantly affect the relationships with customers and the effectiveness of listening and learning strategies. It may also force the organization to redefine customer groups and market segments.

- A variety of listening and learning strategies are commonly used by top-performing organizations. Increasingly, companies interact with customers via multiple modes. Some examples of listening and learning strategies include:

  - Close integration with key customers

  - Rapid innovation and field trials of products and services to better link research and development (R&D) and design to the market

  - Close tracking of technological, competitive, and other factors that may bear upon customer requirements, expectations, preferences, or alternatives

  - Defining the customers' value chains and how they are likely to change

  - Focus groups with leading-edge customers

– Use of critical incidents, such as complaints, to understand key service attributes from the point of view of customers and customer-contact employees

– Interviewing lost customers to determine the factors they use in their purchase decisions

– Survey/feedback information, including information collected on the Internet

– Win/loss analysis relative to competitors

Finally, the organization must have a system in place to improve its customer listening and learning strategies to keep current with changing business needs and directions. If the organization competes in a rapidly changing environment, it may need to evaluate and improve its customer listening and learning strategies more frequently. The organization should be able to demonstrate that it has made appropriate improvements to ensure its techniques for understanding customer requirements and priorities keep pace with changing business needs.

3.1 Customer and Market Knowledge

How the organization determines requirements, expectations, and preferences of target or potential customers and markets to anticipate their needs and to develop business opportunities

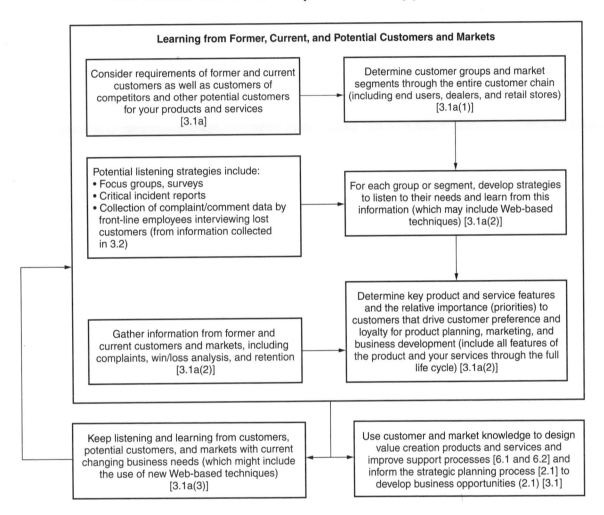

3.1 Customer and Market Knowledge Item Linkages

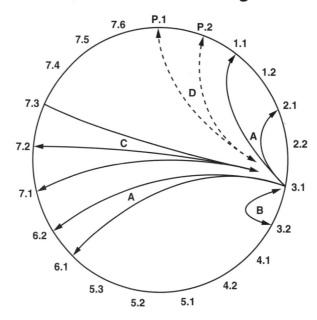

	NATURE OF RELATIONSHIP
A	Customer input and related information about current and future customer and market requirements and preferences [3.1a(2)] are used for strategic planning [2.1a], to design value creation products and services and revise work processes [6.1a(2, 3, and 4)], and to help leaders set directions for the organization [1.1a(1)].
B	Customer complaints [3.2a(3)] are used to help assess current customer expectations and refine requirements [3.1a(2)]. Information about customer requirement priorities [3.1a(2)] is used to build instruments and better target questions to assess customer satisfaction [3.2b(1)] and better follow up on recent transactions [3.2b(2)].
C	Customer satisfaction, complaint, and product and service data and trends [7.1a(2) and 7.2a] and market data [7.3a(2)] are used to help validate customer expectations and refine requirements [3.1a(2)]. In addition, processes to gather intelligence about customer requirements [3.1] are used to define and report customer satisfaction and product and service quality results [7.1 and 7.2].
D	The products and services reported in P.1b(2) were determined using the processes described in 3.1a(2). The information in P.1b(2) helps examiners identify the kind of results, broken out by customer and market segment, which should be reported in Items 7.1 and 7.2.

	IF YOU DON'T DO WHAT THE CRITERIA REQUIRE . . .
Item Reference	**Possible Adverse Consequences**
3.1a(1)	The failure to classify or group customers or markets into meaningful segments may make it difficult to identify and differentiate key requirements that may be critical to one group but not another. For example, frequent or high-volume customers may have different expectations than infrequent or low-volume customers. Dealers may have different requirements than end users. Unless these differences are understood, it may be difficult for the organization to customize information collection techniques as well as programs, products, and services according to the needs and expectations of different groups of customers.
3.1a(2)	Different techniques may be needed to understand the requirements of different groups of customers. The failure to listen and learn about the key customer requirements for products and services, especially those features that are most important to customer purchasing decisions, may make it difficult to design and develop those products and services that are most likely to delight (or even satisfy) customers and increase market share. In addition to gathering feedback directly from current and former customers, the organization should collect and analyze complaint and lost customer data to gain additional insights into unmet requirements and present opportunities. If an organization does not know why it lost or gained customers, it is more difficult to deliver the right products and services to keep customers.
3.1a(3)	The failure to systematically evaluate the processes used to listen and learn about customer requirements may make it difficult to identify specific areas needing change. For example, it does not do much good to create a survey to identify customer requirements if the questions asked on the survey are not the right questions. Incorrect information generated by this survey may cause the organization to design and deliver the wrong products or services. Furthermore, it does little good to use a written survey tool when face-to-face interviews may be a better way to acquire accurate and actionable information. The failure to evaluate the effectiveness of the approaches used to identify and prioritize customer requirements may make it difficult to keep up with changing customer and market needs and gather critical information necessary for strategic planning [Item 2.1a(2)] as well as the design and development of new value creation products and services [Item 6.1a(3)].

3.1 CUSTOMER AND MARKET KNOWLEDGE—SAMPLE EFFECTIVE PRACTICES

A. Customer and Market Knowledge

- Various systematic methods are used to gather data and identify current requirements and expectations of customers (for example, surveys, focus groups, and the use of Web-based systems).

- Key product and service features are defined. Product and service features refer to all important characteristics and to the performance of products and services that customers experience or perceive throughout their use. Factors that bear on customer preference and loyalty—for example, those features that enhance or differentiate products and services from competing offerings—are defined in measurable terms.

- Customer requirements are identified or grouped by customer segments. These segments are consistently used for planning, data analysis, product and service design, production, and delivery processes, and for reporting and monitoring progress.

- Customer data such as complaints and gains or losses of customers are used to support the identification or validation of key customer requirements.

- Fact-based, systematic methods are used to identify the future requirements and expectations of customers. These are tested for accuracy and estimation techniques are improved.

- Customers of competitors are considered and processes are in place to gather expectation data from potential customers.

- Effective listening and learning strategies include:

  - Close monitoring of technological, competitive, societal, environmental, economic, and demographic factors that may bear on customer requirements, expectations, preferences, or alternatives

  - Focus groups with demanding or leading-edge customers

  - Training of front-line employees in customer listening

  - Use of critical incidents in product or service performance or quality to understand key service attributes from the point of view of customers and front-line employees

  - Interviewing lost customers

  - Win/loss analysis relative to competitors

  - Analysis of major factors affecting key customers

- Tools such as forced- or paired-choice analysis are used (where customers select between options A and B, A and C, B and C, and so on). Using this technique, organizations quickly prioritize requirements and focus on delivering those that make the greatest impact on satisfaction, repeat business, and loyalty.

- Methods to listen and learn from customers are evaluated and improved through several cycles. Examples of factors that are evaluated include:

  - The adequacy and timeliness of customer-related information

  - Improvement of survey design

  - Approaches for getting reliable and timely information—surveys, focus groups, customer-contact personnel

  - Improved aggregation and analysis of information

- Best practices for gathering customer requirements and forecasting are identified and used to make improvements.

3.2 CUSTOMER RELATIONSHIPS AND SATISFACTION (45 PTS.) PROCESS

Describe how your organization builds relationships to acquire, satisfy, and retain customers, to increase customer loyalty, and to develop new opportunities. Describe also how your organization determines customer satisfaction.

Within your response, include answers to the following questions:

a. Customer Relationship Building

(1) How do you build relationships to acquire customers, to meet and exceed their expectations, to increase loyalty and repeat business, and to gain positive referrals?

(2) What are your key access mechanisms for customers to seek information, conduct business, and make complaints? How do you determine key customer contact requirements for each mode of customer access? How do you ensure that these contact requirements are deployed to all people and processes involved in the customer response chain?

(3) What is your complaint management process? How do you ensure that complaints are resolved effectively and promptly? How are complaints aggregated and analyzed for use in improvement throughout your organization and by your partners?

(4) How do you keep your approaches to building relationships and providing customer access current with business needs and directions?

b. Customer Satisfaction Determination

(1) How do you determine customer satisfaction and dissatisfaction? How do these determination methods differ among customer groups? How do you ensure that your measurements capture actionable information for use in exceeding your customers' expectations, securing their future business, and gaining positive referrals? How do you use customer satisfaction and dissatisfaction information for improvement?

(2) How do you follow up with customers on products, services, and transaction quality to receive prompt and actionable feedback?

(3) How do you obtain and use information on your customers' satisfaction relative to customers' satisfaction with your competitors and/or industry benchmarks?

(4) How do you keep your approaches to determining satisfaction current with business needs and directions?

Notes:

N1. Customer relationship building [3.2a] might include the development of partnerships or alliances with customers.

N2. Determining customer satisfaction and dissatisfaction (3.2b) might include use of any or all of the following: surveys, formal and informal feedback, customer account histories, complaints, win/loss analysis, and transaction completion rates. Information might be gathered on the Internet, through personal contact or a third party, or by mail.

N3. Customer satisfaction measurements might include both a numerical rating scale and descriptors for each unit in the scale. Actionable customer satisfaction measurements provide useful information about specific product and service features, delivery, relationships, and transactions that bear upon the customers' future actions—repeat business and positive referral.

N4. Your customer satisfaction and dissatisfaction results should be reported in Item 7.1.

Item 3.2 describes processes that examine the impact of products and services on customer relationships and satisfaction. In particular, this Item looks at the organization's processes for building customer relationships and determining customer satisfaction, with the aim of acquiring new customers, retaining existing customers, and developing new opportunities. Relationships provide an important means for organizations to understand and manage customer expectations and to develop new business. Also, customer-contact employees may provide vital information to build partnerships and other longer-term relationships with customers.

Overall, Item 3.2 emphasizes the importance of obtaining actionable information, such as feedback and complaints from customers. To be actionable, the information gathered should meet two conditions:

- Customer responses should be tied directly to key product, service, and business processes, so that opportunities for improvement are clear.

- Customer responses should be translated into cost/revenue implications to support the setting of improvement and change priorities.

The first part of this Item [3.2a(1)] looks at the organization's processes for providing easy access for customers and potential customers to seek information or assistance and/or to comment and complain.

- This access makes it easy to get timely information from customers about issues that are of real concern to them. Timely information, in turn, is transmitted to the appropriate place in the organization to drive improvements or new levels of product and service.

- Information from customers should be actionable. To be actionable, information should be tied to key business processes, and used to determine cost/revenue implications for improvement priority setting.

Organizations must also determine key customer-contact requirements and how these vary for different modes of access, and make sure all employees who are involved in responding to customers understand these requirements. As part of this response, the organization is asked to describe key access mechanisms for customers to seek information, conduct business, and make complaints. Also important is how customer-contact requirements are deployed along the entire response chain.

- Customer-contact requirements essentially refer to customer expectations for service after contact with the organization has been made. Typically, the organization translates customer-contact requirements into customer service standards. Customer-contact requirements should be set in measurable terms to permit effective monitoring and performance review.

- A good example of a measurable customer-contact requirement might be the customer expectation that a malfunctioning computer would be back online within 24 hours of the request for service. Another example might be the customer requirement that a knowledgeable and polite human being is available within 10 minutes to resolve a problem with software. In both cases, a clear requirement and a measurable standard were identified.

- A bad example of a customer service standard might be "we get back to the customer as soon as we can." With this example, no standard of performance is defined. Some customer-contact representatives might get back to a customer within a matter of minutes. Others might take hours or days. The failure to precisely define the contact requirement makes it difficult to allocate appropriate resources to meet that requirement consistently.

- These customer service standards must be deployed to all employees who are in contact with customers. Such deployment needs to take account of all key points in the response chain— all units or individuals in the organization that make effective interactions possible. These standards then become one source of information to evaluate the organization's performance in meeting customer-contact requirements.

Organizations should capture, aggregate, analyze, and learn from the complaint information and comments they receive. A prompt and effective response and solutions to customer needs and desires are a source of satisfaction and loyalty.

- Effective complaint management requires the prompt and courteous resolution of complaints. This leads to recovery of customer confidence. Customer loyalty and confidence is enhanced when problems are resolved by the first person the customer contacts. In fact, prompt resolution of problems helps to ensure higher levels of loyalty than if the customer never had a problem in the first place. Even if the organization ultimately resolves a problem, the likelihood of maintaining a loyal customer is reduced by 10 percent when that customer is referred to another place or person in the organization.

- The organization must also have a mechanism for learning from complaints and ensuring that design/production/delivery process employees receive information needed to eliminate the causes of complaints. Effective elimination of the causes of complaints involves aggregation of complaint information from all sources for evaluation and use in overall organizational improvement—both design and delivery stages (see Items 6.1 and 6.2).

- Complaint aggregation, analysis, and root-cause determination should lead to effective elimination of the causes of complaints and to priority setting for process, product, and service improvements. Successful outcomes require effective deployment of information throughout the organization.

For long-term success, organizations should build strong relationships with customers since business development and product/service innovation increasingly depend on maintaining close relationships with customers.

- Organizations should keep approaches to all aspects of customer relationships current with changing business needs and directions, since approaches to and bases for relationships may change quickly.

- Organizations should also develop an effective process to determine the levels of satisfaction and dissatisfaction for the different customer groups, including capturing actionable information that reflects customers' future business and/or positive referral intentions. Satisfied customers are a requirement for loyalty, repeat business, and positive referrals.

The second part of this Item [3.2b] looks at how the organization determines customer satisfaction and dissatisfaction.

- The organization must gather information on customer satisfaction and dissatisfaction, including any important differences in approaches for different customer groups or market segments. This highlights the importance of the measurement scale in determining those factors that best reflect customers' market behaviors—repurchase, new business, and positive referral. The organization must keep its approaches to determining customer satisfaction current with changing business needs and directions. Changing business needs and directions might include new modes of customer access, such as the Internet. In such cases, key contact requirements might include online security for customers and access to personal assistance.

- The organization should systematically follow-up with customers regarding products, services, and recent transactions to receive feedback that is prompt and actionable. Prompt feedback enables problems to be identified quickly to help prevent them from recurring.

- The organization should determine the satisfaction levels of the customers of competitors in order to identify threats and opportunities to improve future performance. Such information might be derived from the organization's own comparative studies or from independent studies. The factors that lead to customer preference are of critical importance in understanding factors that drive markets, potentially affect longer-term competitiveness, and are particularly helpful during strategic planning.

The customer satisfaction data gathered from the complaint management process in Item 3.2a ensure timely resolution of problems and can help recover or build customer loyalty. Data from the complaint processes in Item 3.2a are collected at the customer's convenience. However, data collected by survey or similar means, as required by Item 3.2b, produce information at the convenience of the organization. Customers complain when they have a problem. They do not tend to hold their complaint until the organization finds it convenient to ask them.

Although the complaint-type customer feedback (from Item 3.2a) is timely, it is often difficult to develop reliable trend data. The processes in Item 3.2b make it easier to track satisfaction over time. Both techniques are required to fully understand the dynamics that build loyalty, retention, and positive referral. To be effective, both techniques should be used to drive improvement actions.

3.2 Customer Relationships and Satisfaction

How customer satisfaction is determined, relationships strengthened, and current products and services enhanced to support customer- and market-related planning

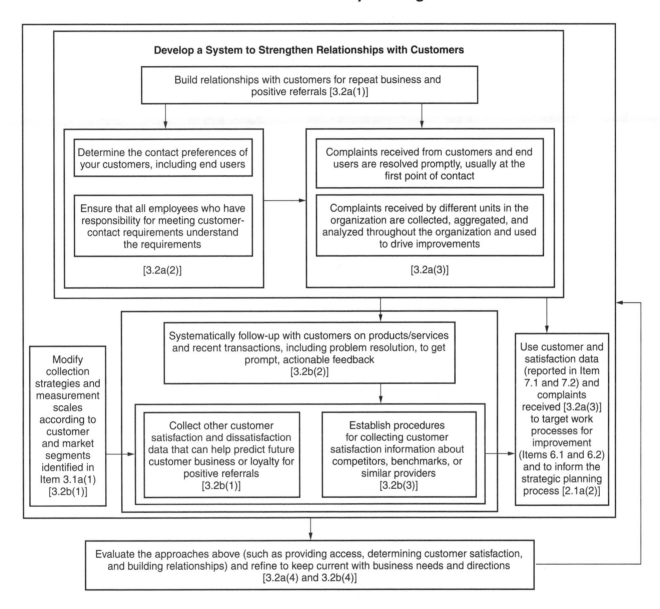

3.2 Customer Relationships and Satisfaction Item Linkages

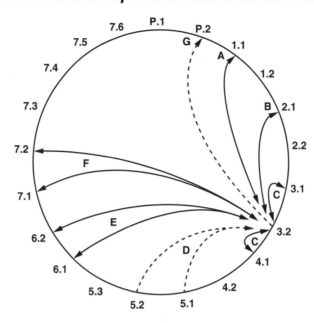

	NATURE OF RELATIONSHIP
A	The climate establishing customer-focused priorities and customer-contact requirements (service standards) for customer service personnel [3.2a(2)] is driven by top leadership [1.1a(1)]. They receive useful information from those customers to improve management decision making. Customer relationships/complaint data [3.2a(3)] and satisfaction data [3.2b(1 and 2)] are typically used by senior leaders to review performance [1.1c(1 and 2)] and set priorities for action [1.1c(3)].
B	Information about customer satisfaction [3.2b(1 and 2)] and complaints [3.2a(3)] collected by customer-contact employees is used in the planning process [2.1a(2)]. In addition, strategic objectives [2.1b(1)] influence customer relationship management [3.2a] and customer satisfaction determination processes [3.2b] by identifying key focus areas.
C	Information concerning customer requirements and expectations [3.1a] and benchmark data [4.1a(2)] are used to help identify, set, and deploy customer contact requirements (service standards) [3.2a(2)]. Customer complaint data [3.2a(3)] are analyzed [4.1b] and used to help assess customer requirements and expectations [3.1a(2)].
D	Training [5.2] and feedback, reward, and recognition tied to customer satisfaction [5.1b] should enhance the ability of customer-contact employees [3.2a(2)] to understand requirements and develop the skills to resolve complaints promptly and satisfy customers [3.2a(3)].
E	Information collected through customer relations employees [3.2a(2 and 3)] is used to enhance design of products and services and to improve value creation and support processes [6.1 and 6.2].

Continued

	NATURE OF RELATIONSHIP *Continued*
F	Information and complaints from customer relations processes [3.2a(3)] can help in the design of customer satisfaction measures [3.2b(1)] and produce data on customer satisfaction [7.1] and related product and service quality [7.2]. In addition, customer satisfaction results [7.1] are used to set customer contact requirements (service standards) [3.2a(2)]. Efforts of improved accessibility and responsiveness in complaint management [3.2a(3 and 4)] should result in improved complaint response time, effective complaint resolution, and a higher percentage of complaints resolved on first contact. These results should be reported in 7.1 and/or 7.2.
G	Processes in Item 3.2b(3) produce information about the satisfaction of competitors' customers, which is needed to create the description for P.2a(1 and 2).

	IF YOU DON'T DO WHAT THE CRITERIA REQUIRE . . .
Item Reference	**Possible Adverse Consequences**
3.2a(1)	The failure to build lasting relationships and loyalty with customers makes it easier for customers to "jump ship" when problems arise. Loyal customers are twice as likely to use your products and services than those who are simply satisfied. The TARP Studies have found that the cost to win a new customer versus retain a current customer varies from 2:1 to 20:1.* If the organization lacks a disciplined approach for building relationships and cultivating loyalty, the benefits of having loyal customers become hit-or-miss opportunities. For example, in many manufacturing companies today, service is a key differentiator. Products that were once considered specialty items, such as personal computers, are now commodities. Therefore, service can become the factor that differentiates companies and cultivates loyal customers. Furthermore, since it is more costly to acquire a new customer than to keep an existing customer, organizations can avoid unnecessary expenses by building relationships and strengthening the loyalty of current customers. Loyal customers are far more likely to provide positive referrals than a dissatisfied or even minimally satisfied customer.
	*From J. Goodman. "Basic Facts on Customer Complaint Behavior and the Impact of Service on the Bottom Line." *Competitive Advantage* (June 1999): 1–5. The article can be read at http://www.e-satisfy.com/basicfacts.pdf .
3.2a(2)	Customer contact requirements (sometimes called customer service standards) help define the customers' expectations for service after initiating a contact, question, or complaint. For example, a large, direct-order computer company surveyed its customers and determined that they expected to have a technician helping solve their problem within 10 minutes of making the initial contact. By knowing the customer contact requirements and the hour-to-hour call volume, the organization was able to put enough technicians in place to ensure the average response time was nine minutes or less. The failure to understand and meet customer contact requirements and make it easy for customers to contact the organization makes it more difficult to build loyalty and learn quickly about customer problems.
3.2a(3)	Once the organization learns about a customer problem, the speed and efficiency with which it resolves that problem contributes greatly to customer loyalty and willingness to make positive referrals. The failure to resolve a problem to the customer's satisfaction at the first point of contact cuts almost in half the likelihood of maintaining a loyal customer. In addition, the failure to collect, aggregate, analyze, and use complaint data to drive improvements throughout the organization (and as appropriate to key suppliers or partners) increases the likelihood that the problem will recur again and again. Failing to prevent the problem from recurring directly adds cost but no value to the products or services delivered to customers. Rework associated with recurring problems is a pure waste of resources and can be a significant source of customer dissatisfaction.

Continued

	IF YOU DON'T DO WHAT THE CRITERIA REQUIRE . . . *Continued*
3.2a(4)	The failure to systematically evaluate the processes used to build relationships, resolve complaints, and prevent them from recurring may make it difficult to identify specific areas needing change. Making it easy for customers to complain but not resolving those complaints effectively and promptly may create even higher levels of dissatisfaction. Ignorance about the effectiveness of customer access and complaint resolution processes may blind the organization to a problem of its own creation, especially in a highly competitive arena where customer and market requirements can change quickly. Without an ongoing system to evaluate and improve processes to build relationships and satisfy customers, current processes may not be able to keep up with changing business or market demands.
3.2b(1)	The failure to accurately determine customer satisfaction and dissatisfaction may make it difficult for the organization to make timely adjustments to the products and services it offers. Furthermore, if the data collection processes do not help the organization understand what drives customer behavior, the organization may not know until it is too late (the customer goes elsewhere) that they have a serious problem. The failure to predict customer behavior and the likelihood for positive referral also makes it difficult to forecast product demand, which may create supply chain difficulties, such as excessive inventories or excessive delays in restocking. In addition, the failure to take into account differences in customer or market segments and adjust the techniques for collecting customer satisfaction and dissatisfaction data appropriately may cause the organization to collect inaccurate or unreliable information, which threatens the accuracy of the organization's decision making and planning.
3.2b(2)	The longer an organization waits to gather customer satisfaction data, the more time it takes to identify and correct a problem. Organizations that fail to follow up with customers whenever a transaction occurs and learn about problems promptly increase the likelihood that other customers will experience the same problem because it will not have been identified or corrected. Similarly, organizations that fail to follow up with customers may be unaware of elements that drive dissatisfaction and disloyalty that could be spread to other parts of the organization or to other products and services.
3.2b(3)	By failing to obtain information on the satisfaction of the competitors' customers, the organization may not learn what it must do differently to satisfy and acquire (win over) the customers of its competitors.
3.2b(4)	Organizations that do not evaluate the effectiveness of their techniques to determine customer satisfaction and dissatisfaction run the risk of making bad decisions based on misleading or even useless information. It does little good to gather customer satisfaction data unless the organization asks the right questions. Failing to ask the right questions rarely produces accurate, actionable information to support effective decision making. Moreover, the failure to evaluate the effectiveness of the approaches used to assess customer satisfaction may make it difficult to keep up with changing customer and market needs and gather critical information necessary for strategic planning as well as the development of new or improved products and services.

3.2 CUSTOMER RELATIONSHIPS AND SATISFACTION—SAMPLE EFFECTIVE PRACTICES

A. Customer Relationships

- Several methods are used to ensure ease of customer contact, 24 hours a day if necessary (for example, toll-free numbers, pagers for contact personnel, Web sites, e-mail, surveys, interviews, focus groups, electronic bulletin boards).

- Customer-contact employees are empowered to make decisions to address customer concerns.

- Adequate staff members are available to maintain effective customer contact, within the time limits expected by customers.

- Measurable performance expectations are set for employees whose job brings them in regular contact with customers. The performance of employees against these expectations is tracked.

- A system exists to ensure that customer complaints are resolved promptly and effectively by the first point of contact. This often means training customer-contact employees and giving them authority for resolving a broad range of problems.

- Complaint data are tracked, analyzed, and used to initiate prompt corrective action to prevent the problem from recurring.

- Training and development plans and replacement procedures exist for customer-contact employees. These processes have been measured and refined.

- Measurable customer-contact requirements (service standards) have been derived from customer expectations (for example, timeliness, courtesy, efficiency, thoroughness, and completeness).

- Requirements for building relationships are identified and may include factors such as product knowledge, employee responsiveness, and various customer contact methods.

- A systematic approach is in place to evaluate and improve service levels, customer-focused decision making, and customer relationships.

B. Customer Satisfaction Determination

- Several customer satisfaction indicators are used (for example, repeat-business measures, praise letters, and direct measures using survey questions and interviews).

- Comprehensive satisfaction and dissatisfaction data are collected and segmented or grouped to enable the organization to predict customer behavior (likelihood of remaining a customer).

- Customer satisfaction and dissatisfaction measurements include both a numerical rating scale and descriptors assigned to each unit in the scale. An effective (actionable) customer satisfaction and dissatisfaction measurement system provides the organization with reliable information about customer ratings of specific product and service features and the relationship between these ratings and the customers' likely market behavior.

- Customer dissatisfaction indicators include complaints, claims, refunds, recalls, returns, repeat services, litigation, replacements, performance rating downgrades, repairs, warranty work, warranty costs, misshipments, and incomplete orders.

- Satisfaction data are collected from former customers.

- Competitors' customer satisfaction is determined using external or internal studies. This information is used to refine services and product features.

- Procedures are in place and evaluated to ensure that customer contact is initiated to follow-up on recent transactions to build relationships. Data from these contacts are used.

- The process of collecting complete, timely, and accurate customer satisfaction and dissatisfaction data is regularly evaluated and improved. Customer preferences, by customer segment, are considered when designing procedures to determine satisfaction levels. Some prefer surveys, others focus groups, and others prefer face-to-face interactions. Several improvement cycles are evident.

4 Measurement, Analysis, and Knowledge Management—90 Points

*The **Measurement, Analysis, and Knowledge Management** Category examines how your organization selects, gathers, analyzes, manages, and improves its data, information, and knowledge assets.*

The Measurement, Analysis, and Knowledge Management Category is the main point within the Criteria for all key information about effectively measuring and analyzing performance and managing organizational knowledge to drive improvement and organizational competitiveness.

This category is like the "motherboard" on a personal computer. All information flows into and out of it. In the simplest terms, Category 4 is the "brain center" for the alignment of the organization's operations and its strategic objectives. Moreover, since information and analysis might themselves be a source of competitive advantage and productivity growth, the category also may have strategic value and its capabilities should be considered as part of the strategic planning process.

Measurement, Analysis, and Knowledge Management evaluates the selection, management, and effectiveness of use of information and data to support processes, action plans, and the performance management system. Systems to analyze, review, capture, store, retrieve, and distribute data to support decision making are also evaluated.

Measurement and Analysis of Organizational Performance

- This Item looks at the mechanical processes associated with data collection, information, and measures (including comparative data) for planning, decision making, improving performance, and supporting action plans and operations.

- The Item also looks at the analytical processes used to make sense out of the data. In addition, it looks at how these analyses are deployed throughout the organization and used to support organization-level review, decision making, and planning.

Information and Knowledge Management

- This Item looks at how the organization ensures that needed data and information are accessible to employees, suppliers and partners, and customers as needed and appropriate to support decision making. This Item also seeks to ensure that hardware and software are reliable and user-friendly throughout the organization. In many organizations, people with minimal computer skills must be able to access and use data to support decision making.

- The data system must provide for and ensure data integrity, reliability, accuracy, timeliness, security, and confidentiality.

4.1 MEASUREMENT AND ANALYSIS OF ORGANIZATIONAL PERFORMANCE (45 PTS.)
PROCESS

Describe how your organization measures, analyzes, aligns, and improves its performance data and information at all levels and in all parts of your organization.

Within your response, include answers to the following questions:

a. Performance Measurement

(1) How do you select, collect, align, and integrate data and information for tracking daily operations and for tracking overall organizational performance? How do you use these data and information to support organizational decision making and innovation?

(2) How do you select and ensure the effective use of key comparative data and information to support operational and strategic decision making and innovation?

(3) How do you keep your performance measurement system current with business needs and directions? How do you ensure that your performance measurement system is sensitive to rapid or unexpected organizational or external changes?

b. Performance Analysis

(1) What analyses do you perform to support your senior leaders' organizational performance review? What analyses do you perform to support your organization's strategic planning?

(2) How do you communicate the results of organizational-level analyses to work group and functional-level operations to enable effective support for their decision making?

Notes:

N1. Performance measurement is used in fact-based decision making for setting and aligning organizational directions and resource use at the work unit, key process, departmental, and whole organization levels.

N2. Comparative data and information [4.1a(2)] are obtained by benchmarking and by seeking competitive comparisons. "Benchmarking" refers to identifying processes and results that represent best practices and performance for similar activities, inside or outside your organization's industry. Competitive comparisons relate your organization's performance to that of competitors in your markets.

N3. Analysis includes examining trends; organizational, industry, and technology projections; and comparisons, cause-effect relationships, and correlations intended to support your performance reviews, help determine root causes, and help set priorities for resource use. Accordingly, analysis draws upon all types of data: customer-related, financial and market, operational, and competitive.

N4. The results of organizational performance analysis should contribute to your senior leaders' organizational performance review in 1.1c and organizational strategic planning in Category 2.

N5. Your organizational performance results should be reported in Items 7.1-7.6.

Item 4.1, the Measurement and Analysis of Organizational Performance, looks at the selection, collection, alignment, integration, management, analysis, and use of data and information in support of organizational decision making, planning, and performance improvement. The processes and systems required by this item:

- Provide a key foundation for consistently good decision making.

- Serve as a central collection and analysis point in the management system to guide the organization's process management toward the achievement of key business results and strategic objectives.

The first part of this Item, Performance Measurement [4.1a], requires the organization to select and use measures to better track daily operations and enhance decision-making accuracy. It should select and integrate measures for monitoring overall organizational performance.

- Data alignment and integration are key concepts for successful implementation of the performance measurement system. They are viewed in terms of extent and effectiveness of use to meet performance assessment needs. Alignment and integration include how measures are aligned throughout the organization, how they are integrated to yield organization-wide measures, and how performance measurement requirements are deployed by senior leaders to track work group and process-level performance on key measures targeted for organization-wide significance and/or improvement.

- Comparative data should be selected and used to help drive performance improvement. These requirements address the major components of an effective performance measurement system.

The organization should show how competitive comparisons and benchmarking data are selected and used to help drive performance improvement.

- The use of competitive and comparative information is important to all organizations. The major premises for using competitive and comparative information are: 1) the organization needs to know where it stands relative to competitors and best practices; 2) comparative and benchmarking information often provides the impetus for significant ("breakthrough") improvement or change; and 3) preparation for comparing performance information frequently leads to a better understanding of the processes and their performance. Benchmarking information also may support business analyses and decisions relating to core competencies, alliances, and outsourcing.

- Effective selection and use of competitive comparisons and benchmarking information require: 1) determination of needs and priorities; 2) criteria for seeking appropriate sources for comparisons—from within and outside the organization's industry and markets; and 3) use of data and information to set stretch targets and to promote major or breakthrough improvements in areas most critical to the organization's competitive strategy.

Item 4.1a also examines how the organization's performance measurement system keeps current with changing business needs. This involves ongoing evaluation and demonstrated refinement.

The second part of this Item, Performance Analysis [4.1b], examines how the organization analyzes data to support decision making. Isolated facts and data do not usually provide an effective basis for setting organizational priorities and effective decision making. Accordingly, close alignment is needed between analysis and organizational performance review and between analysis and organizational planning. This ensures that analysis is relevant to decision making and that decision making is based on relevant data and information.

Effective decision making usually requires leaders to understand cause–effect connections among and between processes and business/performance results. Process actions and their results may have many resource implications. High-performing organizations find it necessary to have support systems that provide an effective analytical basis for decisions because resources for improvement are limited and cause–effect connections are often unclear. In addition, organizations must have the ability to perform effective analyses to support senior leaders' assessment of overall organizational performance and strategic planning. Moreover, the results of organizational-level analysis must be effectively communicated by leaders to support decision making throughout the organization and ensure those decisions are aligned with business results, strategic objectives, and action plans.

Accordingly, systematic processes must be in place for analyzing all types of data and to determine overall organizational health, including key business results, action plans, and strategic objectives. In addition, organizations must evaluate the effectiveness of their analytical processes and make improvements based on the evaluation.

Facts, rather than intuition, are used to support most decision making at all levels based on the analyses conducted to make sense out of the data collected. Analyses that organizations typically conduct to gain an understanding of performance and needed actions vary widely depending on the type of organization, size, competitive environment, and other factors. These analyses help the organization's leaders understand the following:

- How product and service improvement correlates with key customer indicators such as customer satisfaction, customer retention, and market share

- Cost/revenue implications of customer-related problems and effective problem resolution

- Interpretation of market share changes in terms of customer gains and losses and changes in customer satisfaction

- The impact of improvements in key operational performance areas such as productivity, cycle time, waste reduction, new-product introduction, and defect levels

- Relationships between employee/organizational learning and value added per employee

- Financial benefits derived from improvements in employee safety, absenteeism, and turnover

- Benefits and costs associated with education and training, including Internet-based, or e-learning opportunities

- Benefits and costs associated with improved organizational knowledge management and sharing

- The extent to which identifying and meeting employee requirements correlate with employee retention, motivation, and productivity

- Cost/revenue implications of employee-related problems and effective problem resolution

- Individual or aggregate measures of productivity and quality relative to competitors

- Cost trends relative to competitors

- Relationships among product/service quality, operational performance indicators, and overall financial performance trends as reflected in indicators such as operating costs, revenues, asset utilization, and value added per employee

- Allocation of resources among alternative improvement projects based on cost/ benefit implications or environmental/ community impact

- Net earnings derived from quality, operational, and human resource performance improvements

- Comparisons among business units showing how quality and operational performance improvement affect financial performance

- Contributions of improvement activities to cash flow, working capital use, and shareholder value

- Profit impacts of customer retention

- Cost/revenue implications of new market entry, including global market entry or expansion

- Cost/revenue, customer, and productivity implications of engaging in and/or expanding e-commerce/e-business and use of the Internet and intranets

- Market share versus profits

- Trends in economic, market, and shareholder indicators of value

The availability of electronic data and information of many kinds (for example, financial, operational, customer-related, accreditation/regulatory) and from many sources (for example, internal, third-party, and public sources; the Internet; Internet tracking software) permits extensive analysis and correlations. Effectively using and prioritizing this wealth of information are important to the success of top-performing organizations.

4.1 Measurement and Analysis of Organizational Performance

How the organization measures, aligns, improves, analyzes, and uses information and data to support decision making for key processes and to improve performance at all levels and parts of the organization

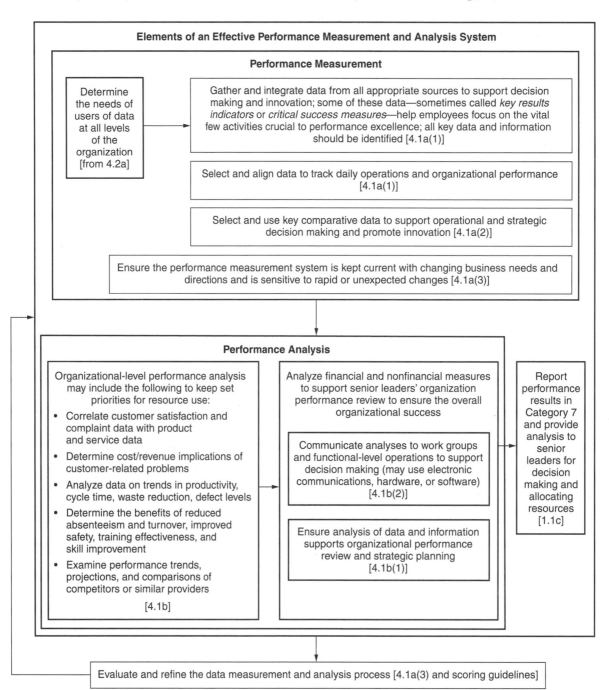

4.1 Measurements and Analysis of Organizational Performance Item Linkages

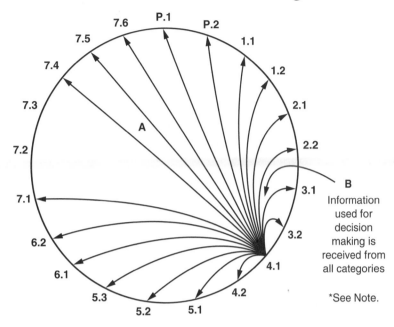

NATURE OF RELATIONSHIP

A	Data and information are collected and analyzed [4.1] and made available [4.2] for developing the Organizational Profile [P.1 and P.2], planning [2.1a(2)], setting strategic objectives [2.1b(1)], day-to-day leadership decisions [1.1], setting public responsibility standards (regulatory, legal, ethical) for community involvement [1.2], reporting performance results [7.1, 7.2, 7.3, 7.4, 7.5, and 7.6], improving work processes [6.1 and 6.2] and human resource systems [5.1, 5.2, and 5.3], determining customer requirements [3.1], managing customer complaints and building customer relations [3.2a], and determining customer satisfaction [3.2b].
B	Data and information used to support analysis, decision making, and continuous improvement [4.1] are received from all processes. Information from customer satisfaction data [7.1] are analyzed [4.1b] and used to help determine ways to assess customer requirements [3.1a(2)], to determine appropriate standards or required levels of customer service [3.2a(2)], and to design instruments to assess customer satisfaction [3.2b(1)]. Data and information are received from the following areas and analyzed to support decisions: human resources capabilities, including work system efficiency, initiative, and self-direction [5.1a(1)]; training and development needs [5.2a(2 and 3)] and effectiveness [5.2a(4)]; and safety, retention, absenteeism, organizational effectiveness, and well-being and satisfaction [5.3]. Data are aggregated and analyzed [4.1] to improve value creation [6.1] and support work processes [6.2] that will reduce cycle time, waste, and defect levels. Performance data from all parts of the organization are integrated and analyzed [4.1] to assess performance in key areas such as customer-related performance [7.1], product and service quality [7.2], operational performance [7.5], financial and market performance [7.3], human resource performance [7.4], and regulatory and legal compliance [7.6] relative to competitors or similar providers in all areas.

*Note: Because the information collected and used for decision making links with all other Items, all of the linkage arrows will not be repeated on the other item maps. Only the most relevant will be repeated.

IF YOU DON'T DO WHAT THE CRITERIA REQUIRE . . .	
Item Reference	**Possible Adverse Consequences**
4.1a(1)	The failure to systematically gather appropriate data and information from throughout the organization to support the daily operational and organizational decision making can create an environment where decisions are typically based on intuition, gut feel, or guesswork. Furthermore, information gathered in this way may ignore some of the linkages critical to sustaining high performance in an organization. Decisions based on intuition or guesswork tend to be highly variable, which introduces error. Furthermore, in an environment where decisions are based on intuition it is usually the boss' intuition that drives the decision, which can lead to the disengagement of the people in the organization. Decisions made in this manner erode the organization's efforts to promote employee empowerment and innovation [Item 1.1a(2)]. Finally, the failure to integrate data and information may make it difficult to monitor overall organizational performance. Disjointed, nonintegrated data are difficult to consolidate and report in a manageable, easy-to-understand "dashboard" to support effective decision making.
4.1a(1)	Data and information provide a basis for decision making at all levels of the organization: top leaders use the data to make decisions about the direction of the organization, and employees use data to make decisions about operational matters. Unless measures are selected and aligned to provide the right information, at the right time, in the right format, the decisions of the leaders and the employees are likely to be suboptimized. Moreover, although the failure to gather appropriate data tends to reduce decision-making quality, spending resources to gather data and information that do not support decision making throughout the organization (useless data) typically adds unnecessary cost. It is difficult to collect the right data and information if the organization has failed to determine what data are needed to support decision making at all levels. In addition, the failure to collect appropriate information makes it more difficult to monitor performance against goals [Item 1.1c(1)], effectively communicate expectations throughout the organization [Item 1.1a(1)], and deploy actions needed to carry out strategy [Item 2.2a].
4.1a(2)	The failure to collect and effectively use the right comparative data makes it difficult for the organization to learn and take appropriate action. Learning from the best helps provoke an understanding of what systems and processes may be required to make quantum leaps in performance as well as the levels that must be reached to achieve the leadership position projected during the planning process [Item 2.2b]. For example, comparisons showing that the organization's projected performance outpaces the industrial average will have little meaning if the best competitor's rate of improvement is greater. Furthermore, if an organization collects comparative data from world-class benchmarks, but does not effectively use comparative data for planning [Item 2.1a(2)], to identify areas needing breakthrough performance, or set improvement priorities [Item 1.1c(2)], then it is simply wasting resources. If an organization does not collect comparative performance outcome data, it is not able to determine if its own rate of progress is sufficient to keep it ahead of the competition or evaluate the strength of its own performance results [required by Category 7].

	IF YOU DON'T DO WHAT THE CRITERIA REQUIRE . . . Continued
Item Reference	**Possible Adverse Consequences**
4.1a(3)	Organizations that fail to improve the speed and accuracy of decision making typically do not perform well in a competitive environment. Without a process to evaluate the information system and how well it responds to the needs of the business, organizations may not know they are collecting insufficient or incorrect data and information. In addition, organizations may not know if the data effectively support daily operations and organizational decision making. They may not know if the resources spent to collect benchmarking and comparison data are producing appropriate benefits.
4.1b(1)	The lack of a system to analyze and make sense out of raw data may make it difficult for senior leaders to understand cause-and-effect relationships, root causes of problems, and the impact of various processes on performance outcomes. This may make it more difficult for leaders to identify specific areas within the organization where improvement is required. It also makes it more difficult for leaders to effectively set priorities. Consider the following examples: a) without a cost–benefit analysis it is more difficult to determine whether project A or project B should receive support, because it is difficult to know which project is likely to be of greater benefit to the organization; b) calculating C_{pk} (the capability of a process) helps leaders understand the extent to which their key processes are in control or need adjustment (the raw run data cannot support this kind of decision making); and c) failing to understand root causes makes it more difficult to prevent problems from recurring, which adds cost but not value.
4.1b(1)	Strategy identifies the things an organization must do to be successful in the future. Many actions must be taken in an organization to ensure strategic objectives are achieved. Data analysis helps leaders understand critical relationships between actions and outcomes to effectively allocate resources and achieve desired results. The failure to examine and understand the relationship between performance outcomes, action plans, and strategic objectives may cause senior leaders to make inappropriate decisions about the allocation of limited resources. This means that the organization may not realize the maximum benefit from the expenditure of those resources. For example, failing to understand the correlation between product and service quality improvement and improved customer satisfaction and retention may cause the leader to divert resources to less important activities.
4.1b(2)	Employees and managers at all levels of the organization need useful information to support decision making. The failure to ensure that people at every level understand the impact that their work has on overall organizational performance makes it more difficult for them to identify and understand why they need to perform at certain agreed levels and why change may need to occur. Without this information, employees and managers throughout the organization must rely on intuition or incomplete data to support decision making—typically reducing the accuracy of those decisions and, in some cases, suboptimizing the overall performance of the organization.

4.1 MEASUREMENT AND ANALYSIS OF ORGANIZATIONAL PERFORMANCE—SAMPLE EFFECTIVE PRACTICES

A. Performance Measurement

- Above all, data and information are favored as a decision-making support tool, rather than a quick and easy reliance on intuition or "gut feel."

- Data collected at the individual worker level are consistent across the organization to permit consolidation and organization-wide performance monitoring.

- The cost of quality (including rework, delay, waste, scrap, errors) and other financial concerns are measured for internal operations and processes.

- Data are maintained on employee-related issues of satisfaction, morale, safety, education and training, use of teams, and recognition and reward.

- A systematic process exists for data review and improvement, standardization, and easy employee access to data. Training on the use of data systems is provided as needed.

- Data used for management decisions' focus on critical success factors are integrated with work processes for the planning, design, and delivery of products and services.

- A systematic process is in place for identifying and prioritizing comparative information and benchmark targets.

- Research has been conducted to identify best-in-class organizations, which may be competitors or noncompetitors. Critical business processes or functions are the subject of benchmarking. Activities such as those that support the organization's goals and objectives, action plans, and opportunities for improvement and innovation are the subject of benchmarking. Benchmarking also covers key products, services, customer satisfiers, suppliers, employees, and support operations.

- The organization reaches beyond its own business to conduct comparative studies.

- Benchmark or comparison data are used to improve the understanding of work processes and to discover the best levels of performance that have been achieved. Based on this knowledge, the organization sets goals or targets to stretch performance as well as drive innovations.

- A systematic process is in place to improve the use of benchmark or comparison data in the understanding of all work processes.

B. Performance Analysis

- Systematic processes are in place for analyzing all types of data and to determine overall organizational health, including key business results, action plans, and strategic objectives. Part of the process is a method to evaluate the effectiveness of the analysis process and improve upon it.

- Facts, rather than intuition, are used to support most decision making at all levels based on the analyses conducted to make sense out of the data collected.

- The analysis process itself is analyzed to make the results more timely and useful for decision making for quality improvement at all levels.

- Analysis processes and tools, and the value of analyses to decision making, are systematically evaluated and improved.

- Analysis is linked to work groups to facilitate decision making (sometimes daily) throughout the organization.

- Analysis techniques enable meaningful interpretation of the cost and performance impact of organization processes. This analysis helps people at all levels of the organization make necessary trade-offs, set priorities, and reallocate resources to maximize overall organization performance.

4.2 INFORMATION AND KNOWLEDGE MANAGEMENT (45 PTS.) PROCESS

Describe how your organization ensures the quality and availability of needed data and information for employees, suppliers and partners, and customers. Describe how your organization builds and manages its knowledge assets.

Within your response, include answers to the following questions:

a. Data and Information Availability

(1) How do you make needed data and information available? How do you make them accessible to employees, suppliers and partners, and customers, as appropriate?

(2) How do you ensure that hardware and software are reliable, secure, and user friendly?

(3) How do you keep your data and information availability mechanisms, including your software and hardware systems, current with business needs and directions?

b. Organizational Knowledge

(1) How do you manage organizational knowledge to accomplish:

- The collection and transfer of employee knowledge

- The transfer of relevant knowledge from customers, suppliers, and partners

- The identification and sharing of best practices

(2) How do you ensure the following properties of your data, information, and organizational knowledge:

- Integrity
- Reliability
- Accuracy

- Timeliness
- Security
- Confidentiality

Notes:

N1. Data and information availability [4.2a] are of growing importance as the Internet, e-business, and e-commerce are used increasingly for business-to-business and business-to-consumer interactions and intranets become more important as a major source of organizationwide communications.

N2. Data and information access [4.2a(1)] might be via electronic and other means.

The first part of this Item, Data and Information Availability [4.2a], examines how the organization ensures the availability of high-quality, timely data and information for all key users—employees, suppliers/partners, and customers. Top-performing organizations make data and information available and accessible to all appropriate users. The organization's hardware systems and software must be reliable and user friendly, facilitating full access and encouraging routine use.

- As the sources of data and information and the number of users within the organization grow dramatically, systems to manage information technology often require significant resources. Top-performing organizations consider the management of information technology as a strategic imperative. The expanding use of electronic information within organizational operations, more comprehensive knowledge networks, new data from the Internet, and increasing business-to-business and business-to-consumer communications challenges make it absolutely critical that the organization develop systems to ensure data reliability and availability in a user-friendly format.

- Data and information are especially important in business networks, alliances, and supply chains. Information management systems should facilitate the use of data and information and should recognize the need for rapid data validation and reliability assurance, given the increasing use of electronic data transfer.

The second part of this Item, Organizational Knowledge [4.2b], focuses on the need to transfer knowledge from employees, customers, suppliers, and partners for the benefit of the organization. It also includes the sharing of practices that might benefit the organization and key partners.

Required data and information should meet user needs, including integrity (completeness—tells the whole story), reliability (consistency), accuracy (correctness), timeliness (available when needed), and appropriate levels of security and confidentiality (free from tampering and inappropriate release).

- Organizations must ensure data and information reliability since reliability is critical to good decision making, successful monitoring of operations, and successful data integration for assessing overall performance.

- Processes should be in place to protect against external threats, including attacks from hackers, viral infections, power surges, and other storm-related damage.

- Processes should be in place to protect against system failure, which may damage critical data. This may require redundant systems as well as effective backup and storage of data.

Finally, as with the other items required for performance excellence, the organization must systematically evaluate and improve data-availability mechanisms, software, and hardware to keep them current with changing business needs and directions.

4.2 Information and Knowledge Management

How the organization ensures the quality and availability of data and information for employees, suppliers and partners, and customers

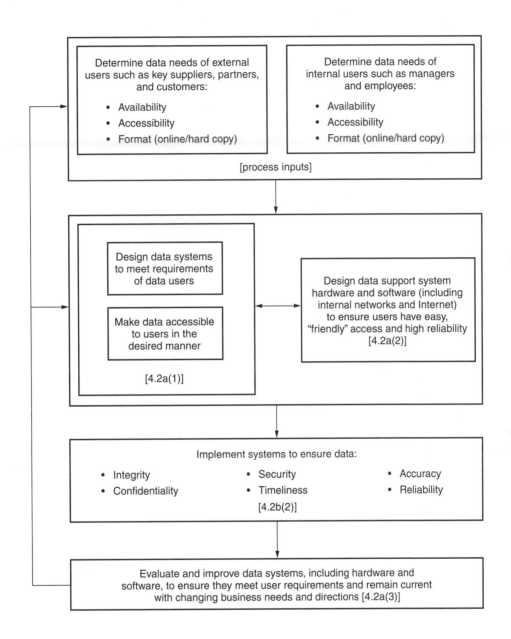

4.2 Information and Knowledge Management Item Linkages

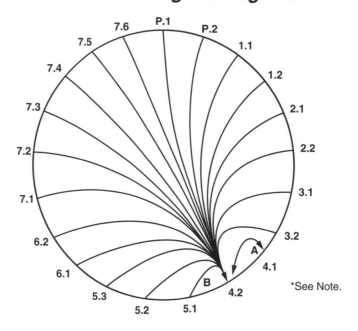

NATURE OF RELATIONSHIP	
A	Information and Knowledge Management [4.2] enables the data flow within the organization and indirectly interacts with all other items (similar to the relationships identified and reported in the Item 4.1 diagram). The simplest way to show these relationships is to tie this Item [4.2] with the Measurement and Analysis of Organizational Performance Item [4.1].
B	To ensure that hardware and software systems are reliable and user friendly [4.2a(2)], information from the following types of system users is gathered: leaders [Category 1]; planners [Category 2]; customer relationships and contact staff [Category 3]; information specialists [Category 4]; human resource personnel, managers, and employees [Category 5]; operations workers and managers [Category 6]; and people who monitor and interpret results [Category 7] for use in decision making.

*Note: Because the information collected and used for decision making links with all other Items, all of the linkage arrows will not be repeated on the other item maps. Only the most relevant will be repeated.

IF YOU DON'T DO WHAT THE CRITERIA REQUIRE . . .	
Item Reference	**Possible Adverse Consequences**
4.2a(1)	Getting the right information to the right people at the right time and in the right format enables effective decision making. Just as different types of employees in an organization need different data to support decision making, they may need to access information in different ways. Similarly, customers and suppliers may need access to information to facilitate ordering and delivery of required products and services. The failure to provide appropriate access to data may make it more difficult for employees to make timely decisions about work, for customers to place orders for products and services, or lead to disruptions in the supply chain. Providing inappropriate access for individuals inside or outside the organization may compromise data confidentiality and security or even violate certain privacy statutes.
4.2a(2)	The breadth, depth, and speed of decision making continue to increase as artificial intelligence plays a larger and larger role in our lives. Hardware and software are at the heart of this phenomenon. More people than ever before are being asked to interact with computers. In the best-performing organizations, employees frequently use computers to access data and use them to develop relevant analyses that enable better decisions about their work. People with very little computer literacy must now enter and retrieve data from these systems. A user interface that may be easily understood by information management technicians may be incomprehensible to a line worker, customer, or supplier. The failure to make these systems reliable and easy to use (user friendly) makes it difficult, if not impossible, for some people to use them effectively. This may create significant problems for organizations, particularly those venturing into areas where e-commerce plays a larger and larger role. Consider, for example, a bank that wants to expand and promote distance banking via the Internet or through home-to-bank modem connections. If the software is not reliable and very user friendly, many customers may be unwilling or unable to take advantage of these services. This may limit the organization's ability to achieve strategic and/or market-share goals that should have been considered during the strategy development process [Item 2.1a(2)].
4.2a(3)	In a rapidly changing world, access to information and the use of that information to provide insight and help decision making can provide a strategic advantage. Rapid data availability is becoming more and more critical for business success, especially in e-business situations. In some industries such as banking, a few seconds can make the difference between capitalizing on currency rate fluctuations or being hurt by them. As product and delivery cycle times grow shorter, the need for rapid access to information grows greater. Without evaluating the suitability of data and information systems, and making refinements based on this evaluation, the organization leaves itself open to falling behind and not being able to respond rapidly to changing business needs and directions.
4.2b(1)	Knowledge is of little or no use unless the people who need it, have it. Knowledge sequestered in one corner of an organization cannot benefit the entire organization unless it is transferred to other employees in other units. The same is true for knowledge held by key customers, suppliers, and partners. Knowledge withheld is knowledge (and resources) wasted.

Continued

	IF YOU DON'T DO WHAT THE CRITERIA REQUIRE . . . *Continued*
Item Reference	**Possible Adverse Consequences**
4.2b(2)	Decisions that are based on data and information may be compromised if the data are inaccurate or unreliable. For example, when a data entry error is made and goes unnoticed (sometimes referred to as "garbage in, garbage out"), it could drive decisions to deliver the wrong product at the wrong time to the wrong customer. At the very least this is likely to cause the product to be returned and restocked, adding cost but not value. The lack of timely information may cause decisions to be delayed inappropriately. Consider, for example, an organization that conducts an employee (or customer) satisfaction survey but does not analyze or make the data available for eight months. This not only sends a message to the organization that employee (or customer) concerns are unimportant, it also makes it difficult to identify real problems that may be contributing to customer dissatisfaction, low worker morale, and poor productivity.
4.2b(2)	Concerns about security, data loss, sophisticated hackers, and increased customer requirements for better access and availability place steadily increasing demands on hardware and software systems. The failure to keep these systems current may expose them to internal or external threats. For example, the failure to update virus protections frequently and maintain up-to-date, effective firewalls can expose the computer system (and the organization) to catastrophic and costly losses. (Please note that this Item does not require improvements in software and hardware simply for the sake of buying new gadgets. Improvements should help support changing business needs and directions—as a means to an end, not the end itself. This is another example where a cost–benefit data analysis [Item 4.1b(2)] may be crucial to making good decisions about maintaining appropriate software and hardware systems.)

4.2 INFORMATION AND KNOWLEDGE MANAGEMENT— SAMPLE EFFECTIVE PRACTICES

A. Data and Information Availability

- Users of data help determine what data systems are developed and how data are accessed.

- Every person has access to the data they need to make decisions about their work, from top leaders to individual workers or teams of workers.

- The performance measurement system is systematically evaluated and refined. Improvements have been made to reduce cycle time for data collection and to increase data access, reliability, and use.

- Data are protected against misuse from external sources through encryption and randomly changing user passwords.

- Procedures required to interface with the hardware and software are designed to meet the needs and capabilities of all computer users, to ensure that no one is excluded.

- Disciplined, automatic file backup occurs. Backup data are stored in a secure, external facility.

- Hardware and software systems have been protected against external threats from hackers, viral threats, water, and electrical damage. Protection systems are updated as appropriate (for example, viral updates are made several times daily).

- Data systems are benchmarked against best-in-class systems and continually refined.

B. Organizational Knowledge

- All key work processes are documented and stored in a searchable and accessible database and used to share improvements and avoid rework associated with reinventing effective processes.

- A data and knowledge exchange is in place to receive useful knowledge and information from customers, suppliers, partners and other key stakeholders. The system is automated for easy update and access. Face-to-face and/or electronic meetings are held regularly to share information.

- A "sunset" review is conducted to determine what data no longer need to be collected and can be dropped.

- A data reliability (consistency) team routinely and randomly checks data. Systems are in place to minimize or prevent human error in data entry and analysis.

5 Human Resource Focus—85 Points

*The **Human Resource Focus** Category examines how your organization's work systems and employee learning and motivation enable employees to develop and utilize their full potential in alignment with your organization's overall objectives and action plans. Also examined are your organization's efforts to build and maintain a work environment and employee support climate conducive to performance excellence and to personal and organizational growth.*

Human Resource Focus addresses key human resource practices—those directed toward creating a high-performance workplace and toward developing employees to enable them and the organization to adapt to change. The category covers human resource development and management requirements in an integrated manner, aligned with the organization's strategic directions. Included in the focus on human resources is a focus on the work environment and the employee support climate.

To ensure the basic alignment of human resource management with overall strategy, the Criteria also include human resource planning as part of organizational planning in the Strategic Planning Category. Human resource focus also evaluates how the organization enables employees to develop and use their full potential.

Work Systems

- Design, organize, and manage work and jobs to optimize employee performance and potential.

- Performance feedback to employees and recognition and reward practices support objectives for customer satisfaction, high-performance objectives, and employee and organization learning goals.

- Identify skills and capabilities needed by potential (future) employees, and then recruit, hire, and effectively retain them.

Employee Learning and Motivation

- Deliver, evaluate, and reinforce appropriate training to achieve action plans and address organization needs including building knowledge, skills, and abilities to improve employee development and performance.

- Enhance employee motivation and career progression.

Employee Well-Being and Satisfaction

- Improve employee safety, well-being, development, and satisfaction and maintain a work environment free from distractions to high performance.

- Systematically evaluate employee well-being, satisfaction, and motivation and identify improvement priorities that promote key business results.

5.1 WORK SYSTEMS (35 PTS.)
PROCESS

Describe how your organization's work and jobs enable employees and the organization to achieve high performance. Describe how compensation, career progression, and related work-force practices enable employees and the organization to achieve high performance.

Within your response, include answers to the following questions:

a. Organization and Management of Work

(1) How do you organize and manage work and jobs to promote cooperation, initiative, empowerment, innovation, and your organizational culture? How do you organize and manage work and jobs to achieve the agility to keep current with business needs?

(2) How do your work systems capitalize on the diverse ideas, cultures, and thinking of your employees and the communities with which you interact (your employee hiring and your customer communities)?

(3) How do you achieve effective communication and skill sharing across work units, jobs, and locations?

b. Employee Performance Management System

How does your employee performance management system, including feedback to employees, support high-performance work? How does your employee performance management system support a customer and business focus? How do your compensation, recognition, and related reward and incentive practices reinforce high performance work and a customer and business focus?

c. Hiring and Career Progression

(1) How do you identify characteristics and skills needed by potential employees?

(2) How do you recruit, hire, and retain new employees? How do you ensure that the employees represent the diverse ideas, cultures, and thinking of your employee hiring community?

(3) How do you accomplish effective succession planning for leadership and management positions, including senior leadership? How do you manage effective career progression for all employees throughout the organization?

Notes:

N1. "Employees" refers to your organization's permanent, temporary, and part-time personnel, as well as any contract employees supervised by your organization. Employees include team leaders, supervisors, and managers at all levels. Contract employees supervised by a contractor should be addressed in Category 6.

N2. "Your organization's work" refers to how your employees are organized or organize themselves in formal and informal, temporary, or longer-term units. This might include work teams, process teams, project teams, customer action teams, problem-solving teams, centers of excellence, functional units, remote (e.g., at-home) workers, cross-functional teams, and departments—self-managed or managed by supervisors. "Jobs" refers to responsibilities, authorities, and tasks of individuals. In some work systems, jobs might be shared by a team.

N3. Compensation and recognition [5.1b] include promotions and bonuses that might be based upon performance, skills acquired, and other factors. Recognition includes monetary and nonmonetary, formal and informal, and individual and group mechanisms.

This Item [5.1] looks at the organization's systems for work and jobs, compensation, career progression, employee performance management, motivation, recognition, communication, and hiring, with the aim of enabling and encouraging all employees to contribute effectively and to the best of their ability. These systems are intended to foster high performance, to result in individual and organizational learning, and to enable adaptation to change.

- Work and jobs should be designed in such a way as to allow employees to exercise optimum discretion and decision making, resulting in higher involvement and better performance. *In order to exercise effective decision making, employees need access to appropriate data and analyses concerning their work.* (This links to the information and knowledge management systems required in Category 4.) Unless employees have access to data to support effective decision making and understand how to analyze and interpret data, their decisions, by default, revert to intuition—which is highly variable. Managers are less likely to permit employees to substitute their intuition for that of managers. Therefore, employee decision making is likely to be limited, even if managers were inclined to release decisions to subordinates. Accordingly, systems to promote employee empowerment and agility should ensure employees have the authority to make decisions about their work, as well as data and analysis systems to support effective and consistently good decisions.

- Work and job factors important to consider include simplification of job classifications (less specialization and work isolation), which can be addressed by cross-training, job rotation, use of teams (including self-directed teams), and changes in work layout and location. Another important method to combat worker isolation is to foster communication across functions and work units, maintain a focus on customer requirements, and create an environment of knowledge sharing and respect.

- High-performance work is also enhanced by systems that promote employee flexibility, innovation, knowledge and skill sharing, alignment with organizational objectives, customer focus, and rapid response to changing business needs and requirements of the marketplace. Work should support the achievement of organizational objectives. Creativity and innovation from all employees should be specifically required, measured, and recognized. Suggestion boxes are not enough. The number of innovative ideas actually *implemented* per person is a better indicator of innovation and idea quality than the number if ideas *proposed*.

- Hierarchical, command-and-control management styles work directly against fast response and high-performance capability. Agility reflects the speed with which employees and the organization do their work, including rapid response to changing needs and requirements. Work that is bogged down with bureaucratic inefficiencies cannot be agile. Unnecessary layers of management approval typically add delay and cost but not value.

- Developing and sustaining high-performance work systems requires ongoing education and training, and information systems (see Category 4) that ensure adequate information availability. To help employees realize their full potential, many organizations use individual development plans prepared with the input of each employee and designed to address their career and learning objectives.

The best organizations put in place an employee performance management system that provides measurable feedback to employees, supports high-performance objectives, and supports a customer and business focus. Furthermore, employee compensation, recognition, and reward are aligned to support these business objectives. In addition, to ensure all employees understand their responsibilities, systems exist to promote effective communication and cooperation, at all levels of the organization.

- Once the organization determines its key strategic objectives, it should review compensation, reward, and recognition systems to ensure they support those objectives. The failure to do this creates an environment where employees are focused on one set of activities (based on their compensation plan), but the organization has determined that another set of activities (the action plans to achieve the strategic objectives) is necessary for success.

- Compensation and recognition systems must be matched to support the work necessary for business success. Consistent with this, compensation and recognition might be tied to demonstrated skills and peer evaluations. Compensation and recognition approaches also might include profit sharing, rewarding exemplary team or unit performance, and links to customer satisfaction and loyalty measures or other business objectives.

The organization must perform effective succession planning for senior leadership and managers at all levels of the organization. The rate of new knowledge acquisition is increasing throughout the world.

Significantly more new knowledge is causing change to occur faster than ever before in history. To manage effectively in this climate of rapid change, organizations must prepare their future leaders and managers. The best organizations do not wait for vacancies to occur before they think about the requirements and skills needed. Succession planning enables organizations to identify future skill needs against current skill gaps, enabling them to recruit and develop the necessary human resources.

Finally, organizations must profile, recruit, and hire employees who will meet skill requirements required to position the organization for future success. Obviously, the right work force is a key driver of high performance.

- As the pool of skilled talent continues to shrink, it becomes more important than ever for organizations to specifically define the capabilities and skills needed by potential employees and create a work environment to attract them. Accordingly, it is critical to take into account characteristics of diverse populations to make sure appropriate support systems exist that make it possible to attract skilled workers.

5.1 Work Systems

How the organization's work and job design, compensation, career progression, and related work force practices enable and encourage all employees to contribute effectively to achieving high performance

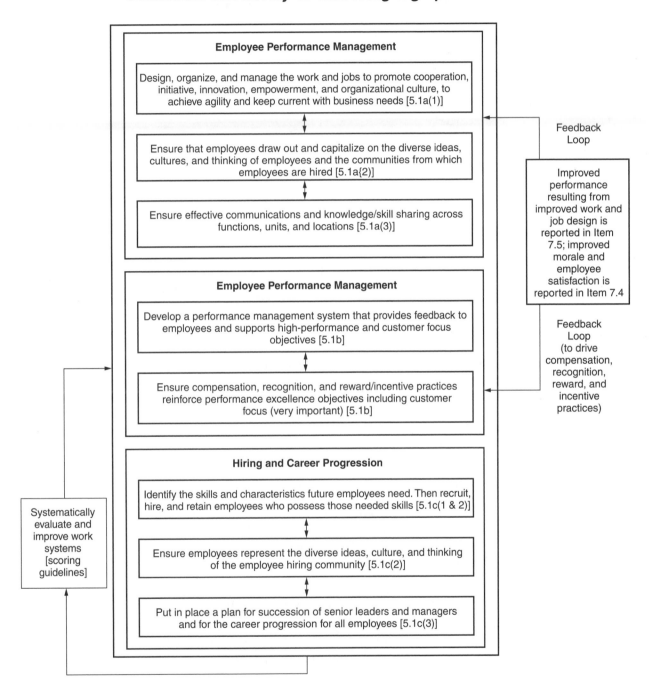

Employee Performance Management

Design, organize, and manage the work and jobs to promote cooperation, initiative, innovation, empowerment, and organizational culture, to achieve agility and keep current with business needs [5.1a(1)]

Ensure that employees draw out and capitalize on the diverse ideas, cultures, and thinking of employees and the communities from which employees are hired [5.1a{2}]

Ensure effective communications and knowledge/skill sharing across functions, units, and locations [5.1a(3)]

Employee Performance Management

Develop a performance management system that provides feedback to employees and supports high-performance and customer focus objectives [5.1b]

Ensure compensation, recognition, and reward/incentive practices reinforce performance excellence objectives including customer focus (very important) [5.1b]

Hiring and Career Progression

Identify the skills and characteristics future employees need. Then recruit, hire, and retain employees who possess those needed skills [5.1c(1 & 2)]

Ensure employees represent the diverse ideas, culture, and thinking of the employee hiring community [5.1c(2)]

Put in place a plan for succession of senior leaders and managers and for the career progression for all employees [5.1c(3)]

Feedback Loop

Improved performance resulting from improved work and job design is reported in Item 7.5; improved morale and employee satisfaction is reported in Item 7.4

Feedback Loop (to drive compensation, recognition, reward, and incentive practices)

Systematically evaluate and improve work systems [scoring guidelines]

5.1 Work Systems Item Linkages

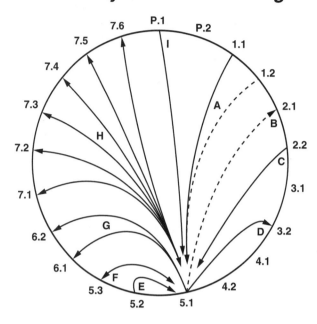

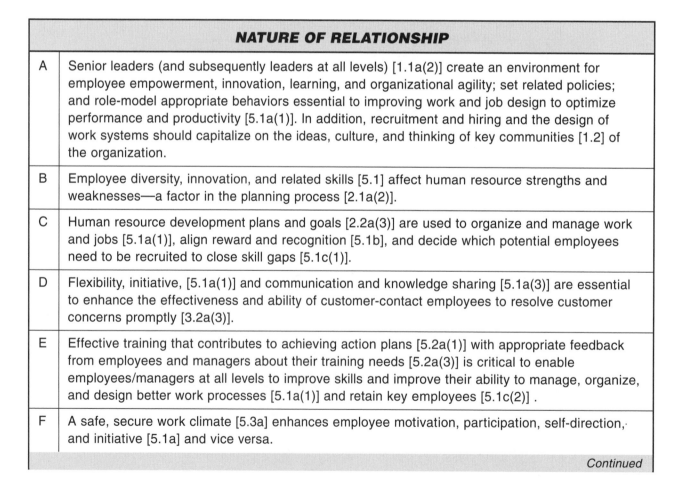

	NATURE OF RELATIONSHIP
A	Senior leaders (and subsequently leaders at all levels) [1.1a(2)] create an environment for employee empowerment, innovation, learning, and organizational agility; set related policies; and role-model appropriate behaviors essential to improving work and job design to optimize performance and productivity [5.1a(1)]. In addition, recruitment and hiring and the design of work systems should capitalize on the ideas, culture, and thinking of key communities [1.2] of the organization.
B	Employee diversity, innovation, and related skills [5.1] affect human resource strengths and weaknesses—a factor in the planning process [2.1a(2)].
C	Human resource development plans and goals [2.2a(3)] are used to organize and manage work and jobs [5.1a(1)], align reward and recognition [5.1b], and decide which potential employees need to be recruited to close skill gaps [5.1c(1)].
D	Flexibility, initiative, [5.1a(1)] and communication and knowledge sharing [5.1a(3)] are essential to enhance the effectiveness and ability of customer-contact employees to resolve customer concerns promptly [3.2a(3)].
E	Effective training that contributes to achieving action plans [5.2a(1)] with appropriate feedback from employees and managers about their training needs [5.2a(3)] is critical to enable employees/managers at all levels to improve skills and improve their ability to manage, organize, and design better work processes [5.1a(1)] and retain key employees [5.1c(2)] .
F	A safe, secure work climate [5.3a] enhances employee motivation, participation, self-direction, and initiative [5.1a] and vice versa.

Continued

		NATURE OF RELATIONSHIP	*Continued*
	G	High-performance and flexible work systems [5.1a(1)] are essential to improving value-adding and related business processes [6.1]. Effective performance feedback, compensation, and recognition [5.1b] are essential to improving value-creation and support processes [6.1 and 6.2].	
	H	Compensation, incentives, recognition, and rewards [5.1b] are based in part on performance results [Category 7]. Improvements in work and job design, innovation, empowerment, [5.1a(1)] sharing, and communication [5.1a(3)] can result in improved performance and business results [Category 7]. Processes to improve initiative and empowerment [5.1a(1)] can enhance all performance results [Category 7].	
	I	Employee characteristics such as educational levels, work force and job diversity, the existence of bargaining units, the use of contract employees, and other special requirements [P.1a(3)] help set the context for determining the requirements for knowledge and skill sharing across work units, jobs, and locations [5.1a(3)] and skills needed of potential employees [5.1c(1)].	

IF YOU DON'T DO WHAT THE CRITERIA REQUIRE . . .	
Item Reference	**Possible Adverse Consequences**
5.1a(1)	The alignment of strategic objectives and the work to accomplish them is vital to the success and optimum performance of the organization. Once strategic objectives, time lines [Item 2.1b(1)], and related actions [Item 2.2a(1)] have been identified and deployed to all levels of the organization, leaders and managers can more effectively organize employees (or they can organize themselves) to carry out the necessary work. In addition, appropriate responsibilities, authorities, and other tasks should be defined to ensure the actions are aligned (consistent) at all levels and effectively carried out. If the organization and management of work and jobs are not aligned to support strategic objectives and related actions, the organization may waste resources by failing to optimize the work that is done.
5.1a(2)	The failure to capitalize on diverse ideas, cultures, and thinking may limit the organization's ability to be innovative and empowered [Item 5.1a(1)]. This in turn may limit the organization's ability to meet the challenges of today's highly competitive environment.
5.1a(3)	The failure to promote cooperation among work units often contributes to redundancy and working at cross-purposes. The failure to promote knowledge and skill sharing often forces the organization to duplicate efforts in the search for more effective and efficient processes. The failure to share knowledge also contributes to isolationism within an organization and prevents "pockets of excellence" from spreading. Frequently, employees organized in a hierarchical, command-and-control environment find individual initiative, empowerment, and innovation stifled, reducing morale and further eroding productivity and responsiveness.
5.1b	In order to optimize performance, work throughout the organization must be fully aligned to support strategic objectives, time lines [Item 2.1b(1)], and related action plans [Item 2.2a(1)]. The action plans should be deployed fully throughout the organization at all levels with appropriate quantitative measures developed to monitor progress [Item 2.2a(4)]. The work of individual employees, when taken together, should enable the organization to achieve its strategic objectives. There are two questions that are fundamental to the work endeavors that employee feedback should address: 1) are the right things being done (the vital few); and 2) are they being done right (correctly). The failure to provide feedback to employees about their performance may make it more difficult for them to determine if they are doing the right thing in support of business strategy or if they are doing things in the right way (process discipline). It forces them to decide for themselves if they are doing a good job. In addition, the failure to provide feedback causes the organization to miss an opportunity to reinforce a customer and business focus. After all, "what gets measured gets done." The alignment of what is "expected" and what is "rewarded" sends strong messages throughout the organization about what is really important. Failing to align appropriate compensation, recognition, rewards, and incentives with the strategic objectives may also contribute to a lack of focus amongst the work force, allowing employees to substitute their own ideas instead of being driven/guided by the reinforcement of management. Many employees equate compensation with the activities the organization wants to achieve. For example, if achieving profitability is critical for organization success, the organization typically rewards people for achieving financial goals. Everyone clearly understands the importance of "profit" because their own compensation and rewards are tied to it. Similarly, the failure to provide rewards, recognition, or compensation that support a customer focus may cause employees to believe that customers are unimportant. Rewards (or the absence of them) drive behavior and motivate people to respond in certain ways.

Continued

	IF YOU DON'T DO WHAT THE CRITERIA REQUIRE . . . *Continued*
Item Reference	**Possible Adverse Consequences**
5.1c(1)	Skill mapping is a process that many high-performing organizations practice to compare the skills it needs to achieve strategic objectives with the skills its work force currently possesses. When a skill gap is identified, organizations are able to more effectively make decisions as to whether they need to recruit, hire, and/or train appropriate employees. The failure to identify characteristics and skills needed by potential employees increases the likelihood of not having appropriate staff in the right places when needed.
5.1c(2)	In a competitive labor market, slowness in recruiting and inefficiencies in hiring may introduce delays that allow competitors to hire the best before your organization can act. Inefficient recruitment and bureaucratic bungling in the hiring process also provide a glimpse of the true management system and can scare off the best prospective employees. In addition, the hiring process represents a terrific opportunity to attract and hire employees with diverse ideas and cultures, without which it will be difficult to capitalize on diverse ideas, cultures, and thinking. This in turn may limit the organization's ability to be innovative and empowered [Item 5.1a(1)], and to meet the challenges of today's highly competitive environment.
5.1c(3)	In the face of worldwide shortages of highly skilled employees, an organization's failure to conduct effective succession planning (both for senior leaders and for key positions throughout the organization) could threaten organizational stability in the long term and create immediate performance problems in the short term. When critical personnel shortages exist within an organization, it is frequently unable to carry out key objectives. If succession planning does not look ahead at least as far as it might take to acquire or train replacement personnel, the organization may lack the talent it needs to fulfill its promises to customers or other key stakeholders.

5.1 WORK SYSTEMS—SAMPLE EFFECTIVE PRACTICES

A. Organization and Management of Work

- Fully using the talents of all employees is a basic organizational value.

- Managers use cross-functional work teams to break down barriers, improve effectiveness, and meet goals.

- Teams have access to data and are authorized to make decisions about their work (not just make recommendations).

- Employee opinion is sought (and obtained) regarding work design and work processes.

- Prompt and regular feedback is provided to teams and individuals regarding their performance. Feedback covers both results and processes.

- Although lower-performing organizations use teams for special improvement projects (while the "regular work" is performed using traditional approaches), higher-performing organizations use teams and self-directed employees as the way regular work is done.

- Self-directed or self-managed work teams are used throughout the organization. They have authority over matters such as budget, hiring, and team membership and roles.

- A systematic process is used to evaluate and improve the effectiveness and extent of employee involvement.

- Many indicators of employee involvement effectiveness exist, such as the improvements in time or cost reduction produced by teams.

B. Employee Performance Management System

- The performance management system provides feedback to employees that supports their ability to contribute to a high-performing organization.

- Compensation, recognition, and rewards/incentives are provided for generating improvement ideas. In addition, a system exists to encourage and provide rapid reinforcement for submitting improvement ideas.

- Compensation, recognition, and rewards/incentives are provided for results, such as for reductions in cycle time and exceeding target schedules with error-free products or services at less-than-projected cost.

- Employees, as well as managers, participate in creating the compensation, recognition, and rewards/incentives practices and help monitor their implementation and systematic improvement.

- The organization evaluates its approaches to employee performance and compensation, recognition, and rewards to determine the extent to which employees are satisfied with them, the extent of employee participation, and the impact of the system on improved performance (reported in Item 7.4).

- Evaluations are used to make improvements. The best organizations have several improvement cycles. (Multiple improvement cycles can occur within one year.)

- Performance measures exist for employee involvement, self-direction, and initiative. Goals for these measures are expressed in measurable terms. These measurable goals form at least a good part of the basis for performance recognition.

- Recognition, reward/incentives, and compensation are influenced by customer satisfaction ratings as well as other performance measures.

C. Hiring and Career Progression

- Employee skill mapping is in place to define current skills of employees and compare to skills that are needed now and in the future. The resulting gap or surplus drives decisions to retrain, relocate, or recruit.

- The need for diverse ideas and cultures among employees is specifically considered during the skill mapping and recruitment process to ensure employees are able to provide the perspective needed to drive innovation and creativity.

- A formal system is in place to develop future leaders. This includes providing training and practice in high-performance leadership techniques. Leaders receive specific training and practice using Baldrige Criteria and performance improvement systems.

- Demonstrated proficiency in the use of the Baldrige Criteria is a prerequisite to leadership advancement.

- Future leaders serve as examiners in the Baldrige process, state quality award process, or internal award process.

5.2 EMPLOYEE LEARNING AND MOTIVATION (25 PTS.)
PROCESS

Describe how your organization's employee education, training, and career development support the achievement of your overall objectives and contribute to high performance. Describe how your organization's education, training, and career development build employee knowledge, skills, and capabilities.

Within your response, include answers to the following questions:

a. Employee Education, Training, and Development

(1) How do employee education and training contribute to the achievement of your action plans? How do your employee education, training, and development address your key needs associated with organizational performance measurement, performance improvement, and technological change? How does your education and training approach balance short- and longer-term organizational objectives with employee needs for development, learning, and career progression?

(2) How do employee education, training, and development address your key organizational needs associated with new employee orientation, diversity, ethical business practices, and management and leadership development? How do employee education, training, and development address your key organizational needs associated with employee, workplace, and environmental safety?

(3) How do you seek and use input from employees and their supervisors and managers on education and training needs? How do you incorporate your organizational learning and knowledge assets into your education and training?

(4) How do you deliver education and training? How do you seek and use input from employees and their supervisors and managers on options for the delivery of education and training? How do you use both formal and informal delivery approaches, including mentoring and other approaches, as appropriate?

(5) How do you reinforce the use of new knowledge and skills on the job?

(6) How do you evaluate the effectiveness of education and training, taking into account individual and organizational performance?

b. Motivation and Career Development

How do you motivate employees to develop and utilize their full potential? How does your organization use formal and informal mechanisms to help employees attain job- and career-related development and learning objectives? How do managers and supervisors help employees attain job- and career-related development and learning objectives?

Note:

Education and training delivery [5.2a(4)] might occur inside or outside your organization and involve on-the-job, classroom, computer-based, distance learning, and other types of delivery (formal or informal).

This Item [5.2] looks at the organization's system for work force education, training, and on-the-job reinforcement of knowledge and skills, as well as systems for motivation and employee career development with the aim of meeting ongoing needs of employees and a high-performance workplace.

To help the organization achieve its high-performance objectives, education and training must be effectively designed, delivered, reinforced on the job, evaluated, and improved. To optimize organization effectiveness, the education and training system should place special emphasis on meeting individual career progression and organizational business needs.

- Education and training needs might vary greatly depending on the nature of the organization's work, employee responsibility, and stage of organizational and personal development. These needs might include knowledge-sharing skills, communications, teamwork, problem solving, interpreting and using data, meeting customer requirements, process analysis and simplification, waste and cycle-time reduction, and priority setting based on strategic alignment or cost/benefit analysis. Education needs also might include basic skills, such as reading, writing, language, and arithmetic.

Organizations should consider job and organizational performance in education and training design and evaluation. Education and training should tie to action plans, and balance short- and longer-term individual and organizational objectives. Employees and their supervisors should help determine training needs and contribute to the design and evaluation of education and training, because these individuals frequently are best able to identify critical needs and evaluate success.

- Education and training delivery might occur inside or outside the organization and could involve on-the-job, classroom, computer-based, distance learning (including web-based instruction), or other types of delivery. Training also might occur through developmental assignments (including mentoring and apprenticeship) within or outside the organization.

- When evaluating education and training, leaders should identify specific measures of effectiveness as a critical component of evaluation. Such measures might address impact on individual, unit, and organizational performance, impact on customer-related performance, and cost/benefit analysis of the training. Training evaluation should at least cover the extent of knowledge and skills transfer (whether the employees learned anything) and the extent to which they use these new skills and knowledge on the job.

- Although this Item does not require specific training for customer-contact employees, the Item does require that education and training "keep current with business and individual needs" and "address performance excellence." If an objective of the organization is to enhance customer satisfaction and loyalty, it may be critical to identify job requirements for customer-contact employees and then provide them with appropriate training . Such training is increasingly important and common among high-performing organizations. It frequently includes: acquiring critical knowledge and skills with respect to products, services, and customers; skills on how to listen to customers; recovery from problems or failures; and learning how to manage customer expectations effectively.

Organizations should ensure that training and education contribute to high performance. This may require organizations to provide training in the use of performance excellence tools.

- This training may be similar to the "quality" training organizations provided in the past. Training may focus on the use of performance measures, skill standards, quality control methods, benchmarking, problem-solving processes, and performance improvement techniques.

- This training should also address high-priority needs such as technological change, ethical business practices, management and leadership development, orientation of new employees, safety, diversity, and performance measurement and improvement. Succession planning and leadership development [examined in Item

5.1c(3)] typically require organizations to provide specialized training and development to key individuals identified as possible successors.

Unless knowledge and skills acquired in training are reinforced on the job, they are quickly and easily forgotten—even after a few days. Accordingly, leaders, managers, and supervisors throughout the organization must promptly ensure that employees actually use the skills acquired through recent training. In fact, one of the measures of leadership effectiveness may consider the extent to which leaders reinforce these skills among their employees.

Finally, to help employees realize their full potential, many organizations prepare individual development plans with every employee to address their career and learning objectives.

To achieve optimum employee productivity, your organization must understand and address the factors promoting and inhibiting motivation. A better understanding of these factors could be developed through exit interviews with departing employees, as well as through feedback from employee satisfaction surveys.

5.2 Employee Learning and Motivation

How the organization's education, training, and career development support the achievement of overall objectives, contribute to high performance, and build employee knowledge, skills, and capabilities

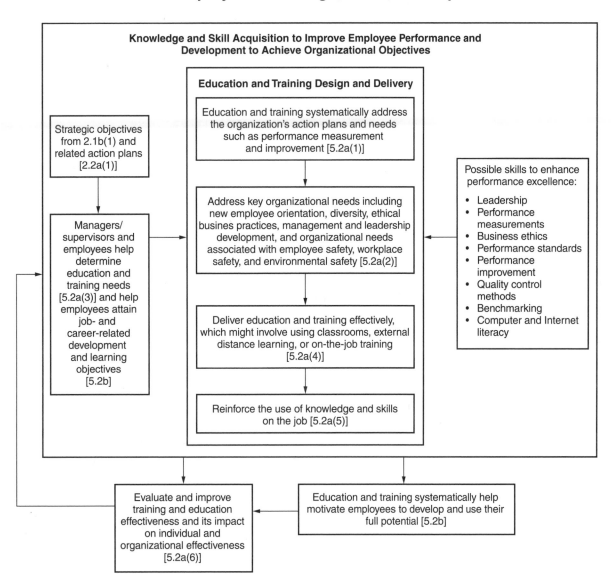

Knowledge and Skill Acquisition to Improve Employee Performance and Development to Achieve Organizational Objectives

Education and Training Design and Delivery

Education and training systematically address the organization's action plans and needs such as performance measurement and improvement [5.2a(1)]

Strategic objectives from 2.1b(1) and related action plans [2.2a(1)]

Managers/ supervisors and employees help determine education and training needs [5.2a(3)] and help employees attain job- and career-related development and learning objectives [5.2b]

Address key organizational needs including new employee orientation, diversity, ethical busines practices, management and leadership development, and organizational needs associated with employee safety, workplace safety, and environmental safety [5.2a(2)]

Deliver education and training effectively, which might involve using classrooms, external distance learning, or on-the-job training [5.2a(4)]

Reinforce the use of knowledge and skills on the job [5.2a(5)]

Possible skills to enhance performance excellence:

- Leadership
- Performance measurements
- Business ethics
- Performance standards
- Performance improvement
- Quality control methods
- Benchmarking
- Computer and Internet literacy

Evaluate and improve training and education effectiveness and its impact on individual and organizational effectiveness [5.2a(6)]

Education and training systematically help motivate employees to develop and use their full potential [5.2b]

5.2 Employee Learning and Motivation Item Linkages

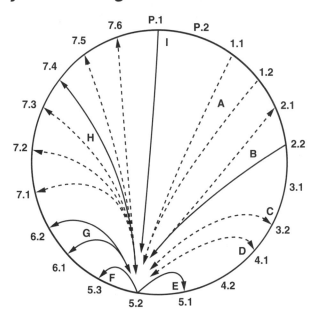

	NATURE OF RELATIONSHIP
A	Leaders [1.1a(2)] are responsible for supporting appropriate skill development of all employees through training and development systems and reinforcing learning on the job [5.2a(5)]. In addition, specific training may be required to ensure employees understand ethical and regulatory requirements [1.2a and b].
B	Human resource plans [2.2a(3)] (which were developed to support strategic objectives [2.1b(1)]) are used to help align training [5.2a(1)] to ensure employees and managers possess appropriate knowledge, skills, and ability.
C	Training [5.2] can enhance capabilities of customer-contact employees and strengthen customer relationships [3.2a(2 and 3)].
D	Key measures and benchmarking data [4.1a(2)] are used to improve training [5.2]. Information regarding training effectiveness [5.2] is analyzed [4.1b] to support planning and operational decision making.
E	Effective training [5.2a] enables managers at all levels to improve their ability to design, organize, and manage better work processes that promote empowerment, innovation [5.1a(1)], creativity, and sharing [5.1a(3)]; make performance feedback and recognition and reward more relevant [5.1b]; enhance succession planning [5.1c(3)]; and recruit and retain the best employees [5.1c(2)].
F	Effective environmental safety training [5.2a(2)] is critical to maintaining and improving a safe, healthful work environment [5.3a] and employee motivation and well-being [5.3b].
G	Training [5.2a(2)] is essential to managing change and improving work effectiveness and innovation [6.1 and 6.2]. In addition, training requirements [5.2] are defined in part by process requirements [6.1 and 6.2].

Continued

	NATURE OF RELATIONSHIP *Continued*
H	Results of improved training and development [5.2] are reported in 7.4. In addition, results pertaining to customer satisfaction [7.1], product and service quality [7.2], financial and market performance [7.3], organizational effectiveness [7.5], and social responsibility [7.6] reflect, in part, and are monitored to assess training effectiveness [5.2a(6)].
I	Employee characteristics such as educational levels, work force and job diversity, and other special requirements [P.1a(3)] help set the context for determining appropriate training needs by employee segment [5.2a(1)].

IF YOU DON'T DO WHAT THE CRITERIA REQUIRE . . .	
Item Reference	**Possible Adverse Consequences**
5.2a(1)	Strategic objectives [Item 2.1b] define what the organization must achieve to be successful in the future. Action plans [Item 2.2a(1)] define the things the organization must do to achieve the strategic objectives. If employees lack the necessary skills to carry out required actions, the strategic plan may fail. Education and training that do not contribute to the achievement of action plans may be a waste of resources. Managers have a responsibility to help employees attain their job- and career-related learning and development objectives [Item 5.2b]. If managers fail to take advantage of appropriate education and training to help employees with work-related development, learning, and career progression, they run the risk of weakening morale and motivation as well as contributing to employee obsolescence. This may adversely impact employee job security and employability and undermine the organization's ability to maintain a viable work force to compete effectively.
5.2a(2)	Today's best-performing organizations have found that the following four areas are instrumental in optimizing performance and winning in a highly competitive environment: 1) new-employee orientation (acculturation); 2) diversity (capitalizing on diverse ideas and cultures); 3) ethical business practices; and 4) management development. The failure to effectively address these factors as a part of employee education, training, and development may adversely affect the organization's ability to achieve its strategic objectives. The failure to provide effective employee orientation may make it difficult to get new employees to achieve organizational objectives. Poor employee orientation may contribute to higher accident rates, higher compensation claims, and lost productivity. The failure to understand and take advantage of diverse ideas and cultures may limit the organization's creativity and innovation and contribute to falling behind competitors. The failure to follow ethical business practices gives rise to corruption, dishonesty, and ultimate business failure (Enron, for example). The failure to develop better managers and leaders may make it more difficult to develop strategic objectives, fully engage employees, and optimize individual or organizational performance.
5.2a(3)	Employees and managers who are closest to the work usually understand best what skills are required (and missing) to do the work effectively. Failing to obtain and use input from these employees and their supervisors may result in the development of inappropriate or ineffective education and training opportunities. Providing ineffective or inappropriate training can waste resources in two ways: 1) the cost of paying employees' salary during training, the cost of facilities, and the cost of instruction; and 2) the cost to the organization of lost productivity while employees are participating in training.
5.2a(4)	The failure to deliver education and training using appropriate methods, consistent with the learning styles and needs of the students, usually suboptimizes the effectiveness of training. If students do not acquire relevant knowledge, skills, or abilities from education and training, the organization has wasted resources. If students do learn new skills and acquire new abilities but those new skills and abilities are not used on the job, the organization has also wasted resources. If the students use the new skills and abilities on the job and it makes no difference to organizational performance or career progression, the organization has again wasted resources.

Continued

IF YOU DON'T DO WHAT THE CRITERIA REQUIRE . . . *Continued*	
Item Reference	**Possible Adverse Consequences**
5.2a(5)	If it is worth training an employee to acquire new skills and abilities, it is important to reinforce the use of those new skills when the employee returns to the job. The failure to reinforce the use of recently acquired knowledge and skills on the job may cause those new skills and abilities to become obsolete and quickly forgotten. Accordingly, the cost of training and the cost of lost productivity while the employee is receiving the training represent wasted resources. Most importantly, when the newly acquired skills are not utilized, the value of those skills and potential productivity gains are lost. Losses of this nature can materially impact an organization's rate of growth and its ability to achieve strategy objectives.
5.2a(6)	The failure to evaluate and improve the effectiveness of training makes it difficult to optimize individual or organizational performance. Ineffective or inefficient training and education wastes resources directly (cost of training) and indirectly (cost of lost opportunity and productivity while employee is receiving training).
5.2b	An organization that fails to develop and use the full potential of its employees wastes significant resources. This waste can be classified into two categories: 1) the failure to develop existing potential and take advantage of it; and 2) the failure to use skills and abilities that already exist. This waste is equivalent to running an operation at less than optimum capacity; for example, paying an employee for 40 hours of work but asking for only 20, or going out and hiring additional people when the potential for skills development already exists but goes unrecognized. To make matters worse, employees usually recognize when their skills are underused and their productivity suffers further erosion, or they seek job opportunities outside the organization where they can develop and advance more fully, or both.

5.2 EMPLOYEE LEARNING AND MOTIVATION—SAMPLE EFFECTIVE PRACTICES

A. Employee Education, Training, and Development

- Managers and employees conduct systematic needs analyses to ensure that skills required to perform work are routinely assessed, monitored, and maintained.

- Clear linkages exist between strategic objectives and education and training. Skills are developed based on work demands and employee needs.

- Training plans are developed based on employee input.

- Employee career and personal development options, including development for leadership, diversity, new-employee orientation, and safety, are enhanced through formal education and training. Some development uses on-the-job training, including rotational assignments or job exchange programs.

- The organization uses various methods to deliver training to ensure that it is suitable for employee knowledge and skill levels.

- To minimize travel costs, all training is examined to determine if electronic or distance delivery options are viable.

- Training is linked to work requirements, which managers reinforce on the job. Just-in-time training is preferred (rather than just-in-case training) to help ensure that the skills will be used immediately after training.

- Employee feedback on the appropriateness of the training is collected and used to improve course delivery and content.

- The organization systematically evaluates training effectiveness on the job. Performance data are collected on individuals and groups at all levels to assess the impact of training.

- Employee satisfaction with courses is tracked and used to improve training content, training delivery, instructional effectiveness, and the effectiveness of supervisory support for the use of training on the job.

- Training design and delivery is systematically refined and improved based on regular evaluations.

B. Motivation and Career Development

- Formal career plans are in place for each employee. Progress against these plans is evaluated and adjustments are made to ensure they remain relevant.

- Employees receive incentives such as bonuses or other rewards for developing additional career-enhancing skills.

5.3 EMPLOYEE WELL-BEING AND SATISFACTION (25 PTS.)
PROCESS

Describe how your organization maintains a work environment and an employee support climate that contribute to the well-being, satisfaction, and motivation of all employees.

Within your response, include answers to the following questions:

a. Work Environment

(1) How do you improve workplace health, safety, security, and ergonomics? How do employees take part in improving them? What are your performance measures or targets for each of these key workplace factors? What are the significant differences in workplace factors and performance measures or targets if different employee groups and work units have different work environments?

(2) How do you ensure workplace preparedness for emergencies or disasters? How do you seek to ensure business continuity for the benefit of your employees and customers?

b. Employee Support and Satisfaction

(1) How do you determine the key factors that affect employee well-being, satisfaction, and motivation? How are these factors segmented for a diverse work force and for different categories and types of employees?

(2) How do you support your employees via services, benefits, and policies? How are these tailored to the needs of a diverse work force and different categories and types of employees?

(3) What formal and informal assessment methods and measures do you use to determine employee well-being, satisfaction, and motivation? How do these methods and measures differ across a diverse work force and different categories and types of employees? How do you use other indicators, such as employee retention, absenteeism, grievances, safety, and productivity, to assess and improve employee well-being, satisfaction, and motivation?

(4) How do you relate assessment findings to key business results to identify priorities for improving the work environment and employee support climate?

Notes:

N1. Specific factors that might affect your employees' well-being, satisfaction, and motivation [5.3b(1)] include effective employee problem or grievance resolution; safety factors; employees' views of management; employee training, development, and career opportunities; employee preparation for changes in technology or the work organization; the work environment and other work conditions; management's empowerment of employees; information sharing by management; workload; cooperation and teamwork; recognition; services and benefits; communications; job security; compensation; and equal opportunity.

N2. Approaches for employee support [5.3b(2)] might include providing counseling, career development and employability services, recreational or cultural activities, non-work-related education, day care, job rotation or sharing, special leave for family responsibilities or community service, home safety training, flexible work hours and location, outplacement, and retirement benefits (including extended health care).

Continued

Notes: *Continued*

N3. Measures and indicators of well-being, satisfaction, and motivation [5.3b(3)] might include data on safety and absenteeism, the overall turnover rate, the turnover rate for customer contact employees, employees' charitable contributions, grievances, strikes, other job actions, insurance costs, workers' compensation claims, and results of surveys. Survey indicators of satisfaction might include employee knowledge of job roles, employee knowledge of organizational direction, and employee perception of empowerment and information sharing. Your results relative to such measures and indicators should be reported in Item 7.4.

N4. Setting priorities [5.3b(4)] might draw upon your human resource results presented in Item 7.4 and might involve addressing employee problems based on their impact on your business results.

This Item [5.3] looks at the organization's work environment, the employee support climate, and how employee satisfaction is determined, for the purpose of enhancing the well-being, satisfaction, and motivation of all employees, while recognizing their diverse needs.

The first part of this Item [5.3a] looks at systems the organization has in place to provide a safe, secure, and healthful work environment for all employees, taking into account their differing work environments and associated requirements. Employees should help identify and improve factors important to workplace safety and security. The organization should identify appropriate measures and targets for key workplace factors so that status and progress can be tracked.

- The organization should be able to show how it includes such factors in its planning and improvement activities. Important factors in this Area to Address include establishing appropriate measures and targets for employee safety, security, and health. Organizations should also recognize that employee groups might experience very different environments and need different services to ensure workplace safety.

- Organizations should also have a workplace preparedness plan in place in case of emergencies or disasters. Part of the plan should focus on ensuring business continuity for the benefit of both employees and customers. Such plans should provide for rapid recovery and minimize disruptions to the work of employees and the

products, services, and programs delivered to customers.

The second part of this Item [5.3b] looks at how the organization determines key factors that affect employee well-being, satisfaction, and motivation. The organization must provide appropriate services, benefits, and policies to enhance employee well-being, satisfaction, and motivation. The best organizations develop a holistic view of employees as key stakeholders. Most organizations, regardless of size, have many opportunities to contribute to employees' well-being, satisfaction, and motivation. These organizations place special emphasis on the variety of approaches used to satisfy a diverse work force with differing needs and expectations in order to reduce attrition and increase motivation.

- Examples of services, facilities, activities, and other opportunities are: personal and career counseling; career development and employability services; recreational or cultural activities; formal and informal recognition; non-work-related education; day care; special leave for family responsibilities and/or for community service; home safety training; flexible work hours and benefits packages; outplacement services; and retiree benefits, including extended health care and access to employee services. Also, these services might include career enhancement activities such as skills assessments, helping employees develop learning objectives and plans, and conducting employability assessments.

- As the work force becomes more diverse (including employees who may work in other countries for multinational companies) it becomes more important to consider and support the needs of those employees with different services.

High-performing organizations also used both formal and informal assessment methods and measures to determine employee well-being, satisfaction, and motivation. These methods and measures are tailored to assess the differing needs of a diverse work force. In addition, indicators other than employee opinion surveys (for example, employee turnover, grievances, complaints, and absenteeism) are used to support the assessment. Taken together, these methods and measures ensure that assessment findings are relevant and relate to key business results in order to identify key priorities for improvement.

Many factors might affect employee motivation, well-being, and satisfaction. Although satisfaction with pay and promotion potential is important, this factor might not be adequate to understand all the factors that contribute to the overall climate for motivation and high performance.

- For this reason, high-performing organizations usually consider a variety of factors that might affect well-being, satisfaction, and motivation, such as effective employee problem and grievance resolution; safety; employee development and career opportunities; employee preparation for changes in technology or work organization; work environment and management support; workload; communication, cooperation, and teamwork; job security; appreciation of the differing needs of diverse employee groups; recognition; benefits; compensation; and organizational support for serving customers.

- In addition to direct measurement of employee satisfaction and well-being through formal or informal surveys, some other indicators of satisfaction and well-being include: absenteeism, turnover, grievances, strikes, accidents, lost-time injuries, and worker's compensation claims. Information and data on the well-being, satisfaction, and motivation of employees are actually used in identifying improvement priorities. Priority setting might draw upon human resource results reported in Item 7.4 and might involve addressing employee problems based on the impact on organizational performance. Factors inhibiting motivation need to be prioritized and addressed. The failure to address these factors is likely to result in even greater problems, which may not only impact human resource results (Item 7.4), but adversely affect customer satisfaction (Item 7.1), product and service quality (Item 7.2), financial performance (Item 7.3), organizational effectiveness (7.5), and public responsibility (Item 7.6).

5.3 Employee Well-Being and Satisfaction

How the organization maintains a work environment and employee support climate that supports the well-being, satisfaction, and motivation of employees

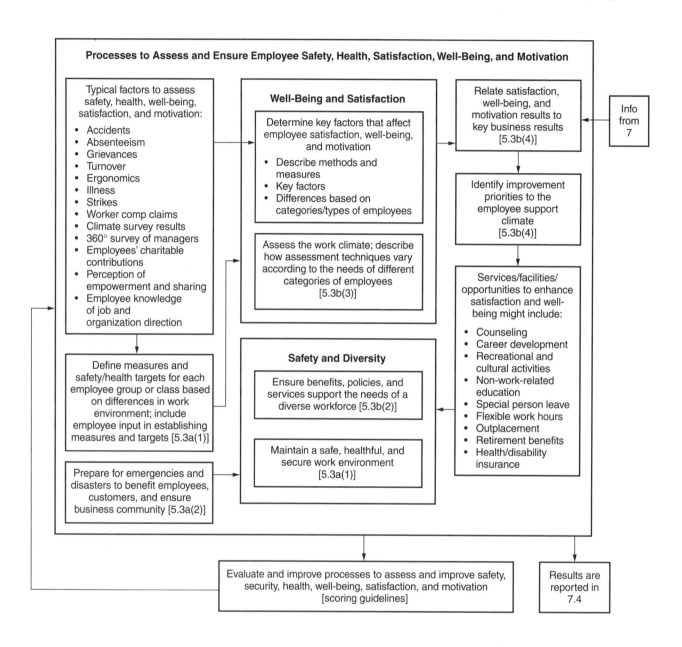

5.3 Employee Well-Being and Satisfaction Item Linkages

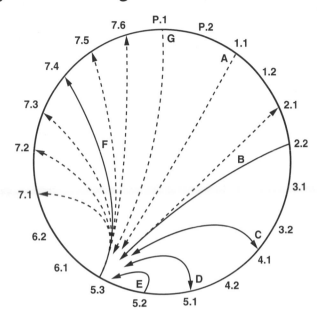

NATURE OF RELATIONSHIP	
A	Leaders [1.1a(2)] are responsible for creating an environment that fosters employee empowerment, innovation, and organizational agility, consistent with effective systems to enhance employee health, safety, security, satisfaction, well-being, and motivation [5.3a].
B	Human resource development plans [2.2a(3)] typically address or set the context for safety, security, motivation, satisfaction, and well-being systems [5.3]. Employee motivation and satisfaction, safety, security, and disaster-recovery processes [5.3] may be important to consider in the process of developing strategy [2.1a(2)].
C	Key benchmarking data [4.1a(2)] are used to design processes to enhance employee motivation and well-being [5.3b]. Information regarding employee well-being and motivation [5.3b(3)] is used to gain a better understanding of problems and performance capabilities to support strategic planning [4.1b(1)].
D	High motivation [5.3] enhances employee empowerment and initiative (self-direction) and innovation [5.1a(1)], and vice versa.
E	Effective training [5.2] is critical to maintaining and improving a safe, secure, healthful work environment and providing an appropriate emergency or disaster response [5.3a] and improved employee motivation, satisfaction, and well-being [5.3b].
F	Systems that enhance employee motivation, satisfaction, and well-being [5.3] can boost financial and market performance [7.3], customer satisfaction [7.1], product and service quality [7.2], organizational effectiveness and productivity [7.5], and social responsibility [7.6]. Specific results of employee well-being and satisfaction systems are reported in 7.4.
G	Employee characteristics such as educational levels, work force and job diversity, the existence of bargaining units, the use of contract employees, and other special requirements [P.1a(3)] may help set the context for tailoring benefits, services, and satisfaction assessment methods for employees according to various types and categories [5.3a and b(1, 2, and 3)].

	IF YOU DON'T DO WHAT THE CRITERIA REQUIRE . . .
Item Reference	**Possible Adverse Consequences**
5.3a	The failure to improve workplace health, safety, security, and ergonomics may increase employee accidents and illness, reduce employee effectiveness, and negatively impact morale and motivation. Poor working conditions can distract employees, reduce productivity, and increase errors, rework, cycle time, and waste, to name a few. Failing to involve employees in the identification of potential health, safety, security, and ergonomics issues may cause the organization to overlook and fail to correct those problems. If significant variation exists in the work environment for different employee groups or work units, employees are likely to face different workplace health, safety, security, and ergonomic issues. For example, carpal tunnel syndrome (repetitive stress injuries) may be a problem for those who do substantial keypunching but not for certain employees on the shop floor. Those employees may be more concerned about injury from lifting heavy objects. Accordingly, the failure to define performance measures and establish targets for each key environmental factor and each distinct employee group increases the likelihood the problems will go unnoticed and those employees will be distracted from their work, suboptimizing performance. In addition, the failure to plan and prepare for emergencies and disasters makes the organization vulnerable to serious disruptions of service, which may hurt both employees and customers, and damage the stability of the business.
5.3b(1)	Factors that affect employee well-being, satisfaction, and motivation can vary significantly from organization to organization or within an organization from site to site, or among different groups of employees in the same organization. The failure to determine the key factors affecting employee well-being, satisfaction, and motivation for each employee or segment may make it difficult to identify key problems and take appropriate corrective action. The inability to identify and correct these problems can reduce employee morale and motivation, which, in turn, hurts productivity and ultimately customer satisfaction.
5.3b(2)	Just as different employee groups may have different needs for safety, different groups of employees may need different support services and benefits to keep them from being distracted in their work. For example, in one company employees located in an extremely rural area lost an entire day of work traveling to a dentist or physician to deal with a toothache or a minor medical problem. Positioning a trailer with dental and health professionals near the plant entrance minimized the time employees had to be absent from work due to a medical problem. A sister plant in the same company, located near a major metropolitan area, had plenty of dentists and physicians nearby and determined that its employees would be better served by an in-house exercise and wellness program. When an organization fails to identify and tailor benefits and services to the needs of its diverse work force, it may increase distractions and reduce optimum employee participation and performance. Suboptimum employee performance hurts productivity.

Continued

	IF YOU DON'T DO WHAT THE CRITERIA REQUIRE . . . *Continued*
Item Reference	**Possible Adverse Consequences**
5.3b(3)	Because the factors that affect employee well-being, satisfaction, and motivation can vary significantly among the diverse groups of employees, if an organization fails to differentiate assessment methods and measures it may not be able to determine accurately the existence of problems and take appropriate corrective action. The failure to identify and correct a problem that adversely affects employee well-being, satisfaction, and motivation can contribute to operational inefficiency, waste resources, and reduce product and service quality and customer satisfaction. Failing to consider data that relate to employee well-being and satisfaction such as absenteeism, grievances, and undesired employee attrition may also prevent a problem from being identified and corrected. Finally, the "one-size-fits-all" method of assessing employee well-being and satisfaction (such as the *annual* climate survey) may fail to take into account parts of the organization that may be undergoing change and facing more turmoil than other parts of the organization. For organizations that are relatively stable, an annual survey may be appropriate. However, for organizations (or parts of organizations) that face a more volatile, unstable environment, more frequent assessments may be required. The failure to ask the right questions, at the right time, and in the right manner may prevent the organization from learning about and correcting serious problems that may adversely affect performance and productivity.
5.3b(4)	When deciding what actions to take to improve the work environment (based on the results of appropriate surveys and related data), organizations may waste resources if they do not set priorities for improvement that are likely to optimize business results. In the example above [5.3b(2)], the plant manager could have installed a workout room and shower facilities rather than a health services trailer. However, analysis revealed that exercise facilities would have minimum impact on productivity, whereas the health care trailer would save hundreds of days each year in lost time due to employee absenteeism. Organizations risk wasting resources if they fail to understand the likely impact on business results of the improvement priorities they set in response to employee satisfaction assessment findings.

5.3 EMPLOYEE WELL-BEING AND SATISFACTION—SAMPLE EFFECTIVE PRACTICES

A. Work Environment

- Issues and concerns relating to employee health, safety, security, and workplace environment are used to design the work environment for all groups of employees. Plans exist and processes are in place to optimize working conditions and eliminate adverse conditions.

- Root causes for health, safety, and security problems are systematically identified and eliminated. Corrective actions are communicated widely to help prevent the problem in other parts of the organization.

- Targets are set and reviewed for all key health, safety, security, and ergonomic factors affecting the employees' work environment. Employees are directly involved in setting these targets.

- A documented and tested emergency-recovery plan is in place and all employees are trained and understand the processes they will follow.

- Disaster-recovery processes are in place and serious tests (drills) are conducted to simulate emergency response to minimize problems and risks to employees and customers in the event of a real crisis. These procedures were developed based on benchmarking other organizations that faced crises.

B. Employee Support and Satisfaction

- Special activities and services are available for employees. These are quite varied, depending on the needs of different employee categories. Examples include the following:

  - Flexible benefits plan including: health care, on-site day care, dental, portable retirement, education (both work and non-work-related), maternity, paternity, and family illness leave

  - Group purchasing power program where the number of participating merchants is increasing steadily

  - Special facilities for employee meetings to discuss their concerns

- Senior leaders build a work climate that addresses the needs of a diverse work force. Recruitment and training are tools to enhance the work climate.

- Key employee satisfaction opinion indicators are gathered periodically based on the stability of the organization (organizations in the midst of rapid change conduct assessments more frequently). Supervisors, managers, and leaders take consistent and prompt action to improve conditions identified through these employee satisfaction surveys.

- On-demand electronic surveys are available for quick response and tabulations any time managers need employee satisfaction feedback. Whenever the survey is completed, managers always follow up promptly to make improvements identified by the survey that relate to key business results.

- Satisfaction data are derived from employee focus groups, employee satisfaction survey results, turnover, absenteeism, and other data that reflect employee satisfaction.

- Managers use the results of these surveys to focus improvements in work systems and enhance employee satisfaction. Actions to improve satisfaction are clearly tied to assessments so employees understand the value of the assessment, and the improvement initiatives do not appear random or capricious.

- Employee satisfaction indicators are correlated with drivers of business success to help identify where resources should be placed to provide maximum business benefit.

- Methods to improve how employee satisfaction is determined are systematically evaluated and improved. Techniques to actually improve employee satisfaction and well-being are, themselves, evaluated and refined consistently.

6 Process Management—85 Points

*The **Process Management** Category examines the key aspects of your organization's process management, including key product, service, and business processes for creating customer and organizational value and key support processes. This Category encompasses all key processes and work units.*

Process Management is the focal point within the Criteria for all key work processes. Built into the category are the central requirements for efficient and effective process management: effective design, a prevention orientation, linkage to suppliers and partners and a focus on supply chain integration, operational performance, cycle time, and evaluation, continuous improvement, and organizational learning.

Organizational agility, cost reduction, and cycle-time reduction are increasingly important in all aspects of process management and organizational design.

- Agility refers to an organization's ability to adapt quickly and effectively to changing requirements. Depending on the nature of the organization's strategy and markets, flexibility might mean rapid changeover from one product to another, rapid response to changing demands, or the ability to produce a wide range of customized services. Agility might demand special strategies such as implementing modular designs, sharing components, sharing manufacturing lines, and providing specialized training. Agility also increasingly involves outsourcing decisions, agreements with key suppliers, and novel partnering arrangements.

- Cost and cycle-time reduction often involve many of the same process management strategies as achieving agility. Thus, it is crucial to utilize key measures for these requirements in the overall process management.

Process management contains two Items that evaluate the management of product and service processes, business processes, and support processes.

Value Creation Processes

(Core and key business processes required to produce and deliver the organization's main products and services and deliver value to customers and other key stakeholders and improve market and financial position)

- Design, develop, and introduce products and services to meet customer requirements, operational performance requirements, and market requirements.

- Use customer feedback, supplier feedback, and in-process measures to control and improve the performance of these processes.

- Ensure a rapid, efficient, trouble-free introduction.

- Manage and continuously improve operating processes.

Support Processes

(Provide support to value creation and business processes)

- Design, develop, and provide products and services to meet internal customer requirements.

- Use internal customer feedback and in-process measures to control and improve the performance of these processes.

- Manage and continuously improve support processes.

6.1 VALUE CREATION PROCESSES (50 PTS.)
PROCESS

Describe how your organization identifies and manages its key processes for creating customer value and achieving business success and growth.

Within your response, include answers to the following questions:

a. Value Creation Processes

(1) How does your organization determine its key value creation processes? What are your organization's key product, service, and business processes for creating or adding value? How do these processes create value for the organization, your customers, and your other key stakeholders? How do they contribute to profitability and business success?

(2) How do you determine key value creation process requirements, incorporating input from customers, suppliers, and partners, as appropriate? What are the key requirements for these processes?

(3) How do you design these processes to meet all the key requirements? How do you incorporate new technology and organizational knowledge into the design of these processes? How do you incorporate cycle time, productivity, cost control, and other efficiency and effectiveness factors into the design of these processes? How do you implement these processes to ensure they meet design requirements?

(4) What are your key performance measures or indicators used for the control and improvement of your value creation processes? How does your day-to-day operation of these processes ensure meeting key process requirements? How are in-process measures used in managing these processes? How are customer, supplier, and partner input used in managing these processes, as appropriate?

(5) How do you minimize overall costs associated with inspections, tests, and process or performance audits, as appropriate? How do you prevent defects and rework, and minimize warranty costs, as appropriate?

(6) How do you improve your value creation processes to achieve better performance, to reduce variability, improve products and services, and keep the processes current with business needs and directions? How are improvements shared with other organizational units and processes?

Notes:

N1. Your key value creation processes are those most important to "running your business" and maintaining or achieving a sustainable competitive advantage. They are the processes that involve the majority of your organization's employees and produce customer, stockholder, and other key stakeholder value. They include the processes through which your organization adds greatest value to its products and services. They also include the business processes most critical to adding value to the business itself, resulting in success and growth.

Continued

Notes:

Continued

N2. Key value creation processes differ greatly among organizations, depending on many factors. These factors include the nature of your products and services, how they are produced and delivered, technology requirements, customer and supplier relationships and involvement, outsourcing, importance of research and development, role of technology acquisition, information and knowledge management, supply chain management, mergers and acquisitions, global expansion, and sales and marketing. Responses to Item 6.1 should be based upon the most critical requirements and processes for your products, services, and business.

N3. To achieve better process performance and reduce variability, you might implement approaches such as a Lean Enterprise System, Six Sigma methodology, use of ISO 9000:2000 standards, or other process improvement tools.

N4. To provide as complete and concise a response as possible for your key value creation processes, you might want to use a tabular format identifying the key processes and the attributes of each as called for in questions 6.1a(1)–6.1a(6).

N5. The results of improvements in product and service performance should be reported in Item 7.2. The results of operational improvements in your product and service design and delivery processes and key business processes should be reported in Item 7.5.

This Item [6.1] looks at both key design processes for products and services and their related production and delivery processes that create value for the organization, its customers, and stakeholders. Descriptions must be provided of the key processes, their specific requirements, and an explanation of how performance relative to these requirements is determined and maintained. Increasingly, these requirements might include the need for agility—speed and flexibility—to adapt to change.

- Design approaches could differ significantly depending upon the nature of products and services—whether the products/services are entirely new, variants, or involve major or minor process changes. Factors that might need to be considered in design include: safety, long-term performance, environmental impact, "green" manufacturing, measurement capability, process capability, manufacturability, maintainability, variability in customer expectations requiring product/service options, supplier capability, and documentation.

- Effective design must consider cycle time and efficiency of production and delivery processes.

Detailed mapping of manufacturing or service processes and redesigning or reengineering those processes to achieve higher levels of efficiency, as well as to meet changing customer requirements, may be helpful. The best organizations have mechanisms in place that promote learning from past design projects.

- New technology, including e-technology, should be incorporated into the design of products and services. The use of e-technology might include new ways of electronically sharing information with suppliers/partners, communicating with customers and giving them continuous (24/7) access, and transferring automated information from in-service products requiring maintenance in the field.

- Frequently, defective design processes require organizations to capture information from customer complaint data using the processes described in Item 3.2a. Immediate access to customer complaint data allows the organization to make design or production changes quickly to prevent problems from occurring or recurring.

- The best-performing organizations consider requirements of suppliers and/or business partners at the design stage. This minimizes the chances that important design issues are not achievable because of supplier and/or partner limitations. Similarly, effective design systems take into account all stakeholders in the value chain.

- To enhance design process efficiency, all related design and production activities should be coordinated within the organization. Coordination of design, production, and delivery processes involves all work units and/or individuals who take part in production/delivery and whose performance materially affects overall process outcome. This might include key business functions or processes such as R&D, marketing, design, product/process engineering, and key suppliers. If many design projects are carried out in parallel, or if the organization's products require parts, equipment, and facilities that are used for other products, coordination of resources frequently provides a means to significantly reduce unit costs and time to market.

- Design processes should cover all key operational performance requirements and appropriate coordination and testing to ensure effective product/service launch without need for rework.

- The best-performing organizations accurately and completely define key production/delivery processes, their key performance requirements, and key performance measures. These requirements and measures provide the basis for maintaining and improving products, services, and production/delivery processes. These organizations also define how performance relative to these requirements is determined and maintained. Increasingly, these requirements usually include the need for agility—speed and flexibility—to adapt to change.

- Top organizations minimize the need for inspections, tests, and audits to avoid rework and warranty costs, because they have implemented processes to prevent problems from occurring in the first place. Sometimes these processes involve error-proofing, which makes it impossible to do the wrong thing the wrong way (for example, electrical cords on today's appliances have one plug blade wider than the other to prevent it from being inserted incorrectly into a wall outlet).

- Organizations also use key measurements at critical points in processes to minimize problems and costs. These activities should occur at the earliest points possible in processes to minimize problems and costs that may result from unacceptable deviation in performance. Achieving expected performance frequently requires setting performance levels or standards to guide decision making. When deviations occur, corrective action is required to restore the performance of the process to its design specifications. Depending on the nature of the process, the corrective action could involve technical and/or human considerations. Proper corrective action involves changes at the source (root cause) of the deviation. Effective corrective action minimizes the likelihood of this type of deviation occurring again or anywhere else in the organization.

- The best-performing organizations have a system in place to evaluate and improve production/delivery processes to achieve better process efficiency and better products and services. Better performance means not only better quality from the customers' perspective but also results in better financial and operational performance—such as productivity. A variety of process improvement approaches are commonly used. These approaches include:

  - Sharing successful strategies across the organization

  - Process analysis and research (for example, process mapping, optimization experiments, and error-proofing)

  - Technical and business research and development

– Benchmarking

– Using alternative technology

– Using information from customers of the processes—within and outside of the organization

New process improvement approaches might also involve the use of cost data to evaluate alternatives and set improvement priorities. Taken together, these approaches offer a wide range of possibilities, including complete redesign of key processes to achieve new levels of operational excellence.

In addition to designing and delivering core value creation products and services, this Item [6.1] also covers the design and delivery of key business processes. Business processes include the organization's key nonproduct and nonservice processes. A nonproduct/nonservice business process is one that is critical to the future success and business growth of the organization but does not involve actually producing products or services for end users (value creation products and services). Key business processes frequently relate to an organization's strategic objectives and critical success factors. As such, it might be useful to consider them as "strategic business processes." These are not core business activities. However, they may be considered as more critical than ordinary support activities (which are examined in Item 6.2).

Key business processes might include the following:

• Processes for innovation, including empowering employees to generate and implement new ideas.

• R&D, involving dedicated units and distributing R&D responsibility throughout the organization.

• Technology acquisition (which may involve partnering), acquisitions, mergers, invention, or other techniques.

• Information and knowledge management, which goes beyond traditional information technology or information management activities. Knowledge management often supports knowledge transfer and knowledge sharing among all organizational units at all levels and sites within an organization.

• Mergers and acquisitions, including global expansion initiatives.

• Project management, to ensure on-time and consistent development of new programs, products, and services.

• Sales and marketing, to strengthen and expand new markets, including e-commerce.

• Supply chain management, supplier partnering, and outsourcing. For many organizations, supply chain management is an increasingly important factor in achieving productivity and profitability goals and overall business success. Suppliers and partners are receiving increasing strategic attention as organizations reevaluate and outsource their core functions. Supply chain management processes typically fulfill two purposes: to help improve the performance of suppliers and partners; and in turn, contribute to better internal operational performance. Supply chain management might include processes for supplier selection, with the aim of reducing the total number of suppliers and increasing preferred supplier and partnering agreements.

6.1 Value Creation Processes

How the organization identifies and manages its key processes for creating customer value and achieving business success and growth

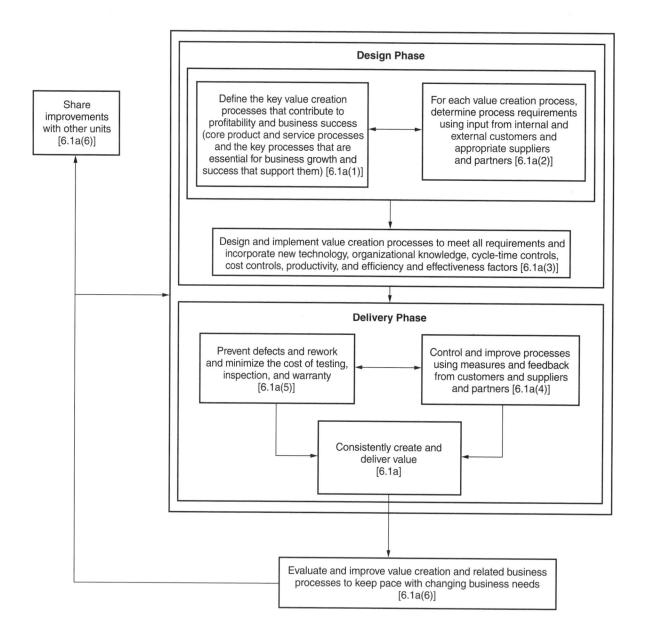

6.1 Value Creation Process Item Linkages

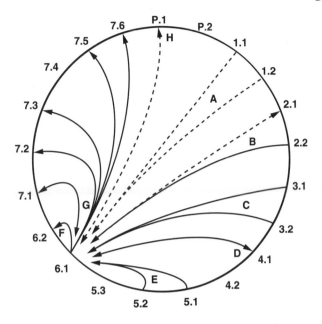

	NATURE OF RELATIONSHIP
A	Senior leaders and the governance system [1.1] have a responsibility for ensuring that value creation and business processes critical for growth and success are designed [6.1a(2)] consistent with organizational objectives, including those relating to social responsibility and good corporate citizenship [1.2a].
B	Organizational value creation process strengths and weaknesses [6.1] are considered as part of the planning process [2.1a(2)]. Action plans, deployed to the work force [2.2a], are used to align actions to design [6.1a(1, 2, and 3] and perform critical value creation and business services [6.1a(3 and 4)].
C	Customer requirements and preferences [3.1a(2)], customer questions [3.2a(2)], complaints/complaint resolution [3.2a(3)], and satisfaction/dissatisfaction [3.2b(1, 2, and 3)] are used to identify requirements for critical value creation and business processes [6.1a(2)].
D	Key business processes such as R&D, knowledge management, and information technology [6.1] are used to help identify and prioritize benchmarking targets [4.1a(2)]. Benchmarking data [4.1a(2)] are used to improve key value creation and business processes [6.1].
E	High-performance, flexible work systems [5.1a(1)], effective recognition [5.1b], and training [5.2] are essential to improving value-adding and related business processes [6.1].
F	Value creation processes [6.1], as customers of support processes [6.2], help define requirements and set priorities for support processes.

Continued

	NATURE OF RELATIONSHIP	*Continued*
G	Information about customer satisfaction [7.1] is used to target improvement efforts in key value creation and business processes [6.1]. Improved value creation and business processes [6.1] can be reflected in better customer satisfaction [7.1] and better product and service quality [7.2], better financial results [7.3], operational efficiency [7.5a(1 and 2)], and social responsibility/ regulatory compliance [7.6].	
H	Information in P.1a(1) derives from the value creation processes [6.1] and helps set the context for examiner review of these processes.	

	IF YOU DON'T DO WHAT THE CRITERIA REQUIRE . . .
Item Reference	**Possible Adverse Consequences**
6.1a(1)	The requirements of design processes can vary significantly within an organization depending on the nature of the products and services being delivered to customers. Design processes may also vary based on whether the products and services are new or only involve minor variations to current product and service offerings. In any event, a design process that fails to consider the key requirements for products and services, and other factors such as environmental impact, process capability, measurement capability, customer service expectations, supplier capability, and customer documentation requirements (such as found in ISO 9000), may make it difficult or impossible for the organization to achieve desired results (satisfy customers) in an efficient and profitable manner.
	In an effort to ensure the design process is consistent and effective, organizations frequently develop elaborate checkpoints or "gates" that must be passed as part of bringing a new product or service into the marketplace. The gates serve a twofold purpose: 1) assuring the focus on customer requirements is maintained throughout the design process and responds to changing customer and market demands; and 2) assuring design maturity is on track. The first deals with fully responding to customer requirements by providing value in the eyes of the customer. The second addresses the ability of the organization to do this in an efficient, effective, and profitable manner. Design processes that are not capable of incorporating changing customer or market requirements into products and services in a timely fashion may find it difficult to remain agile and competitive. For example, an organization that receives customer change requirements at a faster pace than they can implement the changes can be virtually paralyzed. Unwieldy design systems often lead to frustrated employees, excessive delay, and ultimately dissatisfied customers and lost business. When faced with rapidly changing technology, customer requirements, or market demands, inflexible or cumbersome design processes can render a once-good design obsolete before it ever gets to market.

Continued

	IF YOU DON'T DO WHAT THE CRITERIA REQUIRE . . .
Item Reference	**Possible Adverse Consequences**
6.1a(2)	An organization that fails to accurately identify the performance requirements of its value creation and related key business processes may find it difficult to design and optimize those processes to meet customer expectations. Design flaws produce undesired results and nonconforming products and services. This, in turn, requires even more rework or more people-intensive services, which can add significant delay and prevent the organization from achieving its objectives. When these processes fail to meet requirements, resources are wasted and the objectives of the organization may be jeopardized.
6.1a(3)	Organizations that fail to consider all key operational performance requirements when designing key business processes frequently find that the system they designed is not optimum. Design flaws produce undesired results, as well as nonconforming products and services. These, in turn, require even more rework. The failure to consistently meet the requirements of customers may increase the likelihood of downstream problems with the design, production, and delivery of core products and services.
	In today's highly competitive, global economy, speed and agility are important factors that distinguish the best-performing organizations from the rest. The best-performing organizations provide their customers with value faster (speed) and across a wider range of customer areas (agility) than their competition. The speed and agility offered by new technologies enhance that value. Consequently, the leaders are able to distinguish their organizations in chosen markets, keeping their current customers and acquiring new ones. Increasingly, the failure to use the appropriate technologies limits the organization's ability to keep pace with aggressive competitors. These organizations may have the latest computers, but those computers may not be used effectively to accelerate delivery of the things that are important to customers. One *Fortune 500* company, learning that its customers placed a premium on accurate bills being delivered on time, acquired and implemented new technology to dramatically speed up its billing cycle. Unfortunately, the billing process itself was not capable of rendering an accurate invoice. Customers received their inaccurate invoices faster than ever. Using technology to accelerate a bad process only produces unsatisfactory results faster. The failure to incorporate the appropriate technologies can have significant adverse effects on an organization's ability to bring value to its customers and to operate in an efficient and effective manner.
	Eliminating unnecessary steps in any work process tends to reduce variation (increasing quality), reduce cycle time, and reduce cost. In addition, learning from the successes and mistakes of others helps prevent employees from repeating the same problems (which add rework, waste, and delay). When designing new products and services and related production and delivery systems, the failure to consider factors such as cost control, new technology, variability, and ways to enhance productivity and efficiency typically adds unnecessary cost, delay, and rework, making it more difficult to meet increasing demands of customers and the marketplace.

Continued

	IF YOU DON'T DO WHAT THE CRITERIA REQUIRE . . . *Continued*
Item Reference	**Possible Adverse Consequences**
6.1a(4)	The best-performing organizations are able to consistently deliver products and services that meet key performance requirements. They do this by identifying key processes, monitoring them regularly, and improving then continuously. The failure to ensure consistent day-to-day operation of production and delivery processes increases the likelihood of defects, which contribute to rework, waste, delay, and excessive costs. Organizations can always tell if a process is producing desired results by waiting for those results and checking to see if the end product and service meet customer and operational requirements. Unfortunately, waiting for the end of the process to learn that it has not produced desired results is time-consuming and expensive, since most costs may have already been sunk. The earlier an organization can determine if a process is not likely to produced desired results, the earlier it can take corrective action to minimize rework, scrap, delay, and unnecessary cost. In addition, the failure to collect and analyze in-process data makes it more difficult for employees to know when to adjust a process to make it work better. Inappropriate or unnecessary adjustments can actually increase variation and decrease productivity quality. Customers can usually determine quickly if the products and services they receive meet (or exceed) their requirements. They are in a good position to provide near real-time feedback that will enable employees to make adjustments to meet requirements. The failure to gather and use this information makes it more difficult for organizations to make timely changes to reduce rework costs and increase customer satisfaction.
6.1a(5)	High-performing organizations do not rely on excessive inspection and testing to determine if process requirements are likely to be met. Conceptually, the only time to inspect is when the outcome is not known. Instead, these organizations design process controls that let them know how well the process is performing during each of its critical steps. They develop processes that prevent problems using tools and techniques such as error-proofing. The best that testing or inspection can hope to accomplish is to uncover and correct a problem before the customer is disrupted. Although this is better than causing problems for customers, it is still more costly to fix the problem than to prevent it from happening in the first place.
6.1a(6)	Organizations that fail to systematically evaluate and improve production and delivery systems and processes often seem to lag behind the competition. Consider two comparable organizations, each using similar processes to develop and deliver similar products and services. Let's also assume that the organizations are equally competitive today. However, one organization has embedded into its work processes an ongoing evaluation and improvement of its design, production, and delivery systems; the other has not. As time passes the first organization begins to see the impact of improved work processes. It is able to produce goods and services faster, better, and cheaper than its competitor. It has been able to pass a portion of its cost savings on to its customers

	IF YOU DON'T DO WHAT THE CRITERIA REQUIRE . . . *Continued*
	(lowering prices), keeping the rest as increased profit. As a result of better, more timely, and less-expensive products, it is acquiring greater market share—at the expense of its competitor—and making its stockholders exceedingly happy as its share price increases. In addition, the first organization has been able to accelerate performance by sharing improvements with other organizational units so they can get better as well. The organization that does not systematically improve continues to fall further and further behind in a highly competitive environment (or as the popular adage acclaims: today, if you're standing still, you're falling behind). The failure to share effective practices with other organizational support units may cause them to waste time and other resources in redundant work—work that adds cost but not value.

6.1 VALUE CREATION PROCESSES—SAMPLE EFFECTIVE PRACTICES

A. Value Creation Processes (Which Includes Key Business Processes)

- A systematic, iterative process (such as quality function deployment) is used to maintain a focus on the voice of the customer and convert customer requirements into product or service design, production, and delivery.

- Product design requirements are systematically translated into process specifications, with measurement plans to monitor process consistency.

- The work of various functions is coordinated to bring the product or service through the design-to-delivery phases. Functional barriers between units have been eliminated organization-wide.

- Concurrent engineering is used to operate several processes (for example, product and service planning, R&D, manufacturing, marketing, supplier certification) in parallel as much as possible, rather than operating in sequence. All activities are closely coordinated through effective communication and teamwork.

- Internal process capacity and supplier capability, using measures such as C_{pk}, are reviewed and considered before production and delivery process designs or plans are finalized.

- Market, design, production, service, and delivery reviews occur at defined intervals or as needed.

- Steps are taken (such as design testing or prototyping) to ensure that the production and delivery process will work as designed, and will meet customer requirements.

- Design processes are evaluated and improvements are made so that future designs are developed faster (shorter cycle time), at lower cost, and with higher quality, relative to key product or service characteristics that predict customer satisfaction.

- Performance requirements and customer requirements are set using facts and data and are monitored using statistical or other process control techniques.

- Value creation delivery processes are measured and tracked. Measures (quantitative and qualitative) should reflect or assess the extent to which customer requirements are met, as well as production consistency.

- For processes that produce defects (out-of-control processes), root causes are quickly and systematically identified and corrective action is taken to prevent their recurrence.

- Corrections are monitored and verified. Improvements are shared throughout the organization.

- Processes are systematically reviewed to improve productivity, reduce cycle time and waste, and increase quality.

- Tools are used—such as flowcharting, work redesign, and reengineering—throughout the organization to improve work processes.

- Benchmarking, competitive comparison data, or information from customers of the process (in or out of the organization) are used to gain insight to improve processes.

- Information about customer requirements, complaints, concerns, and reactions to products and services are captured "near-real time" and used directly by workers to improve the value creation and delivery processes.

- Key business processes, which are critical to the success of the organization and support core production and delivery activities, are formally identified. For each of these key business processes, a formal process exists to understand customer requirements, translate those requirements into efficient processes, measure their effectiveness, and systematically improve.

- Improvements in key business processes are made with the same rigor and concern for the internal and external customer as improvements in value creation processes.

- All key business processes are subject to continuous review and improvements in performance and customer satisfaction.

- Key business processes are systematically reviewed to improve productivity, reduce cycle time and waste, and increase quality. Improvements in these processes are shared throughout the organization.

6.2 SUPPORT PROCESSES (35 PTS.)
PROCESS

Describe how your organization manages its key processes that support your value creation processes.

Within your response, include answers to the following questions:

a. Support Processes

(1) How does your organization determine its key support processes? What are your key processes for supporting your value creation processes?

(2) How do you determine key support process requirements, incorporating input from internal and external customers, and suppliers and partners, as appropriate? What are the key requirements for these processes?

(3) How do you design these processes to meet all the key requirements? How do you incorporate new technology and organizational knowledge into the design of these processes? How do you incorporate cycle time, productivity, cost control, and other efficiency and effectiveness factors into the design of the processes? How do you implement these processes to ensure they meet design requirements?

(4) What are your key performance measures or indicators used for the control and improvement of your support processes? How does your day-to-day operation of key support processes ensure meeting key performance requirements? How are in-process measures used in managing these processes? How are customer, supplier, and partner input used in managing these processes, as appropriate?

(5) How do you minimize overall costs associated with inspections, tests, and process or performance audits, as appropriate? How do you prevent defects and rework?

(6) How do you improve your support processes to achieve better performance, to reduce variability, and to keep the processes current with business needs and directions? How are improvements shared with other organizational units and processes?

Notes:

N1. Your key support processes are those that are considered most important for support of your organization's value creation processes, employees, and daily operations. These might include finance and accounting, facilities management, legal, human resource, project management, and administration processes.

N2. The results of improvements in your key support processes and key support process performance results should be reported in Item 7.5.

This Item [6.2] looks at the organization's key support processes in order to improve overall operational performance. The organization must ensure its key support processes are designed to meet all internal operational and customer requirements.

The requirements of this Item are similar to the requirements in Item 6.1.

- Support processes are those that support daily operations and product and/or service delivery but are not usually designed in detail with the products and services. The support process requirements usually do not depend significantly upon product and service characteristics. Instead, support process design requirements usually depend significantly upon internal customer requirements, and they must be coordinated and integrated to ensure efficient and effective linkage and performance.

- Support processes might include finance and accounting, software services, public relations, transportation services, food services, human resource services, legal services, plant and facilities management, and secretarial and other administrative services.

As with value creation processes described in Item 6.1, the organization must ensure that the day-to-day operation of its key support processes consistently meets the key performance requirements. To do this, in-process measures are defined to permit rapid identification and correction of potential problems. As with other work processes, key support processes should incorporate mechanisms to obtain and use customer feedback to help identify problems and take prompt, corrective action. The organization should also minimize costs associated with inspection, tests, and audits through use of prevention-based processes, as in Item 6.1.

Finally, organizations should systematically evaluate and improve their key support processes to achieve better performance and to keep them current with changing business needs and directions. Top organizations evaluate and improve the performance of key support processes. Four approaches to evaluating and improving support processes are frequently used:

1. Process analysis and research

2. Benchmarking

3. Use of alternative technology

4. Use of information from customers of the processes

As with value creation processes, a systematic, fact-based approach to improving support processes presents a wide range of possibilities, including complete redesign of key processes or steps within the processes.

6.2 Support Processes

How the organization identifies and manages its key processes that support value creation processes

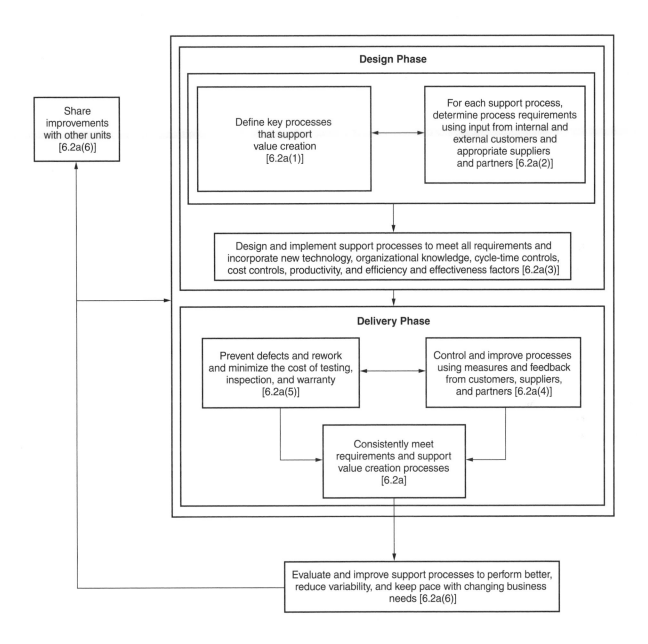

6.2 Support Process Item Linkages

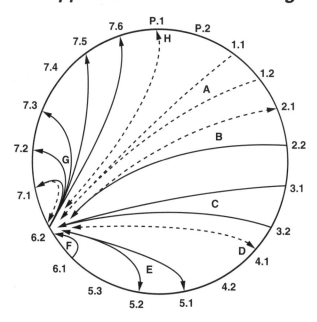

	NATURE OF RELATIONSHIP
A	Senior leaders and the governance system [1.1] have a responsibility for ensuring that support processes are designed [6.2a(2)] consistent with organizational objectives, including those relating to social responsibility and good corporate citizenship [1.2a].
B	Organizational support process strengths and weaknesses [6.2] are considered as part of the planning process [2.1a(2)]. Action plans, deployed to the work force [2.2a], are used to align actions to help ensure that support services [6.2] meet the requirements needed to carry out the action plans.
C	Customer complaints [3.2a(3)], and satisfaction/dissatisfaction [3.2b(1 and 2)] may be used to identify requirements for support processes [6.2a(2)] or provide feedback to help manage those processes [6.2a(4)].
D	Critical support processes [6.2a] may be used to help identify and prioritize benchmarking targets [4.1a(2)]. Benchmarking data [4.1a(2)] are used to improve support work processes [6.2].
E	High-performance work systems [5.1a(1)] and effective recognition [5.1b] and training [5.2a] are essential to improving support work processes [6.2]. In addition, design and delivery of effective support services [6.2] can help promote cooperation and strengthen agility [5.1a(1)] and training [5.2a].
F	Value creation processes [6.1], as customers of support processes [6.2], help define requirements and set priorities for support processes.
G	Information about customer satisfaction [7.1] can be used to target improvement efforts in support processes [6.2]. Improved support processes [6.2] can be reflected in better customer satisfaction [7.1], product and service quality [7.2], financial results [7.3], operational efficiency [7.5], and social responsibility/regulatory compliance [7.6].
H	Information in P.1a(1) derives in part from the support processes [6.2] and helps set the context for examiner review of these processes.

IF YOU DON'T DO WHAT THE CRITERIA REQUIRE . . .	
Item Reference	**Possible Adverse Consequences**
6.2a(1)	The requirements of support processes can vary significantly within an organization depending on the nature of the core products and services that these business processes must support. If a work process has not been identified as a value creation process or key business process, it is a support process, reviewed under the requirements of Item 6.2.
6.2a(2)	An organization that fails to accurately identify the performance and operational requirements of its support processes may find it difficult to design those processes to meet internal customer expectations. When support processes fail to meet requirements, resources are wasted and the achievement of objectives may be jeopardized.
6.2a(3)	Organizations that fail to consider all key operational performance requirements when designing support processes frequently find that the system they design does not meet internal customer requirements. Design flaws produce undesired results and nonconforming support products and services. This, in turn, usually requires even more rework and disrupts core work processes.
6.2a(4)	The failure to consistently meet the requirements of support process customers may increase the likelihood of downstream problems with the design, production, and delivery of core (value creation) products and services. Without key measures or indicators of process performance, it is difficult for employees to determine if a process is working as it should. Without in-process measures, employees must generally wait until they get the results at the end of the line to determine if the support processes worked as intended. The failure to collect and analyze in-process data makes it more difficult for employees to know when to adjust a process to make it work better. Inappropriate or unnecessary adjustments can actually increase variation and decrease product quality. Internal customers can usually determine quickly if the products and services they receive meet requirements. The failure to gather and make timely use of feedback from internal customers makes it more difficult for organizations to reduce rework costs and increase customer satisfaction.
6.2a(5)	High-performing organizations do not rely on excessive inspection and testing to determine if support process requirements are likely to be met. Instead, these organizations develop processes that prevent problems using tools and techniques such as error-proofing. The best that testing or inspection can hope to accomplish is to uncover and correct a problem before the internal customer is disrupted. However, it is still more costly to fix the problem than to prevent it from happening in the first place.
6.2a(6)	Support processes that do not improve may cause the support function to become so ineffective that it becomes a good target for outsourcing. These support process units may not be able to effectively provide critical support to core product and service delivery units within the parent organization and may contribute to the erosion of overall capability in the parent organization. The failure to share effective practices with other organization support units may cause them to waste time and other resources in redundant work—work that adds cost but not value.

6.2 SUPPORT PROCESSES— SAMPLE EFFECTIVE PRACTICES

A. Support Processes

- A formal process exists to understand internal customer requirements for all support processes, translate those requirements into efficient service delivery, and measure their effectiveness.

- Specific improvements in support services are made with the same rigor and concern for the internal and external customer as improvements in value creation processes.

- All key support services are subject to continuous review and improvements in performance and customer satisfaction.

- Systems are in place to ensure process performance is maintained, and customer requirements are met. In-process measures are defined and monitored to ensure early alert of problem.

- Root causes of problems are systematically identified and corrected for processes that produce defects.

- Corrections are monitored and verified. Processes used and results obtained should be systematic and integrated throughout the organization.

- Support processes are systematically reviewed to improve productivity, reduce cycle time and waste, and increase quality. Improvement ideas are routinely implemented and shared throughout the organization.

- Work process simplification and performance improvement tools are applied to support processes with measurable sustained results.

- Measurable goals and related actions are used to drive higher levels of support process performance.

- Benchmarking, competitive comparison data, or information from customers of the process (in or out of the organization) are used to gain insight to improve processes.

7 Business Results—450 Points

*The **Business Results** Category examines your organization's performance and improvement in key business areas—customer satisfaction, product and service performance, financial and marketplace performance, human resource results, operational performance, and governance and social responsibility. Also examined are performance levels relative to those of competitors.*

The Business Results Category provides a results focus that encompasses customers' evaluation of the organization's products and services, overall financial and market performance, the results of all key processes and process improvement activities and governance, fiscal accountability, and ethical behavior as a part of practicing good citizenship.

Through this focus, the Criteria's purposes—superior value of offerings as viewed by customers and the marketplace, superior organizational performance reflected in operational, legal, ethical, and financial indicators, and organizational and personal learning—are maintained. Category 7 can provide "real-time" information (measures of progress) for evaluation and improvement of processes, products, and services, aligned with overall organizational strategy.

Taken together, business results present a balanced scorecard of organizational performance. Historically, businesses have been far too preoccupied with financial performance. Many performance reviews focused almost exclusively on achieving (or failing to achieve) expected levels of financial performance. As such, the results were considered "unbalanced."

- Financial results are considered "lagging" indicators of business success. Financial results are the net of all the good processes, bad processes, satisfied customers, dissatisfied customers, motivated employees, disgruntled employees, effective suppliers, and sloppy suppliers, to name a few. By the time financial indicators become available, bad products and dissatisfied customers have already occurred.

- The second most lagging indicator is customer satisfaction. By definition, customers must experience the product or service before they are in a position to comment on their satisfaction with that product or service. As with financial results, customer satisfaction is affected by many variables including process performance, employee motivation and morale, and supplier performance.

- On the other hand, leading indicators help organizations predict subsequent customer satisfaction and financial performance. Leading indicators include operational effectiveness and employee well-being and satisfaction. Supplier and partner performance, because it affects an organization's own operating performance, is also a leading indicator of customer satisfaction and financial performance.

Taken together, these measures represent a balance between leading and lagging indicators and enable decision makers to identify problems early and take corrective action.

Category 7 requires organizations to report current levels and improvement trends for the following:

- Customer satisfaction and dissatisfaction and customer-perceived value broken out by appropriate customer groups and market segments

- Product and service performance important to customers

- Financial and marketplace performance

- Human resource performance including work systems, employee learning, and employee well-being and satisfaction

- Operational performance such as cycle time, productivity, supplier performance, and the accomplishment of organizational strategy and action plans

- Governance and social responsibility including fiscal accountability, ethical behavior, regulatory and legal compliance, and support of key communities

For all of these areas, organizations must include appropriate comparative data to enable examiners to define what "good" means. Otherwise, even though performance may be improving, it is difficult to determine whether the level of performance is good.

7.1 CUSTOMER-FOCUSED RESULTS (75 PTS.)
RESULTS

Summarize your organization's key customer-focused results, including customer satisfaction and customer-perceived value. Segment your results by customer groups and market segments, as appropriate. Include appropriate comparative data.

Provide data and information to answer the following questions:

a. Customer-Focused Results

(1) What are your current levels and trends in key measures or indicators of customer satisfaction and dissatisfaction? How do these compare with competitors' levels of customer satisfaction?

(2) What are your current levels and trends in key measures or indicators of customer-perceived value, including customer loyalty and retention, positive referral, and other aspects of building relationships with customers, as appropriate?

Notes:

N1. Customer satisfaction and dissatisfaction results reported in this Item should relate to determination methods and data described in Item 3.2.

N2. Measures and indicators of customers' satisfaction with your products and services relative to customers' satisfaction with competitors might include objective information and data from your customers and from independent organizations.

Item 7.1 looks at the organization's customer-focused performance results to demonstrate how well the organization has been satisfying its customers and delivering product and service quality that lead to satisfaction, loyalty, and positive referral.

Organizations must provide data to demonstrate current levels, trends, and appropriate comparisons for key measures and/or indicators of:

- Customer satisfaction, dissatisfaction, and satisfaction relative to competitors

- Customer loyalty (retention), positive referral, and customer-perceived value

- Product and service performance relating to key drivers of customers' satisfaction and retention

Top-performing organizations use all relevant data to determine and help predict the organization's performance as viewed by customers. Relevant data and information include:

- Customer satisfaction and dissatisfaction

- Retention, gains, and losses of customers and customer accounts

- Customer complaints and warranty claims

- Customer-perceived value based on quality and price

- Awards, ratings, and recognition from customers and independent rating organizations

Organizations should provide appropriate comparisons for key measures and/or indicators to permit the assessment of the strength or "goodness" of the organization's performance.

7.1 Customer-Focused Results

The organization's key customer-focused results, customer satisfaction, and customer-perceived value

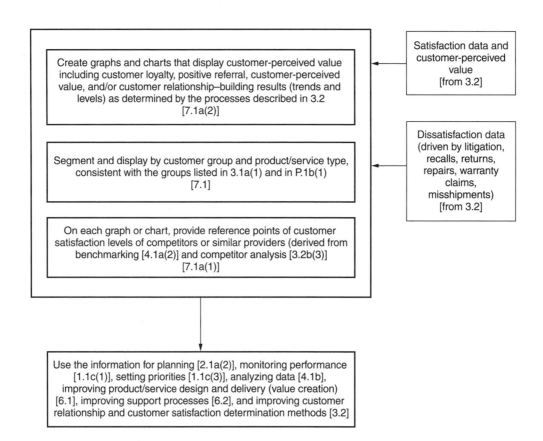

Create graphs and charts that display customer-perceived value including customer loyalty, positive referral, customer-perceived value, and/or customer relationship–building results (trends and levels) as determined by the processes described in 3.2
[7.1a(2)]

Segment and display by customer group and product/service type, consistent with the groups listed in 3.1a(1) and in P.1b(1)
[7.1]

On each graph or chart, provide reference points of customer satisfaction levels of competitors or similar providers (derived from benchmarking [4.1a(2)] and competitor analysis [3.2b(3)]
[7.1a(1)]

Satisfaction data and customer-perceived value
[from 3.2]

Dissatisfaction data (driven by litigation, recalls, returns, repairs, warranty claims, misshipments)
[from 3.2]

Use the information for planning [2.1a(2)], monitoring performance [1.1c(1)], setting priorities [1.1c(3)], analyzing data [4.1b], improving product/service design and delivery (value creation) [6.1], improving support processes [6.2], and improving customer relationship and customer satisfaction determination methods [3.2]

7.1 Customer-Focused Results Item Linkages

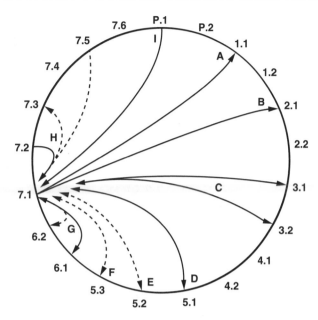

	NATURE OF RELATIONSHIP
A	Data on levels of satisfaction of customers [7.1] are monitored by senior leaders [1.1c(1)].
B	Data on customer satisfaction and loyalty [7.1a(2)] are used for strategic planning [2.1a(2)].
C	Processes used to gather intelligence about current customer requirements [3.1a(2)], strength of customer relations [3.2a(1)], and to determine customer satisfaction [3.2b(1)] produce customer satisfaction results data [7.1a]. In addition, customer satisfaction results [7.1] are used to help set customer-contact requirements (service standards) [3.2a(2)] and better understand customer requirements and preferences [3.1a(2)].
D	Recognition and rewards [5.1a] should be based, in part, on customer satisfaction results [7.1]. Innovation, empowerment, and initiative developed by effective work systems [5.1a] can foster better customer satisfaction [7.1]
E	Customer satisfaction data [7.1] are monitored, in part, to assess training effectiveness [5.2a(6)]. In addition, results pertaining to customer satisfaction [7.1] can be improved with effective training [5.2].
F	Systems to enhance employee motivation, satisfaction, and well-being (including disaster prevention and recovery systems) [5.3] can produce higher levels of customer satisfaction [7.1]. Improved customer satisfaction can affect the morale and motivation of customer-contact employees.

Continued

NATURE OF RELATIONSHIP		*Continued*
G	Data on satisfaction and dissatisfaction of customers [7.1a(1)] are used to help design and improve value creation [6.1] and support [6.2] processes. These processes [6.1 and 6.2] have a direct effect on customer satisfaction/dissatisfaction and loyalty [7.1].	
H	Better product and service quality [7.2] and operational [7.5a] results can enhance customer-focused results [7.1]. Better customer satisfaction [7.1] can improve financial and market performance [7.3].	
I	The information in P.1b(1) helps examiners identify the kind of results, broken out by customer and market segment, that should be reported in Item 7.1.	

IF YOU DON'T DO WHAT THE CRITERIA REQUIRE . . .	
Item Reference	Possible Adverse Consequences
7.1	Failing to provide comparison data makes it difficult for leaders (or Baldrige examiners) to determine if the level of performance reported is good. Failing to provide results data for at least most areas of importance to the organization makes it difficult to determine if performance is getting better in key areas. Finally, the failure to provide this information as part of a Baldrige Award assessment is likely to reduce the score and may even prevent an organization from receiving a site visit (during which time additional results data are usually obtained).

7.1 CUSTOMER-FOCUSED RESULTS—SAMPLE EFFECTIVE RESULTS

A. Customer-Focused Results

- Trends and indicators of customer satisfaction and dissatisfaction (including complaint data), segmented by customer groups, are provided in graph and chart form for all key measures. Multiyear data are provided.

- All indicators show steady improvement. (Indicators include data collected in Area 3.2b, such as customer assessments of products and services, customer awards, and customer retention.)

- All indicators compare favorably to competitors or similar providers.

- Graphs and information are accurate and easy to understand.

- Data are not missing.

- Results data are supported by customer feedback, customers' overall assessments of products and services, customer awards, and indicators from design and production/delivery processes of products and services.

7.2 PRODUCT AND SERVICE RESULTS (75 PTS.)
RESULTS

Summarize your organization's key product and service performance results. Segment your results by product groups, customer groups, and market segments, as appropriate. Include appropriate comparative data.

Provide data and information to answer the following questions:

a. Product and Service Results

What are your current levels and trends in key measures or indicators of product and service performance that are important to your customers? How do these results compare with competitors' performance?

Note:

Product and service results reported in this Item should relate to the key product and service features identified as customer requirements or expectations in P.1b(2) based on information gathered in Items 3.1 and 3.2. The measures or indicators should address factors that affect customer preference, such as those included in P.1, Note 3 and Item 3.1, Note 3.

Item 7.2 looks at the organization's product and service quality results to demonstrate how well the organization has been delivering products and services that lead to satisfaction, loyalty, and positive referral.

Organizations must provide data to demonstrate current levels, trends, and appropriate comparisons for key measures and/or indicators of product and service performance relating to key drivers of customers' satisfaction and retention as well as indicators of customers' views and decisions relative to future purchases and relationships. These measures of product and service performance are derived from customer-related information gathered in Items 3.1 and 3.2.

The correlations between product and service performance and customer indicators are a critical tool that helps managers:

- Define and focus on key quality and customer requirements.

- Identify product and service differentiators in the marketplace.

- Determine cause–effect relationships between your product and service attributes and evidence of customer satisfaction and loyalty, as well as positive referrals.

The correlations might reveal emerging or changing market segments, the changing importance of requirements, or even the potential obsolescence of offerings.

Product/service performance results appropriate for recording in this Item might be based upon one or more of the following:

- Internal (organizational) measurements

- Field performance

- Data collected by the organization or for the organization

- Customer surveys on product and service performance

- Attributes that cannot be accurately assessed through direct measurement (for example, ease of use) or when variability in customer expectations makes the customer's perception the most meaningful indicator (for example, courtesy)

7.2 Product and Service Results

Key product and service performance results segmented by product groups, customer groups, and market segments

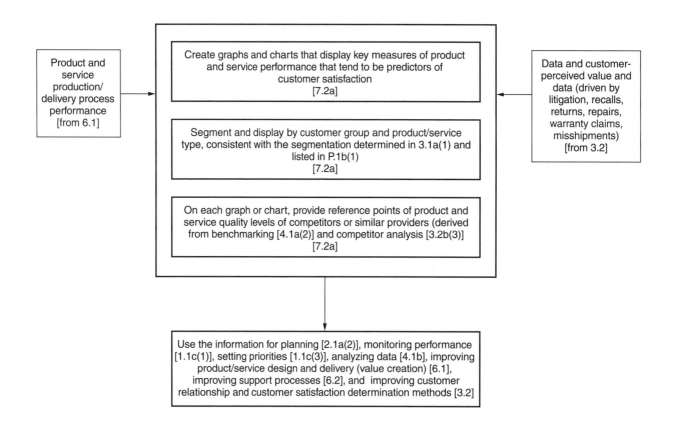

7.2 Product and Service Results Item Linkages

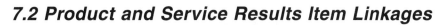

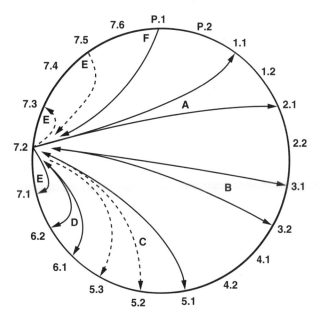

NATURE OF RELATIONSHIP	
A	Data on product and service quality [7.2] are monitored by senior leaders [1.1c(1)] and are used for strategic planning [2.1a(2)].
B	Processes used to gather intelligence about current customer requirements [3.1a(2)], strength of customer relations [3.2a(1)], and to determine customer satisfaction [3.2b(1)] produce product and service results data [7.2]. In addition, product and service quality results [7.2] are used to help set customer-contact requirements (service standards) [3.2a(2)] and better understand customer requirements and preferences [3.1a(2)].
C	Recognition and rewards [5.1a] should be based, in part, on product and service quality results [7.2]. Innovation, empowerment, and initiative developed by effective work systems [5.1a] can foster better product and service quality [7.2] Product and service quality data [7.2] are monitored, in part, to assess training effectiveness [5.2]. In addition, results pertaining to product and service quality [7.2] can be improved with effective training [5.2]. Systems to enhance employee motivation, satisfaction, and well-being (including disaster-prevention and recovery systems) [5.3] can produce higher levels of product and service quality [7.2]. Improved product and service quality can affect the morale and motivation of customer-contact employees.
D	Data on product and service quality [7.2] may be used to help design and improve value creation [6.1] and support [6.2] processes. These processes [6.1 and 6.2] can have a direct effect on product and service quality [7.2].
E	Better product and service quality [7.2] results can enhance customer-focused results [7.1]. Better product and service quality [7.2] can improve financial and market performance [7.3].
F	The information in P.1b(1) helps examiners identify the kind of product and service quality results, broken out by customer and market segment, that should be reported in Item 7.2.

IF YOU DON'T DO WHAT THE CRITERIA REQUIRE . . .	
Item Reference	**Possible Adverse Consequences**
7.2	Failing to provide comparison data makes it difficult for leaders (or Baldrige examiners) to determine if the level of performance reported is good or not. Failing to provide results data for at least most areas of importance to the organization makes it difficult to determine if performance is getting better in key areas. Finally, the failure to provide this information as part of a Baldrige Award assessment is likely to reduce the score and may even prevent an organization from receiving a site visit (during which time additional results data are usually obtained).

7.2 PRODUCT AND SERVICE RESULTS—SAMPLE EFFECTIVE RESULTS

A. Product and Service Results

- Data are presented for the most relevant product or service quality indicators collected through the processes described in Item 3.2 (some of which may be referenced in the Organizational Profile).

- Operational data are presented that correlate with, and help predict, customer satisfaction. These data show consistently improving trends and levels that compare favorably with competitors.

- All indicators show steady improvement. (Indicators include data collected in Item 6.1, such as product and service quality levels and on-time delivery.)

- All or most indicators compare favorably to competitors or similar providers.

- Graphs and information are accurate and easy to understand.

- Data are not missing.

7.3 FINANCIAL AND MARKET RESULTS (75 PTS.)
RESULTS

Summarize your organization's key financial and marketplace performance results by market segments, as appropriate. Include appropriate comparative data.

Provide data and information to answer the following questions:

a. Financial and Market Results

(1) What are your current levels and trends in key measures or indicators of financial performance, including aggregate measures of financial return and economic value, as appropriate?

(2) What are your current levels and trends in key measures or indicators of marketplace performance, including market share or position, business growth, and new markets entered, as appropriate?

Note:

Responses to 7.3a(1) might include aggregate measures such as return on investment (ROI), asset utilization, operating margins, profitability, profitability by market or customer segment, liquidity, debt to equity ratio, value added per employee, and financial activity measures.

Item 7.3 looks at the organization's financial and market results to provide a complete picture of financial and marketplace success and challenges.

Organizations should provide data demonstrating levels, trends, and appropriate comparisons for key financial, market, and business indicators. Measures reported in this Item are used by senior leaders to assess organization-level performance.

- Appropriate financial measures and indicators might include:

  - Revenue
  - Profits
  - Market position
  - Order-to-cash cycle time
  - Earnings per share
  - Returns

- Marketplace performance measures might include:

  - Market share
  - Measures of business growth
  - New product and geographic markets entered (including exports)
  - Entry into e-commerce markets
  - Percent of sales from new products

Organizations should provide appropriate comparisons for key measures and/or indicators to permit the assessment of the strength or "goodness" of the organization's performance.

7.3 Financial and Market Results

Results of improvement efforts using key measures and/or indicators of financial and market performance

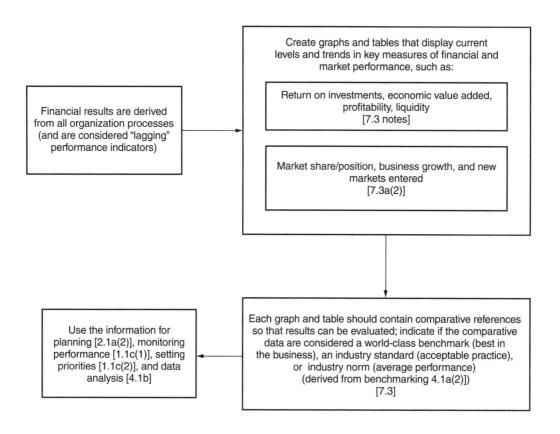

Financial results are derived from all organization processes (and are considered "lagging" performance indicators)

Create graphs and tables that display current levels and trends in key measures of financial and market performance, such as:

Return on investments, economic value added, profitability, liquidity
[7.3 notes]

Market share/position, business growth, and new markets entered
[7.3a(2)]

Each graph and table should contain comparative references so that results can be evaluated; indicate if the comparative data are considered a world-class benchmark (best in the business), an industry standard (acceptable practice), or industry norm (average performance) (derived from benchmarking 4.1a(2)])
[7.3]

Use the information for planning [2.1a(2)], monitoring performance [1.1c(1)], setting priorities [1.1c(2)], and data analysis [4.1b]

7.3 Financial and Market Results Item Linkages

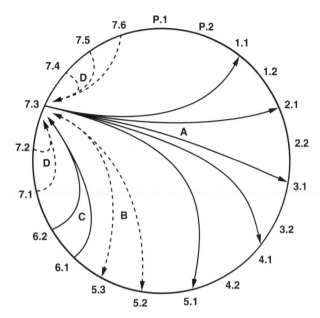

	NATURE OF RELATIONSHIP
A	Financial [7.3a] and market [7.3b] results are used for strategic planning [2.1a(2)]; understanding market requirements and customer preferences [3.1a(2)]; leadership monitoring [1.1c(1)]; priority setting [1.1c(3)]; and analysis [4.1b].
B	Financial results [7.3a] are monitored, in part, to assess training effectiveness [5.2] and could be used as a partial basis for compensation, recognition, and reward [5.1b]. In addition, results pertaining to financial and market performance [7.3a], reflect, in part, training effectiveness [5.2]. Employee motivation and well-being [5.3] affect financial performance results [7.3], and vice versa.
C	Financial [7.3a] and market [7.3b] results are enhanced by improvements in value creation processes [6.1] and support processes [6.2]. Those processes may be modified or improved based on financial and market performance.
D	Better financial [7.3a] and market [7.3b] results (lagging indicators) can be driven by better customer satisfaction [7.1], product and service quality [7.2], employee motivation and morale [7.4], operational effectiveness [7.5] results, and compliance with laws and regulations and good ethical behavior [7.6].

IF YOU DON'T DO WHAT THE CRITERIA REQUIRE . . .	
Item Reference	**Possible Adverse Consequences**
7.3	Failing to provide comparison data makes it difficult for leaders (or Baldrige examiners) to determine if the level of performance reported is good. Failing to provide results data for at least most areas of importance to the organization makes it difficult to determine if performance is getting better in key areas. Finally, the failure to provide this information as part of a Baldrige Award assessment is likely to reduce the score and may even prevent an organization from receiving a site visit (during which time additional results data are usually obtained).

7.3 FINANCIAL AND MARKET RESULTS—SAMPLE EFFECTIVE RESULTS

A. Financial and Market Results

- Key measures and indicators of organization market and financial performance address the following areas:

  - Effective use of materials, energy, capital, and assets

  - Asset utilization

  - Market share, business growth, new markets entered, and market shifting

  - Return on equity

  - Operating margins

  - Pre-tax profit

  - Earnings per share

  - Generating enough revenue to cover expenses (not-for-profit and public sector)

  - Operating within budget (government sector)

- Measures and indicators show steady improvement.

- All key financial and market data are presented.

- Comparative data include industry best, best competitor, and other appropriate benchmarks.

7.4 HUMAN RESOURCE RESULTS (75 PTS.)
RESULTS

Summarize your organization's key human resource results, including work system performance, and employee learning, development, well-being, and satisfaction. Segment your results to address the diversity of your workforce and the different types and categories of employees, as appropriate. Include appropriate comparative data.

Provide data and information to answer the following questions:

a. Human Resource Results

(1) What are your current levels and trends in key measures or indicators of work system performance and effectiveness?

(2) What are your current levels and trends in key measures of employee learning and development?

(3) What are your current levels and trends in key measures or indicators of employee well-being, satisfaction, and dissatisfaction?

Notes:

N1. Results reported in this Item should relate to activities described in Category 5. Your results should be responsive to key process needs described in Category 6 and to your organization's action plans and human resource plans described in Item 2.2.

N2. Appropriate measures and indicators of work system performance and effectiveness [7.4a(1)] might include job and job classification simplification, job rotation, work layout improvement, employee retention and internal promotion rates, and changing supervisory ratios.

N3. Appropriate measures and indicators of employee learning and development [7.4a(2)] might include innovation and suggestion rates, courses completed, learning, on-the-job performance improvements, and cross-training rates.

N4. For appropriate measures of employee well-being and satisfaction [7.4a(3)], see item 5.3 Notes.

Item 7.4 looks at the organization's human resource results to demonstrate how well the organization has created, maintained, and enhanced a positive, productive, learning, and caring work environment.

Organizations should provide data demonstrating current levels, trends, and appropriate comparisons for key measures and/or indicators of employee well-being, satisfaction, dissatisfaction, and development.

The best-performing organizations also provide data and information on the organization's work system performance and effectiveness, showing favorable comparisons with industry leaders.

- Results reported might include generic or organization-specific factors.

  - Generic factors might include: safety, absenteeism, turnover, satisfaction, and complaints (grievances). For some measures, such as absenteeism and turnover, local or regional comparisons may be most appropriate.

  - Organization-specific factors are related to the human resource results of employee well-being and satisfaction. These factors might include: extent of training or cross-training, and the extent and success of systems that promote self-directed and empowered employees.

- Results measures reported for work system performance might include: improvement in job classification, job rotation, work layout, and improved employee decision making. Results reported might include input data, such as extent of training, but the emphasis should be on data that show effectiveness and improvement of outcomes.

Organizations should provide appropriate comparisons for key measures and/or indicators to permit the assessment of the strength or "goodness" of the organization's performance.

7.4 Human Resource Results

Results of human resource improvement efforts using key measures and/or indicators of such performance

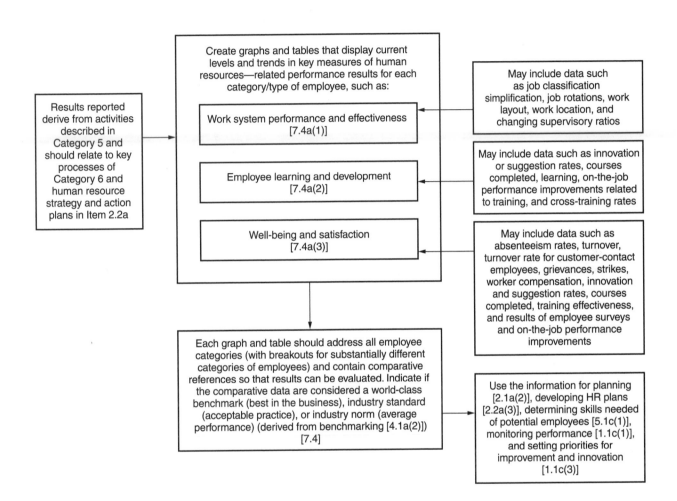

Results reported derive from activities described in Category 5 and should relate to key processes of Category 6 and human resource strategy and action plans in Item 2.2a

Create graphs and tables that display current levels and trends in key measures of human resources—related performance results for each category/type of employee, such as:

Work system performance and effectiveness [7.4a(1)]

Employee learning and development [7.4a(2)]

Well-being and satisfaction [7.4a(3)]

May include data such as job classification simplification, job rotations, work layout, work location, and changing supervisory ratios

May include data such as innovation or suggestion rates, courses completed, learning, on-the-job performance improvements related to training, and cross-training rates

May include data such as absenteeism rates, turnover, turnover rate for customer-contact employees, grievances, strikes, worker compensation, innovation and suggestion rates, courses completed, training effectiveness, and results of employee surveys and on-the-job performance improvements

Each graph and table should address all employee categories (with breakouts for substantially different categories of employees) and contain comparative references so that results can be evaluated. Indicate if the comparative data are considered a world-class benchmark (best in the business), industry standard (acceptable practice), or industry norm (average performance) (derived from benchmarking [4.1a(2)]) [7.4]

Use the information for planning [2.1a(2)], developing HR plans [2.2a(3)], determining skills needed of potential employees [5.1c(1)], monitoring performance [1.1c(1)], and setting priorities for improvement and innovation [1.1c(3)]

7.4 Human Resource Results—Item Linkages

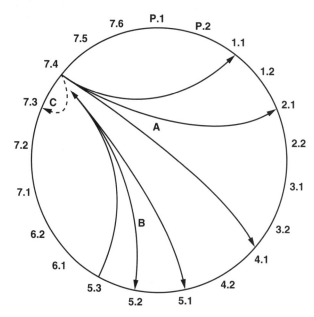

	NATURE OF RELATIONSHIP
A	Human resource results [7.4] are reported and used for planning [2.1a(2)], for monitoring organizational performance [1.1c(1)], and analysis [4.1b].
B	Human resource results derive from and are enhanced by improving work systems and enhancing flexibility, and by strengthening employee recognition systems [5.1], training [5.2], and well-being and satisfaction [5.3]. In addition, human resource results data [7.4] are monitored, in part, to assess training effectiveness [5.2].
C	Better financial [7.3a] and market [7.3b] results (lagging indicators) can be driven by better employee motivation and morale [7.4].

IF YOU DON'T DO WHAT THE CRITERIA REQUIRE . . .	
Item Reference	**Possible Adverse Consequences**
7.4	Failing to provide comparison data makes it difficult for leaders (or Baldrige examiners) to determine if the level of performance reported is good or not. Failing to provide results data for at least most areas of importance to the organization makes it difficult to determine if performance is getting better in key areas. Finally, the failure to provide this information as part of a Baldrige Award assessment is likely to reduce the score and may even prevent an organization from receiving a site visit (during which time additional results data are usually obtained).

7.4 HUMAN RESOURCE RESULTS—SAMPLE EFFECTIVE RESULTS

A. Human Resource Results

- The results reported in Item 7.4 derive from activities described in Category 5 and the human resource plans from Item 2.2a(3).

- Multiyear data are provided to show sustained performance.

- All results show steady improvement.

- Data are not missing. If human resource results are declared important, related data are reported.

- Comparison data for benchmark or competitor organizations are reported, and the organization compares favorably.

- Trend data are reported for employee satisfaction with working conditions, safety, retirement package, and other employee benefits. Satisfaction with management is also reported.

- Trends for declining absenteeism, grievances, employee turnover, strikes, and worker compensation claims are reported.

- Data reported are segmented for all employee categories.

7.5 ORGANIZATIONAL EFFECTIVENESS RESULTS (75 PTS.)
RESULTS

Summarize your organization's key operational performance results that contribute to the achievement of organizational effectiveness. Segment your results by product groups and market segments, as appropriate. Include appropriate comparative data.

Provide data and information to answer the following questions:

a. Organizational Effectiveness Results

(1) What are your current levels and trends in key measures or indicators of the operational performance of your key value creation processes? Include productivity, cycle time, supplier and partner performance, and other appropriate measures of effectiveness and efficiency.

(2) What are your current levels and trends in key measures or indicators of the operational performance of your key support processes? Include productivity, cycle time, supplier and partner performance, and other appropriate measures of effectiveness and efficiency.

(3) What are your results for key measures or indicators of accomplishment of organizational strategy and action plans?

Notes:

N1. Results reported in Item 7.5 should address your key operational requirements and progress toward accomplishment of your key organizational performance goals as presented in the Organizational Profile and in Items 1.1, 2.2, 6.1, and 6.2. Include results not reported in Items 7.1–7.4.

N2. Results reported in Item 7.5 should provide key information for analysis (Item 4.1) and review of your organizational performance (Item 1.1) and should provide the operational basis for customer-focused results (Item 7.1), product and service results (Item 7.2), and financial and market results (Item 7.3).

Item 7.5 looks at the organization's key operational performance results to demonstrate organizational effectiveness in both value creation and support processes and the achievement of key goals and strategic objectives. Organizations should provide data in this item if it does not belong in other Category 7 Items (7.1, 7.2, 7.3, 7.4, or 7.6).

This item encourages the organization to develop and include unique and innovative measures to track business development and operational improvement. However, all key areas of business and operational performance should be covered by measures that are relevant and important to the organization.

Measures and/or indicators of operational effectiveness and efficiency might include:

- Reduced emission levels, waste-stream reductions, by-product use, and recycling

- Internal responsiveness indicators such as cycle times, production flexibility, lead times, set-up times, and time to market

- Business-specific indicators such as innovation rates and increased use of e-technology, product and process yields, Six Sigma initiative results, and delivery performance to request

- Supply chain indicators such as reductions in inventory and incoming inspections, increases in quality and productivity, improvements in electronic data exchange, and reductions in supply chain management costs

- Indicators of strategic goal achievement

Organizations should provide appropriate comparisons for key measures and/or indicators to permit the assessment of the strength or "goodness" of the organization's performance.

7.5 Organizational Effectiveness Results

Results of improvement efforts that contribute to achievement of organizational effectiveness

Organizational Effectiveness Results

Create graphs and tables that display current levels of sustained trends of key operational performance results that contribute to strategic objectives

Key process performance improvement results are derived from *value creation* processes in Items 6.1, including productivity, cycle time, supplier and partner performance, and other efficiency and effectiveness measures important to the organization
[7.5a(1)]

Key process performance improvement results are derived from *support* processes in Items 6.2, including productivity, cycle time, supplier and partner performance, and other efficiency and effectiveness measures important to the organization
[7.5a(2)]

Results supporting accomplishment of strategy and action plans
[7.5a(3)]

Each graph and table should contain comparative references so that results can be evaluated; indicate if the comparative data are considered a world-class benchmark (best in the business), or industry norm (average performance) (derived from benchmarking [4.1a(2)])
[7.5]

Results provide data for analysis [4.1b] and performance review
[1.1c(1)]

7.5 Organizational Effectiveness Results Item Linkages

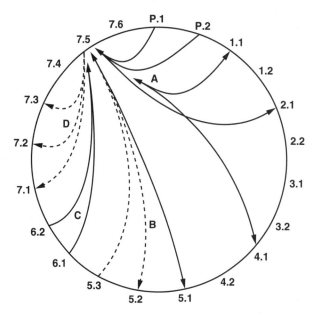

	NATURE OF RELATIONSHIP
A	Organizational effectiveness results [7.5] are reported and used for planning [2.1a(2)], management improvement, performance monitoring and priority setting [1.1c], and analysis [4.1b]. Progress in addressing strategic challenges, as described in P.2b, and strategic objectives listed in 2.1b(1), should be reported in Item 7.5a(3). [Note that the strategic challenges identified in P.2b should be consistent with the strategic objectives in 2.1b(1).] Performance related to the key suppliers and distributors listed in P.1b(2) should be reported in 7.5a(1 and 2)].
B	Organizational effectiveness results [7.5] are used to provide employee feedback and drive rewards and recognition [5.1b] and training and employee development [5.2]. Processes to improve employee initiative and flexibility [5.1a(1)] and employee safety, security, morale, motivation, and well-being [5.3], and better align recognition and reward to desired performance outcomes [5.1b] may enhance performance results [7.5].
C	Designing value creation processes to meet customer requirements [6.1a(3)] and improve product and service delivery and consistency [6.1a(4)] and support service processes [6.2] should affect organizational effectiveness performance outcomes [7.5].
D	Organizational effectiveness results [7.5] contribute to financial and market results [7.3], product and service quality [7.2], and customer-focused results [7.1].

IF YOU DON'T DO WHAT THE CRITERIA REQUIRE . . .	
Item Reference	**Possible Adverse Consequences**
7.5	Failing to provide comparison data makes it difficult for leaders (or Baldrige examiners) to determine if the level of performance reported is good. Failing to provide results data for at least most areas of importance to the organization makes it difficult to determine if performance is getting better in key areas. Finally, the failure to provide this information as part of a Baldrige Award assessment is likely to reduce the score and may even prevent an organization from receiving a site visit (during which time additional results data are usually obtained).

7.5 ORGANIZATIONAL EFFECTIVENESS RESULTS— SAMPLE EFFECTIVE RESULTS

A. Organizational Effectiveness Results

- Indices and trend data are provided in graph and chart form for all operational performance measures identified in 1.1, 6.1, and 6.2, relevant organizational goals (2.2) and strategic objectives (2.1b), and the key business factors identified in the Organizational Profile and not reported elsewhere in Category 7. Multiyear data are reported.

- Most to all indicators show steady improvement.

- Product and service quality measures and indicators address requirements such as accuracy, timeliness, and reliability. Examples include defect levels, repeat services, meeting product or service delivery or response times, and availability levels. However, if these measures predict customer satisfaction, they should be moved to Item 7.1.

- Operational performance measures address:

  - Productivity, efficiency, and effectiveness, such as productivity indices, and product/service design improvement measures

  - Cycle-time reductions

- Comparative data include industry best, best competitor, industry average, and appropriate benchmarks. Data are also derived from independent surveys, studies, laboratory testing, or other sources.

- Data are not missing. (For example, do not show a steady trend from 1999 to 2003 but leave out 2002.)

- Data are not aggregated, since aggregation tends to hide poor performance by blending it with good performance. Charts and graphs break out and report trends separately.

7.6 GOVERNANCE AND SOCIAL RESPONSIBILITY RESULTS (75 PTS.) RESULTS

Summarize your organization's key governance and social responsibility results, including evidence of fiscal accountability, ethical behavior, legal compliance, and organizational citizenship. Segment your results by business units, as appropriate. Include appropriate comparative data.

Provide data and information to answer the following questions:

a. Governance and Social Responsibility Results

(1) What are your key current findings and trends in key measures or indicators of fiscal accountability, both internal and external, as appropriate?

(2) What are your results for key measures or indicators of ethical behavior and of stakeholder trust in the governance of your organization?

(3) What are your results for key measures or indicators of regulatory and legal compliance?

(4) What are your results for key measures or indicators of organizational citizenship in support of your key communities?

Notes:

N1. Responses to 7.6a(1) might include financial statement issues and risks, important internal and external auditor recommendations, and management's response to these matters.

N2. For examples of measures of ethical behavior and stakeholder trust [7.6a(2)], see Note 2 to Item 1.2.

N3. Regulatory and legal compliance results [7.6a(3)] should address requirements described in 1.2a. Organizational citizenship results [7.6a(4)] should address support for the key communities discussed in 1.2c.

Item 7.6 looks at key results in the area of social responsibility that reflect the behavior of an ethical organization that is a good citizen in its communities. In this Item, provide data and information on key measures or indicators of organizational accountability, stakeholder trust, and ethical behavior as well as regulatory and legal compliance and citizenship.

Although there is an increased focus nationally on issues of governance, ethics, and board and leadership accountability, the best-performing organizations practice and demonstrate high standards of overall conduct. The failure to do so may threaten an organization's public trust, which may threaten its long-term success, if not its survival. Boards and senior leaders should track performance measures that relate to governance and social responsibility on a regular basis and emphasize this performance in stakeholder communications.

Measures should include environmental and regulatory compliance and highlight noteworthy achievements in these areas, as appropriate. Results also should include indicators of support for key communities and other public purposes.

Summarize and report any sanctions or adverse findings (including independent audit findings) under law, regulation, or contract the organization has received during the past three years, including the nature of the incidents and their current status.

Organizations should provide appropriate comparisons for key measures and/or indicators to permit the assessment of the strength or "goodness" of the organization's performance.

7.6 Governance and Social Responsibility Results

Results of improvement efforts that contribute to achievement of key governance and social responsibility results, including fiscal accountability ethical behavior, legal compliance, and organizational citizenship

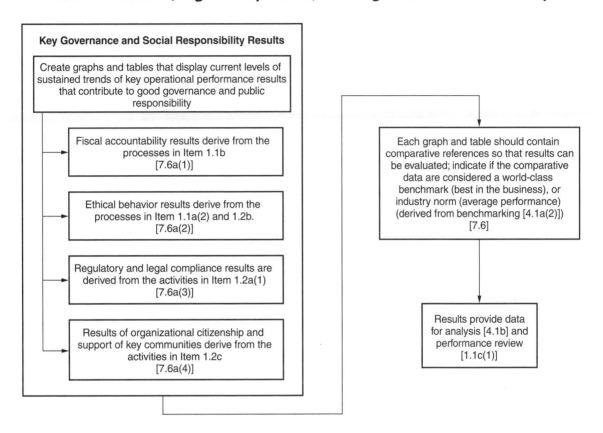

7.6 Governance and Social Responsibility Results Item Linkages

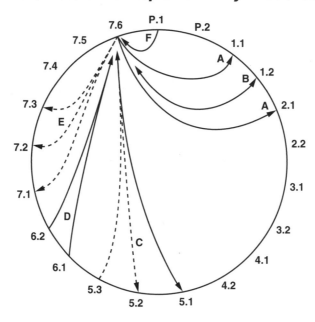

	NATURE OF RELATIONSHIP
A	Governance and social responsibility results that relate to fiscal accountability, ethical behavior, and regulatory compliance [7.6a(1, 2, and 3)] are used for planning [2.1a(2)], management improvement, performance monitoring, and priority setting [1.1c].
B	Results for regulatory and legal compliance and citizenship, related to the activities in Item 1.2, should be reported in 7.5b. In addition, these results are monitored to determine if process changes are needed.
C	Employee motivation, satisfaction, and well-being [5.3] affect governance, and social responsibility results may affect ethical behavior and regulatory compliance [7.6a(2 and 3)]. In addition, results pertaining to these key areas [7.6] should be reflected, in part, in employee feedback [5.1b] and are monitored to assess training effectiveness [5.2].
D	Product and service delivery and consistency [6.1] and support service processes [6.2] affect regulatory compliance and possible ethical results [7.6a(2 and 3)].
E	Governance and social responsibility results [7.6] may affect financial and market results [7.3], product and service quality [7.2], and customer-focused results [7.1].
F	The regulatory requirements described in P.1a(5) define the related performance results that should be reported in 7.6a(3).

IF YOU DON'T DO WHAT THE CRITERIA REQUIRE . . .	
Item Reference	Possible Adverse Consequences
7.6	Failing to provide comparison data makes it difficult for leaders (or Baldrige examiners) to determine if the level of performance reported is good. Failing to provide results data for at least most areas of importance to the organization makes it difficult to determine if performance is getting better in key areas. Finally, the failure to provide this information as part of a Baldrige Award assessment is likely to reduce the score and may even prevent an organization from receiving a site visit (during which time additional results data are usually obtained).

7.6 GOVERNANCE AND SOCIAL RESPONSIBILITY RESULTS— SAMPLE EFFECTIVE RESULTS

A. Governance and Social Responsibility Results

- Indices and trend data are provided in graph and chart form for all regulatory and legal compliance requirements identified in Item 1.2(1) and P.1a(5).

- Results address public responsibilities such as environmental improvements and the increased use of technologies, materials, and work processes that are environmentally friendly.

- Ethical behavior is demonstrated by a large percentage of independent board members. In addition, independent audits demonstrate full compliance with ethics rules established by the organization.

- Areas of community support demonstrate increasing efforts to strengthen local community services, education, and health care, the environment, and related trade and business associations.

- Data indicate most measures of regulatory compliance exceed requirements. Performance is leading the industry. No sanctions or violations have been reported.

- Data show sustained improvements in waste reduction and energy efficiency.

- Resources allocated to support key communities, consistent with business strategy, demonstrate positive desired results, increasing in effectiveness over time.

- Most to all indicators show steady improvement.

- Comparative data include industry best, best competitor, industry average, and appropriate benchmarks. Data are also derived from independent surveys, studies, laboratory testing, or other sources.

- Data are not missing. (For example, do not show a steady trend from 1998 to 2002, but leave out 2001.)

- Data are not aggregated, since aggregation tends to hide poor performance by blending it with good performance. Charts and graphs break out and report trends separately.

Tips on Preparing a Baldrige Award Application

Applications are put together by every conceivable combination of teams, committees, and individual efforts, including consultants. There is no "right" or "best" way to do it. There are, however, lessons that have been learned and are worth considering because they contribute to people and organizations growing and improving.

Author's note: Gathering process information from across the organization is essential to prepare an accurate and complete Baldrige application. Over the past several years, I have helped many organizations conduct assessments and apply for awards. During this time, I have prepared a Microsoft® Word template to help writing teams gather information and prepare to write. The application template provided on the CD that is included with this book facilitates the collection of critical information and makes it easier to write a Baldrige application. A sample of the completed portion of the template appears in Figure 32.

The thoughts that follow are intended to generate conversation and learning. They are not intended to present a comprehensive treatment of the subject.

Getting the Fingerprints of the Organization on the Application

How do we put together a "good" application? To be "good" from a technical perspective, it must both be accurate and respond fully to the multiple requirements of the Criteria.

To be effective, the application must be more than technically accurate. The organization must reflect a sense of commitment and ownership for the application. Ownership requires a role for people throughout the organization as well as top leadership. The actual "putting of words on paper" can be accomplished in a variety of ways. However, ignoring this larger question of ownership exposes the organization to developing a sterile, disjointed, or unrecognizable document that diminishes its value as a vehicle of growth.

The Spirit and Values in an Application

Like it or not, the team or individual that is responsible for developing an application will be closely watched by everyone in the organization. The people coordinating the development of the application need to be perceived as "walking the talk." They need to be seen as believers and role models for what is being written. In the midst of the pressure of putting together an application, a few values have to be continuously brought to the forefront:

- Continuous improvement must be fully embedded into all management processes and work processes.

- The application describes the system used to run the business. This includes not just a description of the pieces, but also the linkages among the activities that make the organization function effectively.

- Put your best foot forward, but do not exaggerate.

Core Values and Recurring Themes

In a document as complex and fact-filled as a Baldrige Award application, make sure key messages are clearly communicated. There are 11 Core Values and the application must address all of them. The organization needs to decide at the onset what key messages reflect the drivers of business success. These key messages should be reflected in each category and tie together the entire application. This is one of the reasons it becomes so important to design and write the Organizational Profile early and well. Too many applicants ignore the importance of the Organizational Profile as an organizing tool. An effective Organizational Profile clearly identifies those things that are important to the business, impor-

How Senior Leaders:	Set	Deploy
Organizational Values	• Conduct planning retreat by the leadership team • Reviewed at quarterly progress reviews and updated annually in planning process	• Employee orientation • Training for all employees • Balanced scorecard assessments • Personal performance plans
Short-Term Directions	• Set as part of annual unit planning process	• Discussed in monthly meetings with all employees during progress reviews • Performance tracked monthly • Tied to bonuses and merit pay for all employees
Longer-Term Directions	• Set as part of annual unit planning process	• Discussed in Annual Report to all employees and stakeholders/stockholders

How Senior Leaders:	Description of How Performance Expectations are Used to:
Focus on Creating and Balancing Value for Customers	• Matrix of customer segments, common, and conflicting requirements defined • Discussed in planning and goal-setting meetings with all employees • Scorecard results determine compensation and bonuses
Focus on Creating and Balancing Value for Other Stakeholders	• Set as part of annual planning process • Stockholders, community, suppliers included in scorecard—segments, common, and conflicting requirements defined • Discussed in planning and goal-setting meetings with all employees • Scorecard results determine compensation and bonuses

How Senior Leaders:	Description
Determine that the processes described above are effective and how these processes have been systematically improved	• After expectations are set and communicated, to check deployment and understanding, brief employee interviews are made randomly at all levels in the organization. Although most employees were aware of the direction, values, and performance expectations, this knowledge was not consistent within three functional areas. Special briefings were conducted in those areas and new performance elements were included in the work plans of supervisors and managers in those areas. Subsequent random checks six months later revealed that deployment was widespread (gaps closed).

Figure 32 Example of Completing Selected Elements of Item 1.1a(1).

*Note: See the CD-ROM in the back of this book for the complete collection matrix

tant to its customers and stakeholders, and important to the future of the business. These selected themes guide the development of the application. We are often asked, "How many themes should an organization focus on?" The answer really depends on how many the organization actually uses. Try focusing on three.

Tests for Reasonableness

During the development of an application, there are "tests" that need to be conducted periodically with two groups of people: the senior executive team and customer-contact or individual contributor (front-line) employees.

With senior executive teams, the issue is the rate of growth of those items undergoing intensive improvement efforts and under the direct sponsorship of senior executives. Every Baldrige application effort should use the occasion to drive significant business process improvements throughout the organization. The development of an application offers an opportunity to review and improve these initiatives. Each improvement of an existing process is a candidate for inclusion in an application to demonstrate progress.

At the customer-contact or front-line employee level, conduct a "reality check." Determine whether the application as written reflects the way the business is run. When people are given the opportunity to review an application during the developmental stages, several things happen:

- Front-line people can comment on how closely the write-up reflects reality. It provides the writer(s) an opportunity to calibrate those words with reality.

- It forces the customer-contact employee to take a top-level view—which can be a learning experience in itself.

- It forces the writer to walk in the shoes of the individual contributor—again learning.

Test the Application

As an application comes together, a question asked by everyone—particularly the leadership team—is, "How well are we doing; what's the score?" Although the real value of an application is continuous improvement, the competitive nature of people also comes to

the forefront. After all, that spirit helps drive people to higher levels of excellence. Nurture that spirit.

The best means of getting an objective review is to have people familiar with the Baldrige process, but unbiased with respect to the organization and its processes, examine the application. It is surprising how differently outsiders view the workings of the business. The important aspect of this review is obviously the skill of the reviewers or examiners. The value to the organization is threefold:

- An early assessment—which sets expectations and eliminates surprises

- An opportunity for an early start on improvement initiatives

- A test of understandability by outsiders—which every application ultimately has to pass

Take Time to Celebrate/ Continuously Improve

Developing an application is tough work. At the end of the day, the application represents: 1) a document highlighting the accomplishments and future aspirations of the organization; 2) a plan for getting there; and 3) an operations manual for new people entering the business.

At key milestones in the development of an application, it is important to take time to celebrate the accomplishments just completed. The celebration should be immediate, inclusive, and visible. Such a celebration raises questions within the organization, and it raises expectations—all of which are critical when trying to change and improve the overall performance of the organization. It also presents a perfect opportunity to promote improvement initiatives.

Some Closing Thoughts

In the words of David Kearns, former CEO of Xerox and one of the greatest leaders of performance excellence in the world, "Quality is a journey without an end." Every company today is faced with the struggle to bring about change—and the pace quickens each year. Baldrige is a mechanism that can help focus the energy for change in a most productive manner. Used properly, it can help companies break out of restrictive paradigms and continue on the journey to top levels of performance excellence.

2004 CRITERIA RESPONSE GUIDELINES

The guidelines given in this section are offered to assist Criteria for Performance Excellence users in responding most effectively to the requirements of the 19 Criteria Items. Writing an application for the Baldrige Award involves responding to these requirements in 50 or fewer pages.

The guidelines are presented in three parts:

1. General guidelines regarding the Criteria booklet, including how the Items are formatted

2. Guidelines for responding to Process Items

3. Guidelines for responding to Results Items

General Guidelines

Read the Entire Criteria Booklet

The main sections of the booklet provide an overall orientation to the Criteria, including how responses are to be evaluated for self-assessment or by award examiners. You should become thoroughly familiar with these Criteria booklet sections:

- Criteria for Performance Excellence

- Scoring System

- Glossary of Key Terms

- Category and Item Descriptions

Review the Item format and understand how to respond to the Item requirements.

The Item format shows the different parts of Items, the role of each part, and where each part is placed. It is especially important to understand the Areas to Address and the Item Notes. Each Item and Area to Address is described in greater detail in the Category and Item Descriptions section.

Each Item is classified as either Process or Results, depending on the type of information required. Guidelines for responding to Process Items are on page 56 of the 2004 Baldrige Criteria booklet. Guidelines for responding to Results Items are on page 57 of the booklet.

Item requirements are presented in question format. Some Areas to Address include multiple questions. Responses to an Item should contain responses to all questions; however, each question need not be answered separately. Responses to multiple questions within a single Area to Address may be grouped, as appropriate to your organization. These multiple questions serve as a guide in understanding the full meaning of the information being requested.

Start by Preparing the Organizational Profile

The Organizational Profile is the most appropriate starting point. The Organizational Profile is intended to help everyone—including organizations using the Criteria for self-assessment, application writers, and reviewers—to understand what is most relevant and important to your organization's business and to its performance.

In addition, read the information describing the linkages, sample effective practices, and process flow diagrams presented in this book. In particular, be certain to understand how the various requirements of the Criteria are integrated into a comprehensive management system. Then gather data using the electronic application template provided with this book.

Guidelines for Responding to Process Items

Although the Criteria focus on key performance results, these results by themselves offer little diagnostic value. For example, if some results are poor or are improving at rates slower than your competitors', it is important to understand why this is so and what might be done to accelerate improvement. The purpose of Process Items is to permit diagnosis of your organization's most important processes—the ones that yield fast-paced organizational performance improvement and contribute to key business results. Diagnosis and feedback depend heavily on the content and completeness of your Item responses. For this reason, it is important to respond to these Items by providing your key process information. Guidelines for organizing and reviewing such information follow.

Understand the Meaning of "How"

Process Items include questions that begin with the word "how." Responses should outline your key process information that addresses approach, deployment, learning, and integration. Responses lacking such information, or merely providing an example, are referred to in the Scoring Guidelines as "anecdotal information."

Understand the Meaning of "What"

Two types of questions in Process Items begin with the word "what." The first type of question requests basic information on key processes and how they work. Although it is helpful to include who performs the work, merely stating who does not permit diagnosis or feedback. The second type of question requests information on what your key findings, plans, objectives, goals, or measures are. These latter questions set the context for showing alignment and integration in your performance management system. For example, when you identify key strategic objectives, your action plans, human resource development plans, some of your performance measures, and some results reported in Category 7 should be expected to relate to the stated strategic objectives.

Show That Processes Are Systematic

Ensure that the response describes a systematic approach, not merely an anecdotal example. Systematic approaches are repeatable and predictable, and involve the use of data and information for evaluation, subsequent improvement, and learning. In other words, the approaches are consistent over time, build in learning and evaluation, and show maturity. Scores above 50 percent rely on clear evidence that approaches are systematic, evaluated, and refined.

Show Deployment

Ensure that the response gives clear and sufficient information on deployment in different parts of the organization. For example, one must be able to distinguish from a response whether an approach described is used in one, some, most, or all parts of the organi-

zation. If the process you describe is widely used in the organization, be sure to state where it is deployed.

Deployment can be shown compactly by using summary tables that outline what is done in different parts of the organization. This is particularly effective if the basic approach is described in a narrative.

Show Evidence of Learning

Processes should include evaluation and improvement cycles, as well as the potential for breakthrough change. Process improvements should be shared with other appropriate units of the organization to enable organizational learning.

Show Integration

Integration shows process, plan, measures, and action alignment and harmonization that generate organizational effectiveness and efficiencies.

Show Focus and Consistency

The response demonstrates that the organization is focused on key processes and on improvements that offer the greatest potential to improve business performance and accomplish organization action plans.

There are four important factors to consider regarding focus and consistency:

1. The Organizational Profile should make clear what is important.

2. The Strategic Planning Category, including the strategic objectives and action plans, should highlight areas of greatest focus and describe how deployment is accomplished.

3. Descriptions of organizational-level analysis and review (Items 4.1 and 1.1) should show how the organization analyzes and reviews performance information to set priorities.

4. The Process Management Category should highlight product, service, support, and supplier processes that are key to overall performance.

Showing focus and consistency in the Process Items and tracking corresponding measures in the Results Items should improve business performance.

Respond Fully to Item Requirements

Ensure that the response fully addresses all important parts of each Item and each Area to Address. Missing or incomplete information will be interpreted by examiners as a system deficiency—a gap in process. All Areas to Address should be addressed and checked in final review. Individual components of an Area to Address may be addressed individually or together.

Cross-Reference When Appropriate

As much as possible, each Item response should be self-contained. However, some responses to different Items might be mutually reinforcing. It is then appropriate to refer to the other responses, rather than to repeat information. In such cases, key process information should be given in the Item requesting this information. For example, employee education and training should be described in detail in Item 5.2. References elsewhere to education and training would then reference, but not repeat, this detail.

Use a Compact Format

Applicants should make the best use of the 50 application pages permitted. Use flowcharts, tables, and "bulletized" presentation of information.

Refer to the Scoring Guidelines

The evaluation of item responses is accomplished by consideration of the Criteria Item requirements and the maturity of the organization's approaches, breadth of deployment, extent of learning. and integration of other elements of the performance management system, as described in the Scoring Guidelines. Therefore, applicants need to consider both the Criteria and the Scoring Guidelines in preparing responses. *In particular, remember that in order to score over 50 percent, organizations must have in place a fact-based evaluation process and corresponding improvements at least for the basic Item requirements. The Scoring Guidelines make this requirement applicable to all items in Categories 1 through 6. Even if the Criteria questions for the Item do not ask for a description of techniques, it will help the examiners give you full credit for your*

processes if an explanation is provided to show how the processes are systematically evaluated and refined. List the process improvements that have been made during the last three to four years.

GUIDELINES FOR RESPONDING TO RESULTS ITEMS

The Baldrige Criteria place great emphasis (and 45 percent of the score) on results. All Results Items remain the same in Category 7 for 2004. Items 7.1, 7.2, 7.3, 7.4, 7.5, and 7.6 call for results related to all key requirements, stakeholders, and goals.

Focus on Reporting the Most Critical Business Results

Results reported should cover the most important requirements for business success highlighted in the Organizational Profile and the Strategic Planning, Customer and Market Focus, and Process Management Categories, and included in responses to other Items, such as Human Resource Focus (Category 5) and Process Management (Category 6).

Four key requirements for effective reporting of results data include the following:

- Performance levels that show performance on a meaningful measurement scale.

- Trends to show directions of results and rates of change.

- Comparisons to show how results compare with those of other, appropriately selected organizations.

- Breadth and importance of results to show that all important results are included and segmented, that is, by important customer, employee, process, and product line groups.

Actual Time Time Periods for Tracking Trends

No minimum period of time is required for trend data. However, results data might span five years or more for some results. Time intervals between data points should be meaningful for the specific measures reported. Trends might be much shorter for some of the organization's more recent improvement activities. Because of the importance of showing deployment and focus, new data should be included even if trends and comparisons are not yet well established. It may be better, however, to report four quarterly measures covering a one-year period than two measures for the beginning and end of the year. The four measures help to demonstrate a sustained trend (if one exists).

Compact Presentation

Many results can be reported compactly by using graphs and tables. Graphs and tables should be labeled for easy interpretation. Results over time or compared with others should be "normalized"—presented in a way (such as with the use of ratios) that takes into account various size factors. For example, reporting safety trends in terms of lost workdays per 100 employees would be more meaningful than total lost workdays, if the number of employees has varied over the time period or if you are comparing your results to organizations varying in size from yours.

Integrate Results with Text

Descriptions of results and the results themselves should be in close proximity in the Award application. Trends that show a significant positive or negative change should be explained. Use figure numbers that correspond to Items. For example, the third figure for Item 7.2 should be 7.2-3 (see Figure 33).

Figure 33 illustrates data an applicant might present as part of a response to Item 7.2, Product and Service Results. In the Organizational Profile, in Item 2.1b(1), and in Item 3.1, the applicant has indicated on-time delivery as a key customer requirement.

Using the graph, the following characteristics of clear and effective data presentation are illustrated:

- A figure number is provided for reference to the graph in the text.

- Both axes and units of measure are clearly labeled.

- Trend lines report data for a key business requirement—on-time delivery.

- Results are presented for several years.

- Appropriate comparisons are clearly shown.

- The organization shows, using a single graph, that its three divisions separately track on-time delivery.

- If different segments or components exist, show each as a separate measure. Avoid aggregating data when the segments are meaningful.

- An upward-pointing arrow appears on the graph, indicating that increasing values are "good." (A downward-pointing arrow would indicate that decreasing values are "good.") The "desired direction" arrows may seem obvious to the authors of the application, but some desired directions are not obvious to examiners who are not familiar with certain data displays.

To help interpret the Scoring Guidelines, the following comments on the graphed results in the previous sample would be appropriate.

- The current overall organization performance level is very good to excellent. This conclusion is supported by the comparison with competitors and with a "world-class" level.

- The organization exhibits an overall excellent improvement trend.

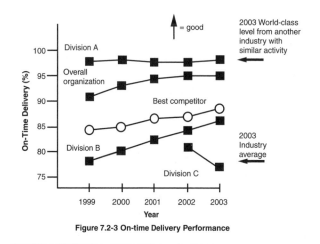

Figure 7.2-3 On-time Delivery Performance

Figure 33 Linking results with text.

- Division A is the current performance leader—showing sustained high performance and a slightly positive trend. Division B shows rapid improvement. Its current performance is near that of the best industry competitor but trails the world-class level.

- Division C—a new division—is having early problems with on-time delivery. (The applicant should analyze and explain the early problems in the application text.) Its current performance is not yet at the level of the best industry competitor.

Complete Data

Be sure that results data are displayed for all relevant customer, financial, market, human resource, operational performance, and supplier performance characteristics. If you identify relevant performance measures and goals in other parts of the analysis (for example, Categories 1 through 6), be sure to include the results of these performance characteristics in Category 7. As each relevant performance measure is identified in the assessment process, create a blank chart and label the axes. Define all units of measure, especially if they are industry-specific or unique to the applicant. As data are collected, populate the charts. If expected data are not provided in the application, examiners may assume that the trends or levels are not good. Missing data drive the score down in the same way that poor trends do.

After you complete all of the data in Category 7, review the Organizational Profile and the processes described in Categories 1 through 6. Make a list of all of the results that an examiner would expect to find in Category 7. Then, cross-check this list with the data provided in Category 7. If any "expected" data are missing, be sure to add the appropriate charts or graphs.

Many examiners actually prepare a list of results that appear to be relevant based on information provided in the application. I refer to this list as a "table of expected results." (See page 320)

Break Out Data

This point, mentioned earlier, bears repeating: avoid aggregating the data. Where appropriate, break data into meaningful components. If you serve several dif-

ferent customer groups, display performance and satisfaction data for each group. As Figure 34 demonstrates, only one of the three trends is positive, although the average is positive. Examiners will seek component data when aggregate data are reported. Presenting aggregate data instead of meaningful component data is likely to reduce the score.

Data and Measures

Comparison data are required for all items in Category 7. These data are designed to demonstrate how well the organization is performing. To judge performance excellence, one must possess comparison data. In Figure 35, performance is represented by the line connecting the squares. Clearly the organization is improving, but how "good" is it? Without comparison data, answering that question is difficult.

Now consider the chart with comparison data added (Figure 36).

Note the position of three hypothetical comparisons, represented by the letters A, B, and C. Consider the following two scenarios:

1. If A represents the industry average and both B and C represent competitors, then examiners would conclude that your organization's performance was substandard, even though it is improving.

2. If A represents a best-in-class (benchmark) organization and B represents the industry aver-

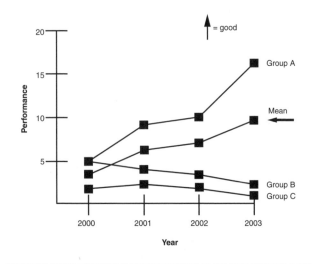

Figure 34 Breakout group data.

age, then examiners would conclude that your organizational performance is very good.

In both scenarios, the organizational performance remained the same, but the examiner's perception of it changed based on changes in comparison data.

Measures

Agreeing on relevant measures is difficult for organizations in the early phases of quality and performance improvement. The task is easier if the following guidelines are considered:

- *Clearly define customer requirements.* Clear customer requirements are easier to measure. Clearly defined customer requirements require probing and suggesting. For example, the customer of a new computer wants the equipment to be reliable. After probing to find what "reliable" means, we discover that: a) the customer expects it to work all of the time; b) prompt appearance by a repair technician at the site if it does stop working; c) immediate access to parts; and d) the ability to fix it right the first time.

- *For each of the four requirements defined, identify a measure.* For example, mean time between failures is one indicator of reliability, but it does not account for all of the variation in customer satisfaction. Since the customer is concerned with run time, we must assess how long it took the repair technician to arrive at the site, diagnose the problem, and fix it. Measures include time in hours, days, weeks between failures, time in minutes between the service call and the computer regaining capability (time to fix), time in minutes waiting for parts, and the associated costs in terms of cash and worker effort.

- *Collect and report data.* Several charts might be required to display these factors, or one chart with several lines.

Refer to the Scoring Guidelines

Considerations in the evaluation of Item responses include the Criteria Item requirements and the significance of the results trends, actual performance levels, relevant comparative data, alignment with important elements of your performance management system, and the strength of the improvement process relative to the Scoring Guidelines. Therefore, you need to consider both the Criteria and the Scoring Guidelines.

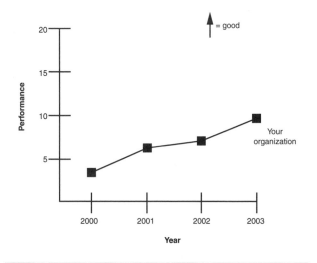

Figure 35 Getting better.

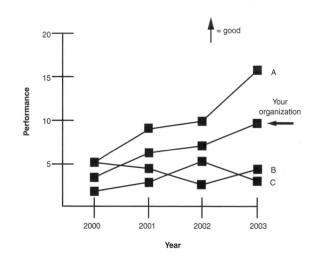

Figure 36 Comparison data.

Fees for the 2004 Award Cycle

Award Category	Eligibility Fee	Application Fee*	Supplemental Section Fee (if applicable)**	Site Visit Fee Usual Range (if applicable)***
Manufacturing	$150	$5000*	$2000	$20,000–$35,000
Service	$150	$5000*	$2000	$20,000–$35,000
Small Business	$150	$2000*	$1000	$10,000–$17,000
Education Not-for-profit	$150	$ 500*	$ 250	$ 1500
Education For-profit >500 faculty/staff	$150	$5000*	$2000	$20,000–$35,000
Education For-profit 500 or fewer faculty/staff	$150	$2000*	$1000	$10,000–$17,500
Health Care >500 staff	$150	$5000*	$2000	$20,000–$35,000
Health Care 500 or fewer staff	$150	$2000*	$1000	$10,000–$17,500

*An additional processing fee of $1250 is required for applications submitted on CD. Note that applications submitted on CD must be postmarked by May 13, 2004.

**Supplemental sections are not applicable for applicants with (a) a single performance system that supports all of their product and/or service lines and (b) products or services that are essentially similar in terms of customers/users, technology,types of employees, and planning.

***Site Visit Review Fee

This fee is paid only by applicants receiving site visits. The fee is set when visits are scheduled and is dependent on a number of factors, including the number of sites to be visited, the number of Examiners assigned, and the duration of the visit.

Site visit fees for applicants with more than 500 employees in the manufacturing, service, for-profit education, and health care sectors usually range between $20,000 and $35,000. However, the site visit fee for small businesses, for-profit education organizations with 500 or fewer faculty/staff, and health care organizations with 500 or fewer staff is approximately one-half that rate. In 2004, the site visit fee for not-for-profit education organizations is $1500. All site visit fees are due to ASQ two weeks after completion of the site visit.

Step 1, Eligibility Certification Package.

Organizations filing an Eligibility Certification Package may nominate one senior member of their staff to serve on the Board of Examiners. Organizations that wish to reserve a place on the Board for a staff member must submit their Eligibility Certification Package by March 12, 2004. If an organization chooses not to nominate someone to the Board, the due date for the Eligibility Certification Package is April 13, 2004.

Step 2, Application Package

The Application Package may be submitted in either CD/PDF format or on paper.

If submitted in CD/PDF format, the Application Package must be postmarked no later than May 13, 2004. If submitted on paper, 25 copies of the Application Package must be postmarked no later than May 27, 2004.

Scoring System

Scoring dimensions are classified according to the kinds of information and/or data being reviewed. The two types of Items and their designations are:

1. Process (for the 13 Items in Categories 1 through 6)

2. Results (for the six Items in Category 7)

Applicants should furnish information relating to these dimensions. Specific factors for these dimensions are described below.

Process

Process refers to the methods the organization uses and improves to address the Item requirements in Categories 1–6. The four factors used to evaluate process are Approach, Deployment, Learning, and Integration (A–D–L–I).

Approach refers to:

- The methods used to accomplish the process.

- The appropriateness of the methods to the Item requirements

- The effectiveness of use of the methods

- The degree to which the approach is repeatable and based on reliable data and information (for example, systematic)

Deployment refers to the extent to which:

- The approach is applied in addressing Item requirements relevant and important to your organization

- The approach is applied consistently

- The approach is used by all appropriate work units

Learning refers to:

- Refining the approach through cycles of evaluation and improvement

- Encouraging breakthrough change to the approach through innovation

- Sharing of refinements and innovation with other relevant work units and processes in the organization

Integration refers to the extent to which:

- The approach is aligned with your organizational needs identified in other Criteria Item requirements

- The measures, information, and improvement systems are complementary across processes and work units

- The plans, processes, results, analysis, learning, and actions are harmonized across processes and work units to support organization-wide goals

In Process Items, (Categories 1–6). approach–deployment–learning–integration are linked to emphasize that descriptions of approach should always indicate the deployment—consistent with the specific requirements of the Item. As processes mature, their description also should indicate how cycles of learning, as well as integration with other processes and work units, occur. Although the approach–deployment–learning–integration factors are linked, feedback to Award applicants reflects strengths and/or opportunities for improvement in any or all of these factors.

Results

Results refers to the organization's ouputs and outcomes in achieving the requirements in Items 7.1–7.6. The four factors used to evaluate results include:

- Current level of performance

- Rate (that is, slope of trend data) and breadth (how widely deployed and shared) of your performance improvements

- Performance relative to appropriate comparisons and/or benchmarks

- Linkage of results measures (often through segmentation) to important customer, product and service, market, process, and action plan performance requirements identified in the Organizational Profile and in Process Items

Results Items call for data showing performance levels, improvement rates, and relevant comparative data for key measures and indicators of organizational performance. Results Items also call for data on breadth of performance improvements. This is directly related to deployment and organizational learning; if improvement processes are widely shared and deployed, there should be corresponding results. A score for a Results Item is thus a composite based upon overall performance, taking into account the rate and breadth of improvements and their importance to the Item requirements and your business.

"Importance" As a Scoring Factor

The two evaluation dimensions described previously are critical to evaluation and feedback. However, another critical consideration in evaluation and feedback is the importance of your reported process and results to your key business factors. The areas of greatest importance should be identified in your Organizational Profile and in Items such as 2.1, 2.2, 3.1, 5.1, and 6.1. Your key customer requirements, competitive environment, key strategic objectives, and action plans are particularly important.

Assignment of Scores

The following guidelines should be observed in assigning scores to Item responses:

- All Areas to Address should be included in Item responses. Also, responses should reflect what is important to your organization.

- In assigning a score to an Item, first decide which scoring range (for example, 50 to 65 percent) is most descriptive of the organization's achievement level as presented in the Item response. "Most descriptive of the organization's achievement level" represents the best fit and can include some gaps in one or more of the A-D-L-I (process) factors or results factors for the chosen scoring range. An organization's achievement level is based on a holistic view of either the four process or four results factors in aggregate and not on a tallying or averaging of independent assessments against each of the four factors. Assigning the actual score within the chosen range requires evaluating whether the Item response is closer to the statements in the next higher or next lower scoring range.

- A Process Item score of 50 percent represents an approach that meets the overall requirements of the Item, that is deployed consistently and to most work units covered by the Item, that has been through some cycles of improvement and learning, and that addresses the key organizational needs. Higher scores reflect greater achievement, demonstrated by broader deployment, significant organizational learning, and increased integration.

- A Results Item score of 50 percent represents a clear indication of improvement trends and/or good levels of performance with appropriate comparative data in the results areas covered in the Item and important to the business. Higher scores reflect better improvement rates and/or levels of importance, better comparative performance, and broader coverage and integration with business requirements.

CALIBRATION GUIDELINES

Defining scoring terms may help reduce unnecessary variability. I have frequently asked examiners to define, in terms of percent, the meaning of "most." Some define "most" as 51 percent. Others have a higher standard, even up to 90 percent. Defining "good" and "very good" is even more difficult. To reduce this variability, the following guidelines are suggested:

Few: Up to 15 percent (major gaps in deployment exist)

Some: Greater than 15 percent to 30 percent (deployed, although in the early stages)

Many: Greater than 30 percent to 50 percent (well-deployed, although deployment may vary in some areas)

Most: Greater than 50 percent to 80 percent (well-deployed, with no apparent gaps in most areas)

Nearly All: Greater than 80 percent to less than 100 percent (fully deployed, with no significant gaps in any areas or work units)

All: 100 percent

Good: *For example, better than average for relevant competitors or similar providers; above industry average.*

Very Good: *For example, in the top quartile of competitors or similar providers.*

Excellent: *For example, at or near the top of competitors or similar providers; top 5 percent; best benchmark; better than best competitor.*

Score	Baldrige Scoring Guidelines Process
0% or 5%	• No systematic approach is evident; information is anecdotal. (A) • Little or no deployment of an approach is evident. (D) • No evidence of an improvement orientation; improvement is achieved through reacting to problems. (L) • No organizational alignment is evident; individual areas or work units operate independently. (I)
10%, 15%, 20%, or 25%	• The beginning of a systematic approach to the basic requirements of the Item is evident. (A) • The approach is in the early stages of deployment in most areas or work units, inhibiting progress in achieving the Basic requirements of the Item. (D) • Early stages of a transition from reacting to problems to a general improvement orientation are evident. (L) • The approach is aligned with other areas or work units largely through joint problem solving. (I)
30%, 35%, 40%, or 45%	• An effective, systematic approach, responsive to the basic requirements of the Item, is evident. (A) • The approach is deployed, although some areas or work units are in early stages of deployment. (D) • The beginning of a systematic approach to evaluation and improvement of key processes is evident. (L) • The approach is in early stages of alignment with your basic organizational needs identified in response to the other Criteria Categories. (I)
50%, 55%, 60%, or 65%	• An effective, systematic approach, responsive to the overall requirements of the Item, is evident. (A) • The approach is well deployed, although deployment may vary in some areas or work units. (D) • A fact-based, systematic evaluation and improvement process and some organizational learning are in place for improving the efficiency and effectiveness of key processes. (L) • The approach is aligned with your organizational needs identified in response to the other Criteria Categories. (I)
70%, 75%, 80%, or 85%	• An effective, systematic approach, responsive to the multiple requirements of the Item, is evident. (A) • The approach is well deployed, with no significant gaps. (D) • Fact-based, systematic evaluation and improvement and organizational learning are key management tools; there is clear evidence of refinement and innovation as a result of organizational-level analysis and sharing. (L) • The approach is integrated with your organizational needs identified in response to the other Criteria Items. (I)
90%, 95%, or 100%	• An effective, systematic approach, fully responsive to the multiple requirements of the Item, is evident. (A) • The approach is fully deployed without significant weaknesses or gaps in any areas or work units. (D) • Fact-based, systematic evaluation and improvement and organizational learning are key organization-wide tools; refinement and innovation, backed by analysis and sharing, are evident throughout the organization. (L) • The approach is well integrated with your organizational needs identified in response to the other Criteria Items. (I)

Score	Baldrige Scoring Guidelines Results
0% or 5%	• There are no business results or poor results in areas reported. • Trend data are either not reported or show mainly adverse trends. • Comparative information is not reported. • Results are not reported for any areas of importance to your organization's key business requirements.
10%, 15%, 20%, or 25%	• A few business results are reported; there are some improvements and/or early good performance levels in a few areas. • Little or no trend data are reported. • Little or no comparative information is reported. • Results are reported for a few areas of importance to your organization's key business requirements.
30%, 35%, 40%, or 45%	• Improvements and/or good performance levels are reported in many areas addressed in the item requirements. • Early stages of developing trends are evident. • Early stages of obtaining comparative information are evident. • Results are reported for many areas of importance to your organization's key business requirements.
50%, 55%, 60%, or 65%	• Improvement trends and/or good performance levels are reported for most areas addressed in the item requirements. • No pattern of adverse trends and no poor performance levels are evident in areas of importance to your organization's key business requirements. • Some trends and/or current performance levels—evaluated against relevant comparisons and/or benchmarks—show areas of good to very good relative performance. • Business results address most key customer, market, and process requirements.
70%, 75%, 80%, or 85%	• Current performance is good to excellent in most areas of importance to the item requirements. • Most improvement trends and/or current performance levels are sustained. • Many to most reported trends and/or current performance levels—evaluated against relevant comparisons and/or benchmarks—show areas of leadership and very good relative performance. • Business results address most key customer, market, process, and action plan requirements.
90%, 95%, or 100%	• Current performance is excellent in most areas of importance to the item requirements. • Excellent improvement trends and/or sustained excellent performance levels are reported in most areas. • Evidence of industry and benchmark leadership is demonstrated in many areas. • Business results fully address key customer, market, process, and action plan requirements.

PROCESS TERMS

Systematic

Look for evidence of a system—a repeatable, predictable process that uses data and information to promote improvement and learning—that is used to fulfill the requirements of the Item. The application should briefly describe the system, explain how it works and describe the refinements that have been made. The application must communicate the nature of the system to people who are not familiar with it. This is essential to achieve the 30 percent scoring threshold.

Integrated

Determine the extent to which the system is integrated or interconnected with other elements of the overall management system. Show the linkages across categories for key themes such as those displayed earlier for each Item. Consider the extent to which the work of senior leaders is integrated. For example:

1. Senior executives (Item 1.1) are responsible for shaping and communicating the organization's values and performance expectations throughout the leadership system and work force.

2. They develop relationships with key customers (Item 3.2) and monitor customer satisfaction (Item 7.1), related product and service quality (Item 7.2), and organization performance results (Items 7.3, 7.4, 7.5, and 7.6).

3. With this in mind, senior executives participate in strategy development (Item 2.1) and ensure the alignment of the workplace to achieve strategic objectives (Item 2.2).

4. Leaders must convert goals and strategic objectives into measurable milestones and time lines [Item 2.1b(1)] to serve as a basis for monitoring performance [Item 1.1c(1)] and setting improvement priorities [Item 1.1c(3)]. (Time lines [2.1b(1)] should be set to coincide with the review cycle of senior leaders. If they review progress quarterly, then quarterly time lines or milestones should be set.)

5. This information, when properly collected and analyzed (Item 4.1), helps them plan and monitor progress better and make more informed decisions to optimize customer satisfaction and operational and financial performance.

6. Senior executives may also become involved in supporting new structures to improve employee performance and motivation (Item 5.1), training effectiveness (Item 5.2), and employee well-being and satisfaction (Item 5.3).

Similar relationships (linkages) exist between other items. In the application, highlight these linkages to demonstrate integration.

Prevention-Based

Prevention-based systems are characterized by actions to minimize or prevent the existence or recurrence of problems. In an ideal world, all systems would produce perfect products and flawless service. Since that rarely happens, high-performing organizations are able to act quickly to recover from a problem (fight the fire) and then take action to identify the root cause of the problem and prevent it from surfacing again. The nature of the problem, its root cause, and appropriate corrective action is communicated to all relevant employees so that they can implement the corrective action in their area before the problem arises.

Continuous Improvement

Continuous improvement is a bedrock theme for top performing organizations. It is the method that helps organizations establish and keep their competitive edge. Continuous improvement involves the fact-based evaluation and improvement of processes crucial to organizational success. Evaluation and improvement completes the high-performance management cycle. Fact-based continuous improvement evaluations can be complex statistical processes, or as simple as a focus group discussing *and recording* what went right, what went wrong, and how it could be done better. The key to optimum performance lies in the pervasive evaluation and improvement of all processes. By practicing systematic, pervasive, continuous improvement, time becomes the organization's ally. Consistent fact-based evaluation and refinement practices with correspondingly good deployment can drive the score to 60 percent or 70 percent, and higher.

Complete

Each Item contains one or more Areas to Address. Many Areas to Address contain several parts. Failure to address all Areas and parts can push the score lower. If an Area to Address or part of an Area does not apply to your organization, it is important to explain why. Otherwise, examiners may conclude that the system is incomplete.

Anecdotal

If your application narrative describes a process or procedure that is random, ad hoc, or anecdotal and does not address the Criteria in a predictable, disciplined manner, it is worth very little (zero points).

Deployment

The extent to which processes are widely used by organization units affects scoring. For example, a systematic approach that is well-integrated, evaluated consistently, and refined routinely may be worth 70 percent or more. However, if that process is not in place in all key parts of the organization, the score may be reduced, perhaps significantly, depending on the nature and extent of the deployment gap.

Major gaps are expected to exist at the 5 percent to 25 percent level. At the 30 percent and higher levels, no major gaps exist, although some units may still be at the early stages of development. At the 70 percent to 85 percent level, no major gaps exist and the approach is well-integrated with organizational needs identified in other parts of the Criteria.

Summary

For each Item examined, the process is rated as follows:

- Anecdotal: zero percent to 5 percent
- Beginnings of a systematic approach to meet *basic* Item requirements (perhaps recently piloted or implemented process): 10 percent to 25 percent

- Effective, systematic approach in place to meet *basic* Item requirements: 30 to 35 percent
- Effective, systematic approach in place to meet *basic* Item requirements, with the beginnings (planned or piloted) of a process to evaluate and improve: 40 to 45 percent
- Effective, systematic approach in place to meet *overall* Item requirements, with fact-based evaluation process in place: 50 percent
- Effective, systematic approach in place to meet *overall* Item requirements, with fact-based evaluation process in place and at least one cycle of refinements based on the evaluation: 60 to 65 percent
- Effective, systematic approach in place to meet *multiple* Item requirements, with fact-based evaluation process in place and multiple cycles of refinement, innovation, and integration based on the evaluation: 70 percent to 85 percent
- Integrated: 70 percent to 100 percent
- Refined: 60 percent to 100 percent
- Widely used, with no significant gaps in deployment: 70 percent or greater

Systematic, integrated, prevention-based, and continuously improved systems that are widely used are generally easier to describe than undeveloped systems. Moreover, describing activities or anecdotes does not convince examiners that an integrated, systematic process is in place. In fact, simply describing activities and anecdotes suggests that an integrated system does not exist. However, by tracing critical success threads through the relevant Items in the Criteria, the organization demonstrates that its system is integrated and fully deployed.

To demonstrate system integration, pick several critical success factors and show how the organization manages them. For example, trace the leadership focus on performance.

- Identify performance-related data that are collected to indicate progress against goals [Item 4.1].

- Show how performance data are analyzed [Item 4.1], reviewed by senior leaders [Item 1.1c(1)], and used to set priorities for work and resources [Item 1.1c(3)].

- Show how performance effectiveness is considered in the planning process [Item 2.1a] and how work at all levels is aligned to increase performance [Item 2.2a].

- Demonstrate the impact of human resource management [Item 5.1] and training [Item 5.2] on performance and show how both tie to the strategy and human resource plans [Item 2.2a(3)].

- Show how value creation and support processes [Items 6.1 and 6.2] are enhanced to improve results.

- Report the results of improved performance [Items 7.1, 7.2, 7.3, 7.4, 7.5, and 7.6] and be sure all key results are reported with key comparative or benchmark data included.

- Determine how improved product and service quality [Item 7.2] affects customer satisfaction levels [Item 7.1].

- Show how customer requirements and preferences [Item 3.1] and concerns [Item 3.2] are used to drive the selection of key measures [Item 4.1] and impact design and delivery processes [Items 6.1 and 6.2].

Note that the application is limited to 50 pages, not including the five-page Organizational Profile. This may not be sufficient to describe in great detail the process, results, integration, and refinement of all systematic critical success factors, goals, or processes. Thus, it is better to pick the most important few, indicate them as such, and then thoroughly describe the threads and linkages throughout the application.

Clarifying the Requirements for Basic-, Overall-, and Multiple-Level Scoring

INTRODUCTION

The Baldrige Criteria, together with the Scoring Guidelines, are supposed to help Examiners identify the key strengths and vital few areas needing improvement to help leaders focus their resources on the steps needed to get to the next developmental level. Unfortunately, for several years, national and state Examiners have tended to "nit-pick" applicants by citing minute, inconsequential opportunities for improvement—even when basic or fundamental processes were not in place. Because of the tendency to "nit-pick," scores were inappropriately low and comments were not properly focused.

To avoid this problem, the Baldrige Award office redefined the Scoring Guidelines to focus attention on a hierarchy of requirements moving from "basic" to "overall" to "multiple." The purpose of this hierarchy was to keep Examiners focused on the most important factors each applicant needed to put in place to get to the next level and not turn the examination process into a compliance checklist.

In other words, the strengths comments were supposed to describe the processes and systems an applicant had in place that supported or justified the score assigned. The opportunities for improvement were supposed to identify the processes or systems that were not in place that kept the organization from moving to the next higher level. By listing insignificant issues (nits) in the feedback report, an applicant might spend resources fixing a problem that had relatively low impact and overlook a key area essential for growth and improvement.

I believe that the Baldrige Award office was correct in identifying the need to prevent Examiners from "nit-picking" while getting them to focus on the vital few issues. To achieve this objective, it is essential that all Examiners reviewing applications for a state, regional, or "in-house" Baldrige-based recognition program interpret the Criteria and scoring guidelines consistently. Unfortunately, the process and definitions presented in the 2003 and 2004 Criteria and Scoring Guidelines do not achieve this objective.

From my experience in training thousands of Examiners each year on the use of the Baldrige criteria, I have found that the greatest source of unacceptable variation is caused by Examiners focusing on different aspects of the Criteria during the review process. The lack of clarity in defining precisely what systems and/or processes are required for each scoring level and for each Item forces Examiners to decide for themselves the elements of each Item they deem more critical than others. With many different opinions of what constitutes basic and overall requirements, Examiners' comments and scores have not been consistent, either from team to team or Examiner to Examiner. For example, in recent Examiner training classes conducted, I asked the Examiners to follow the Baldrige definitions and list the factors they would look for as a basic requirement of "Organizational Leadership" [Item 1.1]. Each class generated a list similar to the following.

The applicant organization and its senior leaders must have in place processes to:

- Set direction

- Set expectations

- Empower employees

- Focus on customers

- Deploy values

- Set values

- Communicate values and directions to employees

- Engage in two-way communication with employees and customers

- Protect stockholder interests

- Hold managers accountable

- Review organizational performance

- Assess progress relative to goals

- Identify priorities for improvement

- Improve their personal leadership effectiveness

The list of "basic" requirements that the individual Examiners produced (required for a score of 10 to 45 percent), more accurately defines most of the "multiple" level requirements (needed for a score of 70 to 85 percent). With this kind of variation on Item 1.1, a relatively straightforward Item, imagine the differences a team of 6 to 10 Examiners will have interpreting the requirements of the 13 Items in Categories 1 through 6 that use the Approach-Deployment scoring guidelines. It is difficult to conduct a consistently accurate assessment when each Examiner's interpretation of the "basic" and "overall" requirements is so varied.

During the past two years, several states and in-house organizational award programs pilot tested and subsequently implemented a new approach produces more consistently accurate assessments in both the government and private sectors. This technique provides Examiners with a more precise and consistent definition of "basic" and "overall" requirements for each Item (the multiple level requirements are already precise).

By providing consistent definitions of basic requirements, overall requirements, and multiple requirements, Examiners have been able to more accurately and consistently assess, score, and provide meaningful feedback to participating organizations or quality award applicants.

Official Baldrige Definitions

This section presents the actual definitions (in bold italic type) from the Baldrige Award Office that created the confusion.

Basic Requirements

The term "basic requirements" refers to the most central concept of an Item. Basic requirements are the fundamental theme of that Item. In the Criteria, the basic requirements of each Item are presented as the Item title.

Meeting the basic requirements of the Item could result in a score at the 10 to 45 percent levels depending on the level of development of the basic systems and on the extent of deployment of those systems.

Accordingly, for Item 1.1, an organization can meet the "basic" requirements by providing "Organizational Leadership" (the title of item 1.1). For Item 2.1, the organization must have a process for "Strategy Development" (also undefined). What do these terms mean? What does "strategy development process" include? There is simply not enough information presented by these terms to ensure a consistent review, which is critical to ensure appropriate feedback and an accurate score.

Overall Requirements

The term "overall requirements" refers to the topics Criteria users need to address when responding to the central theme of an Item. Overall requirements address the most significant features of the Item requirements. In the Criteria, the overall requirements of each Item are presented as an introductory sentence(s) printed in bold.

Meeting the overall requirements of the Item could result in a score at the 50, 55, 60 or 65 percent level depending on the maturity of the overall systems, the extent of deployment of those systems, and the extent of systematic evaluation and refinement, and integration of those systems.

More detail is provided to define the "overall" level than is provided for the "basic" level. However, the explanation is still too limited to enable Examiners to provide a consistent review, appropriate feedback, and an accurate score.

For example, under the requirements of Item 1.1, senior leaders must "guide the organization" and "review organizational performance." The organization must also describe its governance system." Under Item 2.1, the organization must have a system in place to establish "strategic objectives" and enhance its "competitive position." Ask any 10 people what systems might be needed to meet these requirements and you will receive 10 different answers.

Multiple Requirements

The term "multiple requirements" refers to the individual questions Criteria users need to answer within each Area to Address. These questions constitute the details of an Item's requirements. They are presented in black text under each Item's Area(s) to Address

Meeting the multiple requirements of the Item could result in a score at the 70 to 100 percent levels, depending on the maturity of the multiple systems, the extent of deployment of those systems, and the extent of systematic evaluation, refinement, innovation, and improved integration of those systems.

Unlike the "basic" and "overall" definitions, the "multiple" level definitions are quite clear. Sufficient detail is provided to enable Examiners to identify the elements of management systems and processes that must be in place to score at the 70 percent or higher level.

Importance As a Scoring Factor

Examiners must determine the extent to which the management systems and processes are responsive to the organization's key business requirements and changing business needs, (especially at the 50 percent and higher scoring bands). Accordingly, Examiners should consider the extent to which processes in the application appear to support or respond to key business needs that were expressed in the Organizational Profile and in Items such as:

- 2.1 Strategic objectives

- 2.2 Action plans and measures that derive from the strategic objectives and are deployed to all levels of the organization

- 3.1 The definition of customer segments, their requirements, and preferences for products and services that are most likely to drive loyalty

- 5.1 Work systems and systems to align employee feedback, reward, recognition, and

compensation with high-performance, business, and customer-focused objectives

- 6.1 Key value creation and business processes critical to organizational success and growth

Key customer requirements, competitive environment, strategic objectives, and action plans are particularly important to consider when determining the relevance of the systems and processes described in the application.

Clarifications for Scoring

The definitions on the following pages are intended to help improve consistency of interpretation and are offered as guidelines only. Prior to using these clarifying statements, the cognizant award program should reach consensus that the Basic, Overall, and Multiple requirements listed on the following pages appropriately capture the levels and meaning of the criteria.

Examiners please remember that the notes at the end of each Item provide additional clarification about information that is expected as part of the review.

- The word "should" creates an expectation that the process is in place. For example, Note 2 for Item 1.1 indicates that, "Senior leaders' organizational performance reviews (1.1c(1)) should be informed by organizational performance analyses described in 4.1b and guided by strategic objectives and action plans described in Items 2.1 and 2.2." This means that Examiners will be looking for, and expect to find these linkages.

- The word "might" is meant to suggest alternatives or examples, but not establish the expectation that the process is required. For example, the same Note 2 in 1.1 indicates that "Senior leaders' organizational performance reviews might be informed by internal or external Baldrige assessments." This means that Examiners cannot require such reviews to be used to assess organizational performance or capabilities and should not write an Opportunity for Improvement comment or lower the score if the organizations senior leaders do not use such reviews.

To make the following clarifying tables more complete, the scoring guidelines are presented in the first column as a reminder of the key points in the scoring for each level. The process scoring guidelines for the 70-85 percent level and the 90-100 percent levels have been grouped together in the tables because these scoring levels all require the multiple level requirements to be met.

Remember, the following analysis is presented only as a guideline that state, local, and in-house recognition programs may want to consider in order to help their Examiners provide more consistent and meaningful scoring and feedback to applicants.

1.1 Organizational Leadership *(70 points possible)*	
Scoring Guidelines	**Expected Observations**
10, 15, 20, or 25% The beginning of a systematic approach to the basic requirements of the Item is evident. (A) The approach is in the early stages of deployment in most areas or work units, inhibiting progress in achieving the basic requirements of the Item. (D) Early stages of a transition from reacting to problems to a general improvement orientation are evident. (L) The approach is aligned with other areas or work units largely through joint problem solving. (I)	*1.1 Organizational Leadership.* Senior leaders are in the beginning stages of establishing and implementing systems and/or processes to lead the organization and review organizational performance. *The values and approaches that guide the organization and its senior leaders are not widely understood. The organizational review processes are not uniform and may overlook measures important to organizational success. Reacting to problems is widespread; working to prevent problems is in the beginning stages.*
30, 35, 40, or 45% An effective, systematic approach, responsive to the basic requirements of the Item, is evident. (A) The approach is deployed, although some areas or work units are in early stages of deployment. (D) The beginning of a systematic approach to evaluation and improvement of key processes is evident. (L) The approach is in early stages of alignment with basic organizational needs identified in response to the other Criteria Categories. (I)	*1.1 Organizational Leadership.* Senior leaders have effective, systematic processes in place to lead the organization and review organizational performance. *The values and approaches that guide the organization and its senior leaders are generally understood. The organizational review processes generally consider key measures of organizational success but a few measures may be overlooked. Senior leaders are beginning to evaluate and may have made some improvements in these processes.*
50, 55, 60, or 65% An effective, systematic approach, responsive to the overall requirements of the Item, is evident. (A) The approach is well-deployed, although deployment may vary in some areas or work units. (D) A fact-based, systematic evaluation and improvement process and some organizational learning are in place for improving the efficiency and effectiveness of key processes. (L) The approach is aligned with organizational needs identified in response to the other Criteria Items. (I)	*1.1 Organizational Leadership.* Senior leaders have effective, systematic processes in place to do the following: a. *Senior Leadership Direction.* Communicate and reinforce directions and performance expectations with a focus on delivering value to key customers. b. *Organizational Governance.* Ensure management accountability for the organization's actions and the protection of stakeholder interests. c. *Organizational Performance Review.* Review organizational performance and progress relative to goals/strategic objectives. *The leadership processes are generally aligned with organizational needs. Some relatively minor gaps may exist in the deployment of these processes in some parts of the organization. However, there is a systematic, fact-based process in place to evaluate and improve the efficiency/effectiveness of some of the key elements of (a), (b), and/or (c) above.*

Continued

1.1 Organizational Leadership *(70 points possible)* Continued	
Scoring Guidelines	**Expected Observations**
70, 75, 80, or 85% An effective, systematic approach, responsive to the multiple requirements of the Item, is evident. (A) The approach is well-deployed, with no significant gaps (D). Fact-based, systematic evaluation and improvement and organizational learning are key management tools; there is clear evidence of refinement and innovation as a result of organizational-level analysis and sharing. (L) The approach is integrated with your organizational needs identified in response to the other Criteria Items. (I) **90, 95, or 100%** An effective, systematic approach, fully responsive to the multiple requirements of the Item, is evident. (A) The approach is fully deployed without significant weaknesses or gaps in any areas or work units. (D). Fact-based, systematic evaluation and improvement and organizational learning are key organization-wide tools; refinement and innovation, backed by analysis and sharing, are evident throughout the organization. (L) The approach is well-integrated with your organizational needs identified in response to the other Criteria Items. (I)	*1.1 Organizational Leadership.* Senior leaders have well-deployed, effective, systematic processes in place to do the following: a. *Senior Leadership Direction* (1) Senior leaders— • Set and deploy organizational values, short- and longer-term directions, and performance expectations. • Include a focus on creating and balancing value for customers and other stakeholders in their performance expectations. • Communicate organizational values, directions, and expectations through the leadership system, to all employees, and to key suppliers and partners. • Ensure two-way communication on these topics. (2) Senior leaders create an environment— • For empowerment, innovation, and organizational agility • For organizational and employee learning. • That fosters and requires legal and ethical behavior. b. *Organizational Governance.* The organization addresses the following key factors in its governance system: • Management accountability for the organization's actions • Fiscal accountability • Independence in internal and external audits • Protection of stockholder and stakeholder interests, as appropriate c. *Organizational Performance Review* (1) Senior leaders review organizational performance and capabilities and use these reviews to— • Assess organizational success, competitive performance, and progress relative to short- and longer-term goals. • Assess organizational ability to address changing organizational needs. (2) Key performance measures regularly reviewed by senior leaders are defined and key recent performance review findings are reported. (3) Senior leaders translate organizational performance review findings into priorities for continuous and breakthrough improvement of key business results and into opportunities for innovation. These priorities and opportunities are deployed throughout the organization and, when appropriate, to affected suppliers and partners to ensure organizational alignment. (4) The performance of senior leaders, including the chief executive and, as appropriate, members of the board of directors is systematically evaluated. Senior leaders use organizational performance review findings to improve both their own leadership effectiveness and that of the board and leadership system, as appropriate. *The approach is well-deployed with no significant gaps. In addition, there is a systematic, fact-based process in place to evaluate and improve (a), (b), and (c) above with clear evidence of innovation, learning, and organizational sharing which results in refinements and improved or excellent organization-wide integration, consistent with organizational needs.*

Notes:

N1. Organizational directions [1.1a(1)] relate to creating the vision for the organization and to setting the context for strategic objectives and action plans described in Items 2.1 and 2.2.

N2. Senior leaders' organizational performance reviews [1.1c] should be informed by organizational performance analyses described in 4.1b and guided by strategic objectives and action plans described in Items 2.1 and 2.2. Senior leaders' organizational performance reviews also might be informed by internal or external Baldrige assessments.

N3. Leadership performance evaluation [1.1c(4)] might be supported by peer reviews, formal performance management reviews (5.1b), and formal and/or informal employee and other stakeholder feedback and surveys.

N4. Organizational performance results should be reported in Items 7.1 – 7.6.

1.2 Social Responsibility *(50 points possible)*	
Scoring Guidelines	**Expected Observations**
10, 15, 20, or 25% The beginning of a systematic approach to the basic requirements of the Item is evident. (A) The approach is in the early stages of deployment in most areas or work units, inhibiting progress in achieving the basic requirements of the Item. (D) Early stages of a transition from reacting to problems to a general improvement orientation are evident. (L) The approach is aligned with other areas or work units largely through joint problem solving. (I)	*1.2 Social Responsibility.* The organization in the beginning stages of establishing systems and processes to address the organization's responsibilities to the public such as complying with laws and regulations. *Major gaps exist where the processes do not cover many key regulatory or legal requirements in many parts of the organization. Reacting to problems related to social responsibility is widespread; working to prevent problems is in the beginning stages.*
30, 35, 40, or 45% An effective, systematic approach, responsive to the basic requirements of the Item, is evident. (A) The approach is deployed, although some areas or work units are in early stages of deployment. (D) The beginning of a systematic approach to evaluation and improvement of key processes is evident. (L) The approach is in early stages of alignment with basic organizational needs identified in response to the other Criteria Categories. (I)	*1.2 Social Responsibility.* The organization has effective, systematic processes in place to address the organization's responsibilities to the public such as complying with laws and regulations. *The processes cover most key regulatory or legal requirements in most parts of the organization.* *The organization is beginning to evaluate and may have made some improvements in key elements of these processes.*
50, 55, 60, or 65% An effective, systematic approach, responsive to the overall requirements of the Item, is evident. (A) The approach is well-deployed, although deployment may vary in some areas or work units. (D) A fact-based, systematic evaluation and improvement process and some organizational learning are in place for improving the efficiency and effectiveness of key processes. (L) The approach is aligned with organizational needs identified in response to the other Criteria Items. (I)	*1.2 Social Responsibility.* The organization has effective, systematic processes in place to do the following: a. *Responsibilities to the Public.* Address regulatory and other legal requirements; anticipate public concerns and address risks to the public. b. *Ethical Behavior.* Ensure ethical behavior in most parts of the organization. c. *Support of Key Communities.* Strengthen and support key communities important to the organization. *The social responsibility processes are generally aligned with organizational needs. Some relatively minor gaps may exist in the deployment of these processes in some parts of the organization. However, there is a systematic, fact-based process in place to evaluate and improve the efficiency/effectiveness of some of the key elements of (a), (b), and/or (c) above.*

Continued

1.2 Social Responsibility *(50 points possible)Continued*	
Scoring Guidelines	**Expected Observations**
70, 75, 80, or 85% An effective, systematic approach, responsive to the multiple requirements of the Item, is evident. (A) The approach is well-deployed, with no significant gaps (D). Fact-based, systematic evaluation and improvement and organizational learning are key management tools; there is clear evidence of refinement and innovation as a result of organizational-level analysis and sharing. (L) The approach is integrated with your organizational needs identified in response to the other Criteria Items. (I)	*1.2 Social Responsibility* . The organization has well-deployed, effective, systematic processes in place to do the following: a. *Responsibilities to the Public* (1) Address the impacts on society of the organization's products, services, and operations. Put in place appropriate compliance processes, measures, and goals for achieving and surpassing regulatory and legal requirements. Put in place key processes, measures, and goals for addressing risks associated with products, services, and operations. (2) Anticipate public concerns with current and future products, services, and operations. Prepare for these concerns in a proactive manner.
90, 95, or 100% An effective, systematic approach, fully responsive to the multiple requirements of the Item, is evident. (A) The approach is fully deployed without significant weaknesses or gaps in any areas or work units. (D). Fact-based, systematic evaluation and improvement and organizational learning are key organization-wide tools; refinement and innovation, backed by analysis and sharing, are evident throughout the organization. (L) The approach is well integrated with your organizational needs identified in response to the other Criteria Items. (I)	b. *Ethical Behavior.* Ensure ethical behavior in all stakeholder transactions and interactions. Put processes in place with appropriate measures or indicators for monitoring ethical behavior throughout the organization, with key partners, and in the governance structure. c. *Support of Key Communities.* Identify, support, and strengthen key communities and determine areas of emphasis for organizational involvement and support. Senior leaders and employees contribute to improving these communities. *The approach is well-deployed with no significant gaps. In addition, there is a systematic, fact-based process in place to evaluate and improve (a), (b), and (c) above with clear evidence of innovation, learning, and organizational sharing which results in refinements and improved or excellent organization-wide integration, consistent with organizational needs.*

Notes:

N1. Social responsibilities in areas critical to business also should be addressed in Strategy Development [Item 2.1] and in Process Management [Category 6]. Key results, such as results of regulatory and legal compliance or environmental improvements through use of "green" technology or other means, should be reported as Governance and Social Responsibility Results [Item 7.6].

N2. Measures or indicators of ethical behavior [1.2b] might include the percentage of independent board members, measures of relationships with stockholder and non-stockholder constituencies, and results of ethics reviews and audits.

N3. Areas of community support appropriate for inclusion in 1.2c might include efforts to strengthen local community services, education, and health, the environment, and practices of trade, business, or professional associations.

N4. The health and safety of employees are not addressed in Item 1.2; you should address these employee factors in Item 5.3.

2.1 Strategy Development *(40 points possible)*	
Scoring Guidelines	**Expected Observations**
10, 15, 20, or 25% The beginning of a systematic approach to the basic requirements of the Item is evident. (A) The approach is in the early stages of deployment in most areas or work units, inhibiting progress in achieving the basic requirements of the Item. (D) Early stages of a transition from reacting to problems to a general improvement orientation are evident. (L) The approach is aligned with other areas or work units largely through joint problem solving. (I)	*2.1 Strategy Development.* The organization is in the beginning stages of developing its strategic objectives. *Major gaps exist where the strategic planning process does not consider many business requirements or challenges (which may have been presented in the organizational profile) that are key to future business success and essential to effective strategic planning. Reacting to problems in the planning process is widespread; working to prevent problems is in the beginning stages.*
30, 35, 40, or 45% An effective, systematic approach, responsive to the basic requirements of the Item, is evident. (A) The approach is deployed, although some areas or work units are in early stages of deployment. (D) The beginning of a systematic approach to evaluation and improvement of key processes is evident. (L) The approach is in early stages of alignment with basic organizational needs identified in response to the other Criteria Categories. (I)	*2.1 Strategy Development.* The organization has effective, systematic processes in place to develop its strategic objectives. *The planning and related strategic objectives cover some business requirements or challenges (which may have been presented in the organizational profile) that are key to future business success and essential to effective strategic planning. The organization is beginning to evaluate and may have made some improvements in key elements of these processes.*
50, 55, 60, or 65% An effective, systematic approach, responsive to the overall requirements of the Item, is evident. (A) The approach is well-deployed, although deployment may vary in some areas or work units. (D) A fact-based, systematic evaluation and improvement process and some organizational learning are in place for improving the efficiency and effectiveness of key processes. (L) The approach is aligned with organizational needs identified in response to the other Criteria Items. (I)	*2.1 Strategy Development* The organization has effective, systematic processes in place to do the following: a. *Strategy Development Process.* Examine key organizational strengths, weaknesses, opportunities, and threats that cover most business requirements or challenges (which may have been presented in the organizational profile) that are key to future business success and essential to effective strategic planning. b. *Strategic Objectives.* Develop clear strategic objectives to enhance competitive position, overall performance, and future success. *The planning processes are generally aligned with organizational needs. Some relatively minor gaps may exist in the process of planning and setting strategic objectives. However, there is a systematic, fact-based process in place to evaluate and improve the key elements of (a) and (b) above.*

Continued

2.1 Strategy Development *(40 points possible)*	*Continued*
Scoring Guidelines	**Expected Observations**

70, 75, 80, or 85% An effective, systematic approach, responsive to the multiple requirements of the Item, is evident. (A) The approach is well-deployed, with no significant gaps (D). Fact-based, systematic evaluation and improvement and organizational learning are key management tools; there is clear evidence of refinement and innovation as a result of organizational-level analysis and sharing. (L) The approach is integrated with your organizational needs identified in response to the other Criteria Items. (I)

90, 95, or 100% An effective, systematic approach, fully responsive to the multiple requirements of the Item, is evident. (A) The approach is fully deployed without significant weaknesses or gaps in any areas or work units. (D). Fact-based, systematic evaluation and improvement and organizational learning are key organization-wide tools; refinement and innovation, backed by analysis and sharing, are evident throughout the organization. (L) The approach is well-integrated with your organizational needs identified in response to the other Criteria Items. (I)

2.1 Strategy Development. The organization has well-deployed, effective, systematic processes in place to do the following:

a. *Strategy Development Process*
  (1) Define the overall strategic planning process including key steps, key participants, short- and longer-term planning time horizons, and a description of these timing horizons and the manner by which the strategic planning process addresses these timing horizons.
  (2) Collect and analyze data and information relevant to strategic planning and ensure that strategic planning addresses the key factors listed below:
    i.   Customer and market needs, expectations, and opportunities
    ii. Competitive environment and capabilities relative to competitors
    iii. Technological and other key innovations or changes that might affect products, services, and operations
    iv. Internal strengths and weaknesses, including human and other resources
    v.   Opportunities to redirect resources to higher-priority products, services, or areas
    vi. Financial, societal and ethical, regulatory, and other potential risks
    vii. Changes in the national or global economy
    viii. Factors unique to the organization, including partner and supply chain needs, strengths, and weaknesses

b. *Strategic Objectives*
  (1) Define key strategic objectives and the timetable for accomplishing them. Define the most important goals for these strategic objectives.
  (2) Ensure that strategic objectives—
    • Address the challenges identified in response to P.2 in the Organizational Profile.
    • Balance short-term and longer-term challenges and opportunities.
    • Balance the needs of all key stakeholders.

The approach is well-deployed with no significant gaps. In addition, there is a systematic, fact-based process in place to evaluate and improve (a) and (b) above with clear evidence of innovation, learning, and organizational sharing which results in refinements and improved or excellent organization-wide integration, consistent with organizational need.

Notes:

N1. "Strategy development" refers to the organization's approach (formal or informal) to preparing for the future. Strategy development might utilize various types of forecasts, projections, options, scenarios, and/or other approaches to envisioning the future for purposes of decision making and resource allocation.

N2. "Strategy" should be interpreted broadly. Strategy might be built around or lead to any or all of the following: new products, services, and markets; revenue growth via various approaches, including acquisitions; and new partnerships and alliances. Strategy might be directed toward becoming a preferred supplier, a local supplier in each of major customers' markets, a low-cost producer, a market innovator, or a high-end or customized product or service provider.

N3. Strategies to address key challenges [2.1b(2)] might include rapid response, customization, lean or virtual manufacturing, rapid innovation, ISO 9000:2000 registration, Web-based supplier and customer relationship management, and product and service quality. Responses to Item 2.1 should focus on specific challenges—those most important to business success and to strengthening the organization's overall performance.

N4. Item 2.1 addresses overall organizational strategy, which might include changes in services, products, and product lines. However, the Item does not address product and service design; you should address these factors in Item 6.1, as appropriate.

2.2 Strategic Deployment *(45 points possible)*	
Scoring Guidelines	**Expected Observations**
10, 15, 20, or 25% The beginning of a systematic approach to the basic requirements of the Item is evident. (A) The approach is in the early stages of deployment in most areas or work units, inhibiting progress in achieving the basic requirements of the Item. (D) Early stages of a transition from reacting to problems to a general improvement orientation are evident. (L) The approach is aligned with other areas or work units largely through joint problem solving. (I)	*2.2 Strategy Deployment.* The organization is in the beginning stages of developing its action plans to carry out the strategic objectives. *Major gaps exist where the action plans do not cover many elements essential to effective deployment of strategic objectives. Reacting to problems in the process of developing and deploying strategic plans and actions is widespread; working to prevent problems is in the beginning stages*
30, 35, 40, or 45% An effective, systematic approach, responsive to the basic requirements of the Item, is evident. (A) The approach is deployed, although some areas or work units are in early stages of deployment. (D) The beginning of a systematic approach to evaluation and improvement of key processes is evident. (L) The approach is in early stages of alignment with basic organizational needs identified in response to the other Criteria Categories. (I)	*2.2 Strategy Deployment.* The organization has effective, systematic processes in place to convert its strategic objectives into action plans. *Action plans have been developed for most strategic objectives and deployed to most areas important to the organization. The organization is beginning to evaluate and make some improvements in the key elements of these processes.*
50, 55, 60, or 65% An effective, systematic approach, responsive to the overall requirements of the Item, is evident. (A) The approach is well-deployed, although deployment may vary in some areas or work units. (D) A fact-based, systematic evaluation and improvement process and some organizational learning are in place for improving the efficiency and effectiveness of key processes. (L) The approach is aligned with organizational needs identified in response to the other Criteria Items. (I)	*2.2 Strategy Deployment.* The organization has effective, systematic processes in place to do the following: a. *Action Plan Development and Deployment.* Convert strategic objectives into action plans and related performance measures or indicators. b. *Performance Projection.* Project future performance levels for key measures or indicators. *The processes of developing and deploying action plans are generally aligned with organizational needs. Some relatively minor gaps may exist in the deployment of these processes in some parts of the organization. However, there is a systematic, fact-based process in place to evaluate and improve the efficiency/effectiveness of some of the key elements of (a), and/or (b) above*

Continued

2.2 Strategic Deployment *(45 points possible)*	*Continued*
Scoring Guidelines	**Expected Observations**

70, 75, 80, or 85% An effective, systematic approach, responsive to the multiple requirements of the Item, is evident. (A) The approach is well-deployed, with no significant gaps (D). Fact-based, systematic evaluation and improvement and organizational learning are key management tools; there is clear evidence of refinement and innovation as a result of organizational-level analysis and sharing. (L) The approach is integrated with your organizational needs identified in response to the other Criteria Items. (I)
 	
90, 95, or 100% An effective, systematic approach, fully responsive to the multiple requirements of the Item, is evident. (A) The approach is fully deployed without significant weaknesses or gaps in any areas or work units. (D). Fact-based, systematic evaluation and improvement and organizational learning are key organization-wide tools; refinement and innovation, backed by analysis and sharing, are evident throughout the organization. (L) The approach is well integrated with your organizational needs identified in response to the other Criteria Items. (I)
	2.2 Strategy Deployment. The organization has well-deployed, effective, systematic processes in place to do the following:
	
	  a. *Action Plan Development and Deployment*
	    (1) Develop and deploy action plans to achieve key strategic objectives. Allocate resources to ensure accomplishment of action plans. Ensure that the key changes resulting from action plans can be sustained.
	    (2) Define key short- and longer-term action plans. Define key changes, if any, in products and services, customers and markets, and in operations.
	    (3) Define key human resource plans that derive from short- and longer-term strategic objectives and action plans.
	    (4) Define key performance measures or indicators for tracking progress with action plans. Ensure that the overall action plan measurement system reinforces organizational alignment and covers all key deployment areas and stakeholders.
	
	  b. *Performance Projection.* Define both short- and longer-term time performance projections horizons for the key performance measures or indicators identified in 2.2a(4). Show how the organization's projected performance compares with competitors' projected performance, key benchmarks, goals, and past performance, as appropriate.
	
	The approach is well-deployed with no significant gaps. In addition, there is a systematic, fact-based process in place to evaluate and improve (a) and (b) above with clear evidence of innovation, learning, and organizational sharing which results in refinements and improved or excellent organization-wide integration, consistent with organizational needs.

Notes:

N1. Strategy and action plan development and deployment are closely linked to other Items in the Criteria. Examples of key linkages are
- Item 1.1 for how senior leaders set and communicate directions;
- Category 3 for gathering customer and market knowledge as input to strategy and action plans and for deploying action plans;
- Category 4 for information, analysis and knowledge management to support key information needs, to support development of strategy, to provide an effective basis for performance measurements, and to track progress relative to strategic objectives and action plans;
- Category 5 for work system needs; employee education, training, and development needs; and related human resource factors resulting from action plans;
- Category 6 for process requirements resulting from action plans; and
- Item 7.5 for specific accomplishments relative to organizational strategy and action plans.

N2. Measures and indicators of projected performance [2.2b] might include changes resulting from new business ventures; business acquisitions or mergers; new value creation; market entry and shifts; and significant anticipated innovations in products, services, and technology.

3.1 Customer and Market Knowledge *(40 points possible)*	
Scoring Guidelines	**Expected Observations**
10, 15, 20, or 25% The beginning of a systematic approach to the basic requirements of the Item is evident. (A) The approach is in the early stages of deployment in most areas or work units, inhibiting progress in achieving the basic requirements of the Item. (D) Early stages of a transition from reacting to problems to a general improvement orientation are evident. (L) The approach is aligned with other areas or work units largely through joint problem solving. (I)	*3.1 Customer and Market Knowledge.* The organization is in the beginning stages of acquiring customer and market knowledge to identify their requirements and/or expectations. *Major gaps exist where the listening and learning (knowledge acquisition) processes do not cover many customer segments or groups essential to effectively understanding their requirements. Reacting to problems in understanding customer requirements is widespread; working to prevent problems is in the beginning stages.*
30, 35, 40, or 45% An effective, systematic approach, responsive to the basic requirements of the Item, is evident. (A) The approach is deployed, although some areas or work units are in early stages of deployment. (D) The beginning of a systematic approach to evaluation and improvement of key processes is evident. (L) The approach is in early stages of alignment with basic organizational needs identified in response to the other Criteria Categories. (I)	*3.1 Customer and Market Knowledge.* The organization has effective, systematic processes in place to acquire (listen and learn about) customer and market knowledge to identify their requirements and/or expectations for most key customer and market segments. *The organization is beginning to evaluate and may have made some improvements in key elements of these processes.*
50, 55, 60, or 65% An effective, systematic approach, responsive to the overall requirements of the Item, is evident. (A) The approach is well-deployed, although deployment may vary in some areas or work units. (D) A fact-based, systematic evaluation and improvement process and some organizational learning are in place for improving the efficiency and effectiveness of key processes. (L) The approach is aligned with organizational needs identified in response to the other Criteria Items. (I)	*3.1 Customer and Market Knowledge.* The organization has effective, systematic processes in place to do the following: a. *Customer and Market Knowledge.* Determine (target) market and customer segments. Listen and learn about customer requirements, expectations, and preferences to determine the relative value and ensure the continuing relevance of products and services and develop new business opportunities. *The customer and market knowledge processes are generally aligned with organizational needs. Some relatively minor gaps may exist in the deployment of these processes in some parts of the organization. However, there is a systematic, fact-based process in place to evaluate and improve the efficiency/effectiveness of some of the key elements of (a) above.*

Continued

3.1 Customer and Market Knowledge *(40 points possible)*	*Continued*
Scoring Guidelines	**Expected Observations**

70, 75, 80, or 85% An effective, systematic approach, responsive to the multiple requirements of the Item, is evident. (A) The approach is well-deployed, with no significant gaps (D). Fact-based, systematic evaluation and improvement and organizational learning are key management tools; there is clear evidence of refinement and innovation as a result of organizational-level analysis and sharing. (L) The approach is integrated with your organizational needs identified in response to the other Criteria Items. (I)	*3.1 Customer and Market Knowledge.* The organization has well-deployed, effective, systematic processes in place to do the following:
	a. *Customer and Market Knowledge*
	(1) Determine or target customers, customer groups, and market segments after considering the requirements of customers of competitors and other potential customers and markets.
	(2) Determine key customer requirements and expectations (including product and service features) and their relative importance to customers' purchasing decisions. To effectively determine customer expectations and preferences—
	• Adjust the methods of determining customer requirements and preferences according to the unique needs of these different groups.
	• Use relevant information from current and former customers, including marketing and sales information, customer loyalty and retention data, win/loss analysis, and complaints in the determination of customer requirements and preferences.
	• Use this information for product and service planning, marketing, process improvements, and business development.
90, 95, or 100% An effective, systematic approach, fully responsive to the multiple requirements of the Item, is evident. (A) The approach is fully deployed without significant weaknesses or gaps in any areas or work units. (D). Fact-based, systematic evaluation and improvement and organizational learning are key organization-wide tools; refinement and innovation, backed by analysis and sharing, are evident throughout the organization. (L) The approach is well-integrated with your organizational needs identified in response to the other Criteria Items. (I)	(3) Keep your listening and learning methods current with business needs and directions.
	The approach is well-deployed with no significant gaps. In addition, there is a systematic, fact-based process in place to evaluate and improve (a) above with clear evidence of innovation, learning, and organizational sharing which results in refinements and improved or excellent organization-wide integration, consistent with organizational needs.

Notes:

N1. Responses to this Item should include the customer groups and market segments identified in P.1b(2).

N2. If products and services are sold to or delivered to end-use customers via other businesses such as retail stores or dealers, customer groups [3.1a(1)] should include both the end users and these intermediate businesses.

N3. "Product and service features" [3.1a(2)] refers to all the important characteristics of products and services and to their performance throughout their full life cycle and the full "consumption chain." This includes all customer purchase experiences and other interactions with the organization that influence purchase decisions. The focus should be on features that affect customer preference and repeat business—for example, those features that differentiate your products and services from competing offerings. Those features might include price, reliability, value, delivery requirements for hazardous materials use, disposal, customer or technical support, and the sales relationship. Key product and service features and purchasing decisions (3.1a(2)] might take into account how transactions occur and factors such as confidentiality and security.

N4. Listening and learning [3.1a(2)] might include gathering and integrating surveys, focus group findings, and Web-based and other data and information that bear upon customers' purchasing decisions. Keeping listening and learning methods current with business needs and directions [3.1a(3)] also might include use of newer technology, such as Web-based data gathering.

3.2 Customer Relationships and Satisfaction *(45 points possible)*	
Scoring Guidelines	**Expected Observations**
10, 15, 20, or 25% The beginning of a systematic approach to the basic requirements of the Item is evident. (A) The approach is in the early stages of deployment in most areas or work units, inhibiting progress in achieving the basic requirements of the Item. (D) Early stages of a transition from reacting to problems to a general improvement orientation are evident. (L) The approach is aligned with other areas or work units largely through joint problem solving. (I)	*3.2 Customer Relationships and Satisfaction.* The organization is in the beginning stages of establishing good relationships with customers and assessing their levels of satisfaction. *Major gaps exist where the relationship building and/or satisfaction determination processes do not cover many customer segments/groups and/or products and services. Reacting to problems in establishing good customer relationships and assessing satisfaction is widespread; working to prevent problems is in the beginning stages.*
30, 35, 40, or 45% An effective, systematic approach, responsive to the basic requirements of the Item, is evident. (A) The approach is deployed, although some areas or work units are in early stages of deployment. (D) The beginning of a systematic approach to evaluation and improvement of key processes is evident. (L) The approach is in early stages of alignment with basic organizational needs identified in response to the other Criteria Categories. (I)	*3.2 Customer Relationships and Satisfaction.* The organization has effective, systematic processes in place to establish good relationships and assess the levels of satisfaction with most customer groups/segments and most products/services. *The organization is beginning to evaluate and may have made some improvements in key elements of these processes.*
50, 55, 60, or 65% An effective, systematic approach, responsive to the overall requirements of the Item, is evident. (A) The approach is well-deployed, although deployment may vary in some areas or work units. (D) A fact-based, systematic evaluation and improvement process and some organizational learning are in place for improving the efficiency and effectiveness of key processes. (L) The approach is aligned with organizational needs identified in response to the other Criteria Items. (I)	*3.2 Customer Relationships and Satisfaction.* The organization has effective, systematic processes in place to do the following: a. *Customer Relationship Building.* Build relationships to acquire, satisfy, and retain customers, increase loyalty, and develop new business. b. *Customer Satisfaction Determination.* Determine customer satisfaction that can be used to meet their requirements and drive improvements. *The processes for building customer relations and assessing satisfaction/dissatisfaction are generally aligned with organizational needs. Some relatively minor gaps may exist in the deployment of these processes in some parts of the organization. However, there is a systematic, fact-based process in place to evaluate and improve the efficiency/effectiveness of some of the key elements of (a) and/or (b) above*

Continued

3.2 Customer Relationships and Satisfaction *(45 points possible)*	Continued
Scoring Guidelines	**Expected Observations**

Scoring Guidelines	Expected Observations
70, 75, 80, or 85% An effective, systematic approach, responsive to the multiple requirements of the Item, is evident. (A) The approach is well-deployed, with no significant gaps (D). Fact-based, systematic evaluation and improvement and organizational learning are key management tools; there is clear evidence of refinement and innovation as a result of organizational-level analysis and sharing. (L) The approach is integrated with your organizational needs identified in response to the other Criteria Items. (I) **90, 95, or 100%** An effective, systematic approach, fully responsive to the multiple requirements of the Item, is evident. (A) The approach is fully deployed without significant weaknesses or gaps in any areas or work units. (D). Fact-based, systematic evaluation and improvement and organizational learning are key organization-wide tools; refinement and innovation, backed by analysis and sharing, are evident throughout the organization. (L) The approach is well-integrated with your organizational needs identified in response to the other Criteria Items. (I)	*3.2 Customer Relationships and Satisfaction.* The organization has well-deployed, effective, systematic processes in place to do the following: a. *Customer Relationship Building* (1) Build relationships to acquire customers, meet and exceed their expectations, increase loyalty and repeat business, and gain positive referrals. (2) Establish— • Access mechanisms to make it easy for customers to seek information, conduct business, and make complaints. • Customer contact requirements for each mode of customer access and ensure that these contact requirements are deployed to all people and processes involved in the customer response chain. (3) Establish an effective complaint management process to ensure that complaints are resolved effectively and promptly. Aggregate and analyze the complaints and use this information to drive improvements throughout the organization and to affected partners. (4) Keep approaches to building relationships and providing customer access current with business needs and directions. b. *Customer Satisfaction Determination* (1) Determine customer satisfaction and dissatisfaction and adjust these determination methods according to the needs of differing customer groups. • Ensure that measurements capture actionable information for use in exceeding your customers' expectations, securing their future business, and gaining positive referrals. • Use customer satisfaction and dissatisfaction information to drive improvements. (2) Follow up with customers on products, services, and transaction quality to receive prompt and actionable feedback. (3) Obtain and use information about your customers' satisfaction relative to the customers' satisfaction with competitors and/or industry benchmarks. (4) Keep your approaches to determining satisfaction current with business needs and directions. *The approach is well-deployed with no significant gaps. In addition, there is a systematic, fact-based process in place to evaluate and improve (a) and (b) above with clear evidence of innovation, learning, and organizational sharing, which results in refinements and improved integration.*

Notes:

N1. Customer relationship building [3.2a] might include the development of partnerships or alliances with customers.

N2. Determining customer satisfaction and dissatisfaction [3.2b] might include use of any or all of the following: surveys, formal and informal feedback, customer account histories, complaints, win/loss analysis, and transaction completion rates. Information might be gathered on the Internet, through personal contact or a third party, or by mail.

N3. Customer satisfaction measurements might include both a numerical rating scale and descriptors for each unit in the scale. Actionable customer satisfaction measurements provide useful information about specific product and service features, delivery, relationships, and transactions that bear upon the customers' future actions—repeat business and positive referral.

N4. Your customer satisfaction and dissatisfaction results should be reported in Item 7.1.

4.1 Measurement and Analysis of Organizational Performance *(45 points possible)*	
Scoring Guidelines	**Expected Observations**
10, 15, 20, or 25% The beginning of a systematic approach to the basic requirements of the Item is evident. (A) The approach is in the early stages of deployment in most areas or work units, inhibiting progress in achieving the basic requirements of the Item. (D) Early stages of a transition from reacting to problems to a general improvement orientation are evident. (L) The approach is aligned with other areas or work units largely through joint problem solving. (I)	*4.1 Measurement and Analysis of Organizational Performance.* The organization is in the beginning stages of establishing effective performance management systems for measuring and analyzing organizational performance. *Major gaps exist where the measures and analyses do not cover many elements essential to effective organizational decision making. Reacting to problems with effective data and analyses to support decision making is widespread; working to prevent problems is in the beginning stages.*
30, 35, 40, or 45% An effective, systematic approach, responsive to the basic requirements of the Item, is evident. (A) The approach is deployed, although some areas or work units are in early stages of deployment. (D) The beginning of a systematic approach to evaluation and improvement of key processes is evident. (L) The approach is in early stages of alignment with basic organizational needs identified in response to the other Criteria Categories. (I)	4.1 Measurement and Analysis of Organizational Performance. The organization has effective, systematic processes in place for measuring and analyzing organizational performance. *Measures and analyses cover many to most areas essential to effective organizational decision making. The organization is beginning to evaluate and may have made some improvements in key elements of these processes.*
50, 55, 60, or 65% An effective, systematic approach, responsive to the overall requirements of the Item, is evident. (A) The approach is well-deployed, although deployment may vary in some areas or work units. (D) A fact-based, systematic evaluation and improvement process and some organizational learning are in place for improving the efficiency and effectiveness of key processes. (L) The approach is aligned with organizational needs identified in response to the other Criteria Items. (I)	*4.1 Measurement and Analysis of Organizational Performance.* The organization has effective, systematic processes in place to do the following: a. *Performance Measurement.* Select and use the right measures to align work and ensure effective decision making to improve performance at most levels and parts of the organization. b. *Performance Analysis.* Analyze data to support effective decision making to improve performance at all levels and in all parts of the organization. *The measurement and analysis processes cover most areas essential to effective organizational decision making and are generally aligned with organizational needs. Some relatively minor gaps may exist in the deployment or use of these processes in some parts of the organization. However, there is a systematic, fact-based process in place to evaluate and improve the efficiency/effectiveness of some of the key elements of (a) and/or (b) above.*

Continued

4.1 Measurement and Analysis of Organizational Performance   *Continued*
(45 points possible)

Scoring Guidelines	Expected Observations

70, 75, 80, or 85% An effective, systematic approach, responsive to the multiple requirements of the Item, is evident. (A) The approach is well-deployed, with no significant gaps (D). Fact-based, systematic evaluation and improvement and organizational learning are key management tools; there is clear evidence of refinement and innovation as a result of organizational-level analysis and sharing. (L) The approach is integrated with your organizational needs identified in response to the other Criteria Items. (I)
 	
90, 95, or 100% An effective, systematic approach, fully responsive to the multiple requirements of the Item, is evident. (A) The approach is fully deployed without significant weaknesses or gaps in any areas or work units. (D). Fact-based, systematic evaluation and improvement and organizational learning are key organization-wide tools; refinement and innovation, backed by analysis and sharing, are evident throughout the organization. (L) The approach is well-integrated with your organizational needs identified in response to the other Criteria Items. (I)
	4.1 Measurement and Analysis of Organizational Performance. The organization has well-deployed, effective, systematic processes in place to do the following:
	
	a. *Performance Measurement*
	  (1) Select, collect, align, and integrate data and information for tracking daily operations and for tracking overall organizational performance. Use these data and information to support organizational decision making and innovation.
	  (2) Select and effectively use key comparative data and information to support operational and strategic decision making and innovation.
	  (3) Keep the performance measurement system current with business needs and directions and ensure the system is sensitive to rapid or unexpected organizational or external changes.
	
	b. *Performance Analysis*
	  (1) Perform appropriate analyses to support senior leaders' organizational performance review and organizational strategic planning.
	  (2) Communicate the results of organizational-level analyses to work group and functional-level operations to enable effective support for their decision making.
	
	The approach is well-deployed with no significant gaps. In addition, there is a systematic, fact-based process in place to evaluate and improve (a) and (b) above with clear evidence of innovation, learning, and organizational sharing which results in refinements and improved or excellent organization wide integration, consistent with organizational needs.

Notes:

N1. Performance measurement is used in fact-based decision making for setting and aligning organizational directions and resource use at the work unit, key process, departmental, and whole organization levels.

N2. Comparative data and information [4.1a(2)] are obtained by benchmarking and by seeking competitive comparisons. "Benchmarking" refers to identifying processes and results that represent best practices and performance for similar activities, inside or outside the organization's industry. Competitive comparisons relate the organization's performance to that of competitors in your markets.

N3. Analysis includes examining trends; organizational, industry, and technology projections; and comparisons, cause-effect relationships, and correlations intended to support the performance reviews, help determine root causes, and help set priorities for resource use. Accordingly, analysis draws upon all types of data: customer-related, financial and market, operational, and competitive.

N4. The results of organizational performance analysis should contribute to the senior leaders' organizational performance review in 1.1c and organizational strategic planning in Category 2.

N5. Organizational performance results should be reported in Items 7.1-7.6.

4.2 Information and Knowledge Management *(45 points possible)*	
Scoring Guidelines	**Expected Observations**
10, 15, 20, or 25% The beginning of a systematic approach to the basic requirements of the Item is evident. (A) The approach is in the early stages of deployment in most areas or work units, inhibiting progress in achieving the basic requirements of the Item. (D) Early stages of a transition from reacting to problems to a general improvement orientation are evident. (L) The approach is aligned with other areas or work units largely through joint problem solving. (I)	*4.2 Information and Knowledge Management.* The organization is in the beginning stages of ensuring that needed information and knowledge are available to support decision making. *Major gaps exist where the needed information and/or knowledge are not available to support organizational decision making and/or learning. Reacting to problems with data availability is widespread; working to prevent problems is in the beginning stages.*
30, 35, 40, or 45% An effective, systematic approach, responsive to the basic requirements of the Item, is evident. (A) The approach is deployed, although some areas or work units are in early stages of deployment. (D) The beginning of a systematic approach to evaluation and improvement of key processes is evident. (L) The approach is in early stages of alignment with basic organizational needs identified in response to the other Criteria Categories. (I)	*4.2 Information and Knowledge Management.* The organization has effective, systematic processes in place to ensure that appropriate information and knowledge are available when needed to support decision making. *Information and knowledge cover most areas essential to effective organizational decision making and/or learning. The organization is beginning to evaluate and may have made some improvements in key elements of these processes.*
50, 55, 60, or 65% An effective, systematic approach, responsive to the overall requirements of the Item, is evident. (A) The approach is well-deployed, although deployment may vary in some areas or work units. (D) A fact-based, systematic evaluation and improvement process and some organizational learning are in place for improving the efficiency and effectiveness of key processes. (L) The approach is aligned with organizational needs identified in response to the other Criteria Items. (I)	*4.2 Information and Knowledge Management.* The organization has effective, systematic processes in place to do the following: a. *Data and Information Availability.* Ensure needed data and information are available when needed by appropriate employees, suppliers and partners, and customers to support decision making. b. *Organizational Knowledge.* (1) Build and manage knowledge assets (information systems) to effectively transfer needed knowledge. (2) Ensure the quality (such as accuracy, reliability, timeliness) of needed data and information. *The knowledge management processes are generally aligned with organizational needs. Some relatively minor gaps may exist in the deployment of these processes in some parts of the organization. However, there is a systematic, fact-based process in place to evaluate and improve the efficiency/effectiveness of some of the key elements of (a) and/or (b) above.*

Continued

4.2 Information and Knowledge Management *(45 points possible)* *Continued*	
Scoring Guidelines	**Expected Observations**
70, 75, 80, or 85% An effective, systematic approach, responsive to the multiple requirements of the Item, is evident. (A) The approach is well-deployed, with no significant gaps (D). Fact-based, systematic evaluation and improvement and organizational learning are key management tools; there is clear evidence of refinement and innovation as a result of organizational-level analysis and sharing. (L) The approach is integrated with your organizational needs identified in response to the other Criteria Items. (I) **90, 95, or 100%** An effective, systematic approach, fully responsive to the multiple requirements of the Item, is evident. (A) The approach is fully deployed without significant weaknesses or gaps in any areas or work units. (D). Fact-based, systematic evaluation and improvement and organizational learning are key organization-wide tools; refinement and innovation, backed by analysis and sharing, are evident throughout the organization. (L) The approach is well-integrated with your organizational needs identified in response to the other Criteria Items. (I)	*4.2 Information and Knowledge Management.* The organization has well-deployed, effective, systematic processes in place to do the following: a. *Data and Information Availability* (1) Make needed data and information available and accessible to employees, suppliers and partners, and customers. (2) Ensure that hardware and software are reliable, secure, and user friendly. (3) Keep data and information availability mechanisms, including software and hardware systems, current with business needs and directions. b. *Organizational Knowledge* (1) Manage organizational knowledge to accomplish: • The collection and transfer of employee knowledge • The transfer of relevant knowledge from customers, suppliers, and partners • The identification and sharing of best practices (2) Ensure the following properties of data, information, and organizational knowledge: • Integrity (completeness) • Timeliness (available when needed) • Reliability(consistency • Security (free from tampering) • Accuracy(correctness) • Confidentiality (no inappropriate release) *The approach is well-deployed with no significant gaps. In addition, there is a systematic, fact-based process in place to evaluate and improve (a) and (b) above with clear evidence of innovation, learning, and organizational sharing which results in refinements and improved or excellent organization-wide integration, consistent with organizational needs.*

Notes:

N1 Data availability [4.2a] is of growing importance as the Internet, e-business, and e-commerce are used increasingly for business-to-business and business-to-consumer interactions and intranets become more important as a major source of organization-wide communications.

N2. Data and information access [4.2a(1)] might be via electronic and other means.

5.1 Work Systems *(35 points possible)*	
Scoring Guidelines	**Expected Observations**
10, 15, 20, or 25% The beginning of a systematic approach to the basic requirements of the Item is evident. (A) The approach is in the early stages of deployment in most areas or work units, inhibiting progress in achieving the basic requirements of the Item. (D) Early stages of a transition from reacting to problems to a general improvement orientation are evident. (L) The approach is aligned with other areas or work units largely through joint problem solving. (I)	*5.1 Work Systems.* The organization is in the beginning stages of ensuring work and jobs enable employees and the organization to achieve high performance (which is usually defined by strategic objectives and related action plans). *Major gaps exist where the work systems do not help most employees to achieve high-performance objectives. Reacting to employee performance problems is widespread; working to prevent problems is in the beginning stages.*
30, 35, 40, or 45% An effective, systematic approach, responsive to the basic requirements of the Item, is evident. (A) The approach is deployed, although some areas or work units are in early stages of deployment. (D) The beginning of a systematic approach to evaluation and improvement of key processes is evident. (L) The approach is in early stages of alignment with basic organizational needs identified in response to the other Criteria Categories. (I)	*5.1 Work Systems.* The organization has effective, systematic processes in place to enable many employees in many parts of the organization to achieve high performance (which is usually defined by strategic objectives and related action plans). *Work and jobs in some parts of the organization do not support (or are just beginning to support) high performance. The organization is beginning to evaluate and may have made some improvements in key elements of these processes.*
50, 55, 60, or 65% An effective, systematic approach, responsive to the overall requirements of the Item, is evident. (A) The approach is well-deployed, although deployment may vary in some areas or work units. (D) A fact-based, systematic evaluation and improvement process and some organizational learning are in place for improving the efficiency and effectiveness of key processes. (L) The approach is aligned with organizational needs identified in response to the other Criteria Items. (I)	*5.1 Work Systems.* The organization has effective, systematic processes in place to do the following: a. *Organization and Management of Work.* Organize and manage work and jobs to enable workers and managers to achieve high performance objectives. b. *Employee Performance Management System.* Ensure compensation practices (such as employee feedback, recognition, and rewards/pay) align with and support the achievement of high performance objectives. c. *Hiring and Career Progression.* Ensure career progression opportunities and related work force practices align with and support the achievement of high-performance objectives. The processes of managing work and reinforcing and recognizing employee performance are generally aligned with organizational needs. *Some relatively minor gaps may exist in the deployment of these processes in some parts of the organization. However, there is a systematic, fact-based process in place to evaluate and improve the efficiency/effectiveness of some of the key elements of (a), (b), and/or (c) above.*

Continued

5.1 Work Systems *(35 points possible)*	Continued
Scoring Guidelines	**Expected Observations**

70, 75, 80, or 85% An effective, systematic approach, responsive to the multiple requirements of the Item, is evident. (A) The approach is well-deployed, with no significant gaps (D). Fact-based, systematic evaluation and improvement and organizational learning are key management tools; there is clear evidence of refinement and innovation as a result of organizational-level analysis and sharing. (L) The approach is integrated with your organizational needs identified in response to the other Criteria Items. (I) **90, 95, or 100%** An effective, systematic approach, fully responsive to the multiple requirements of the Item, is evident. (A) The approach is fully deployed without significant weaknesses or gaps in any areas or work units. (D). Fact-based, systematic evaluation and improvement and organizational learning are key organization-wide tools; refinement and innovation, backed by analysis and sharing, are evident throughout the organization. (L) The approach is well-integrated with your organizational needs identified in response to the other Criteria Items. (I)	*5.1 Work Systems.* The organization has well-deployed, effective, systematic processes in place to do the following: a. *Organization and Management of Work* (1) Organize and manage work and jobs to— • Promote cooperation, initiative, empowerment, innovation, and organizational culture. • Achieve the agility to keep current with business needs. (2) Ensure work systems capitalize on the diverse ideas, cultures, and thinking of employees and the communities with which the organization interacts (considered to be the employee hiring and customer communities). (3) Achieve effective communication and skill sharing across work units, jobs, and locations. b. *Employee Performance Management System* Ensure the employee performance management system, including feedback to employees— • Supports high-performance work. • Supports a customer and business focus. Ensure compensation, recognition, and related reward and incentive practices reinforce high performance and a customer and business focus. c. *Hiring and Career Progression* (1) Identify characteristics and skills needed by potential employees. (2) Recruit, hire, and retain new employees and ensure the employees represent the diverse ideas, cultures, and thinking of the employee hiring community. (3) Accomplish effective succession planning for leadership and management positions, including senior leadership and manage effective career progression for all employees throughout the organization. *The approach is well-deployed with no significant gaps. In addition, there is a systematic, fact-based process in place to evaluate and improve (a), (b), and (c) above with clear evidence of innovation, learning, and organizational sharing which results in refinements and improved or excellent organization-wide integration, consistent with organizational needs.*

Notes:

N1. "Employees" refers to the organization's permanent, temporary, and part-time personnel, as well as any contract employees supervised by the organization. Employees include team leaders, supervisors, and managers at all levels. Contract employees supervised by a contractor should be addressed in Category 6.

N2. The "organization's work" refers to how employees are organized or organize themselves in formal and informal, temporary, or longer-term units. This might include work teams, process teams, project teams, customer action teams, problem-solving teams, centers of excellence, functional units, remote (e.g., at-home) workers, cross-functional teams, and departments—self-managed or managed by supervisors. "Jobs" refers to responsibilities, authorities, and tasks of individuals. In some work systems, jobs might be shared by a team.

N3. Compensation and recognition (5.1b) include promotions and bonuses that might be based upon performance, skills acquired, and other factors. Recognition includes monetary and nonmonetary, formal and informal, and individual and group mechanisms.

5.2 Employee Learning and Motivation *(25 points possible)*	
Scoring Guidelines	**Expected Observations**
10, 15, 20, or 25% The beginning of a systematic approach to the basic requirements of the Item is evident. (A) The approach is in the early stages of deployment in most areas or work units, inhibiting progress in achieving the basic requirements of the Item. (D) Early stages of a transition from reacting to problems to a general improvement orientation are evident. (L) The approach is aligned with other areas or work units largely through joint problem solving. (I)	*5.2 Employee Learning and Motivation.* The organization is in the beginning stages of establishing an effective education and training program to support employee learning and motivation to help employees achieve high performance (which is usually defined by strategic objectives and related action plans). *Major gaps exist where the education and training processes do not help most employees to achieve high performance. Reacting to problems with training and development is widespread; working to prevent problems is in the beginning stages.*
30, 35, 40, or 45% An effective, systematic approach, responsive to the basic requirements of the Item, is evident. (A) The approach is deployed, although some areas or work units are in early stages of deployment. (D) The beginning of a systematic approach to evaluation and improvement of key processes is evident. (L) The approach is in early stages of alignment with basic organizational needs identified in response to the other Criteria Categories. (I)	*5.2 Employee Learning and Motivation.* The organization has effective, systematic, education and training processes in place to support employee learning and motivation to help employees achieve high performance (which is usually defined by strategic objectives and related action plans). *Learning and motivation processes in some parts of the organization do not support (or are just beginning to support) high-performance work. The organization is beginning to evaluate and may have made some improvements in key elements of these processes.*
50, 55, 60, or 65% An effective, systematic approach, responsive to the overall requirements of the Item, is evident. (A) The approach is well-deployed, although deployment may vary in some areas or work units. (D) A fact-based, systematic evaluation and improvement process and some organizational learning are in place for improving the efficiency and effectiveness of key processes. (L) The approach is aligned with organizational needs identified in response to the other Criteria Items. (I)	*5.2 Employee Learning and Motivation.* The organization has effective, systematic processes in place to do the following: a. *Employee Education, Training, and Development.* Build employee knowledge, skills, and capabilities through education and training to help them achieve overall organizational objectives and high performance. b. *Motivation and Career Development.* Build employee knowledge, skills, and capabilities through career development programs to help them achieve overall organizational objectives and high performance. *The processes of training and developing employees are generally aligned with organizational needs. Some relatively minor gaps may exist in the deployment of these processes in some parts of the organization. However, there is a systematic, fact-based process in place to evaluate and improve the efficiency/effectiveness of some of the key elements of (a) and/or (b) above.*

Continued

5.2 Employee Learning and Motivation *(25 points possible)*	*Continued*
Scoring Guidelines	**Expected Observations**

70, 75, 80, or 85% An effective, systematic approach, responsive to the multiple requirements of the Item, is evident. (A) The approach is well-deployed, with no significant gaps (D). Fact-based, systematic evaluation and improvement and organizational learning are key management tools; there is clear evidence of refinement and innovation as a result of organizational-level analysis and sharing. (L) The approach is integrated with your organizational needs identified in response to the other Criteria Items. (I)

90, 95, or 100% An effective, systematic approach, fully responsive to the multiple requirements of the Item, is evident. (A) The approach is fully deployed without significant weaknesses or gaps in any areas or work units. (D). Fact-based, systematic evaluation and improvement and organizational learning are key organization-wide tools; refinement and innovation, backed by analysis and sharing, are evident throughout the organization. (L) The approach is well-integrated with your organizational needs identified in response to the other Criteria Items. (I)

5.2 Employee Learning and Motivation. The organization has well-deployed, effective, systematic processes in place to do the following:

a. *Employee Education, Training, and Development*
  (1) Ensure employee education and training—
    • Contribute to the achievement of action plans
    • Address key needs associated with organizational performance measurement, performance improvement, and technological change.
    • Balance short- and longer-term organizational objectives with employee needs for development, learning, and career progression.
  (2) Ensure employee education, training, and development address key organizational needs associated with—
    • New-employee orientation, diversity, ethical business practices, and management and leadership development.
    • Employee, workplace, and environmental safety.
  (3) Seek and use input from employees and their supervisors and managers to determine education and training need. Incorporate organizational learning and knowledge assets into education and training.
  (4) Deliver education and training based on input from employees and their supervisors and managers regarding options for the delivery of education and training. Use both formal and informal delivery approaches, including mentoring and other approaches, as appropriate.
  (5) Reinforce the use of new knowledge and skills on the job.
  (6) Evaluate the effectiveness of education and training, taking into account individual and organizational performance.

b. *Motivation and Career Development*
Motivate employees to develop and utilize their full potential. Use formal and informal mechanisms, with assistance from managers and supervisors, to help employees attain job- and career-related development and learning objectives.

The approach is well-deployed with no significant gaps. In addition, there is a systematic, fact-based process in place to evaluate and improve (a) and (b) above with clear evidence of innovation, learning, and organizational sharing which results in refinements and improved or excellent organization-wide integration, consistent with organizational needs.

Note:

Education and training delivery [5.2a(4)] *might* occur inside or outside the organization and involve on-the-job, classroom, computer-based, distance learning, and other types of delivery (formal or informal).

5.3 Employee Well-Being and Satisfaction *(25 points possible)*	
Scoring Guidelines	**Expected Observations**
10, 15, 20, or 25% The beginning of a systematic approach to the basic requirements of the Item is evident. (A) The approach is in the early stages of deployment in most areas or work units, inhibiting progress in achieving the basic requirements of the Item. (D) Early stages of a transition from reacting to problems to a general improvement orientation are evident. (L) The approach is aligned with other areas or work units largely through joint problem solving. (I)	*5.3 Employee Well-Being and Satisfaction.* The organization is in the beginning stages of establishing a safe, healthful work environment that contributes to the well-being and satisfaction of employees. *Major gaps exist where the organization has not created a work environment to promote employee well-being and satisfaction. Reacting to employee safety, motivation, and well-being problems is widespread; working to prevent problems is in the beginning stages.*
30, 35, 40, or 45% An effective, systematic approach, responsive to the basic requirements of the Item, is evident. (A) The approach is deployed, although some areas or work units are in early stages of deployment. (D) The beginning of a systematic approach to evaluation and improvement of key processes is evident. (L) The approach is in early stages of alignment with basic organizational needs identified in response to the other Criteria Categories. (I)	*5.3 Employee Well-Being and Satisfaction.* The organization has effective, systematic processes in place to provide a safe, healthful work environment that contributes to the well-being and satisfaction of employees. *Processes in some parts of the organization do not support (or are just beginning to support) employee well-being and satisfaction. The organization is beginning to evaluate and may have made some improvements in key elements of these processes.*
50, 55, 60, or 65% An effective, systematic approach, responsive to the overall requirements of the Item, is evident. (A) The approach is well-deployed, although deployment may vary in some areas or work units. (D) A fact-based, systematic evaluation and improvement process and some organizational learning are in place for improving the efficiency and effectiveness of key processes. (L) The approach is aligned with organizational needs identified in response to the other Criteria Items. (I)	*5.3 Employee Well-Being and Satisfaction.* The organization has effective, systematic processes in place to do the following: a. *Work Environment.* Maintain a safe, healthful work environment that contributes to the well-being, satisfaction, and motivation of all employees. b. *Employee Support and Satisfaction.* Provide benefits and maintain a support climate that contributes to the well-being, satisfaction, and motivation of all employees. *The processes to promote employee well-being and satisfaction are generally aligned with organizational needs. Some relatively minor gaps may exist in some parts of the organization to maintain a work environment and support climate that inhibit the achievement of employee well-being, satisfaction, and motivation. However, there is a systematic, fact-based process in place to evaluate and improve the efficiency/effectiveness of some of the key elements of (a) and/or (b) above.*

Continued

5.3 Employee Well-Being and Satisfaction *(25 points possible)*	*Continued*
Scoring Guidelines	**Expected Observations**

70, 75, 80, or 85% An effective, systematic approach, responsive to the multiple requirements of the Item, is evident. (A) The approach is well-deployed, with no significant gaps (D). Fact-based, systematic evaluation and improvement and organizational learning are key management tools; there is clear evidence of refinement and innovation as a result of organizational-level analysis and sharing. (L) The approach is integrated with your organizational needs identified in response to the other Criteria Items. (I)

90, 95, or 100% An effective, systematic approach, fully responsive to the multiple requirements of the Item, is evident. (A) The approach is fully deployed without significant weaknesses or gaps in any areas or work units. (D). Fact-based, systematic evaluation and improvement and organizational learning are key organization-wide tools; refinement and innovation, backed by analysis and sharing, are evident throughout the organization. (L) The approach is well-integrated with your organizational needs identified in response to the other Criteria Items. (I)

5.3 Employee Well-Being and Satisfaction. The organization has well-deployed, effective, systematic processes in place to do the following:

a. *Work Environment*
   (1) Improve workplace health, safety, security, and ergonomics.
   - Involve employees in workplace improvements.
   - Define performance measures or targets for each of key workplace factors (health, safety, security, and ergonomics).
   - Define significant differences in workplace factors and performance measures or targets, if different employee groups and work units have different work environments.
   (2) Ensure workplace preparedness for emergencies or disasters and ensure business continuity for the benefit of employees and customers.

b. *Employee Support and Satisfaction*
   (1) Determine the key factors that affect employee well-being, satisfaction, and motivation. Segment these factors, as appropriate, to consider the needs of a diverse work force and different categories and types of employees.
   (2) Provide services, benefits, and policies to support employees and tailor these to the needs of a diverse work force and different categories and types of employees.
   (3) Conduct formal and informal assessments to determine (measure) employee well-being, satisfaction, and motivation. Use different methods and measures as appropriate to capture accurate information about the well-being, satisfaction, and motivation across a diverse work force and for different categories and types of employees. Use these and other indicators, such as employee retention, absenteeism, grievances, safety, and productivity, to assess and improve employee well-being, satisfaction, and motivation.
   (4) Establish priorities for improving the work environment and employee support climate by relating assessment findings to key business results.

The approach is well-deployed with no significant gaps. In addition, there is a systematic, fact-based process in place to evaluate and improve (a) and (b) above with clear evidence of innovation, learning, and organizational sharing which results in refinements and improved or excellent organization-wide integration, consistent with organizational needs.

Notes:

N1. Specific factors that might affect employees' well-being, satisfaction, and motivation [5.3b(1)] include effective employee problem or grievance resolution; safety factors; employees' views of management; employee training, development, and career opportunities; employee preparation for changes in technology or the work organization; the work environment and other work conditions; management's empowerment of employees; information sharing by management; workload; cooperation and teamwork; recognition; services and benefits; communications; job security; compensation; and equal opportunity.

N2. Approaches for employee support [5.3b(2)] might include providing counseling, career development and employability services, recreational or cultural activities, nonwork-related education, day care, job rotation or sharing, special leave for family responsibilities or community service, home-safety training, flexible work hours and location, outplacement, and retirement benefits (including extended health care).

N3. Measures and indicators of well-being, satisfaction, and motivation (5.3b(3)] might include data on safety and absenteeism, the overall turnover rate, the turnover rate for customer contact employees, employees' charitable contributions, grievances, strikes, other job actions, insurance costs, worker's compensation claims, and results of surveys. Survey indicators of satisfaction might include employee knowledge of job roles, employee knowledge of organizational direction, and employee perception of empowerment and information sharing. Results relative to such measures and indicators should be reported in Item 7.4.

N4. Setting priorities [5.3b(4)] might draw upon human resource results presented in Item 7.4 and might involve addressing employee problems based on their impact on business results.

Scoring Guidelines	6.1 Value Creation Processes *(50 points possible)*
	Expected Observations
10, 15, 20, or 25% The beginning of a systematic approach to the basic requirements of the Item is evident. (A) The approach is in the early stages of deployment in most areas or work units, inhibiting progress in achieving the basic requirements of the Item. (D) Early stages of a transition from reacting to problems to a general improvement orientation are evident. (L) The approach is aligned with other areas or work units largely through joint problem solving. (I)	*6.1 Value Creation Processes.* The organization is in the beginning stages of establishing key processes for value creation (such as designing and producing core products and services important to creating customer value). *Major gaps exist where key value creation processes have not been developed that are essential to business success and growth. Reacting to problems with design and delivery of core business processes is widespread; working to prevent problems is in the beginning stages.*
30, 35, 40, or 45% An effective, systematic approach, responsive to the basic requirements of the Item, is evident. (A) The approach is deployed, although some areas or work units are in early stages of deployment. (D) The beginning of a systematic approach to evaluation and improvement of key processes is evident. (L) The approach is in early stages of alignment with basic organizational needs identified in response to the other Criteria Categories. (I)	*6.1 Value Creation Processes.* The organization has effective, systematic value creation processes in place (such as designing, producing, and delivering core products and services) important to creating customer value and achieving business success and growth (which is usually defined by strategic objectives and related action plans). *However, in some parts of the organization, effective systematic processes that are essential to value creation and business success and growth are just beginning to emerge. The organization is beginning to evaluate and may have made some improvements in key elements of these processes*
50, 55, 60, or 65% An effective, systematic approach, responsive to the overall requirements of the Item, is evident. (A) The approach is well-deployed, although deployment may vary in some areas or work units. (D) A fact-based, systematic evaluation and improvement process and some organizational learning are in place for improving the efficiency and effectiveness of key processes. (L) The approach is aligned with organizational needs identified in response to the other Criteria Items. (I)	*6.1 Value Creation Processes.* The organization has effective, systematic processes in place to do the following: a. Value Creation Processes. Design and manage key processes to create customer value (such as designing, producing, and delivering core products and services) and achieve business success and growth (which is usually defined by strategic objectives and related action plans). (Design activities for value creation and business processes should ensure key customer requirements are met. Management activities for these processes should ensure that process steps are effectively monitored and controlled to ensure required products and services are consistently delivered.)The value creation processes are generally aligned with organizational needs. *Some relatively minor gaps may exist in the deployment of these processes in some parts of the organization. However, there is a systematic, fact-based process in place to evaluate and improve the efficiency/effectiveness of some of the key elements of (a) above.*

Continued

6.1 Value Creation Processes *(50 points possible)*	*Continued*
Scoring Guidelines	**Expected Observations**

70, 75, 80, or 85% An effective, systematic approach, responsive to the multiple requirements of the Item, is evident. (A) The approach is well-deployed, with no significant gaps (D). Fact-based, systematic evaluation and improvement and organizational learning are key management tools; there is clear evidence of refinement and innovation as a result of organizational-level analysis and sharing. (L) The approach is integrated with your organizational needs identified in response to the other Criteria Items. (I)

90, 95, or 100% An effective, systematic approach, fully responsive to the multiple requirements of the Item, is evident. (A) The approach is fully deployed without significant weaknesses or gaps in any areas or work units. (D). Fact-based, systematic evaluation and improvement and organizational learning are key organization-wide tools; refinement and innovation, backed by analysis and sharing, are evident throughout the organization. (L) The approach is well-integrated with your organizational needs identified in response to the other Criteria Items. (I)

6.1 Value Creation Processes. The organization has well-deployed, effective, systematic processes in place to do the following:

a. *Value Creation Processes*
   (1) Define key product, service, and business processes used to—
       • Create or add value for the organization, its customers, and other key stakeholders.
       • Contribute to profitability and business success.
   (2) Determine and define (list) key value creation process requirements, incorporating input from customers, suppliers, and partners, as appropriate.
   (3) Design these processes to meet all the key requirements including the following:
       • Incorporate new technology and organizational knowledge into the design of these processes.
       • Incorporate cycle time, productivity, cost control, and other efficiency and effectiveness factors into the design of these processes.
       • Implement these processes to ensure they meet design requirements.
   (4) Define key performance measures or indicators used for the control and improvement of value creation processes.
       • Ensure day-to-day operation of these processes consistently meet key process requirements.
       • Ensure in-process measures and appropriate customer, supplier, and partner input are used to manage these processes.
   (5) Minimize overall costs associated with inspections, tests, and process or performance audits, as appropriate, while at the same time prevent defects and rework, and minimize warranty costs, as appropriate.
   (6) Improve value creation processes to—
       • Achieve better performance.
       • Reduce variability.
       • Improve products and services
       • Keep the processes current with business needs and directions and share improvements with other organizational units and processes.

The approach is well-deployed with no significant gaps. In addition, there is a systematic, fact-based process in place to evaluate and improve (a) above with clear evidence of innovation, learning, and organizational sharing which results in refinements and improved or excellent organization wide integration, consistent with organizational needs.

Notes:

N1. Key value creation processes are those most important to "running the business" and maintaining or achieving a sustainable competitive advantage. They are the processes that involve the majority of the organization's employees and produce customer, stockholder, and other key stakeholder value. They include the processes through which the organization adds greatest value to its products and services. They also include the business processes most critical to adding value to the business itself, resulting in success and growth.

N2. Key value creation processes differ greatly among organizations, depending on many factors. These factors include the nature of the products and services, how they are produced and delivered, technology requirements, customer and supplier relationships and involvement, outsourcing, importance of research and development, role of technology acquisition, information and knowledge management, supply chain management, mergers and acquisitions, global expansion, and sales and marketing. Responses to Item 6.1 should be based upon the most critical requirements and processes for products, services, and business.

N3. To achieve better process performance and reduce variability, the organization might implement approaches such as a lean enterprise system, six sigma methodology, use of ISO 9000:2000 standards, or other process improvement tools.

N4. To provide as complete and concise a response as possible for key value creation processes, you might want to use a tabular format identifying the key processes and the attributes of each as called for in questions 6.1a(1)–6.1a(6).

N5. he results of improvements in product and service performance should be reported in Item 7.2. The results of operational improvements in product and service design and delivery processes and key business processes should be reported in Item 7.5.

Scoring Guidelines	**6.2 Support Processes** *(35 points possible)* Expected Observations
10, 15, 20, or 25% The beginning of a systematic approach to the basic requirements of the Item is evident. (A) The approach is in the early stages of deployment in most areas or work units, inhibiting progress in achieving the basic requirements of the Item. (D) Early stages of a transition from reacting to problems to a general improvement orientation are evident. (L) The approach is aligned with other areas or work units largely through joint problem solving. (I)	*6.2 Support Processes.* The organization is in the beginning stages of establishing key processes to support value creation and business success and growth. *Major gaps exist where key value support processes have not been developed. Reacting to problems with design and delivery of support processes is widespread; working to prevent problems is in the beginning stages.*
30, 35, 40, or 45% An effective, systematic approach, responsive to the basic requirements of the Item, is evident. (A) The approach is deployed, although some areas or work units are in early stages of deployment. (D) The beginning of a systematic approach to evaluation and improvement of key processes is evident. (L) The approach is in early stages of alignment with basic organizational needs identified in response to the other Criteria Categories. (I)	*6.2 Support Processes.* The organization has effective, systematic processes in place to support value creation and business success and growth. *However, these support processes are just beginning to emerge in some parts of the organization. The organization is beginning to evaluate and make some improvements in the key elements of these support processes.*
50, 55, 60, or 65% An effective, systematic approach, responsive to the overall requirements of the Item, is evident. (A) The approach is well-deployed, although deployment may vary in some areas or work units. (D) A fact-based, systematic evaluation and improvement process and some organizational learning are in place for improving the efficiency and effectiveness of key processes. (L) The approach is aligned with organizational needs identified in response to the other Criteria Items. (I)	*6.2 Support Processes.* The organization has effective, systematic processes in place to do the following: a. *Support Processes.* Design and manage key processes that support customer value and business success and growth. (Design activities for support processes should ensure all key customer requirements are met. Management activities for support services should ensure that process steps are effectively monitored and controlled to ensure required products and services are consistently delivered.) *The support processes are generally aligned with organizational and value creation needs. Some relatively minor gaps may exist in the deployment of these processes in some parts of the organization. However, there is a systematic, fact-based process in place to evaluate and improve the efficiency/effectiveness of some of the key elements of (a) above.*

Continued

6.2 Support Processes *(35 points possible)*		*Continued*
Scoring Guidelines	**Expected Observations**	

70, 75, 80, or 85% An effective, systematic approach, responsive to the multiple requirements of the Item, is evident. (A) The approach is well-deployed, with no significant gaps (D). Fact-based, systematic evaluation and improvement and organizational learning are key management tools; there is clear evidence of refinement and innovation as a result of organizational-level analysis and sharing. (L) The approach is integrated with your organizational needs identified in response to the other Criteria Items. (I)	*6.2 Support Processes.* The organization has well-deployed, effective, systematic processes in place to do the following:
	
	a. *Support Processes*
	(1) Define key processes that support value creation processes.
	(2) Determine and define (list) key support process requirements, incorporating input from appropriate internal and external customers, suppliers, and partners.
	(3) Design support processes to meet all the key requirements including the following:
	  • Incorporate new technology and organizational knowledge into the design of these processes.
	  • Incorporate cycle time, productivity, cost control, and other efficiency and effectiveness factors into the design of these processes.
	  • Implement these processes to ensure they meet design requirements.
	(4) Define key performance measures or indicators used for the control and improvement of support processes.
	  • Ensure day-to-day operation of these processes consistently meets key process requirements.
	  • Ensure in-process measures and appropriate customer, supplier, and partner input are used to manage these processes.

90, 95, or 100% An effective, systematic approach, fully responsive to the multiple requirements of the Item, is evident. (A) The approach is fully deployed without significant weaknesses or gaps in any areas or work units. (D). Fact-based, systematic evaluation and improvement and organizational learning are key organization-wide tools; refinement and innovation, backed by analysis and sharing, are evident throughout the organization. (L) The approach is well-integrated with your organizational needs identified in response to the other Criteria Items. (I)	(5) Minimize overall costs associated with inspections, tests, and process or performance audits, while at the same time prevent defects and rework, and minimize warranty costs, as appropriate.
	(6) Improve value creation processes to—
	  • Achieve better performance.
	  • Reduce variability.
	  • Improve products and services
	  • Keep the processes current with business needs and directions and share improvements with other organizational units and processes.
	
	The approach is well-deployed with no significant gaps. In addition, there is a systematic, fact-based process in place to evaluate and improve (a) above with clear evidence of innovation, learning, and organizational sharing which results in refinements and improved or excellent organization-wide integration, consistent with organizational needs.

Notes:

N1. Key support processes are those that are considered most important for support of the organization's value creation processes, employees, and daily operations. These might include finance and accounting, facilities management, legal, human resource, project management, and administration processes.

N2. The results of improvements in key support processes and key support process performance results should be reported in Item 7.5.

Category 7 Results

Category 7 uses different scoring guidelines than Categories 1 through 6. No additional clarification has been developed for category 7 since the ambiguities in Process scoring are not present in Results scoring. However, a complete reference guide is included in the CD accompanying this book, which includes Category 7 Criteria and scoring guidelines.

Self-Assessments of Organizations and Management Systems

Baldrige-based self-assessments of organization performance and management systems take several forms, ranging from rigorous and time-intensive to simple and somewhat superficial. This section discusses the various approaches to organizational self-assessment and the pros and cons of each. Curt Reimann, the first director of the Malcolm Baldrige National Quality Award Office and the closing speaker for the 10th Quest for Excellence Conference, spoke of the need to streamline assessments to get a good sense of strengths, opportunities for improvement, and the vital few areas to focus leadership and drive organizational change. Three distinct types of self-assessment will be examined: the written narrative, the Likert-scale survey, and the behaviorally anchored survey.

Full-Length Written Narrative

The Baldrige application development process is the most time-consuming organizational self-assessment process. To apply for the Baldrige Award, applicants must prepare a 50-page written narrative to address the requirements of the performance excellence Criteria. In the written self-assessment, the applicant is expected to describe the processes and programs it has in place to drive performance excellence. The Baldrige application process serves as the vehicle for self-assessment in most state-level quality awards. The process has not changed since the national quality award program was created in 1987 (except for reducing the maximum page limit from 85 pages to 50 pages). (Author's note: The CD attached to the back cover of this book contains a document designed to facilitate the collection of information within an organization to serve as a basis for a complete and thorough written application.)

Over the years, three methods have been used to prepare the full-length, comprehensive written narrative self-assessment.

1. The most widely used technique involves gathering a team of people to prepare the application. The team members are usually assigned one of the seven Categories and asked to develop a narrative to address the Criteria requirements of that Category. The Category writing teams are frequently subdivided to prepare responses Item by Item. After the initial draft is complete, an oversight team consolidates the narrative and tries to ensure processes are linked and integrated throughout. Finally, top leaders review and "scrub" the written narrative to put the best spin on the systems, processes, and results reported.

2. Another technique is similar to that described previously. However, instead of subdividing the writing team according to the Baldrige Categories, the team remains together to write the entire application. In this way, the application may be more coherent and the linkages between business processes are easier to understand. This approach also helps to ensure consistency and integrity of the review processes. With fewer people involved, however, the natural "blind spots" of the team may prevent a full and accurate analysis of the management system. Finally, as with the method described previously, top leaders review and scrub the written narrative.

3. The third method of preparing the written narrative is the least common and involves one person writing for several days to produce the application. Considering the immense amount of knowledge and work involved, it is easy to understand why the third method is used so rarely.

With all three methods, external experts are usually involved. Baldrige Award recipients usually reported they hired consultants to help them finalize their application by sharpening its focus and clarifying linkages.

Pros:

- Baldrige Award–winning organizations report that the discipline of producing a full-length written self-assessment (Baldrige application) helped them learn about their organization and identify opportunities for improvement before the site-visit team arrived. The written narrative self-assessment process clearly helped focus leaders on their organization's strengths and opportunities for improvement—provided that a complete and honest assessment was made.

- The written narrative self-assessment also provides rich information to help examiners conduct a site visit (the purpose of which is to verify and clarify the information contained in the written self-assessment).

Cons:

- Written narrative self-assessments are extremely time and labor intensive. Organizations that use this approach for Baldrige or state applications or for internal organizational review report that it requires between approximately 2000 and 4000 person-hours of effort—sometimes much more. People working on the self-assessment are diverted from other tasks during this period.

- Because the application is closely scrutinized and carefully scrubbed, and because of page limits, it may not fully and accurately describe the actual management processes and systems of the organization. Decisions based on misleading or incomplete information may take the organization down the wrong path.

- Although the written self-assessment provides information to help guide a site visit, examiners cannot determine the depth of deployment because only a few points of view are represented in the narrative.

- Finally, and perhaps most importantly, the discipline and knowledge required to write a meaningful narrative self-assessment is usually far greater than that possessed within the vast majority of organizations. Even the four 1997 Baldrige Award winners hired expert consultants to help them prepare and refine their written narrative.

Short Written Narrative

Two of the most significant obstacles to writing a useful full-length written narrative self-assessment are poor knowledge of the performance excellence Criteria and the time required to produce a meaningful assessment. If people do not understand the Criteria, it takes significantly longer to prepare a written self-assessment. In fact, the amount of time required to write an application/assessment is inversely related to the writers' knowledge of the Criteria. The difficulty associated with writing a full-length narrative has prevented many organizations from participating in state, local, or national award programs.

To encourage more organizations to begin the performance improvement journey, many state award programs developed progressively higher levels of recognition, ranging from "commitment" at the low end, through "demonstrated progress," to "achieving excellence" at the top of the range. Even with progressive levels of recognition, however, the obstacle of preparing a 50-page written narrative prevented many from engaging in the process. To help resolve this problem, several state programs permit applicants who seek recognition at the lower levels to submit a 7- to 20-page "short" written narrative self-assessment. The short form ranges from requiring a one-page description per category to one page per Item (hence the 7- to 20-page range in length).

Pros:

- It clearly takes less time to prepare the short form.

- Because of the reduced effort required to complete the self-assessment, more organizations are beginning the process of assessing and improving their performance.

Cons:

- The short form provides significantly less information to help examiners prepare for the site visit. In some cases, the very short, seven-page version provides examiners with no useful information.

- The short form is usually as closely scrutinized and carefully scrubbed as its full-length cousin. This reduces accuracy and value to both the organization and examiners.

- The knowledge required to write even a short narrative prevents organizations in the beginning stages from preparing an accurate and meaningful assessment.

- Finally, there is not enough information presented in the short form to understand the extent of deployment of the systems and processes covered by the Criteria.

The Survey Approach

Just about everyone is familiar with a Likert-scale survey. These surveys typically ask respondents to rate, on a scale of one to five, the extent to which they strongly disagree or strongly agree with a comment. The following is an example of a simple Likert-scale survey item from the "Are We Making Progress as Leaders" survey released in February 2004 by the Baldrige Award Office of NIST:

Our leadership team shares information about the organization				
1	2	3	4	5
Strongly Disagree				Strongly Agree

A variation on the simple Likert-scale survey item has been developed in an attempt to improve consistency among respondents. Brief descriptors have been added at each level as shown below in the descriptive Likert-scale survey item:

Senior leaders effectively share information about the organization				
1	2	3	4	5
None	Few	Some	Many	Most

Pros:

- The Likert-scale survey is quick and easy to administer. People from all functions and levels within the organization can provide their opinion.

Cons:

- Both the simple and the descriptive Likert-scale survey items are subject to wide ranges of interpretation. One person's rating of "two" and another person's rating of "four" may actually describe the same systems or behaviors. This

problem of scoring reliability raises serious questions about the usefulness of both the simple and the descriptive survey techniques for conducting accurate organizational self-assessments. After all, a quick and easy survey that produces inaccurate data still has low value. That is the main reason why states have not adopted the Likert-scale survey as a tool for conducting the self-assessments, even for organizations in the beginning stages of the quality journey.

The Behaviorally Anchored Survey

A behaviorally anchored survey contains elements of a written narrative and a survey approach to conducting a self-assessment. The method is simple. Instead of brief descriptors such as "strongly agree/strongly disagree" or "none–few–some–many–most," a more complete behavioral description is presented for each level of the survey scale. Respondents simply identify the behavioral description that most closely fits the activities in the organization. In addition, by asking the respondent to describe briefly the processes used by the organization to do what the Baldrige Criteria require, we can simulate the kind of information collected on a site visit, checking deployment and process integration. A sample is shown on the next page.

Since the behavioral descriptions in the survey combine the requirements of the Criteria with the standards from the scoring guidelines, it is possible to produce accurate Baldrige-based scores for Items and Categories for the entire organization and for any subgroup or division.

Figure 37 provides sample scores for the entire organization. The chart below shows the percent scores, on a zero to 100 scale, for each Item. This helps users determine, at a glance, the relative strengths and weaknesses.

Figure 38 shows the ratings by job classification subgroup, in this case, positions of senior leaders and employees. In Figure 37, Item 1.1, Leadership System reflected a rating of 50 percent. According to the breakout in Figure 38, however, senior leaders believe the processes are much stronger (more than 60 percent) than employees (less than 35 percent). This typically indicates incomplete systems development or poor deployment of existing systems and processes required by the Item.

	Improving Leadership Effectiveness throughout the Organization [1.1c(4)]
How well do senior leaders, managers, and supervisors at all levels evaluate and improve their effectiveness?	
1 **Not Evident** ☐	Leaders do not systematically check their own effectiveness or bother to become more effective.
2 **Beginning** ☑	A few leaders use financial and budget results to check their own effectiveness but do not make improvements based on this information.
3 **Basically Effective** ☐	Some leaders and managers effectively use financial and budget results to check their own effectiveness. They use this information to set personal improvement goals but do not consistently make improvements.
4 **Mature** ☐	Many leaders and managers effectively use financial and budget results and other performance results. They use this information to set personal improvement goals. Some have improved their own effectiveness.
5 **Advanced** ☐	Most leaders and managers effectively use financial and budget results and other key performance results to evaluate their own effectiveness. They use this information to set personal improvement goals. Many have improved their own effectiveness. The system to evaluate and improve leadership effectiveness is routinely checked and some refinements have been made.
6 **Role Model** ☐	Nearly all leaders and managers use key performance results and employee feedback to evaluate their own effectiveness. They use this information to set personal improvement goals. Most have improved their own effectiveness. The system to evaluate and improve leadership effectiveness is routinely checked and ongoing refinements have been made.
? or Not Applicable ☐	I do not have enough information to answer this question or it is not applicable to my organization.
Describe how the leaders and managers at all levels use performance data and employee feedback to improve their own effectiveness. List the usual measures that are used to assess leadership effectiveness. How widely is this done in the organization? Describe improvements to this process, if any. Suggest ways to improve this process.	

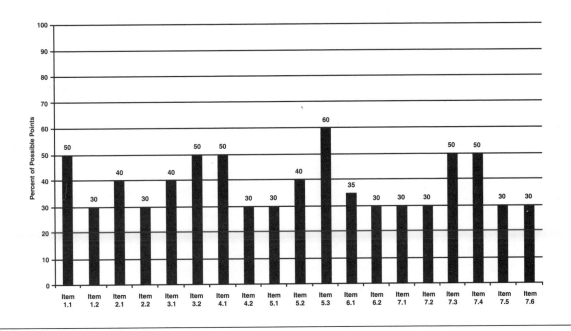

Figure 37 Sample organization overall percent scores by item.

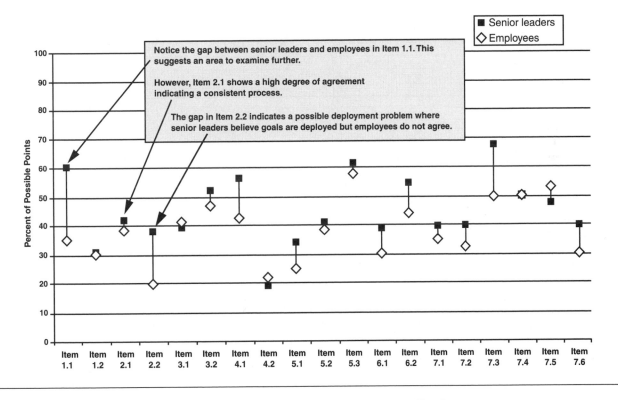

Figure 38 Sample organization position percent scores by item and job classification.

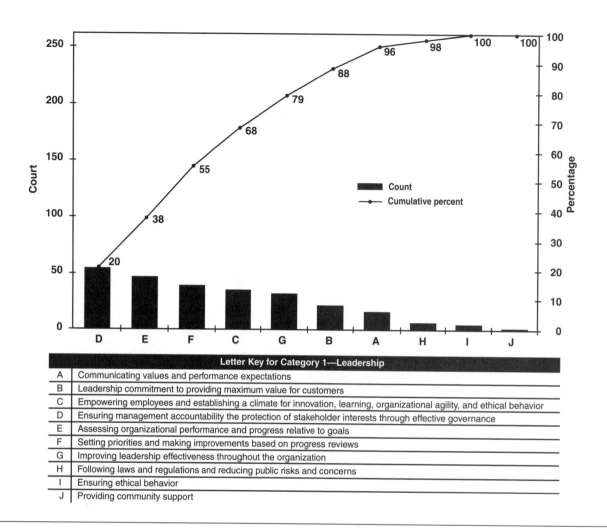

Letter Key for Category 1—Leadership

A	Communicating values and performance expectations
B	Leadership commitment to providing maximum value for customers
C	Empowering employees and establishing a climate for innovation, learning, organizational agility, and ethical behavior
D	Ensuring management accountability the protection of stakeholder interests through effective governance
E	Assessing organizational performance and progress relative to goals
F	Setting priorities and making improvements based on progress reviews
G	Improving leadership effectiveness throughout the organization
H	Following laws and regulations and reducing public risks and concerns
I	Ensuring ethical behavior
J	Providing community support

Figure 39   Category 1—Leadership: analysis of areas most needing improvement.

The Pareto diagram in Figure 39 presents data reflecting the areas respondents believed were most in need of improvement. Continuing with the leadership example, it is clear that respondents believe that leaders need to do a better job of assessing organizational performance and progress relative to goals (theme D), setting priorities and making improvements based on progress reviews (theme E), and improving leadership effectiveness throughout the organization (theme F). This helps examiners focus on which areas in leadership may present the most important opportunities for improvement.

Figure 40 allows examiners to determine what type of employee identified the various improvement priorities. Look at "D" and "F" in Figure 40 and you

will see that employees identified the need to improve these areas by a 2 to 1 margin over senior managers. This tends to indicate a deployment gap and suggests that senior managers are not perceived as effective as they believe themselves to be.

Finally, a complete report of the comments and explanations of the respondents can be prepared and used by examiners and organization leaders for improvement planning.

Pros:

- Descriptive behavioral anchors increase the consistency of rating. That is, one respondent's rating of "two" is likely to reflect the same observed behaviors as another respondent's rating of "two."

1. Leadership

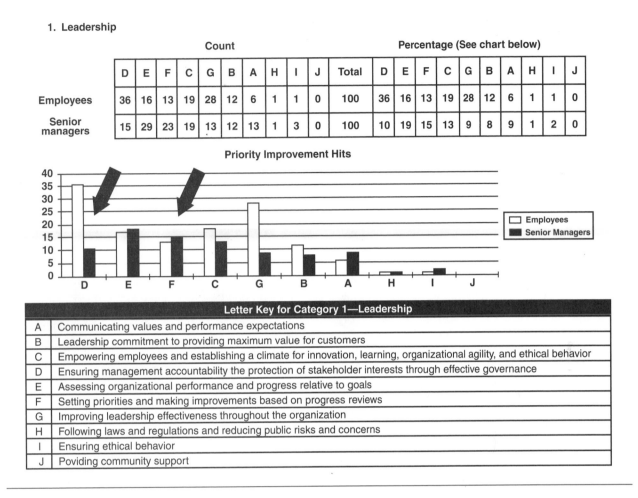

	Count											Percentage (See chart below)									
	D	E	F	C	G	B	A	H	I	J	Total	D	E	F	C	G	B	A	H	I	J
Employees	36	16	13	19	28	12	6	1	1	0	100	36	16	13	19	28	12	6	1	1	0
Senior managers	15	29	23	19	13	12	13	1	3	0	100	10	19	15	13	9	8	9	1	2	0

	Letter Key for Category 1—Leadership
A	Communicating values and performance expectations
B	Leadership commitment to providing maximum value for customers
C	Empowering employees and establishing a climate for innovation, learning, organizational agility, and ethical behavior
D	Ensuring management accountability the protection of stakeholder interests through effective governance
E	Assessing organizational performance and progress relative to goals
F	Setting priorities and making improvements based on progress reviews
G	Improving leadership effectiveness throughout the organization
H	Following laws and regulations and reducing public risks and concerns
I	Ensuring ethical behavior
J	Poviding community support

Figure 40 Priority improvement counts and percentages—by position for the Leadership Category.

- Although completing a behaviorally anchored survey requires more reading than a Likert-scale survey, the amount of time and cost required to complete it is still less than 10 percent of the time and cost required to prepare a written narrative.

- Because it is easy and simple to use, the behaviorally anchored survey does not impose a barrier to participation as does the written narrative. States and companies that use surveys with properly written behavioral anchors find the accuracy of the assessment to be as good and in many cases better than that achieved by the full-length narrative self-assessment, and significantly better than Likert-scale or short narrative assessments. By obtaining input from a cross section of functions, locations, and grade levels throughout the organization, a performance profile can be developed, which not only identifies strengths and opportunities for improvement, but deployment gaps as well—something the written narrative assessments rarely provide.

- For organizations doing business throughout the world, the behaviorally anchored survey—translated into the native language of respondents—permits far greater input than the written narrative.

- Modern techniques involving surveying through Internet access have created an easy way to survey a large, global company.

- Accurate survey data, based on behavioral anchors, can be used to compare or benchmark organizations within and among industries, and can also support longitudinal performance studies.

- Finally, examiners report that the effort required to analyze survey data and plan a site visit is about 50 percent less than the amount of effort required to analyze and prepare for a site visit based on a written narrative. Moreover, they report better information regarding deployment.

Cons:

- Organizations with highly developed performance management systems that seek to apply for top state or national recognition may prefer to practice developing the full-length narrative self-assessment because it is usually required.

- Examiners who are comfortable with the Baldrige application review process, which requires 25 or more hours to conduct an individual review of a full-length narrative self-assessment, initially find it disconcerting to develop comments and plan a site visit based on data gathered from a survey. Different training for examiners is required to develop skills at using survey data to prepare feedback and plan site visits.

Note: The preceding report summary of a behaviorally anchored self-assessment survey is administered by the National Council for Performance Excellence. Readers may contact them by calling 802-655-1922 or by writing to NCPE, 480 Hercules Drive, Colchester, VT 05446. Several state quality awards and many private-sector organizations are using this type of assessment instead of the written narrative form of evaluation. NCPE is the only organization authorized to administer this assessment tool. Any other use is not permitted.

In conclusion:

- The full-length written narrative self-assessment is costly. It provides useful information both to examiners and the organizations completing it. The process of completing the written self-assessment can help more advanced organizations to focus and work together as a team.

- The usefulness of the short-form written self-assessment is marginal, especially for beginning organizations; little useful information is provided to examiners and managers/employees of the organization. Because the short-form written self-assessment takes less time to complete, one barrier to participation is lowered.

- Concerns over the accuracy and inter-rater reliability of the simple and descriptive Likert scales make their use in conducting effective organizational assessments of management systems marginal.

- The behaviorally anchored survey with comments from respondents combines the benefits of survey speed with the accuracy and completeness of a well-developed written narrative self-assessment. In addition, the behaviorally anchored survey can identify gaps in deployment unlike the written narrative self-assessment and is less costly and faster to administer than the written narrative.

More information about business, education, and health care surveys can be obtained from the National Council for Performance Excellence, 480 Hercules Drive, Colchester, VT 05446, (802-655-1922). Its website is: www.PerformanceExcellence.com.

Following is a sample of a behaviorally anchored survey.

2004 Baldrige Business

Organizational Self-Assessment, Behaviorally Anchored Version

Customized Demographic Profile

Each participating organization completes a customized demographic profile (a generic sample follows). In this way, survey data can be analyzed by these variables to help pinpoint specific areas needing improvement. This allows the extent of use (deployment) of management systems to be examined.

Please circle one selection from each column below to indicate your position within the organization.

Position	Location	Function	Org.	Years of Service
• Executive	• North	• Engineering	• 1	• 0 < 1
• Manager	• South	• Sales	• 2	• 1 < 3
• Supervisor	• East	• Human Resources	• 3	• 3 < 5
• Technician	• West	• Finance	• 4	• 5 < 10
• Individual Contributor	• HQ	Marketing	• 5	• 10 +
		• Materials Planning•	Other	
		• Manufacturing		
		• Supply Management		
		• Info Technology		
		• Other		

BALDRIGE IN-DEPTH FOR BUSINESS INSTRUCTIONS

This survey consists of 58 themes or questions that relate to the 2004 Baldrige Performance Excellence Criteria. It is organized into seven "sections," one for each of the seven Performance Excellence Criteria Categories.

- To the best of your knowledge, select a rating (1 to 6) that describes the level of development in your organization. Note that all of the elements of a statement must be true before you can select that level. If one or more is not true, you must go to a lower level. After you have selected the

rating level, please enter the value in the empty box to the right of the row of statements.

➡ Accuracy tip: The rating scale involves your assessment about the extent of use of the required management processes. The following definitions should help you rate this consistently:

✔ Few	less than 15%
✔ Some	15% to less than 30%
✔ Many	30% to less than 50%
✔ Most	50% to less than 80%
✔ Nearly All	80% to less than 99%
✔ All	100%

➤ Time-saving tip: Start reading at level 3. If all parts of the statement are true, go to level 4, if not, drop back to read level 2. After a few answers, save even more time by starting at the number you select most often. Don't waste time by reading from row 1 each time (unless most of your answers are 1).

- If you do not know an answer, enter NA (Not Applicable/Does Not Apply) or ? (Don't Know). If you are unsure of the meaning of a word or phrase, please check the glossary at the end of this booklet.

- After all statements in the first category (Leadership) have been rated, go to the last page in the Leadership category. Follow the directions and identify two areas you believe most need improvement in your organization now. Then, go back to the space below each row of statements you identified as vital to improve. Describe briefly the activities your organization conducts that relate to the topic. Also, please suggest steps that your organization or its leaders could take to improve the processes. Your thoughtful comments are as helpful as the rating itself. If you want to comment on more themes, please do so.

- Continue in the same way to complete all seven Categories.

SUMMARY OF CATEGORY 1: LEADERSHIP

This sample assessment looks at one question in the Leadership Category (see sample question at Figure 41). The full-length assessment of Leadership contains 10 themes: The first part (seven questions 1A through 1G) looks at how senior leaders guide the organization by setting directions and monitoring performance to help assure the long-term success of the organization. Senior leaders should express clear values and set high performance expectations that address the needs of all stakeholders. In addition, an effective governance structure must be in place to ensure management accountability and the protection of stakeholder interests.

- You are asked to comment on the extent to which senior leaders set directions, communicate, and deploy values and performance expectations, and take into account the expectations of customers and other stakeholders. This includes how leaders create an environment for innovation, learning, knowledge sharing, and organizational agility. You are asked how the organizational governance structure ensures accountability for fiscal and management integrity as well as the protection of stakeholder interests. You also are asked how senior leaders review organizational performance, what key performance measures they regularly review, and how review findings are used to drive improvement and change, including improving leaders' effectiveness.

The second part (three questions 1H through 1J) looks at how well the organization meets its responsibilities to the public and how the organization practices good citizenship.

- You are asked how the organization addresses current and future impacts on society in a proactive manner and how it ensures ethical business practices in all stakeholder interactions. The impacts and practices are expected to cover all relevant and important areas—products, services, and operations. You also are asked how the organization, senior leaders, and employees identify, support, and strengthen key communities as part of good citizenship practices.

Leadership Commitment to Providing Maximum Value for Customers [Baldrige reference: 1.1a(1)]

1B. How serious are top leaders about providing maximum value to customers and stakeholders? Do they make it clear that producing value for all customers and stakeholders is critical for success?

Not Evident

1. Leaders focus on short-term business issues, not on value for customers. Leaders react to problems and no consistency is evident.

Beginning

2. A few leaders are just beginning to focus on value for customers. The process is not very effective since it is not used widely in the organization. The process is not evaluated to see how it could be improved.

Basically Effective

3. Some leaders effectively focus on providing maximum value for customers and other stakeholders through their written and verbal communication. They are starting to gather data about the effectiveness of some of these processes.

Mature

4. Many leaders and managers effectively focus on providing maximum value to many customer and stakeholder groups. They sometimes check on the effectiveness of activities that focus on customer value. They gather data to evaluate the effectiveness of these processes but do not usually use the information to make improvements.

Advanced

5. Most leaders and managers effectively focus on providing maximum value to most customers and stakeholders consistent with organizational needs. They regularly check on the effectiveness of customer value activities. They sometimes make improvements. Some sharing of effective practices within the organization is done.

Role Model

6. Nearly all leaders and managers effectively focus on providing maximum value to all key customers and stakeholders consistent with organizational needs. They regularly check on the effectiveness of customer value activities. They make ongoing improvements. They routinely innovate and share the best practices across the organization.

Figure 41 Sample Leadership question.

SUMMARY OF CATEGORY 2: STRATEGIC PLANNING

This sample assessment looks at one question in the Strategic Planning Category (see sample question at Figure 42). The full-length assessment of Strategic Planning contains seven themes.

The first part (three questions 2A through 2C) looks at how the organization develops its strategic plans. The Category stresses that customer-driven quality and operational performance excellence are key strategic issues that need to be integral parts of the organization's overall planning. Specifically:

- Customer-driven quality is a strategic view of quality. The focus is on the drivers of customer satisfaction, customer retention, new markets, and market share—key factors in competitiveness, profitability, and business success.

- Operational performance improvement contributes to short-term and longer-term productivity, growth, and cost/price competitiveness. Building operational capability—including speed, responsiveness, and flexibility—represents an investment in strengthening your competitive fitness.

The second part (four questions 2D through 2G) looks at the way work processes support the organization's strategic directions to help make sure that priorities are carried out.

- The organization must translate its strategic objectives into action plans to accomplish the objectives. The organization must also be able to assess the progress of action plans. The aim is to ensure that strategies are understood and followed by everyone in the organization to help achieve goals.

Developing and Deploying Action Plans Based on Strategic Objectives [Baldrige Reference: 2.2a(1)]

2D. How well do the organization's action plans support its strategic objectives? Do the action plans help all parts of the organization pull together (align) to carry out its strategic objectives? Are appropriate resources allocated to carry out the actions?

Not Evident

1. The organization does not systematically develop action plans to support strategic objectives. They react to problems within the organization and no consistency is evident.

Beginning

2. The organization has developed action plans to support a few strategic objectives. Resources are not effectively allocated to achieve desired actions. The process is not very effective since it is not used widely in the organization. The process is not evaluated to see how it could be improved.

Basically Effective

3. The organization has developed action plans at some levels in the organization to support some strategic objectives. Resources are generally allocated to achieve desired actions. The organization has started to gather data about the effectiveness of some of the process to develop action plans and align resources to achieve them.

Mature

4. The organization has developed action plans at many levels in the organization to support many strategic objectives. Resources are effectively allocated to achieve desired actions. The action plans and resources are sometimes improved to make sure the work of some employees is focused on actions needed to carry out strategic objectives. The organization sometimes gathers data to evaluate the effectiveness of the process to develop action plans and align resources to achieve them but does not usually use the information to make improvements.

Advanced

5. The organization has developed action plans at most levels in the organization to support most strategic objectives. Resources are effectively allocated to achieve desired actions. The approach they use is consistent with organizational needs. The organization regularly gathers data to evaluate the effectiveness of the process to develop action plans and align resources to achieve them. The action plans and resources are sometimes improved to make sure the work of most employees is focused on actions needed to carry out strategic objectives. Some sharing of improved practices to develop and deploy action plans within the organization takes place.

Continued

Role Model

6. The organization has developed action plans at all levels in the organization to support nearly all strategic objectives throughout the organization. Resources are effectively allocated to achieve desired actions. The approach they use is consistent with organizational needs. The action plans and resources are regularly checked to see how well they support objectives. Improvements or changes resulting from the action plans are maintained. Action plans are consistently improved to make sure the work of nearly all employees is focused on actions needed to carry out strategic objectives. They routinely innovate and share the best practices to develop and deploy action plans across the organization.

Figure 42 Sample Strategic Planning question. *(Continued)*

SUMMARY OF CATEGORY 3: CUSTOMER AND MARKET FOCUS

This sample assessment looks at one question in the Customer and Market Focus Category (see sample question at Figure 43). The full-length assessment of Customer and Market Focus contains 10 themes.

The first part (four questions 3A through 3D) looks at how the organization tries to understand what the customers and the marketplace want. The organization must learn about customers and markets to help make sure it understands new customer requirements, offers the right products and services, and keeps pace with changing customer demands and increasing competition.

- You are asked how the organization determines key customer groups and how it segments the markets.

- You are asked how the organization determines the most important product/service features.

- Also, you are asked how the organization improves the way it listens and learns from customers so that it keeps current with changing business needs.

The second part (six questions 3E through 3J) looks at how well the organization builds good relationships with customers to get repeat business and positive referrals. You are also asked how the organi-

Figure 42 Sample Strategic Planning question.

zation gets data on customer satisfaction and dissatisfaction for customers and competitors' customers.

- You are asked how the organization makes it easy for customers and potential customers to get information or assistance and/or to comment and complain.

- You are asked how the organization gathers, analyzes, and learns from complaint information to increase customer satisfaction and loyalty.

- You are asked how the organization builds relationships with customers, since success depends on maintaining close relationships with customers.

- You are asked how the organization determines the satisfaction and dissatisfaction for different customer groups because satisfied customers are necessary for loyalty, repeat business, and positive referrals.

- Finally, you are asked how the organization follows up with customers, and how it determines customer satisfaction relative to competitors so that it may improve future performance.

Basically Effective

3. An effective system is in place to determine requirements of some customer groups or segments for some products and services. The organization has started to gather data about the effectiveness of some of these processes.

Mature

4. An effective system is in place to determine the requirements and preferences of many customer groups or segments for many products and services. These processes are sometimes checked for accuracy and completeness. The organization sometimes gathers data to evaluate the effectiveness of these processes but does not usually use the information to make improvements.

Advanced

5. An effective system is in place to determine the requirements and preferences of most customer groups or segments for most products and services for most of the product/service life cycle. These processes are regularly checked for accuracy and completeness and sometimes improved. Some sharing of improved practices within the organization takes place.

Role Model

6. An effective system is in place to determine what is most important to all customer groups or segments for nearly all products and services for the entire product/service life cycle. These processes are regularly checked for accuracy and completeness and consistently improved. They routinely innovate and share the best practices across the organization

Figure 43 Sample Customer and Market Focus question. *(Continued)*

Understanding What Customers Value Most in Products and Services [Baldrige Reference: 3.1a(2)]

3D. How well does the organization determine the most important requirements and preferences of its various customer groups and market segments that drive their purchasing decisions?

Not Evident

1. The organization does not have an effective process to learn about the requirements of its customers. They react to problems within the organization and no consistency is evident.

Beginning

2. The organization has just started to determine the requirements of a few customer groups or segments for a few products and services. The process is not very effective since it is not used widely in the organization. The process is not evaluated to see how it could be improved.

Continued

Figure 43 Sample Customer and Market Focus question.

SUMMARY OF CATEGORY 4: MEASUREMENT, ANALYSIS, AND KNOWLEDGE MANAGEMENT

This sample assessment looks at one question in the Measurement, Analysis, and Knowledge Management Category (see sample question at Figure 44). The full-length assessment of Measurement, Analysis, and Knowledge Management contains nine themes.

Measurement, analysis, and knowledge management are the "brain center" of an effective management system. Appropriate information and analysis are used to improve decision making at all levels to achieve high levels of performance. Effective measures, properly deployed, help align the organization's operations to achieve its strategic goals as well as protect organizational knowledge. The first part (five questions 4A through 4E) looks at the selection, collection, alignment, and integration of data and information to support effective decision making at all levels. Data and information guide decision making to help the organization achieve key business results and strategic objectives. Measurement, analysis, and knowledge systems serve as a key foundation for achieving innovation and sustaining peak performance.

- The organization must build an effective performance measurement system. It must select, align, and integrate the right measures for tracking daily operations and use those measures for monitoring overall organizational performance. The organization must also make sure that data and information are accurate and reliable.

- Competitive comparisons and benchmarking (best practices) information should be used to help drive innovation and performance improvement.

- The organization should evaluate and improve the performance measurement system to keep it current with changing business needs and able to respond to rapid changes.

- Data and information concerning processes and results (outcomes) from all parts of the organization must be analyzed to support the senior leaders' assessment of overall organizational health, organizational planning, and daily operations.

- Analyses must be communicated to support decision making and strategic planning at all levels of the organization.

The second part (four questions 4F through 4I) looks at how the organization ensures the quality and availability of data and information to support effective decision making for employees and appropriate suppliers, partners, and customers. It also examines building and managing knowledge assets.

- The organization must ensure integrity (completeness) of data and information as well as

ensure they are available, accessible, reliable, accurate, timely, confidential, and secure.

- The organization must identify, manage, collect, and transfer relevant knowledge and best practices.

- For data that are captured, stored, analyzed, and/or accessed through electronic means, the organization must ensure hardware and software reliability, security, and user friendliness.

All of these systems must be evaluated and enhanced to ensure they remain current with changing business needs and directions.

Selecting Measures to Track Daily Operations and Overall Organizational Performance [Baldrige Reference: 4.1a(1 and 3)]

4B. How well does the organization select and align appropriate measures throughout the organization to effectively track daily operations and overall organizational performance?

Not Evident

1. The organization does not systematically collect data to track how well it performs. Intuition or "gut feel" drives most decisions. They react to problems within the organization and no consistency is evident.

Beginning

2. The organization collects data to track financial performance but very few other areas. The process is not very effective since it is not used widely in the organization. The process is not evaluated to see how it could be improved.

Basically Effective

3. The organization collects data to track one or two of the following areas of organizational performance: customer satisfaction; financial; market; product quality; service quality; human resources effectiveness; operational effectiveness; and governance and social responsibility. The organization has started to gather data about the effectiveness of some of these processes

Mature

4. Effective processes are in place to select and collect data to track daily operations and organizational performance in at least three of the following areas: The organization sometimes checks how well the data enable.

Continued

Figure 44 Sample Measurement, Analysis, and Knowledge Management question.

tracking at the different levels. The organization some-times gathers data to evaluate the effectiveness of these processes but does not usually use the information to make improvements.

Advanced

5. Effective processes are in place to select, collect, and align data to track organizational performance in at least five of the following areas: customer satisfaction; financial; market; product quality; service quality; human resources effectiveness; operational effective-ness; and governance and social responsibility. The organization regularly checks how well the data enable tracking and promote alignment at the different levels and sometimes makes improvements. Some sharing of improved practices within the organization takes place. consistent with organizational needs

Role Model

6. Effective processes are in place to select, collect, align and integrate data to track organizational performance in at least six of the following areas: customer satisfac-tion; financial; market; product quality; service quality; human resources effectiveness; operational effective-ness; and governance and social responsibility. The organization regularly checks how well the data enable tracking and promote alignment throughout the organi-zation and makes ongoing improvements. They rou-tinely innovate and share the best practices across the organization.

Figure 44 Sample Measurement, Analysis, and Knowledge Management question. *(Continued)*

SUMMARY OF CATEGORY 5: HUMAN RESOURCE FOCUS

This sample assessment looks at one question in the Human Resource Focus Category (see sample ques-tion at Figure 45). The full-length assessment of Human Resource Focus contains 9 themes.

The first part (three questions 5A through 5C) looks at how well the organization's systems for work and job design, compensation, motivation, recognition, and hiring help all employees reach peak performance.

- You are asked how the organization designs work and jobs to empower employees to exer-cise initiative, innovation, and decision making, resulting in high performance.

- You are asked how the organization compen-sates, recognizes, and rewards employees to support its high-performance objectives (strate-gic objectives) as well as ensuring a customer and business focus.

- Finally, you are asked how the organization recruits and hires employees who will meet its expectations and needs. The right work force is an enabler of high performance.

The second part (three questions 5D through 5F) looks at how well education, training, and career development support high performance.

- You are asked how education and training are designed, delivered, reinforced on the job, and evaluated

- You are also asked about how well the organiza-tion provides training in different areas of per-formance excellence, which includes leadership development.

- In addition, you are asked how employees are motivated to reach their full potential.

The third part (three questions 5G through 5I) looks at the organization's work environment, its employee support climate, and how the organization determines employee satisfaction, with the aim of fostering the well-being, satisfaction, and motivation of all employees.

- You are asked how the organization's work envi-ronment for all employees is safe, secure, and healthful and how well the organization is pre-pared to deal with emergencies and disasters to ensure the business continues to function.

- You are asked how the organization provides benefits and services to enhance employee well-being, satisfaction, and motivation for all employee groups.

- Finally, you are asked how the organization assesses employee well-being, satisfaction, and motivation, and how it relates assessment findings to key business results to set improve-ment priorities.

Providing Feedback, Compensation, and Recognition to Support High-Performance Goals and a Customer and Business Focus [Baldrige Reference: 5.1b]

5B. How well do managers and supervisors at all levels provide feedback to employees and make sure pay, reward, and recognition support high performance and a customer and business focus? [Note that compensation and recognition might include promotions and bonuses based on performance, skills acquired, and other factors contributing to high performance goals. Recognition may be provided to individuals and/or groups and includes monetary and non-monetary and formal and informal techniques.]

Not Evident

1. The organization does not systematically provide effective feedback to employees or tie pay or recognition to high performance work. No consistency is evident.

Beginning

2. The organization provides effective feedback about performance to a few employees. It rarely ties pay and recognition to performance. The process is not very effective since it is not used widely in the organization. The process is not evaluated to see how it could be improved.

Basically Effective

3. The organization provides effective feedback about performance to some employees. It ties pay and recognition to some high performance. The organization has started to gather data about the effectiveness of some of these processes.

Mature

4. The organization provides effective feedback about performance to many employees. It ties pay and recognition to many high performance goals. The organization sometimes gathers data to evaluate the effectiveness of these processes but does not usually use the information to make improvements.

Advanced

5. The organization provides effective feedback about performance to most employees. It ties pay and recognition to most high performance, customer focus, and business goals and strategies, consistent with organizational needs. The organization regularly checks its feedback and compensation processes and improvements are sometimes made. Some sharing of improved reward and recognition practices within the organization takes place.

Continued

Figure 45 Sample Human Resource Focus question.

Role Model

6. The organization provides effective feedback about performance to nearly all employees. It ties pay and recognition to nearly all high performance, customer focus, and business goals and strategies, consistent with organizational needs. The organization regularly checks its feedback and compensation processes and makes ongoing improvements. They routinely innovate and share the best reward and recognition practices across the organization.

Figure 45 Sample Human Resource Focus question. *(Continued)*

SUMMARY OF CATEGORY 6: PROCESS MANAGEMENT

This sample assessment looks at one question in the Process Management Category (see sample question at Figure 46). The full-length assessment of Process Management contains seven themes.

Process Management is the focal point for all key work processes. The first part (four questions 6A through 6D) looks at the organization's key processes for creating customer value, business success, and growth.

- You are asked how key value creation processes are determined using input from customers and suppliers/partners as appropriate.

- You are asked how all key requirements are addressed in the design process. You are also asked how cost control, cycle time, productivity, new technology, and organizational knowledge are considered during the design phase. You should make sure that design processes actually work as expected.

- You are asked how the organization makes sure that value creation processes work consistently and how performance measures are used to get an early alert of potential problems so you can take prompt corrective action.

- You are asked how well the overall costs associated with inspections, tests, and audits are minimized while preventing defects and rework.

- In addition, you are asked how the organization improves its value creation processes to achieve better performance and how it shares these improvements, reduces variability, and keeps processes current with changing business needs.

The last part (three questions 6E through 6G) examines the organization's key support processes, with the aim of improving overall operational performance.

- You are asked how key support processes are designed to meet all the requirements of internal and external customers.

- The day-to-day operation of key support processes should meet the key requirements. In-process measures and internal customer feedback should be used to get an early alert of problems.

- Finally, you are asked how the organization improves its key support processes to achieve better performance.

Understanding Value Creation and Business Processes Requirements [Baldrige Reference: 6.2a(1, 2, and 6)]

6A. How does the organization determine key value creation process requirements using input from customers and suppliers/partners as appropriate? [Note that key value creation and business processes are considered most important to running the business to achieve organizational growth and success. Key value creation processes include the majority of employees and add greatest value to products and services. Value creation processes are sometimes called "core work processes" and define the reason the organization is in business.]

Not Evident

1. The organization does not systematically define key business processes or identify key process requirements based on customer input for value creation and business process. They react to problems within the organization and no consistency in value creation is evident.

Beginning

2. The organization defines a few of the basic process requirements important for value creation and business success. However, specific performance requirements are not well defined. The process is not very effective since it is not used widely in the organization. The process is not evaluated to see how it could be improved.

Continued

Basically Effective

3. Effective processes are in place to identify performance requirements based on customer input for some value creation and business process. The organization has started to gather data about the effectiveness of some of these processes.

Mature

4. Effective processes are in place to accurately and completely identify performance requirements in measurable terms based on customer input for many value creation and business process. The organization sometimes checks the effectiveness of these processes. The organization sometimes gathers data to evaluate the effectiveness of these processes but does not usually use the information to make improvements.

Advanced

6. Effective processes, consistent with organizational needs, are in place to accurately and completely identify performance requirements in measurable terms based on customer and appropriate supplier and partner input for most value creation and business process. The organization regularly checks the effectiveness of these processes, sometimes makes improvements, and sometimes shares the improvements with other organizational units. Some sharing of improved practices within the organization takes place.

Role Model

6. Effective processes, consistent with organizational needs, are in place to accurately and completely identify performance requirements in measurable terms based on customer and appropriate supplier and partner input for nearly all value creation and business process. The organization regularly checks the effectiveness of these processes, makes ongoing improvements, and nearly always shares the improvements with other organizational units. They routinely innovate and share the best practices across the organization.

Figure 46 Sample Process Management question. *(Continued)*

Figure 46 Sample Process Management question.

SUMMARY OF CATEGORY 7: BUSINESS RESULTS

This sample assessment looks at one theme in the Business Results Category (see sample question at Figure 47). The full-length assessment of Business Results contains six themes.

The Business Results Category looks for the results produced by the management systems described in Categories 1 through 6. Results range from lagging performance outcomes such as customer satisfaction, market share, and financial performance to predictive or leading outcomes such as internal operating measures and human resource results. Together, these lagging and leading results create a set of balanced indicators of organizational health, commonly called a "balanced scorecard."

- 7A looks at how well the organization has been satisfying customers and achieving better customer–focused results.

- Question 7B looks at product and service quality that lead to customer satisfaction, loyalty, and positive referral such as fitness-for-use characteristics and on-time delivery.

- Question 7C looks at the strength of the organization's financial and market results.

- Question 7D looks at how well the organization has been creating and maintaining a positive, productive, learning, and caring work environment.

- Question 7E looks at the organization's key operational (internal) performance results with the aim of achieving organizational effectiveness.

- Question 7F looks at key results in the area of societal responsibilities, organization's citizenship, ethical behavior, and compliance with applicable laws and regulations.

Customer-Focused Results [Baldrige Reference: 7.1a(1 and 2)

7A. What are the trends and results for customer satisfaction and dissatisfaction? These include customer loyalty indicators, measures of customer-perceived value, customer retention, and positive referral. [Results data may come from internal measures as well as data from customers and independent organization,]

Not Evident

1. No results or poor results exist.

Beginning

2. Performance levels are good in very few areas that are important to the business.

Basically Effective

3. Performance levels are good in some areas important to the business. The organization is beginning to demonstrate improvement trends and get comparison data.

Mature

4. Performance levels are good in many areas of importance to the organization's key business requirements (such as customer satisfaction, dissatisfaction, and loyalty indicators, measures of customer-perceived value, customer retention, and positive referral) when compared to industry average. Some trends in areas of importance to the organization's key business requirements show growth.

Advanced

5. Performance levels are good to very good in many to most areas of importance to the organization's key business requirements (such as customer satisfaction, dissatisfaction, and loyalty indicators, measures of customer-perceived value, customer retention, and positive referral) when compared to top performing competitors or benchmarks. Unless the actual level of performance is already at the top levels, many to most trends in areas of importance to the organization's key business requirements continue to improve and show sustained growth. No pattern of adverse trends and no poor performance levels are evident in areas of importance to the organization's key business requirements.

Role Model

6. Performance levels are good to excellent in many to most areas of importance to the organization's key business requirements (such as customer satisfaction, dissatisfaction, and loyalty indicators, measures of customer-perceived value, customer retention, and positive referral) when compared to top performing competitors or benchmarks. Unless the actual level of performance is already at the top levels, most trends in areas of importance to the organization's key business requirements continue to improve and show sustained growth. No pattern of adverse trends and no poor performance levels are evident in areas of importance to the organization's key business requirements.

Figure 47 Sample Business Results question.

The Site Visit

INTRODUCTION

Many people and organizations have asked about how to prepare for site visits. This section is intended to help answer those questions and prepare the organization for an on-site examination. It includes rules of the game for examiners and what they are taught to look for. As we all know, the best preparation for this type of examination is to see things through the eyes of the trained examiner.

Before an organization can be recommended to receive the Malcolm Baldrige National Quality Award, it must receive a visit from a team of business assessment experts from the National Board of Examiners. Approximately 25 percent to 30 percent of organizations applying for the Baldrige Award in recent years have received these site visits.

The Baldrige Award site-visit team usually includes at least two senior examiners—one of whom is designated as team leader—and three to eight other examiners. In addition, the team is accompanied by a representative of the National Quality Award Office and a representative of the American Society for Quality (ASQ), which provides administrative services to the Baldrige Award Office under contract.

The site visit team usually gathers at a hotel near the organization's headquarters on the Sunday morning immediately preceding the site visit. During the day, the team makes final preparations and plans for the visit.

Each team member is assigned lead responsibility for one or more categories of the Award Criteria. Each examiner is usually teamed with one other examiner during the site visit. These examiners usually conduct the visit in pairs to ensure the accurate recording of information.

Site visits usually begin on a Monday morning and last one week. By Wednesday or Thursday, most site-visit teams will have completed their on-site review. They retire to the nearby hotel to confer and write their reports. By the end of the week, the team must reach consensus on the findings and prepare a final report for the panel of judges.

Purpose of Site Visits

Site visits help clarify uncertain points and verify self-assessment (that is, application) accuracy. During the site visit, examiners investigate areas most difficult to understand from self-assessments, such as the following:

- Deployment: How widely a process is used throughout the organization

- Integration: Whether processes fit together to support performance excellence

- Process ownership: Whether processes are broadly owned, simply directed, or micromanaged

- Employee involvement: The extent to which employees' participation in managing processes of all types is optimized

- Continuous improvement maturity (learning): The number and extent of improvement cycles and resulting refinements in all areas of the organization and at all levels

Characteristics of Site Visit Issues

Examiners look at issues that are an essential component of scoring and role model determination. They have a responsibility to:

- Clarify information that is missing or vague and verify significant strengths identified from the self-assessment.

- Verify deployment of the practices described in the self-assessment.

Examiners will:

- Concentrate on cross-cutting issues.

- Examine data, reports, and documents.

- Interview individuals and teams.

- Receive presentations from the applicant organization.

Examiners may not conduct their own focus groups or surveys with customers, suppliers, or dealers. Conducting focus groups or surveys would violate confidentiality agreements as well as be statistically unsound.

Discussions with the Applicant Prior to the Site Visit

Prior to the official Baldrige Award site visit, all communication between the applicant organization and its team must be routed through their respective single points of contact. Only the team leader may contact the applicant on behalf of the site-visit team prior to the site visit. This helps ensure consistency of message and communication for both parties. It prevents confusion and misunderstandings. The team leader should provide the applicant organization with basic information about the process. This includes schedules, arrival times, and equipment and meeting room needs.

Applicant organizations usually provide the following information prior to the site-visit team's final planning meeting at the hotel on the day before the site visit starts:

- List of key contacts

- Organization chart

TYPICALLY IMPORTANT SITE VISIT ISSUES

- Role of senior management in leading and serving as a role model
- Independence of governance system to protect stakeholder interests and hold managers accountable
- Degree of involvement and self-direction of employees below upper management
- Comprehensiveness and accessibility of the information system
- Extent that facts and data are used in decision making
- Degree of emphasis on customer satisfaction
- Extent of systematic approaches to work processes
- Training effectiveness
- Use of compensation, recognition, and rewards to promote key values
- Extent that strategic plans align organizational work
- Extent of the use of measurable goals at all levels in the organization
- Evidence of evaluation and improvement cycles in all work processes and in system effectiveness
- Improvements in cycle times and other operating processes
- Extent of integration of all processes—operational and support
- Extent of benchmarking effort

- Facility layout

- Performance data requested by examiners

The team leader, on behalf of team members, will ask for supplementary documentation to be compiled (such as results data brought up to date) to avoid placing an undue burden on the organization at the time of the site visit. The site-visit team will select sites that allow them to examine key issues and check deployment in key areas. This information may or may not be discussed with the applicant prior to the site visit. Examiners will need access to all areas of the organization.

Conduct of Site-Visit Team Members (Examiners)

Examiners are not allowed to discuss findings with anyone but team members. Examiners may not disclose the following to the applicant:

- Personal or team observations and findings

- Conclusions and decisions

- Observations about the applicant's performance systems, whether complimentary or critical

Examiners may not discuss the following with anyone:

- Observations about other applicants

- Names of other award program applicants

Examiners may not accept trinkets, gifts, or gratuities of any kind (coffee, cookies, rolls, breakfast, and lunch are okay), so applicant organizations should not offer them. At the conclusion of the site visit, examiners are not permitted to leave with any of the applicant's materials including logo items or catalogs—not even items usually given to visitors. Examiners will dress in appropriate business attire unless instructed otherwise by the applicant organization.

Opening Meeting

An opening meeting will be scheduled to introduce all parties and set the structure for the site visit. The meeting is usually attended by senior executives and the self-assessment writing team. The opening meeting usually is scheduled first on the initial day of the site visit (8:30 AM or 9:00 AM). The team leader generally starts the meeting, introduces the team, and opens the site visit. Overhead slides and formal presentations are usually unnecessary.

The applicant organization usually has one hour to present any information it believes important for the examiners to know. This includes time for a tour, if necessary.

Immediately after the meeting, examiners usually meet with senior leaders and those responsible for preparing sections of the self-assessment (application), since those people are likely to be at the opening meeting.

Conducting the Site Visit

The team will follow the site-visit plan, subject to periodic adjustments according to its findings. The site-visit team will need a private room to conduct frequent caucuses. Applicant representatives are not present at these caucuses. The team will also conduct evening meetings at the hotel to review the findings of the day, reach consensus, write comments, and revise the site-visit report.

If, during the course of the site visit, someone from the applicant organization believes the team or any of its members are missing the point, the designated point of contact should inform the team leader or the Baldrige Award Office monitor. Also, someone who believes an examiner behaved inappropriately should inform the designated point of contact, who will inform the team leader or the award office monitor.

Employees should be instructed to mark every document given to examiners with the name and work location of the person providing the document. This will ensure that it is returned to the proper person. Records should be made of all material given to team members. Organizational personnel may not ask examiners for opinions and advice. Examiners are not permitted to provide any information of this type during the site visit.

GENERIC SITE-VISIT QUESTIONS

Examiners must verify or clarify the information contained in an application, whether they have determined a process to be a strength or an opportunity for improvement. Examiners must verify the existence of strengths as well as clarify the nature of each opportunity for improvement in the final feedback report.

Before and during the site-visit review process, examiners formulate a series of questions based on the Baldrige Criteria. It is possible to identify a series of generic questions that examiners are likely to ask during the site-visit process, based only on the Baldrige Criteria. Of course, all questions should be tailored to the specific key factors of the organization to be most relevant. The questions in the following section are presented to help prepare applicants and examiners for the site-visit process.

Many times, leaders and employees become focused on the process they have in place today. They often fail to describe how they systematically refined the process and show how it evolved to the process of today. Therefore, after learning how the process works today, all examiners should ask the following questions: "Have you always done it this way? How did you do it before? Why did you change? Do you have additional improvements in the works?"

Category 1—Leadership

1. (To top leaders) How do you set direction and guide the organization? Please share with us the values of your organization. [1.1a(1)]

   - What are your top priorities?

   - How do you ensure that all your employees know these priorities?

   - How do you know how effective you are at communicating these values?

   - How you know your messages to employees are understood as you intended?

2. What does two-way communication mean to you (the leader)? Give me some examples. How widely is the process actually used? [1.1a(1)]

3. What are your key customer or stakeholder segments? [3.1a(1), (2); 1.1a(1)]

- Pick one and ask, what does this customer/ stakeholder group value?

- Are the requirements or value expected of this customer group different from any other group? If so, what are the differences, and how have you ensured that the different or competing interests of these groups are addressed by your organization?

4. What are the ways you communicate throughout the organization and to key partners and suppliers? What kind of information do you communicate? When do you do this? [1.1c(3)]

   - What kinds of communication or feedback do you receive from employees and partners/ suppliers? What do you do with this information? How well do these processes work? How do you know? What has been done to improve them? [1.1a(2)]

5. What is your role in supporting processes to ensure performance excellence? [1.1a(2)]

   - What are the behaviors you want your managers and other employees to emulate? Give me some examples of what you do personally to model these behaviors to employees and managers throughout the organization.

   - How do you encourage innovation and employee empowerment? Give me some examples of improved innovation throughout the organization as a result of your efforts. (Follow up on these examples with other employees.)

   - How do you ensure that middle managers and other subordinates promote employee empowerment and innovation throughout the organization?

   - What does organizational agility mean to you? What are the barriers to this agility you have identified in the organization? Pick some barriers and ask, what have you done to overcome this barrier?

   - What processes have you put in place to ensure that innovations and other knowledge are effectively shared throughout the organization to appropriate managers and employees? How well do these processes work? How do you know? What has been done to improve them?

6. What policies and principles exist in the organization to promote or require ethical and legal behavior? [1.1a(2)]

   • What are some of the most important ethical principles? What processes have you put in place to achieve the desired ethical behavior? How well do these processes work? How do you know? What has been done to improve them?

7. How independent is your board of directors? [1.1b]

   • What percentage of the board is not affiliated with your organization in any way (other than being a board member)?

   • How does your audit function ensure objectivity and independence?

   • Have problems existed in the past where stakeholder interests were threatened? If so, what was done to prevent the possibility of those problems recurring?

   • How does the board make sure managers behave properly and account for their actions in the organization?

   • How would you rate the board's climate of trust? To what extent are distention and disagreement among board members tolerated? Encouraged?

   • What policies are in place to ensure the board remains alert to management problems in the organization?

   • What type of fiscal oversight does the board provide? What problems or issues have emerged in the past three to five years? Pick some and ask, what was the board's reaction to this issue? How was it resolved? What steps were taken to prevent the problem from happening again?

   • What processes have you put in place to ensure the board effectively protects stockholder and shareholder value? How well do these processes work? How do you know? What has been done to improve them?

8. What is the process used to monitor the performance of your organization? How does it relate to the organization's strategic business plan? [1.1c(1)]

   • What measurable goals exist? How are they monitored? How often? How well do these processes work? How do you know? What has been done to improve them?

   • What are the key success factors (or key result areas, critical success factors, key business drivers) for your organization, and how do you use them to drive performance excellence?

   • What percentage of your time is spent on performance review and improvement activities? How do you review performance to assess the organization's health, competitive performance, and progress against key objectives? What key performance measures do you and other senior leaders regularly review?

   • How do top priorities and opportunities for innovation reflect organizational review findings? Have you set or changed priorities for innovation and resource allocation? Please give examples of how this is done.

   • How do you ensure that these priorities and opportunities for innovation are understood and used throughout the organization to align work? (After you identify a top priority for innovation, ask the leader to provide specific examples of how they ensure these priorities are implemented and aligned throughout the organization, as appropriate.) To what extent do these priorities and innovation opportunities involve support from key suppliers and/or partners? (Pick one example of a priority and ask the leader to help you understand how the organization works with affected suppliers or partners.)

✗ 9. What is your process for evaluating the effectiveness of the leadership system? [1.1c(4)]

- How do you include or use employee feedback from the two-way communication (if done) in the evaluation?

- Please identify specific examples where the senior leadership improved the leadership system as a result of these evaluations. How do managers evaluate and improve their personal leadership effectiveness? How are data from organizational performance reviews used here?

10. What are the criteria for promoting and rewarding managers within the organization? [1.1c(4); 5.1b]

- How are you making managers accountable for performance improvement, employee involvement, and customer satisfaction objectives? (Look at some samples of managers' evaluations [chosen at random] and check to see if they reflect refinements based on organizational performance review findings and employee feedback.)

- How have you improved the process of evaluating managers over the years?

- What processes have been put in place to evaluate and improve the effectiveness of the board of directors as a whole and individual board members? How well do these processes work? How do you know? What has been done to improve them?

✗ 11. What do you do to anticipate public concerns over the possible impact of your organization? How do you determine what risks the public faces because of your current and/or future products, services, and operations? What are some examples of risks you have identified? Pick some risks at random and ask, what have you done to reduce the risk or threat to the public? How do you know you are successful in these areas? How do you measure progress? [1.2a(1)]

- What goals have been developed to identify and reduce risks?

- What are the biggest environmental issues your organization faces? As a corporate citizen, what is your process for contributing to and improving the environment and society?

- How do you know that your processes for protecting the public from risks associated with your products, services, and programs are effective? How have you improved these processes?

✗ 12. What are some ways your organization ensures that employees and key partners act in an ethical manner in all business and stakeholder transactions? How is this measured and monitored to ensure compliance? [1.2b]

✗ 13. What support does your organization provide to local communities? Why do you provide this support? How does this support align with organizational priorities and the strategy? [1.2c]

- How do you know that the processes you have in place for identifying and supporting key communities are appropriate?

- How do you know the resource issues allocated for these purposes are appropriately used? Have you always provided this type of support?

- What has been done to improve your efforts to support these communities?

Category 2—Strategic Planning

1. When was the last time the strategic plan was updated? Were you involved in the strategic planning process? What was your role? Who else was involved and what did each contribute? [2.1a(1)]

- How far out does your planning look? Why? Why not shorter or longer?

- How does the overall process for developing strategy work? (If people were involved in the planning process, ask them to recite how the process works without referring to written documentation. We must determine whether a consistent planning process is in place that meets the requirements of the Criteria—we are not testing the ability of senior leaders to read a written document.)

2. What data, information, and other factors did you consider in the development of your strategic plan? [2.1a(2)]

   • Does your organization depend on key suppliers or partners to be successful? If so, which ones? Pick some from their list and ask, how did you consider the needs and capabilities of these suppliers/partners during the process of developing your strategic plan?

   • Does your organization have key competitors that affect your ability to be successful? Which ones? Pick some and ask, what abilities does this competitor possess that may create a problem for your organization. How did you consider the threats posed by this key competitor during the process of developing your strategic plan? How has your plan addressed these potential problems or threats?

   • Is your organization helped or hurt by new technologies? Which ones? Pick some and ask, how did you consider these new technologies during the process of developing your strategic plan?

   • How do you consider the needs of all key customers (or other appropriate stakeholders) in the development of the strategic plan? How do you balance the requirements and preferences of these customers when they are conflicting?

   • What future regulatory, legal, financial, economic, or ethical risks does your organization face? Pick some and ask, how did you determine this was a risk? How did your planning process consider the potential problems presented by this risk when developing your plan?

   • Were you or are you likely to be affected by changes in the national or global economy? If so, in what ways? Help me understand how you considered the likely impact of these problems in your planning process.

   • How has your planning process helped you identify opportunities to redirect resources to more productive uses, such as higher-priority products, services, and programs? Please give some examples of new opportunities and how you capitalized on them as a result of your planning.

   • What have you done to check the accuracy of planning assumptions and projections you used in the past to develop your strategic plan? How accurate have your past planning assumptions been? What have you done to improve the accuracy and effectiveness of your planning process" What refinements have you made during the past few years?

3. How often do you review progress of your key strategic objectives? Please show me the time lines or projections for achieving each objective. How did you develop the projected or expected levels of future performance for each strategic objective (also called time lines)? [2.1b(1)]

4. Review the list of strategic challenges the organization provided in P2. Pick one, then ask: Please show me how you check your objectives to be sure this strategic challenge was addressed. Then repeat the process for another challenge. [2.1b(2)]

   • Can you tell from this information where you expect to be on each objective when you review performance the next time? Next quarter? Next year? In two years? (Note: the frequency of review should be consistent with the review processes described in Item 1.1c(1). For example, if progress toward achieving the customer satisfaction objectives is reviewed quarterly by the senior leadership team, then quarterly time lines or milestones should be defined to permit effective review. In addition, the time lines reported under 2.1b(1) should identify the measurable levels of performance that are expected during these reviews.)

   • How did you determine the appropriate frequency or period to review progress for these objectives?

5. What is the process you use to identify the actions that need to be taken throughout the organization in order to meet your goals or strategic objectives? [2.2a(1)]

   • How do you break the strategic objectives into actions that drive work at all levels of the organization?

   • How do you make sure that every employee knows what work he or she must do to achieve his or her part of the plan?

   • What process is used to figure out what resources are needed to do this work? How are resources allocated to make sure the actions can be completed on schedule? How effective are these processes? How do you know? What improvements in the processes of converting plans to actions and assigning resources have been made in the past few years?

   • How do you determine what people and skills you will need to carry out your strategic objectives and related action plans? What changes have been made in your human resource plan during the past few years to help you achieve your strategic objectives and related action plans? How effective and accurate have your human resource plans been?

6. Another way of examining the issues outlined in No. 5 is as follows: How do you make sure that goals, objectives, and action plans are understood and used throughout the organization to drive and align work? [2.2a(1)]

   • How do you ensure that organizational, work unit, and individual actions and resources are aligned at all levels? (Pick a strategy that the leader has indicated is important to organizational success. Then ask the leader what actions they have determined are critical to achieve the strategy. From the list of actions, pick one or two and ask the leader to explain specifically how resources were allocated to ensure these plans would be accomplished. Then ask how the leader checks to determine if appropriate

resources were allocated. Ask if any improvements have been made in this process over the past few years. Repeat this line of questioning at different levels in the organization to check alignment.)

   • Ask to see an old plan. Pick an action that drove improvement. Determine the extent to which the changes that were put in place have been sustained. If the change was not sustained, determine what process changes were made to ensure that future changes can be sustained. In other words, determine what they learned from the failure and what they did with that knowledge.

7. Describe your long- and short-term plans to meet the recruitment, recognition, safety and security, motivation, development, education, and training needs of the organization that are necessary to carry out the strategic plans. What are the measures of progress to meet these human resource plans?

8. Summarize the organization's human resource plans that are needed to carry out the strategic objectives and related action plans. How do these human resource plans ensure sufficient human resources?

   • What are examples of changes to the human resource plans based on inputs from the strategic planning in the following areas: recruitment, training, compensation, rewards, incentives, fringe benefits, and other programs, as appropriate?

9. What is (summarize) your process for evaluation and improvement of the strategic planning and plan deployment processes, including human resource planning?

   • What are examples of improvements made as a result of these evaluation processes? Where and when did they occur?

   • Why did you decide to focus on these improvements? What facts helped with your decisions on what to improve and how to improve the planning process?

10. How did you determine that the goals or objectives you set were appropriate? How do you know that achieving this goal will make you a leader in the industry or sector? [2.2b]

11. Who do you consider to be your top competitors, and how does your planned performance (goals) compare to theirs and/or similar providers? How did you determine who your top competitors are? [2.2b]

    • At what level do you expect your key competitors or other similar providers to perform during the same period as your plan covers?

    • How did you figure this out?

    • How accurate have your past estimates of your competitor's future performance been? What have you done to make these projections more accurate?

Category 3—Customer and Market Focus

1. Who are your key customers, customer groups, or market segments? [3.1a(1); 3.1a(2)]

    • What was your reason for grouping them this way?

    • How did you determine what your customers expect of you?

    • How does your organization determine short- and long-term customer requirements for each of the customer groups or segments? Do you use the same techniques for all customer groups? Why or why not?

    • How do you know what the customers of your competitors (your potential customers) are getting or want? How have you used this knowledge?

    • How do you use information you learned from customers, including data such as retention rates, complaints, and loyalty to plan products and services, market them, make improvements in them, or develop new business?

2. What are the key requirements of your customers (break out by segment or group)? Are the requirements of potential customers different from the requirements of the customers you presently serve? [3.1a(2)]

    • What is most important or valuable to the different customer groups you serve or want to serve? What features of products and services are most important to getting them and keeping them happy? How do you separate the most important customer requirements from less important requirements?

    • How do you anticipate new or emerging customer requirements? What do you do with this information?

    • How do you evaluate and improve processes for determining customer requirements? What role has new technology or changing business needs played in deciding what improvements to make? Provide some examples of improvements that you have made in the past few years.

3. How do you make it easy for your customers to contact you, get information and assistance, or complain? What do you expect to learn from customer complaints? What have you learned? Please provide examples. [3.2a(2), (3)]

    • What is your process for handling customer complaints? What do you do with the complaint or comment data? (Ask to see some sample complaints and follow the data trail. Determine how the data are analyzed and used to drive improvements.)

    • What does "prompt and effective resolution of a complaint" mean to your organization? What processes do you have in place to ensure complaints are resolved by the first person in your organization to receive the complaint? What skills and authority do your customer contact employees need to resolve complaints promptly and effectively? How do you check to determine if your complaint resolution processes are effective or not?

What improvements have you made in these processes over the past few years?

- What are the customer-contact requirements or service standards? How were they determined? How do you make sure that every employee who comes in contact with customers understands and works to these standards? How do you know the customer contact requirements (standards) are consistently met for all customers throughout the organization?

4. How do you evaluate and improve the customer-relationship process? What are some improvements you've made to the way you strengthen customer relationships and loyalty? How did you decide they were important to make, and when were they made? [3.2a(4)]

5. What are your key measures for customer satisfaction and dissatisfaction? How do these measures provide information on likely future market behavior such as loyalty, repurchase, and referrals? [3.2b(1)]

- What tools and techniques do you use to measure customer satisfaction and dissatisfaction?

- Do you measure satisfaction/dissatisfaction for all key customer groups/segments? What do you do with the information?

6. Describe your process for follow-up with customers after the customer has had contact with the organization or used its products and services? What do you do with feedback you solicit from customers regarding products and services? What triggers follow-up action?

7. What customer satisfaction information do you have about your competitors or benchmarks? What do you do with this information? How do employees use this information in their regular work? What action do they take as a result? Please provide some examples. [3.2b(3)]

8. How do you go about improving the way you determine customer satisfaction and dissatisfaction? Please provide some examples

of how you have improved these techniques over the past several years. [3.2b(3)]

- How do you know appropriate action is taken in response to customer satisfaction data at all levels of the organization?

- How do you know you are asking customers and right questions when trying to determine satisfaction and dissatisfaction? [3.2b(4)]

Category 4—Measurement, Analysis, and Knowledge Management

1. What kind of decisions do you have to make in your job? Show me the data that you collect to help you make these decisions. [4.1a(1)]

- What are the major performance indicators critical to running your organization?

2. How do you determine whether the information you collect and use for decision making is appropriate for tracking your daily work and the performance of the entire organization? [4.1a(1)]

- What criteria do you use for data selection? How do you ensure that all data collected meet these criteria?

3. What is the process you use to determine the relevance of the information to organizational goals and strategic planning? [4.1a(1)]

- Describe how you obtain feedback from the users of the information, the employees, suppliers, and customers who use this information to support their decision making. How is this feedback used to make improvements in the data and information you collect and analyze?

4. You have told us what your top priorities are. How do you benchmark against these? [4.1a(2)]

- Please describe how needs and priorities for selecting comparisons and benchmarking are determined.

- Show us samples of comparative studies and how the resulting information was used to support innovation throughout the organization. Picking some at random, determine:

- Why was the area selected for benchmarking?

- How did you use competitive or comparative performance data?

- How are the results of your benchmarking efforts used to set appropriate goals, make better decisions about work, and set priorities for improvement or innovation?

- How are the results of your benchmarking efforts used to improve work processes?

- How do you evaluate and improve your benchmarking processes to make them more efficient and useful?

5. Please share with us an example of analysis of information important to organizational performance review and strategic planning. [4.1b(1)]

- How are data analyzed to determine relationships between customer information and financial performance; operational data and financial performance; or operational data and human resource requirements and/or performance?

- What data and analyses do you use to understand your people, your customers, and your market to help with strategic planning?

- How widely are these analyses used for decision making throughout the organization at both functional or work-group levels?

- What are you doing to improve the analysis process and make it more useful for organizational and operational decision making?

6. How do you make sure that the analysis needed to support decision making at all levels of the organization is effectively communicated (made available)? Show how the following types of analyses are used to support decision making and innovation or improvements: [4.1b(2)]

- Technology projections

- Cause–effect relationships

- Root cause analysis

- Descriptive analyses such as statistical process control, central tendencies, Pareto analysis, histograms

- Other statistical tools such as correlation analysis, regression and factor analyses, and tests of significance (t-tests, f-tests)

7. How do you make sure that data, information, and analysis needed to support decision making at all levels of the organization are available, timely, and accurate? [4.2a(1)]

8. How do you make sure that your hardware and software systems meet the needs of all users? How do you determine whether the software and hardware are "user friendly?" (Ask what groups use the hardware/software system. Randomly pick a group and ask how the organization makes sure these people can easily use the hardware and software. Then randomly ask some people in a group how their "user-friendliness" requirements were identified and met.) [4.2a(2)]

9. Please show how you make sure software and hardware are up to date. What drives decisions to change or upgrade systems? [4.2a(3)]

10. What are the data security requirements you believe are critical to your system? (For example, certain statutes and regulations, such as the Family and Education Rights and Privacy Act, may require certain levels of security and data protection.) How do you guarantee data and system security and confidentiality? [4.2a(2); 4.2b(2)]

11. How do you make sure relevant knowledge and information are appropriately shared throughout the organization and with appropriate suppliers, partners, and customers? [4.2a(1); 4.2b(1)]

- How are worthy processes and work practices shared among all appropriate employees quickly and effectively? (These processes and practices are also known as best practices, exemplary practices, role model practices or, in Minnesota, pretty good practices.)

12. What do you do to make sure the data that support decision making are complete, tell the whole story (data integrity)? [4.2b(2)]

13. What kind of reliability problems have you experienced with your hardware and software? How have you resolved them? What have you done to prevent these types of problems from happening again? [4.2b(2)]

Category 5—Human Resource Focus

1. What authority do employees have to direct their own actions and make decisions about their work? [5.1a(1)]

   - (To employees) What authority do you have to make decisions about your work, such as resolving problems, improving work processes, and communicating across departments? What have managers done to encourage innovation within the work force?

   - (To all) To what extent do leaders, managers, and supervisors make it easy to change and keep pace with changing business and customer requirements? If extremely agile and flexible were a 10 and slow-moving, bureaucratic, and bound in "red tape" were a one, where would you rate the organization as a whole? Where would you rate your unit?

   - (To managers) How do you empower employees? What do you do to encourage initiative and self-directed responsibility among employees in their regular work and jobs? What are some examples of processes you have used to evaluate and enhance opportunities for employees to take individual initiative and demonstrate self-directed responsibility in designing and managing their work? What have you done to increase employee innovation, where employees actually make improvements, not just suggestions? Show examples of actions taken and improvements made. When were they made?

2. What different cultural groups do you employ? What have you done to draw out and use ideas and thinking of these diverse cultures and types of employees? [5.1a(2)]

3. What do you do to ensure effective communication and knowledge sharing among employees and work units? [5.1a(3)]

   - How do you break down barriers to effective sharing and communication?

   - How do you know the communication is understood correctly?

4. Describe your approach to employee recognition and compensation. [5.1b]

   - What specific reward and recognition programs are in place? Is the reward and recognition the same for all employees? Why are they the same (or different)?

   - How does the organization link recognition, reward, and compensation to achieve high-performance objectives (which are usually stated as strategic objectives or goals)?

   - How do compensation, recognition, and related reward and incentive systems reinforce, strengthen, or support customer focus objectives (for example, customer satisfaction)?

   - (General question for employees) What do you get rewarded for around here? What recognition is offered and why? Are the reward and recognition systems consistent? Fair?

5. How do you figure out what skills will be needed by future (potential) employees? [5.1c(1); 5.1c(2)]

   - How do you attract employees with the right skills your organization needs to be successful? How do you make sure that employees represent the diversity of the general community from which you hire? What diverse employees do you recruit and why? How does this recruitment help you get the right mix of diverse ideas, culture, and thinking?

   - How do you make sure these skills, diverse ideas, and cultures are used to maximum advantage within your organization?

6. What replacement strategy or process do you have in place for key leaders and employees/employee groups throughout the organization? (For example, if the organization knows key senior leaders or a group of engineers/technicians are scheduled to retire, determine what it is doing to fill the gap this retirement makes.) [5.1c(3)]

7. What training is provided for your employees? [5.2a(1)]

   • (From the action plans identified in 2.2, pick some and ask) What training and education is provided to support the achievement of (the selected action plan)?

8. After you determine the key groups or segments of employees within the organization, ask the following question: What training and education do you provide to ensure that you meet the needs of all categories of employees? [5.2a(3)]

   • What training does a new employee receive to obtain the knowledge and skills necessary for success and high performance, including leadership development?

   • What is included in new employee orientation? How do you address key training needs, such as environmental safety, ethical business practices, and diversity?

   • If applicable, how do employees in remote locations participate in training programs?

9. How do you integrate employee, supervisor, and manager feedback into the design and delivery of your training program? (Ask related follow-up questions to supervisors, managers, and employees to determine the extent to which their needs for development, learning, and career progression were identified and considered when designing the education and training approach.) [5.2a(3)]

10. How is your training curriculum designed and delivered? What methods are used to determine what training should be offered and how it should be delivered? [5.2a(4)]

11. How do you make sure that the knowledge and skills acquired during training are actually used and reinforced on the job? Provide some examples (then select from this list and follow up with employees and their supervisors to determine how skills are reinforced on the job). [5.2a(5)]

12. How does your training program affect operational performance goals? How do you know your training improves your business results? Show examples. [5.2a(6)]

13. What is your system for improving training? Please give us some examples of improvements made and when they were made. [5.2a(6)]

14. To what extent is training provided to enhance employee motivation, career development, and progression? What do you (senior leaders, managers, and supervisors) do to develop the full potential of employees? Give examples. [5.2b]

15. What are your standards, performance measures, and targets for employee health, ergonomics, security, and safety? [5.3a(1)]

   • How were they derived?

   • How do you make sure that your approach to health and safety addresses the needs of all employee groups?

16. How do you determine that you have a safe and healthy work environment? How do you measure this? [5.3a(1)]

   • What are your procedures for systematic evaluation and improvement of workplace health, safety, and ergonomics?

   • What have you done to improve workplace health, safety, and ergonomics?

17. What processes or systems have you put in place to prepare for emergencies or disasters that may affect your workplace? [5.3a(2)]

   • How do you know these systems work as intended? What kinds of disruptions have you faced in the past? What was the impact on the workplace and your customers and employees? What have you put in place to reduce the possible impact of such disasters or emergencies?

18. What services, facilities, activities, and benefits are most important to your work force? [5.3b(1)]

    • How did you determine these were the most important? Are they the same for all groups or segments of the work force? If not, how have the services and benefits been modified or tailored to meet the needs of different groups or categories of employees?

19. What are the key elements, conditions, or factors that help or hurt employee well-being, satisfaction, and motivation? [5.3b(1)]

    • How did do you determine that these were the key elements? Are the elements the same for all groups of employees? If not, how do they differ?

20. What are the benefits and services you provide for employees to enhance motivation and satisfaction? [5.3b(2)]

    • To what extent are these customized for different employee types or groups? How did you determine what changes in the benefits and services should be offered?

21. How is employee satisfaction measured? (If a survey is used, ask how they know they are asking the right questions on the survey. Unless they have already told you, ask for some specific examples about how they use other information such as employee retention, absenteeism, grievances, safety, and productivity data to assess and improve employee well-being, satisfaction, and motivation.) [5.3b(3)]

    • What do you do with the information? Provide examples.

    • Please show us how your employee assessment tools (for example, surveys) reflect the key factors you identified that affect employee well-being, satisfaction, and motivation.

22. What do you do to actually improve employee well-being, satisfaction, and motivation systematically? [5.3b(3)]

    • Describe the process you use to analyze employee satisfaction data and other indicators to determine what problems exist that may disrupt or hurt employee well-being, satisfaction, and motivation?

    • How quickly or effectively do you use this information to drive improvements to employee well-being, satisfaction, and motivation?

23. How do you ensure that managers throughout the organization work to improve the climate for employee well-being, satisfaction, and motivation? [5.3b(3)] [Links to 1.1a(2)]

24. When you identify the priorities for improving the work environment to promote employee well-being, satisfaction, and motivation, what factors do you consider? [5.3b(4)]

    • What are the top three or four improvement priorities? (Pick one and ask the leader.) What specific finding from the employee satisfaction survey or other assessment tool did the organization use to identify this priority action? How is this priority for improving work environment likely to affect key business results?

25. What improvements have you made in the process of determining employee satisfaction, well-being, and motivation, and then actually improving the work climate? [Scoring Guidelines]

Category 6—Process Management

1. What new program, product, or service have you designed in the past few years? (Pick one from their list and ask.) What is your process for designing this new or revised product or service to ensure that customer requirements are met and value is created for the customers, the organization, or other stakeholders? Please walk us through the steps. [6.1a(1); 6.1a(2)]

2. What new design technologies, including e-technology, have you used in recent product/service and production/delivery of the projects? [6.1a(3)]

3. How do you test new products or services before they are introduced to be sure they perform as expected and meet all customer and operational requirements? What have you done to prevent errors in the design process? What kinds of problems or troubles have you had with past introductions of new products and services? Provide examples of how you have learned from these problems and prevented them in subsequent product/service designs. [6.1a(3)]

4. What are your key production and delivery processes and their requirements for creating value, including quality and performance indicators? [6.1a(4)]

   - What steps have you taken to improve the effectiveness/efficiency of key work processes, including cycle time?

   - Once you determine that a process may not be meeting measurement goals or performing according to expectations, what process do you use to determine root cause and to bring about process improvement?

   - Please give an example of how a customer request or complaint resulted in an improvement of a current process or the establishment of a new process. How often do customers change their requirements? How do you respond to these changes? How has this process been refined to respond more quickly, especially when customer requirements change more often?

5. Please share with us your list of key business processes, requirements, and associated performance measures, including in-process measures. (Remember that key business processes include critical processes that support value creation and are necessary for business growth and success.) For example, if supply chain management is designated as a key business process, the following series of questions may be useful: What process is in place for managing your supplier chain? Who are your most important [key] suppliers? How do you establish and communicate to your key suppliers the key requirements they must meet so your needs are met? What are the key performance requirements? Please explain how you measure your suppliers' performance and provide feedback to help them improve. [6.1a(1); 6.1a(4)]

   - What are the steps you have taken to design your key business processes to ensure they meet all performance requirements? How do you determine the types of services and outputs needed? How do your key business processes add value to enhance business growth and success?

6. What kinds of tests, audits, or inspections do you routinely conduct to ensure products and services are defect-free and require no rework? Show how you have reduced the need for these tests, audits, or inspections and still eliminated defects and rework. [6.1a(5); 6.2a(5)]

   - What are the steps you have taken to design your key support processes? How do you determine the types of services needed? How do your support services interact with and add value to your operational processes? [6.2a(2)]

   - How does your organization maintain the performance of key support services? Share some examples of processes used to determine root causes of support problems and how you prevent recurrence of problems. How do you monitor costs of these processes? How have you reduced costs? Please give examples. [6.2a(4)]

7. How do you evaluate and improve the process for designing and delivering new value creating business and support processes, and make improvements in cycle time, cost control, productivity, and other effectiveness or efficiency factors? Please provide some examples of

improvements and when they were made. [6.1a(6); 6.2a(6)]

- What process do you have in place to make sure that lessons learned in one part of the organization (or from past improvement efforts) are transferred to others in the organization to save time and prevent rework?

8. Please share with us your list of key support processes, requirements, and associated process measures, including in-process measures. [6.2a(1)]

Category 7—Business Results

Normally, applicants are careful to display "good" results and sometimes neglect to report results that are not as good. The scoring guidelines penalize applicants for failing to provide results that are important to the organization's key business requirements.

To score accurately, examiners must be able to determine what results should be reported in the application that are important to the organization's success. To evaluate Category 7 properly, examiners first develop a list of the results that they "expect" to be provided in Category 7 based on what the organization reported was important to its success. Then, by comparing the list of "expected" results to the results actually provided in the application, examiners can determine what important results are missing.

Usually a description of important results can be found in the Organizational Profile, strategic goals [Item 2.1b], the list of actions required to achieve strategic objectives [Item 2.2a(1)], the priority customer requirements [Item 3.1a(2)], or other places in the application.

Figure 48 represents the type of information that might be presented by an applicant in the Organizational Profile [P.1b(2)], listing Customer Segments and Requirements. Note that three customer segments were identified, each with multiple requirements. This information serves as a basis for "expecting" results related to the satisfaction of these customers with the important product and service features. Accordingly, note that in Figure 49, the first column identifies where these results should be reported [Item 7.2]. The second column lists the customer segments and the specific requirements of each

segment as found in the Organizational Profile (Figure 49). The third column simply identifies the place in the application that the examiner found the reference to expected results. (In case another examiner on the team did not find the expected requirement, little time will be wasted searching for it.) The fourth column indicates whether results were actually reported in 7.2, where they can be found (figure reference), and whether results are improving or not. Column five indicates whether benchmark/comparative data were reported (as required) and how favorably the applicant's performance compares with the benchmark data.

In this way, examiners can easily determine if few, some, many, or most important results were reported. Similarly, applicants should prepare a similar table to make sure the actual results are aligned with the important results.

Most of the site-visit work for Category 7 involves studying reports containing raw data as well as trend and comparison data. All relevant results that were reported in the application should be updated to reflect current conditions.

Comparison data and the rationale for offering the comparison data should be examined to determine if the comparisons are appropriate and relevant. Comparisons are relevant if the applicant is able to present a plausible explanation or link between the comparison data and the data the applicant has reported.

1. What are the customer satisfaction and dissatisfaction trends at this time? [Links to P.1b and Items 3.1 and 3.2] [7.1]

- Please show a breakout of data by customer group or segment.

- What are your current levels and trends for customer loyalty, positive referral, customer-perceived value, and relationship building?

- Please bring your customer satisfaction, dissatisfaction, and related results up to date and close any information gaps that may have been noted in your application.

- How do these customer satisfaction and dissatisfaction trends and levels compare with those of your competitors or similar providers?

2. What are the product/service performance levels at this time? [Links to P.1b and Items 3.1, 3.2, and 6.1] [7.2]

   - Please show a breakout of data by customer group or segment.

   - What are your current levels and trends for how customers perceive your products and service performance?

   - What are the performance results for key products and services that are most critical to customer satisfaction?

   - Please bring your results up to date and close any information gaps that may have been noted in your application.

   - How do these trends and levels compare with those of your competitors or similar providers?

3. What are the current levels and trends showing financial and marketplace performance or economic value? [7.3]

   - Please provide data on key financial measures, such as return on investment (ROI), operating profits (or budget reductions as appropriate), or economic value added.

   - Please provide data on market share or business growth, as appropriate. Identify new markets entered and the level of performance in those markets.

   - Please show a breakout of data by customer and market group or segment.

   - Please bring your financial and marketplace performance results up to date and close any information gaps that may have been noted in your application.

   - Show how these trends and levels compare with those of your competitors or similar providers?

4. What are the current levels and trends showing the effectiveness of your human resource practices? [Links to processes in Category 5] [7.4]

   - Please provide data on key indicators, such as safety/accident record, absenteeism, turnover by category and type of employee/manager, and grievances and related litigation.

   - Please bring your human resource results up to date and close any information gaps that may have been noted in your application.

   - How does performance on these key indicators compare to your competitors, other providers, or benchmarks?

Customer Segments (As Reported by the Applicant)	Key Customer Requirements (As Reported by the Applicant)
Active inpatients, outpatients, home care patients, and families	Access to effective 24/7/365 error-free care, compassionate/caring environment, reliable/consistent information, participation in health care decisions, accommodations for visitors
Potential or inactive patients (no services received within the last three years)	Easy access, courtesy when contacting hospital, accurate answers to inquiries, reputation
Physicians	Knowledgeable, pleasant colleagues/staff; easy access to technology and facilities; real-time clinical information; input into Umbrella policies and decision making; high patient satisfaction

Figure 48 Example of applicant customer segments and corresponding key requirements provided in the Organizational Profile.

5. What are the current levels and trends showing the effectiveness of your value creation and support processes? [Links to Items 6.1 and 6.2] [7.5]

- What are current levels and trends for key design, production, delivery, and business process performance?

- What are current levels and trends for production and cycle time for design, delivery, and production?

- Please show us your supplier/partner performance data trends and current levels

for each key indicator, such as on-time delivery, error rate, and reducing costs. [Links to supply chain issues in Item 6.1 or 6.2 as appropriate]

- Please show us results data that demonstrate the extent to which you accomplished your organizational strategy or strategic objectives. [Links to 2.1b(1) and 2.2a]

- Please bring your data about organizational effectiveness up to date and close any information gaps that may have been noted in your application.

	**Table of Expected Results**
Item Ref.	Expected Results (Based on Info in the Application)	Reference (where you found source)	Actual Result Reported in the Application	Comparison Data Provided?
7.2a		Active inpatient, outpatients, home care patients, and families
	• Rapid access to treatment • Error free care • Caring environment • Consistent information • Participation in HC decisions • Visitor accommodations	Figure 48	No Only indirect results: 7.2-1 overall satisfaction improving 7.2-2 physician care improving No No No	No Yes, above average Yes-in top quartile No No No
7.2a		Inactive / potential patient
	• Easy access • Courtesy • Accurate answers • Reputation	Figure 48	No No No 7.2-7 to 12 Community image, mixed	No No No Yes, above average
7.2a		Physicians
	• Knowledgeable, pleasant staff • Easy access to facilities/tech • Real-time clinical information • Input into policies • High patient satisfaction	Figure 48	7.2-6 Staff courtesy, improving 7.2-5 Ease of access, improving 7.2-3 Timeliness of clinical info, flat 7.2-1 overall patient satisfaction improving Note: additional results were provided that were not listed elsewhere in the application as important: physicians willingness to recommend to other physicians, satisfaction with billing support, facilities quality [7.2-13 to 15]	No No No Yes, above average No

Figure 49 Table of expected results.

- How does your performance on these key indicators compare to your competitors, other providers, or benchmarks?

6. What are the current levels and trends showing the effectiveness of your governance and social responsibility processes? [Links to processes in P.1, P.2, and Items 1.1b and 1.2] [7.6]

  - Please show us your performance data related to fiscal accountability such as financial statement issues and risks and questioned accounting practices, auditor findings and recommendations, and management's response to these issues. [Links to Item 1.2a(1)]

  - Please show us your performance data related to effective governance, holding managers accountable for their actions, and ethical behavior, such as percentages of independent members of the board of directors and results of ethics reviews and audits. [Links to Item 1.2a(2)]

  - What are your results for regulatory/legal compliance? [Links to Item 1.2a(3)]

  - What are your results for organizational citizenship? [Links to Item 1.2c]

  - Please bring your governance and social responsibility results up to date and close any information gaps that may have been noted in your application.

  - How does your performance on these key indicators compare to your competitors, other providers, or benchmarks?

General Cross-Cutting Questions to Ask Employees

- Who are your customers? [Links to 1.1a(1) and 3.1a(1)]

- What are the organization's mission, vision, and values? [Links to 1.1a(1)]

- What is the strategic plan for the organization? What are the organization's goals, and what role do you play in helping to achieve the goals? [Links to 2.1b(1) and 2.2a]

- What kind of training have you received? Was it useful? Who decided what training you should receive? What kind of on-the-job support did you get for using the new skills you learned during training? [Links to 5.2]

- What kinds of decisions do you usually make about your work and the work of the organization? What data or information do you use to help make these decisions? Is this information easily available to help make decisions easier? [Links to 1.1a(2), 4.2a, and 5.1a]

- What activities or work are recognized or rewarded? Is achieving customer satisfaction a critical part of your job? Are your rewards and/or recognition determined in part on achieving certain customer satisfaction levels? If so, explain how this works. [Links to 5.1b]

- Remember to ask the employee how processes are improved. Are improvements based on evaluation or are they random? Be sure to ask if the process you are examining has been improved. Ask how the improvement was identified. Ask what steps are being taken to continue to evaluate and improve the process.

Glossary

This glossary defines and briefly describes key terms used throughout the Criteria that are important to performance management and assessment.

action plans—the term "action plans" refers to specific actions that respond to short- and longer-term strategic objectives. Action plans include details of resource commitments and time horizons for accomplishment. Action plan development represents the critical stage in planning when strategic objectives and goals are made specific so that effective, organization-wide understanding and deployment are possible. In the Criteria, deployment of action plans includes creating aligned measures for work units. Deployment might also require specialized training for some employees or recruitment of personnel.

An example of a strategic objective for a supplier in a highly competitive industry might be to develop and maintain a price leadership position. Action plans could entail designing efficient processes and creating an accounting system that tracks activity-level costs, aligned for the organization as a whole. Deployment requirements might include unit and/or team training in setting priorities based upon costs and benefits. Organizational-level analysis and review likely would emphasize productivity growth, cost control, and quality. See the definition of "strategic objectives" for the description of this related term.

alignment—the term "alignment" refers to consistency of plans, processes, information, resource decisions, actions, results, and analysis to support key organization-wide goals. Effective alignment requires a common understanding of purposes and goals. It also requires the use of complementary measures and information for planning, tracking, analysis, and improvement at three levels: the organizational level, the key process level, and the work unit level. See the definition of "integration" for the description of this related term.

analysis—the term "analysis" refers to an examination of facts and data to provide a basis for effective decisions. Analysis often involves the determination of cause-effect relationships. Overall organizational analysis guides process management toward achieving key business results and toward attaining strategic objectives.

Despite their importance, individual facts and data do not usually provide an effective basis for actions or setting priorities. Effective actions depend on an understanding of relationships, derived from analysis of facts and data.

anecdotal—the term "anecdotal" refers to process information that lacks specific methods, measures, deployment mechanisms, and evaluation/improvement/learning factors. Anecdotal information frequently uses examples and describes individual activities rather than systematic processes.

An anecdotal response to how senior leaders deploy performance expectations might describe a specific occasion when a senior leader visited all company facilities. On the other hand, a systematic process might describe the communication methods used by all senior leaders to deliver performance expectations on a regular basis to all employee locations, the measures used to assess effectiveness of the methods, and the tools and techniques used to evaluate and improve the communication methods.

approach—the term "approach" refers to the methods used by an organization to address the Baldrige Criteria Item requirements. Approach includes the appropriateness of the methods to the Item requirements and the effectiveness of their use.

basic requirements—the term "basic requirements" refers to the topic Criteria users need to address when responding to the most central concept of an Item. Basic requirements are the fundamental theme of that Item. *In the Criteria, the basic requirements of each item are presented as the Item title.* If you are an examiner, see the chapter in this book that provides a detailed explanation of basic, overall, and multiple requirements.

benchmarks—the term "benchmarks" refers to processes and results that represent best practices and performance for similar activities, inside or outside an organization's industry. Organizations engage in benchmarking as an approach to understand the current dimensions of world-class performance and to achieve discontinuous (nonincremental) or breakthrough improvement.

Benchmarks are one form of comparative data. Other comparative data organizations might use include industry data collected by a third party (frequently industry averages), data on competitors' performance, and comparisons with similar organizations in the same geographic area.

customer—the term "customer" refers to actual and potential users of your organization's products or services. Customers include the end users of your products or services, as well as others who might be the immediate purchasers of your products or services, such as wholesale distributors, agents, or companies that further process your product as a component of their product. The Criteria address customers broadly, referencing current and future customers, as well as customers of your competitors.

Customer-driven excellence is a Baldrige core value embedded in the beliefs and behaviors of high-performance organizations. Customer focus impacts and integrates an organization's strategic directions, its value creation processes, and its business results.

See the definition of "stakeholders" for the relationship between customers and others who might be affected by your products or services.

cycle time—the term "cycle time" refers to the time required to fulfill commitments or to complete tasks. Time measurements play a major role in the Criteria because of the great importance of time performance to improving competitiveness. "Cycle time" refers to all aspects of time performance. Cycle-time improvement might include time to market, order fulfillment time, delivery time, changeover time, customer response time, and other key measures of time.

deployment—the term "deployment" refers to the extent to which an organization's approach is applied to the requirements of a Baldrige Criteria Item. Deployment is evaluated on the basis of the breadth and depth of application of the approach to relevant work units throughout the organization.

effective—the term "effective" refers to how well a process or a measure addresses its intended purpose. Determining effectiveness requires the evaluation of how well a need is met by the approach taken and its deployment or by the measure used.

empowerment—the term "empowerment" refers to giving employees the authority and responsibility to make decisions and take actions. Empowerment results in decisions being made closest to the "front line," where work-related knowledge and understanding reside.

Empowerment is aimed at enabling employees to satisfy customers on first contact, to improve processes and increase productivity, and to improve the organization's business results. Empowered employees require information to make appropriate decisions; thus, an organizational requirement is to provide that information in a timely and useful way.

ethical behavior—the term "ethical behavior" refers to how an organization ensures that all its decisions, actions, and stakeholder interactions conform to the organization's moral and professional principles. These principles are the foundation for the organization's culture and values and define "right" from "wrong."

Senior leaders should act as role models for these principles of behavior. The principles apply to all individuals involved in the organization, from employees to members of the board of directors, and need to be communicated and reinforced on a regular basis. Although there is no universal model for ethical behavior, senior leaders should ensure that the organization's mission and vision are aligned with its ethical principles. Ethical behavior should be practiced with all stakeholders, including employees, shareholders, customers, partners, suppliers, and the organization's local community.

While some organizations may view their ethical principles as boundary conditions restricting behavior, well-designed and clearly articulated ethical principles should empower people to make effective decisions with great confidence.

goals—the term "goals" refers to a future condition or performance level that one intends to attain. Goals can be both short-term and longer-term. Goals are ends that guide actions. Quantitative goals, frequently referred to as "targets," include a numerical point or range. Targets might be projections based on comparative data and/or competitive data. The term "stretch goals" refers to desired major, discontinuous (nonincremental) or breakthrough improvements, usually in areas most critical to your organization's future success.

Goals can serve many purposes, including clarifying strategic objectives and action plans to indicate how success will be measured, fostering teamwork by focusing on a common end, encouraging "out-of-the-box" thinking to achieve a stretch goal, and providing a basis for measuring and accelerating progress.

governance—the term "governance" refers to the system of management and controls exercised in the stewardship of your organization. It includes the responsibilities of your organization's owners/shareholders, board of directors, and CEO. Corporate charters, bylaws, and policies document the rights and responsibilities of each of the parties and describe how your organization will be directed and controlled to ensure accountability to owners/shareholders and other stakeholders, transparency of operations, and fair treatment of all

stakeholders. Governance processes may include approving strategic direction, monitoring and evaluating CEO performance, succession planning, financial auditing, establishing executive compensation and benefits, managing risk, disclosure, and shareholder reporting. Ensuring effective governance is important to stakeholders' and the larger society's trust and to organizational effectiveness.

high-performance work—the term "high-performance work" refers to work processes used to systematically pursue ever-higher levels of overall organizational and individual performance, including quality, productivity, innovation rate, and cycle time performance. High-performance work results in improved service for customers and other stakeholders.

Approaches to high-performance work vary in form, function, and incentive systems. High-performance work frequently includes cooperation between management and the work force, which may involve work force bargaining units; cooperation among work units, often involving teams; self-directed responsibility/employee empowerment; employee input to planning; individual and organizational skill building and learning; learning from other organizations; flexibility in job design and work assignments; a flattened organizational structure, where decision making is decentralized and decisions are made closest to the "front line"; and effective use of performance measures, including comparisons. Many high-performance work systems use monetary and nonmonetary incentives based upon factors such as organizational performance, team and/or individual contributions, and skill building. Also, high-performance work processes usually seek to align the organization's structure, work, jobs, employee development, and incentives.

how—the term "how" refers to the processes that an organization uses to accomplish its mission requirements. In responding to "how" questions in the Process Item requirements, process descriptions should include information such as approach (methods and measures), deployment, learning, and integration factors.

innovation—the term "innovation" refers to making meaningful change to improve products, services, and/or processes and to create new value for stakeholders. Innovation involves the adoption of an idea, process, technology, or product that is either new or new to its proposed application.

Successful organizational innovation is a multistep process that involves development and knowledge sharing, a decision to implement, implementation, evaluation, and learning. Although innovation is often associated with technological innovation, it is applicable to all key organizational processes that would benefit from change, whether through breakthrough improvement or change in approach or outputs.

integration—the term "integration" refers to the harmonization of plans, processes, information, resource decisions, actions, results, analysis, and learning to support key organization-wide goals. Effective integration goes beyond alignment and is achieved when the individual components of a performance management system operate as a fully interconnected unit. See the definition of "alignment" for the description of this related term.

key—the term "key" refers to the major or most important elements or factors, those that are critical to achieving your intended outcome. The Baldrige Criteria, for example, refer to key challenges, key plans, key processes, key measures—those that are most important to the organization's success. They are the essential elements for pursuing or monitoring a desired outcome.

knowledge assets—the term "knowledge assets" refers to the accumulated intellectual resources of your organization. It is the knowledge possessed by your organization and its employees in the form of information, ideas, learning, understanding, memory, insights, cognitive and technical skills, and capabilities. Employees, software, patents, databases, documents, guides, policies and procedures, and technical drawings are repositories of an organization's knowledge assets.

Knowledge assets are held not only by an organization but reside within its customers, suppliers, and partners as well. Knowledge assets are the "know-how" that your organization has available to use, to invest, and to grow. Building and managing its knowledge assets are key components for your organization to create value for its stakeholders and to help sustain competitive advantage.

leadership system—the term "leadership system" refers to how leadership is exercised, formally and informally, throughout the organization—the basis for and the way key decisions are made, communicated, and carried out. It includes structures and mechanisms for decision making; selection and development of leaders and managers; and reinforcement of values, directions, and performance expectations.

An effective leadership system respects the capabilities and requirements of employees and other stakeholders, and it sets high expectations for performance and performance improvement. It builds loyalties and teamwork based on the organization's values and the pursuit of shared goals. It encourages and supports initiative and appropriate risk taking, subordinates organization structure to purpose and function, and avoids chains of command that require long, cumbersome decision paths. An effective leadership system includes mechanisms for the leaders to conduct self-examination, receive feedback, and improve.

learning—the term "learning" refers to new knowledge or skills acquired through evaluation, study, experience, and innovation. The Baldrige Criteria include two distinct kinds of learning: organizational and personal. Organizational learning is achieved through research and development, evaluation and improvement cycles, employee and customer ideas and input, best practice sharing, and benchmarking. Personal learning is achieved through education, training, and developmental opportunities that further individual growth.

To be effective, learning should be embedded in the way an organization operates. Learning contributes to a competitive advantage for the organization and its employees. For further description of organizational and personal learning, see the related Core Value and Concept on page 30 of this book.

levels—the term "levels" refers to numerical information that places or positions an organization's results and performance on a meaningful measurement scale. Performance levels permit evaluation relative to past performance, projections, goals, and appropriate comparisons.

measures and indicators—the term "measures and indicators" refers to numerical information that quantifies input, output, and performance dimensions of processes, products, services, and the overall organization (outcomes). Measures and indicators might be simple (derived from one measurement) or composite.

The Criteria do not make a distinction between measures and indicators. However, some users of these terms prefer the term indicator: 1) when the measurement relates to performance but is not a direct measure of such performance (for example, the number of complaints is an indicator of dissatisfaction but not a direct measure of it), and 2) when the measurement is a predictor ("leading indicator") of some more significant performance (for example, increased customer satisfaction might be a leading indicator of market share gain).

mission—the term "mission" refers to the overall function of an organization. The mission answers the question, "What is this organization attempting to accomplish?" The mission might define customers or markets served, distinctive competencies, or technologies used.

multiple requirements—the term "multiple requirements" refers to the individual questions Criteria users need to answer within each Area to Address. These questions constitute the details of an Item's requirements. *Multiple requirements are presented in black text under each Item's Area(s) to Address.* If you are an examiner, see the chapter in this book that provides a detailed explanation of basic, overall, and multiple requirements.

overall requirements—the term "overall requirements" refers to the topics Criteria users need to address when responding to the central theme of an Item. Overall requirements address the most significant features of the Item requirements. *In the Criteria, the overall requirements of each Item are presented as an introductory sentence(s) printed in bold.* If you are an examiner, see the

chapter in this book that provides a detailed explanation of basic, overall, and multiple requirements.

performance—the term "performance" refers to output results and their outcomes obtained from processes, products, and services that permit evaluation and comparison relative to goals, standards, past results, and other organizations. Performance might be expressed in nonfinancial and financial terms. The Baldrige Criteria address four types of performance: 1) Customer-focused, 2) product and service, 3) financial and marketplace, and 4) operational.

"Customer-focused performance" refers to performance relative to measures and indicators of customers' perceptions, reactions, and behaviors. Examples include customer retention, complaints, and customer survey results. These are considered "direct" measures of customer satisfaction since they are "telling" organizations directly about their levels of satisfaction or dissatisfaction. In the Criteria these results are reported in Item 7.1.

"Product and service performance" refers to performance relative to measures and indicators of product and service characteristics important to customers. Examples include product reliability, on-time delivery, customer-experienced defect levels, and service response time. These are considered "indirect" measures of customer satisfaction since the organizations are using measures or indicators of product and service quality to "predict" what the customer is likely to think without actually asking the customer or waiting for the customer to leave. In the Criteria these results are reported in Item 7.2.

"Financial and marketplace performance" refers to performance relative to measures of cost, revenue, and market position, including asset utilization, asset growth, and market share. Examples include returns on investments, value added per employee, debt-to-equity ratio, returns on assets, operating margins, cash-to-cash cycle time, other profitability and liquidity measures, and market gains. In the Criteria these results are reported in Item 7.3.

"Operational performance" refers to human resource, organizational, and ethical performance relative to effectiveness, efficiency, and accountability measures and indicators. Examples include cycle time, productivity, waste reduction, employee turnover, employee cross-training rates, regulatory compliance, fiscal accountability, and community involvement. Operational performance might be measured at the work-unit level, key-process level, and organizational level. In the Criteria these results are reported in Items 7.4, 7.5, and 7.6.

performance excellence—the term "performance excellence" refers to an integrated approach to organizational performance management that results in: 1) delivery of ever-improving value to customers, contributing to marketplace success; 2) improvement of overall organizational effectiveness and capabilities; and 3) organizational and personal learning. The Baldrige Criteria for Performance Excellence provide a framework and an assessment tool for understanding organizational strengths and opportunities for improvement and thus for guiding planning efforts.

performance projections—the term "performance projections" refers to estimates of future performance or goals for future results. Projections may be inferred from past performance, may be based on competitors' performance that must be met or exceeded, may be predicted based on changes in a dynamic marketplace, or may be goals for future performance. Projections integrate estimates of your organization's rate of improvement and change, and they may be used to indicate where breakthrough improvement or change is needed. Thus, performance projections serve as a key management planning tool.

process—the term "process" refers to linked activities with the purpose of producing a product or service for a customer (user) within or outside the organization. Generally, processes involve combinations of people, machines, tools, techniques, and materials in a defined series of steps or actions. In some situations, processes might require adherence to a specific sequence of steps, with documentation (sometimes formal) of procedures and requirements, including well-defined measurement and control steps.

In many service situations, particularly when customers are directly involved in the service,

process is used in a more general way, that is, to spell out what must be done, possibly including a preferred or expected sequence. If a sequence is critical, the service needs to include information to help customers understand and follow the sequence. Service processes involving customers also require guidance to the providers of those services on handling contingencies related to customers' likely or possible actions or behaviors.

In knowledge work such as strategic planning, research, development, and analysis, process does not necessarily imply formal sequences of steps. Rather, process implies general understandings regarding competent performance such as timing, options to be included, evaluation, and reporting. Sequences might arise as part of these understandings.

In the Baldrige Scoring System, process achievement level is assessed. This achievement level is based on four factors that can be evaluated for each of an organization's key processes: Approach, Deployment, Learning, and Integration.

productivity—the term "productivity" refers to measures of the efficiency of resource use. Although the term often is applied to single factors such as staffing (labor productivity), machines, materials, energy, and capital, the productivity concept applies as well to the total resources used in producing outputs. The use of an aggregate measure of overall productivity allows a determination of whether the net effect of overall changes in a process—possibly involving resource trade-offs—is beneficial.

purpose—the term "purpose" refers to the fundamental reason that an organization exists. The primary role of *purpose* is to inspire an organization and guide its setting of values. Purpose is generally broad and enduring. Two organizations in different businesses could have similar purposes, and two organizations in the same business could have different purposes.

results—the term "results" refers to outputs and outcomes achieved by an organization in addressing the requirements of a Baldrige Criteria Item. Results are evaluated on the basis of current performance; performance relative to appropriate comparisons; the rate, breadth, and importance of performance improvements; and the relationship of results measures to key organizational performance requirements.

segment—the term "segment" refers to a part of an organization's overall customer, market, product line or employee base. Segments typically have common characteristics that can be logically grouped. In Results Items, the term refers to disaggregating results data in a way that allows for meaningful analysis of an organization's performance. It is up to each organization to determine the specific factors that it uses to segment its customers, markets, products, and employees.

Understanding segments is critical to identifying the distinct needs and expectations of different customer, market, and employee groups and to tailoring products, services, and programs to meet their needs and expectations. As an example, market segmentation might be based on geography, distribution channels, business volume, or technologies employed. Employee segmentation might be based on geography, skills, needs, work assignments, or job classification.

senior leaders—the term "senior leaders" refers to an organization's senior management group or team. In many organizations, this consists of the head of the organization and his or her direct reports.

stakeholders—the term "stakeholders" refers to all groups that are or might be affected by an organization's actions and success. Examples of key stakeholders include customers, employees, partners, governing boards, stockholders, and local/professional communities.

strategic challenges—the term "strategic challenges" refers to those pressures that exert a decisive influence on an organization's likelihood of future success. These challenges frequently are driven by an organization's future competitive position relative to other providers of similar products or services. While not exclusively so, strategic challenges generally are externally driven. However, in responding to externally driven strategic challenges, an organization may face internal strategic challenges.

External strategic challenges may relate to customer or market needs or expectations; product, service, or technological changes; or financial, societal, and other risks. Internal strategic challenges may relate to an organization's capabilities or its human and other resources.

See the definition of "strategic objectives" for the relationship between strategic challenges and the strategic objectives organizations create to address key challenges.

strategic objectives—the term "strategic objectives" refers to an organization's articulated aims or responses to address major change or improvement, competitiveness issues, and/or business advantages. Strategic objectives generally are focused externally and relate to significant customer, market, product, service, or technological opportunities and challenges (strategic challenges). Broadly stated, they are what an organization must achieve to remain or become competitive. Strategic objectives set an organization's longer-term directions and guide resource allocations and redistributions.

See the definition of "action plans" for the relationship between strategic objectives and action plans and for an example of each.

systematic—the term "systematic" refers to approaches that are repeatable and use data and information so that improvement and learning are possible. In other words, approaches are systematic if they build in the opportunity for evaluation, improvement, and sharing, thereby permitting a gain in maturity. For use of the term, see the Scoring Guidelines.

trends—the term "trends" refers to numerical information that shows the direction and rate of change for an organization's results. Trends provide a time sequence of organizational performance.

A minimum of three data points generally is needed to begin to ascertain a trend. The time period for a trend is determined by the cycle time of the process being measured. Shorter cycle times demand more frequent measurement, while longer cycle times might require longer periods before meaningful trends can be determined.

Examples of trends called for by the Criteria include data related to customer and employee satisfaction and dissatisfaction results, product and service performance, financial performance, marketplace performance, and operational performance, such as cycle time and productivity.

value—the term "value" refers to the perceived worth of a product, service, process, asset, or function relative to cost and relative to possible alternatives.

Organizations frequently use value considerations to determine the benefits of various options relative to their costs, such as the value of various product and service combinations to customers. Organizations need to understand what different stakeholder groups value and then deliver value to each group. This frequently requires balancing value for customers and other stakeholders, such as stockholders, employees, and the community.

value creation—the term "value creation" refers to processes that produce benefit for your customers and for your business. They are the processes most important to "running your business"—those that involve the majority of your employees and generate your products, your services, and positive business results for your stockholders and other key stakeholders.

values—the term "values" refers to the guiding principles and/or behaviors that embody how your organization and its people are expected to operate. Values reflect and reinforce the desired culture of the organization. Values support and guide the decision making of every employee, helping the organization to accomplish its mission and attain its vision in an appropriate manner.

vision—the term "vision" refers to the desired future state of your organization. The vision describes where the organization is headed, what it intends to be, or how it wishes to be perceived.

work systems—the term "work systems" refers to how your employees are organized into formal or informal units to accomplish your mission and your strategic objectives; how job responsibilities are managed; and your processes for compensation, employee performance management, recognition, communication, hiring, and succession planning. Organizations design work systems to align their components to enable and encourage all employees to contribute effectively and to the best of their ability.

Clarifying Confusing Terms

Comparative Information versus Benchmarking

Comparative information includes benchmarking and competitive comparisons. Benchmarking refers to collecting information and data about processes and performance results that represent the best practices and performance for similar activities inside or outside the organization's business or industry. Competitive comparisons refer to collecting information and data on performance relative to direct competitors or similar providers.

For example, a personal computer manufacturer, ABC Micro, must store, retrieve, pack, and ship computers and replacement parts. ABC Micro is concerned about shipping response time, errors in shipping, and damage during shipping. To determine the level of performance of its competitors in these areas, and to set reasonable improvement goals, ABC Micro would gather competitive comparison data from similar providers (competitors). However, these performance levels may not reflect best practices for storage, retrieval, packing, and shipping.

Benchmarking would require ABC Micro to find organizations that execute these processes better than any other organization and examine both their processes and performance levels, such as the catalog company L.L. Bean.

Benchmarking seeks best-practices information. Competitive comparisons look at competitors, whether or not they are the best.

Customer-Contact Employees

Customer-contact employees are any employees who are in direct contact with customers. They may be direct service providers or answer complaint calls. Whenever a customer makes contact with an organi-zation, either in person or by phone or other electronic means, that customer forms an opinion about the organization and its employees. Employees who come in contact with customers are in a critical position to influence customers for the good of the organization, or to its detriment.

Customer Satisfaction versus Customer Dissatisfaction

One is not the inverse of the other. The lack of complaints does not indicate satisfaction, although the presence of complaints can be a partial indicator of dissatisfaction. Measures of customer dissatisfaction can include direct measures through surveys as well as complaints, product returns, and warranty claims.

Customer satisfaction and dissatisfaction are complex areas to assess. Customers are rarely "thoroughly" dissatisfied, although they may dislike a feature of a product or an aspect of service. There are usually degrees of satisfaction and dissatisfaction.

Data versus Information

Information can be qualitative and quantitative. Data lend themselves to quantification and statistical analysis. For example, an incoming inspection might produce a count of the number of units accepted, rejected, and total shipped. This count is considered *data*. These counts add to the base of *information* about supplier quality.

Education versus Training

Training refers to learning about and acquiring job-specific skills and knowledge. Education refers to the general development of individuals. An organization might provide training in equipment maintenance for its workers, as well as support the education of workers through an associate degree program at a local community college.

Empowerment and Involvement

Empowerment generally refers to processes and procedures designed to provide individuals and teams the tools, skills, and authority to make decisions that affect their work—decisions traditionally reserved for managers and supervisors.

Empowerment as a concept has been misused in many organizations. For example, managers may appear to extend decision-making authority under the guise of chartering teams and individuals to make recommendations about their work, while continuing to reserve decision-making authority for themselves.

This practice has given rise to another term—involvement—which describes the role of employees who are asked to become involved in decision making, without necessarily making decisions. Involvement is a practice that many agree is better than not involving employees at all, but still does not optimize their contribution to initiative, flexibility, and fast response.

Measures and Indicators

The Award Criteria do not make a distinction between measures and indicators. However, some users of these terms prefer the term indicator: 1) when the measurement relates to performance but is not a direct or exclusive measure of such performance, for example, the number of complaints is an indicator of dissatisfaction, but not a direct or exclusive measure of it; and 2) when the measurement is a predictor (leading indicator) of some more significant performance, for example, gain in customer satisfaction might be a leading indicator of market share gain.

Operational Performance and Predictors of Customer Satisfaction

Operational performance processes and predictors of customer satisfaction are related but not always the same. Operational performance measures can reflect

issues that concern customers as well as those that do not. Operational performance measures are used by the organization to assess effectiveness and efficiency, as well as predict customer satisfaction.

In the example of the coffee shop, freshness is a key customer requirement. One predictor of customer satisfaction might be the length of time, in minutes, between brewing and serving to guarantee freshness and good aroma. The standard might be 10 minutes or less to ensure satisfaction. Coffee more than 10 minutes old would be discarded.

A measure of operational effectiveness might be how many cups were discarded (waste) because the coffee was too old. The customer does not care if the coffee shop pours out stale coffee, and therefore, that measure is not a predictor of satisfaction. However, pouring out coffee does affect profitability and should be measured and minimized.

Ideally, an organization should be able to identify enough measures of product and service quality to predict customer satisfaction accurately and monitor operating effectiveness and efficiency.

Performance Requirements versus Performance Measures

Performance requirements are an expression of customer requirements and expectations. Sometimes performance requirements are expressed as design requirements or engineering requirements. They are viewed as a basis for developing measures to enable the organization to determine, generally without asking the customer, whether the customer is likely to be satisfied.

Performance measures can also be used to assess efficiency, effectiveness, and productivity of a work process. Process performance measures might include cycle time, error rate, or throughput.

Support Services

Support services are those services that support the organization's product and service delivery core operating processes. Support services might include finance and accounting, management information services, software support, marketing, public relations, personnel administration (job posting, recruitment, and payroll), facilities maintenance and management, secretarial support, and other administration services.

Of course, if an organization is in business to provide a traditional support service such as accounting, then accounting services provided to its external customers become its core work/operating process and are no longer considered a support service. Internal accounting services would continue to be considered a support service.

In the human resources area (Category 5), the Criteria require organizations to manage their human resource assets to optimize performance. However, many human resources support services might also exist such as payroll, travel, position control, recruitment, and employee services. These processes must be designed, delivered, and refined systematically according to the requirements of Item 6.2.

Teams and Natural Work Units

Natural work units reflect the people who normally work together because they are a part of a formal work unit. For example, on an assembly line, three or four people may naturally work together to install a motor in a new car. Hotel employees who prepare food in the kitchen might constitute another natural work unit.

Teams may be formed of people within a natural work unit or may cross existing (natural) organization boundaries. To improve room service in a hotel, for example, certain members of several natural work units, such as the switchboard, kitchen workers, and waiters, may form a special team. This team would not be considered a natural work unit. It might be called a cross-functional work team because its members come from different functions within the organization.

Appendix A: A Global View of Quality

This section describes quality and performance awards from around the globe. It describes their purpose, goals, strategies, models, and core values. Much of the research for this section is based on the references at the end of the section. In addition to recognizing the contribution of these organizations and sponsors, phone numbers or e-mail addresses are listed for our readers so they may pursue more in-depth research on global awards.

There are about 50 national quality organizations around the world:

- Central and Eastern Europe—18 percent

- Western and North Europe—32 percent

- South Europe and Mediterranean—12 percent

- Central and South America and Caribbean—18 percent

- North America—6 percent

- Asia—10 percent

- Africa—4 percent

The majority of the above organizations have these common goals:

- To raise the level and quality of management in organizations

- To support the competitiveness of industry in their country

- To share knowledge and best practices

- To increase emphasis on the methods of quality

Quality awards around the world are based in whole or in part on one of three basic models: The Baldrige model, the Deming model, and the European Quality Award (EQA) model (which, in itself, ties to the Baldrige model). The MBNQA was founded in 1987 and authorized by the U.S. Congress to recognize service, small business, and manufacturing companies. Of the worldwide quality awards, approximately 95 percent use the Baldrige model in part or whole as the basic foundation for their award (including the EQA).

The Deming Prize, the longest-standing of the awards, was established in 1951 by a resolution of the Union of Japanese Scientists and Engineers (JUSE) and named after the great leader in quality, W. Edwards Deming. The Deming Prize was, and continues to be, primarily used in Japan (although several years ago, representatives of the Japanese government benchmarked the Baldrige process and have created a Baldrige-based national quality award). Approximately four percent of the awards (India and Japan's JUSE Award) are based on this model today. (Reference: JUSE Tokyo, Japan +81-3-5379-1227.)

The EQA was initiated in 1992 to recognize high levels of commitment to quality in Europe. Approximately half of the national quality award organizations use the EQA format.

Since the European Quality Award is based on the Malcolm Baldrige Award, they have common or very similar core values as the following table indicates:

EQA Value	Malcolm Baldrige Value
Customer focus	Customer driven
Supplier partnerships	Valuing employees and partners
People development and involvement	Organizational and personal learning
Processes and facts	Management by fact
Continuous improvement and innovation	Managing for innovation
Leadership and consistency of purpose	Visionary leadership
Public responsibility	Public responsibility and citizenship
Results oriented	Focus on results and creating value

The following core values were included in more than 50 percent of the worldwide awards. The Baldrige value follows in parenthesis.

- Customer orientation (customer driven)

- Continuous improvement (organizational and personal learning but was formerly called continuous improvement and learning)

- Participation by everyone (valuing employees and partners)

- Committed leadership (visionary leadership)

- Process orientation (managing for innovation)

- Long-range perspective (focus on the future)

- Public responsibility (public responsibility and citizenship)

- Management by facts (management by fact)

- Prevention (No clear corresponding value, but agility corresponds in part)

- Learn from others (organizational and personal learning)

References on Quality Awards

JUSE. *The Deming Prize Guide for Overseas Companies*. Union of Japanese Scientists and Engineers (JUSE). 1996. Telephone: +81-3-5379-1227 (Japan), Fax +81-3-5379-1227.

HKMA. *Quality for Excellence and Prosperity*. Hong Kong Management Association (HKMA) Quality Award. 1998. Telephone: 2774 8569/2766 3303 (Hong Kong).

EFQM. *The European Quality Award*. European Foundation for Quality Management (EFQM). 1996. Telephone: +32 2 775 35 11 (Brussels).

Bases del Premo Nacional a la Calidad. Republica Argentina. 1996. Telephone/Fax: 541-326-6104 (Argentina). Private-Sector Award.

Australian Business Excellence Framework. 1999. Web site: http://www.apc.org.au.

State of the Quality Organization: A Comparative Review of the Organizations, Their Products and Service and Quality Awards Programs. Report sponsored by the Swedish International Development Agency, Swedish Institute for Quality, and the Xerox Corporation. 1998. More details may be obtained via e-mail to sari@recomate.se or telephoning +46 31 53 00 (Sweden).

Appendix B: Baldrige or ISO 9001

Prepared by John Lawrence and Mark Blazey

There is an ongoing discussion regarding which approach to performance improvement is better: ISO 9001 or Baldrige. The issue is complex as ISO 9001 has made strides to improve the standards to compete better with Baldrige. Both ISO 9001 and Baldrige are useful but they were designed for different purposes. To understand the options, it is appropriate to provide some background information.

BALDRIGE CRITERIA FOR PERFORMANCE EXCELLENCE

The operative goal in the use of the Baldrige Criteria involves achieving *excellence*. If the leadership team is interested in *optimizing* performance and wants to understand how well its entire management system responds to the marketplace and where its strengths and opportunities lie, Baldrige is the choice. More than 50 countries have a Baldrige-based assessment program including the European Quality Award and the Japan Quality Award.

ISO 9001

ISO 9001 is a compliance standard that establishes a basis for certification. By definition a compliance standard sets a *minimum level of acceptable performance*. If the leadership team wants to establish a fundamentally sound, consistent approach to meet basic performance requirements, ISO 9001 is the choice. ISO 9001 standards were developed and are maintained by the International Organization for Standardization in Switzerland and are aligned with standards organizations in 110 countries. ISO 9001 provides a certificate of compliance that is periodically renewable through assessment by third-party organizations.

Comparisons between Baldrige and ISO 9001

Baldrige does not establish minimum standards but requires a variety of continually improving processes that lead to top levels of performance. Baldrige requires leaders to understand the factors that are of critical importance to the business, what is needed to do well, why, how it compares to the competition and the best in the marketplace, and how to improve work processes continually in order to optimize performance. Baldrige requires levels of performance that lead the industry in many areas.

Because ISO 9001 is a compliance standard, it is relatively straightforward: either the organization does what is required by the standard or it does not. Thus, the elements often begin with the words "management shall...." Baldrige does not stipulate the specific steps or process elements an organization must put in place. Baldrige requires processes consistent with business needs and directions, recognizing that different approaches may be required depending on differences among organizations, their people, customers, and markets. Achieving excellence is always more challenging than achieving mediocrity. Accordingly, Baldrige is a more rigorous approach: it forces self-examination and learning and causes the leadership team to question why things are done in a certain way and constantly struggle to improve them. In Baldrige, the *status quo* is an enemy. ISO 9001 prescribes specific techniques to ensure minimum levels of quality are achieved, focusing on the *management of quality*. Baldrige requires integrated systems and processes to optimize performance and enhance the *quality of management*.

ISO 9001 judgments are supposed to be made relative to a clear, prescribed standard: either a process requirement is met or not met. With Baldrige, approaches to management are judged in relation to the strategic imperatives of the business and the degree of deployment, improvement, and integration of the required process. As such, Baldrige conducts a developmental analysis and reports progress on a scale of 0 to 100 percent. But Baldrige looks at more than management processes. Because Baldrige is intended to help organizations achieve excellence, the organization must demonstrate top performance outcomes (results), relative to the best competitors or benchmarks.

ISO 9001 requires the collection and reporting of some performance data but does not expect or require high-performance outcomes. It is possible to be ISO 9001 certified and have poor financial, customer, or operational performance, relative to competitors or the best in the business. It is not possible to receive the Baldrige Award without demonstrating outstanding performance in the areas of customer satisfaction, financial and market performance, human resource performance, operational effectiveness, and public responsibility and citizenship.

In 2000, ISO 9001 standards were modified in an attempt to make them more relevant in a highly competitive business environment. In particular, they added some requirements that the Baldrige Criteria had previously identified as necessary for high performance, such as the need to improve continuously. The ISO 9001 standard (8.5.1) now requires that the organization continually improve the effectiveness of the quality management system through the use of the quality policy, quality objectives, audit results, analysis of data, corrective and preventive actions, and management review. It is a standard that ISO 9001 auditors have had difficulty assessing consistently, since the act of rating "continuous improvement" is highly subjective.

Making the Choice

The choice is simple:

- If your key customers require ISO 9001 certification as a condition of doing business, if you do not face serious competition, or if customer expectations are low, choose ISO 9001.

- If you must survive in a highly competitive environment where customer expectations are high and getting higher, and nothing short of "excellent" performance is acceptable, choose Baldrige.

Indeed, a great many organizations choose ISO 9001 because their customers require them to do so. However, once certified, some go beyond ISO 9001, using the Baldrige Criteria in order to achieve market leadership characterized by competitive advantage and consistently increasing profitability, market growth, and employee security. Make your choice based on what you are trying to accomplish. Both systems have value, provided the system you choose is effectively implemented. The leadership team needs to be fully committed to the choice it makes and provide disciplined leadership every day in carrying out that choice. Leadership commitment, involvement, and consistency are essential to implement either approach. Without effective leadership, neither approach will be of much value and could even waste valuable resources.

Baldrige and ISO 9001 are not mutually exclusive. Some Baldrige winners are also ISO 9001 certified. However, some Baldrige winners would not pass ISO 9001 certification because they do not meet some requirements, usually the failure to "document" work processes. That does not mean that they are poor performers. On the other hand, most ISO 9001 certified organizations would not qualify for the Baldrige Award, usually because their actual performance outcomes and many work processes are only adequate and not considered to be role models within their industries. Figure 50 is a brief matrix showing the gaps and similarities between the two system. *A much more detailed comparative analysis of these two approaches is presented in the CD included with this book.*

This section was prepared by John lawrence of the Quantum Performance Group with input from Mark Blazey.

Categories	Leadership		Strategy		Customer and Market Knowledge		Measurement and Analysis		Human Resources		
Basic Items	1.1	1.2	2.1	2.2	3.1	3.2	4.1	4.2	5.1	5.2	5.3
Baldrige Areas and Requirements	7	4	4	5	3	8	5	5	7	7	6
ISO 9001 Requirements	Organizational Leadership	Social Responsibility	Strategy Development	Strategy Deployment	Customer and Market Knowledge	Customer Relationship and Satisfaction	Measurement and Analysis	Information and Knowledge Management	Work Systems	Employee Learning and Motivation	Employee Well-being and Satisfaction
Number of times ISO 9001 requires a Baldrige Area or Sub Area to Address	6- [a1] 2- [a2] 1- [b] 8- [c1] 0- [c2] 4- [c3] 1- c4] 22 Total	3- [a1] 0- [a2] 1- [b] 1- [c] 4- Total	0- [a1] 2- [a2] 1- [b1] 0- [b2] 3- Total	5- [a1] 0- [a2] 1- [a3] 2- [a4] 0- [b] 8- Total	0- [a1] 2- [a2] 1- [a3] 3- Total	1- [a1] 1- [a2] 2- [a3] 1- [a4] 1- [b1] 1- [b2] 1- [b3] 1- [b4] 9-Total	4- [a1] 0- [a2] 2- [a3] 2- [b1] 2- [b2] 10-Total	2- [a1] 2- [a2] 2- [a3] 4- [b1] 3- [b2] 13-Total	2- [a1] 1- [a2] 1- [a3] 1- [b] 1- [c1] 0- [c2] 0- [c3] 6- Total	2- [a1] 1- [a2] 0- [a3] 0- [a4] 0- [a5] 1- [a6] 0- [b] 3- Total	0- [a1] 1- [a2] 0- [b1] 0- [b2] 1- [b3] 0- [b4] 2- Total
Fraction of Baldrige Areas Addressed by ISO 9001	6/7	3/4	2/4	3/5	2/3	8/8	4/5	5/5	5/7	3/7	2/6

Categories	Process Management		Business Results					
Basic Items	6.1	6.2	7.1	7.2	7.3	7.4	7.5	7.6
Baldrige Areas and Requirements	6	6	2	1	2	3	3	4
ISO Requirements 9001	Value Creation Processes	Support Processes	Customer Focus Results	Product and Service Results	Financial and Market Results	Human Resource Results	Organizational Effectiveness	Governance and Social Responsibility
Number of times ISO 9001 requires a Baldrige Area or Sub Area to Address	2- [a1] 4- [a2] 9- [a3] 19 [a4] 4- [a5] 7- [a6] 45 Total	1- [a1] 2- [a2] 4- [a3] 8- [a4] 1- [a5] 3- [a6] 18-Total	1- [a1] 11-[a2] 2-Total	2- [a] 2- Total	0- [a1] 0- [a2] 0- Total	0- [a1] 0- [a2] 0- [a3] 0-Total	3- [a1] 2- [a2] 2- [a3] 7-Total	0- [a1] 0- [a2] 0- [a3] 0- [a4] 0-Total
Fraction of Baldrige Areas Addressed by ISO 9001	6/6	5/6	2/2	1/1	0/2	0/3	3/3	0/4

Figure 50   Baldrige and ISO 9001 gaps and similarities.

Appendix C: Baldrige or Shingo Prize for Excellence in Manufacturing

The Shingo Prize for Excellence in Manufacturing is sponsored by the College of Business at Utah State University in Logan, Utah. Unlike the ISO 9001 standards, which establish minimum standards for acceptable performance, both Shingo and Baldrige recognize excellence. The Shingo Prize recognizes excellence in manufacturing. Baldrige recognizes excellence in manufacturing as well as service, small business, education, and healthcare. The Shingo Prize criteria are customized to manufacturing, whereas the Baldrige criteria are more generally applicable to all types of organizations in all sectors, including the government and not-for-profit sectors.

Both the Shingo and Baldrige awards use a developmental scoring guideline to separate poor, adequate, and excellence systems and performance outcomes. Shingo emphasizes waste prevention, full use of human resources, and an aggressive strategic focus on high-value-added processes and issues. Baldrige emphasizes continuous improvement, innovation, integration, alignment, and full deployment of systematic, consistent processes. Baldrige is more comprehensive and rigorous than Shingo, as the analysis in Figure 51 indicates.

Manufacturing companies may do well by participating in a Shingo process as part of their journey to excellence. Having won a Shingo Prize, a manufacturing company may strive to a higher level of excellence in the Baldrige Award. For more information about the Shingo Prize for Manufacturing Excellence, visit the Web site at http://www.shingoprize.org.

COMPARING BALDRIGE AND SHINGO REQUIREMENTS

The following summary table (Figure 51) indicates the areas where the Baldrige Criteria and Shingo Prize Criteria contain similar requirements as well as where there is no match. For example, Shingo requires leaders to set direction [1.1a(1) and (2)] and monitor performance [1.1c(1)], but not necessarily use that process to list findings [1.1c(2)], set priorities for improvement, communicate with relevant organizational units and suppliers [1.1c(3)], or evaluate and improve leadership effectiveness [1.1c(4)]. Shingo requires the organization to behave in an ethical manner [1.2b] and support the community [1.2c], but not necessarily anticipate and address concerns the public may have with its products and services, including operations needed to produce them [1.2a(1)].

Shingo requires a planning process to establish and deploy vision, mission, values, strategies, and goals, which relates to Baldrige [2.1a(2)], but Shingo does not require the many planning components of Baldrige [2.1a(2)], the identification of strategic objectives and timelines to accomplish them [2.1b(1)], or a process to ensure the planning process actually addresses all of the strategic challenges the organization faces [2.1b(2)]; Shingo also requires the organization to ensure strategic plans are deployed throughout the organization, similar to Baldrige requirements [2.2a(1, 2, 3, 4)]. However, Shingo does not require the organization to estimate future competitive performance to help set goals that produce leading performance levels [2.2b].

In the area of customer and market knowledge, Shingo requires the organization to develop new markets and expand existing ones. Baldrige requires processes for determining customer and market requirements and the use of that information for new development and growth [3.1a(2)]. Shingo does not require information on the rationale for determining market segments [3.1a(1)] or improving the process for listening and learning about customer and market requirements [3.1a(3)]. Moreover, Shingo requires no specific, systematic processes to develop and improve customer relations, make it easy for customers to complain, handle those complaints promptly, use the complaint information to drive improvements and prevent problem recurrence [3.2a(1, 2, 3, 4)], \assess customer satisfaction and dissatisfaction.[3.2b(1)], follow up on recent transactions [3.2b(2)], and determine the satisfaction of customers of competitors [3.2b(3)]. Shingo does require customer satisfaction data to be reported [part V], including customer awards and audits, which suggests some customer data are collected.

Shingo requires data to support decision making [4.1a(1)], benchmark or comparison data [4.1a(2)], and analyses to support organizational and functional decision making [4.1b(1, 2)]. Shingo does not require processes to improve data collection and use in order to keep current with changing business needs [4.1a(3)]. Shingo requires data be made available to support decision making [4.2a(1)] and to transfer relevant knowledge [4.2b(1)]. Shingo does not require processes to ensure hardware and software reliability [4.2a(2)], processes to improve information systems [4.2a(3)], or processes to ensure data integrity, timeliness, reliability, security, accuracy, or confidentiality [4.2b(2)].

Shingo requires 3 out of 7 Baldrige requirements for Item 5.1. Shingo requires the organization to promote a philosophy that encourages and recognizes innovations, improvements [5.1a(1)], organizational communication [5.1a(3)], and appropriate recognition and reward systems [5.1b]. Shingo does not stipulate that employee feedback and related reward and recognition reinforce high-performance objectives or customer satisfaction as Baldrige does [5.1b]. Shingo does not establish any requirements for the organization to have processes in place to identify characteristics and skills needed by the organization [5.1c(1)], processes that ensure employees represent the diverse ideas, cultures, and thinking of the employee hiring community [5.1c(2)], or effective succession planning and the management of career progression for all employees [5.1c(3)]. Shingo requires 2 out of 7 Baldrige requirements for Item 5.2. Shingo requires the organization to provide training in world-class practices [5.2a(2)] and cooperation with schools to ensure the development of a qualified work force, which enables different methods to deliver effective training [5.2a(4)]. Shingo does not specifically require training to be aligned to support the organization's action plans [5.2a(1)], employee and supervisor input

in identifying training needs, incorporation of the organization's learning and knowledge in education and training [5.2a(3)], processes to reinforce training on the job [5.2a(5)], processes to evaluate and improve training effectiveness taking into account organizational performance [5.2a(6)], or processes to ensure the development and use of employees' full potential [5.2b]. Shingo requires 2 out of 6 Baldrige requirements for Item 5.3. Shingo requires efforts to maintain an ergonomic, clean, and safe work environment for all employees [5.3a(1)] and measures that document employee satisfaction and morale such as employee turnover, absenteeism, and employee surveys [5.3b(3)]. Shingo does not require the organization to ensure work-place preparedness for emergencies or disasters or business continuity for the benefit of your employees and customers [5.3a(2)], to determine the key factors that affect employee well-being, satisfaction, and motivation [5.3b(1)], to provide support services, benefits, and policies that are tailored to the needs of a diverse work force and different categories and types of employees [5.3b(2)], or to relate priorities for improving the work environment and employee support climate to achieving key business results [5.3b(4)].

Shingo covers 5 out of 6 areas of process management in the value creation Item. Shingo does not require the organization to identify the value creation processes [6.1a(1)]. Shingo covers 4 out of 6 areas of process management for support services. Shingo does not require the organization to identify its key support processes [6.2a(1)] or key performance measures or indicators used for the control and improvement of support processes [6.2a(4)]. Shingo does not specifically require in-process measures or the use of customer, supplier, and partner input in managing these processes [6.2a(4)].

Shingo requires results very similar to those required by Baldrige (11 out of 15 areas). The few results that Shingo does not require include indicators of work system performance and effectiveness [7.4a(1)], measures of employee learning and development [7.4a(2)], key measures of fiscal accountability [7.6a(1)], and key measures of ethical behavior and of stakeholder trust in organizational governance [7.6a(2)].

Categories	Leadership		Strategy		Customer and Market Knowledge		Measurement and Analysis		Human Resources		
Basic Items	1.1	1.2	2.1	2.2	3.1	3.2	4.1	4.2	5.1	5.2	5.3
Baldrige Areas and Requirements	7	4	4	5	3	8	5	5	7	7	6
Shingo Requirements	Organizational Leadership	Social Responsibility	Strategy Development	Strategy Deployment	Customer and Market Knowledge	Customer Relationship and Satisfaction	Measurement and Analysis	Information and Knowledge Management	Work Systems	Employee Learning and Motivation	Employee Well-being and Satisfaction
Number of times Shingo requires a Baldrige Area or Sub Area to Address	1- [a1] 4- [a2] 1- [b] 0- [c1] 0- [c2] 0- [c3] 0- [c4] 6 Total	0- [a1] 0- [a2] 1- [b] 2- Total	0- [a1] 1- [a2] 1- [b] 1- [c] 1- Total	3- [a1] 1- [a2] 1- [a3] 2- [a4] 0- [b] 7- Total	0- [a1] 1- [a2] 0- [a3] 1- Total	0- [a1] 0- [a2] 0- [a3] 0- [a4] 0- [b1] 0- [b2] 0- [b3] 0- [b4] 0-Total	4- [a1] 0- [a2] 1- [a3] 2- [b1] 3- [b2] 8-Total	2- [a1] 0- [a2] 0- [a3] 1- [b1] 0- [b2] 3-Total	3- [a1] 0- [a2] 2- [a3] 1- [b] 0- [c1] 0- [c2] 0- [c3] 6- Total	0- [a1] 1- [a2] 0- [a3] 1- [a4] 0- [a5] 0- [a6] 0- [b] 2- Total	1- [a1] 0- [a2] 0- [b1] 0- [b2] 1- [b3] 0- [b4] 2- Total
Fraction of Baldrige Areas Addressed by Shingo	3/7	2/4	1/5	4/5	1/3	0/8	4/5	2/5	3/7	2/7	2/6

Categories	Process Management		Business Results					
Basic Items	6.1	6.2	7.1	7.2	7.3	7.4	7.5	7.6
Baldrige Areas and Requirements	6	6	2	1	2	3	3	4
Shingo Requirements	Value Creation Processes	Support Processes	Customer Focus Results	Product and Service Results	Financial and Market Results	Human Resource Results	Organizational Effectiveness	Governance and Social Responsibility
Number of times Shingo requires a Baldrige Area or Sub Area to Address	0- [a1] 1- [a2] 3- [a3] 3- [a4] 3- [a5] 5- [a6] 15 Total	0- [a1] 2- [a2] 1- [a3] 0- [a4] 3- [a5] 6- [a6] 12-Total	3- [a1] 3- [a2] 6-Total	8- [a] 8- Total	8- [a1] 6- [a2] 14-Total	0- [a1] 0- [a2] 0- [a3] 1-Total	19-[a1] 18-[a2] 11-[a3] 38-Total	0- [a1] 0- [a2] 2- [a3] 1- [a4] 3-Total
Fraction of Baldrige Areas Addressed by ISO 9001	5/6	4/6	2/2	1/1	2/2	1/3	3/3	2/4

Figure 51 Baldrige and Shingo gaps and similarities.

Appendix D: Baldrige or JCAHO

Prepared by Paul Grizzell and Mark Blazey

Healthcare is an industry in a state of transition. Healthcare traditionally has been a "cottage industry" in which an individual physician or small group of physicians provided a wide range of healthcare services to their patients, most of whom had very little healthcare knowledge. Current healthcare has moved to a model in which specialized physicians provide healthcare as part of healthcare systems that may involve affiliated clinics, hospitals, laboratories, and pharmacies. Patients are more knowledgeable than ever, and expect to be viewed as a partner in their healthcare. This transition provides benefits to many involved, but others find the transition difficult for them individually or for their particular role in the system.

In addition, the various "players" in the healthcare system are often at odds with each other. One player's success often hurts another (in the form of decreased revenue). These players include physicians, nurses and other staff, healthcare administration, payers such as managed care providers and insurance companies, employers and various healthcare purchasing groups, and last, but by no means least, the recipients of healthcare services, which include patients and their family. There are few individuals who are not directly impacted by the healthcare system from cradle to grave.

THE NEED FOR A SYSTEMATIC MANAGEMENT SYSTEM

In order to address these issues, it has become necessary for healthcare systems and providers to become more effective and efficient at providing services that meet the requirements of its various constituents. In order to accomplish this, the healthcare organization has to look at the best ways to provide these services, taking into account all staff, healthcare and other processes, relationships with patients and other customers, including payers, and the methods by which leadership sets and communicates the direction of the healthcare organization.

WHAT IS BALDRIGE?

The Malcolm Baldrige Health Care Criteria for Performance Excellence (Baldrige) is a comprehensive, integrated management system that helps an organization focus and align all of its activities to achieve optimum performance. These management activities must focus on meeting customer requirements in a manner that drives toward continual improvement of a balanced set of healthcare organization results.

WHAT IS JCAHO?

The Joint Commission on Accreditation of Healthcare Organizations (JCAHO) focuses on establishing standards, then assessing performance of healthcare organizations against those standards. These standards are focused on healthcare delivery and outcomes. JCAHO, as all compliance-based accreditation standards, requires the implementation of specific processes and measures to ensure minimally acceptable performance against a set of healthcare-specific standards.

WHAT'S THE DIFFERENCE BETWEEN BALDRIGE AND JCAHO?

Both JCAHO and Baldrige play important, integrated roles in helping a healthcare organization improve. JCAHO is a required assessment the organization must go through as a condition of receiving and maintaining accreditation to conduct business. Baldrige is an option, but is one that can help the organization go beyond accomplishing its JCAHO goals to achieve

345

the highest levels of performance possible. The two should not be viewed as competitive business models. In actuality, the two are complementary.

The Baldrige Criteria provide an overall framework of excellence that helps align all activities within the healthcare organization. There is no managed process within the healthcare organization that cannot be framed within the context of the Baldrige Criteria. The results of Baldrige assessments are used by the organization for ongoing improvement—results do not have to be communicated outside the organization.

JCAHO provides a set of minimum standards for healthcare organizations. Healthcare organizations use their performance against these standards as a method of rating and communicating healthcare related performance to potential patients, payers, and employers. Organizations that possess JCAHO accreditation enjoy no competitive advantage over any other JCAHO-accredited organization—unless they do more than is required by JCAHO, and that is where Baldrige helps. By aligning performance excellence activities in a manner that drives to ever-increasing quality, the healthcare organization can set itself apart from competitors and gain a true competitive advantage. The competitive advantage gained is usually not one that is easily copied by competitors, so the advantage is sustainable over time.

WHY USE BOTH BALDRIGE AND JCAHO?

JCAHO provides a prescriptive list of processes and procedures that must be in place to meet minimum standards as well as a method of assessing the quality of a healthcare organization. By setting standards for healthcare organizations, JCAHO helps to ensure that at least minimum levels of safety and quality exist in the industry.

The Baldrige Criteria for Performance Excellence, on the other hand, provides a non-prescriptive method of assessing the processes and performance of the entire healthcare organization with a goal of driving and identifying the organizations that have optimized performance. By being non-prescriptive, Baldrige requires the healthcare organization to frame its management system within the context of its unique orga-

nizational requirements and its overall market and market segments. This allows flexibility in adapting to a changing environment.

Baldrige and JCAHO do not represent conflicting management systems or a competing set of minimum standards. Each provides significantly different value to healthcare organizations for very specific purposes. The use of Baldrige and JCAHO as complementary methods will help the healthcare organization that is committed to establishing processes to ensure competent delivery of healthcare services (JCAHO), and then continue to improve and become more patient- and other customer-focused, process oriented, and results-driven to help the healthcare organization attain peak levels of performance excellence (Baldrige).

COMPARING BALDRIGE AND JCAHO REQUIREMENTS

Figure 52 illustrates the alignment of Joint Commission on Accreditation of Healthcare Organizations (JCAHO) and the Baldrige Criteria for Performance Excellence (Baldrige). The Baldrige requirements are provided in brackets []. Baldrige guides the organization to high levels of excellence, while JCAHO provides a set of standards to help ensure the organization is qualified to deliver healthcare services.

JCAHO requires the organization's leaders to establish a planned, systematic, organization-wide approach to process design and performance measurement, analysis, and improvement [1.1a(1)], however, JCAHO does not require the depth and breadth of senior leadership direction-setting required by Baldrige such as creating value and balance for patients and other customers and stakeholders. JCAHO also does not require leaders to set an environment for empowerment, innovation, organizational agility, and learning [1.1a(2)]. JCAHO requires leaders to ensure that the organization complies with laws and regulation. It does not require the depth of Baldrige in addressing corporate governance [1.1b]. JCAHO requires the healthcare organization to operate according to a code of ethical behavior [1.2b].

Strategic Planning is required by JCAHO, although JCAHO does not require the depth of the Strategy Development Process [2.1a(1)] or the description of Strategic Objectives [2.1b] required by Baldrige. JCAHO does not ask for the Strategic Deployment Action Plan Development and Deployment [2.2a(1,2,3,4)] or the Performance Projection [2.2b] required by Baldrige to help ensure that achieving its goals will position the organization as a healthcare leader.

JCAHO does not address Customer and Market Knowledge other than in providing appropriate healthcare services to patients [3.2a(1)]. JCAHO focuses on clinical care provided to patients—it does not focus on defining the requirements, expectations and preferences of patients, other customers, and markets. Baldrige focuses on understanding the requirements of patients, other customers, and markets, in a manner that will drive the healthcare organization to improvement in a balanced set of measures, including increased market share. JCAHO does not address how the healthcare organization acquires knowledge of patient/customer and healthcare markets [3.2a(1,2,3)], provides access mechanisms for patients [3.2a(2)], manages complaints [3.2a(3)], keeps approaches current with healthcare needs and directions [3.2a(4)] or monitors patient/customer satisfaction [3.2b(1,2,3,4)].

There is strong alignment between Baldrige and JCAHO in the area of Measurement and Analysis of Organizational Performance. JCAHO requires that data be collected to monitor the stability of existing processes, identify opportunities for improvement, identify changes that will lead to improvement, and sustain improvement, as well as to systematically aggregate and analyze data on an ongoing basis. This requirement aligns closely with the Baldrige requirement to select, collect, align, and integrate data [4.1a(1)], and to perform effective analyses of data and information [3.2b(1,2)]. JCAHO does not require the effective use of comparative data [4.1a(2)] or methods to keep performance measurement systems current with healthcare service needs and directions [4.1a(3)]. JCAHO addresses the Baldrige requirements to ensure data reliability and security [4.2a(2)], manage patient-related knowledge effectively [4.2b(1)], but does not address how data availability mechanisms are kept current [4.2a(3)].

JCAHO emphasizes the need to maintain adequate, qualified staff to provide appropriate care to patients. There is a focus on staff that provides clinical care (medical staff, nurses). These standards align closely with Baldrige [5.1a(1,2,3), b, and c(1,2,3)]. The value of training is recognized by JCAHO, which requires continuing education for those with clinical responsibilities [(5.2a(1)] and orientation training for all staff. Baldrige requires further training in diversity, ethical business practices, and management and leadership development [5.2a(2)]. JCAHO requires that the competence of all staff members be assessed, maintained, demonstrated, and improved continually, which aligns with the more detailed staff education, training, and development [5.2a1,2,3,4,5,6)] of Baldrige. JCAHO does not directly address the need for staff motivation and career development [5.2b]. JCAHO addresses the need to reduce risk of infection outbreaks to staff [5.3a(1,2)] and addresses the staff member's request not to participate in any aspect of patient care [5.3b(1)]; otherwise Baldrige addresses staff well-being and satisfaction more deeply, including services, benefits and policies [5.3b(2)], staff satisfaction assessment [5.3b(3)], and alignment of assessment findings to priorities for improvement [5.3b(4)].

JCAHO and Baldrige align most closely in the Baldrige Health Care Processes item [6.1]. This shows JCAHO's strong focus on clinical processes. Both Baldrige and JCAHO require a process orientation to how work is accomplished. JCAHO is much more prescriptive in describing how clinical processes should be managed, including the standard that organized self-governing medical staffs have overall responsibility for the quality of the professional services provided by individuals with clinical privileges. JCAHO is much less prescriptive when describing support process management [6.2], asking simply for internal controls of support processes and processes to measure, assess, and improve the quality of the hospital's governance, management, clinical, and support activities [6.2a(4)].

Baldrige requires a balanced set of measures. JCAHO requires only Health Care Results [7.1a], but in significant detail, including comparative data. Alignment of Baldrige and JCAHO in this category is significant. JCAHO does not require measures on the other 5 Categories of Organizational Performance Results.

This section was prepared by Paul Grizzell of the Performance Leadership Group with input from Mark Blazey.

Categories	Leadership		Strategy		Customer and Market Knowledge		Measurement and Analysis		Human Resources		
Basic Items	1.1	1.2	2.1	2.2	3.1	3.2	4.1	4.2	5.1	5.2	5.3
Baldrige Areas and Requirements	7	4	4	5	3	8	5	5	7	7	6
JCAHO Requirements	Organizational Leadership	Social Responsibility	Strategy Development	Strategy Deployment	Customer and Market Knowledge	Customer Relationship and Satisfaction	Measurement and Analysis	Information and Knowledge Management	Work Systems	Employee Learning and Motivation	Employee Well-being and Satisfaction
JCAHO requires a Baldrige Area or Sub Area to Address	2- [a1] 0- [a2] 3- [b] 0- [c1] 0- [c2] 0- [c3] 0- c4] 5 Total	4- [a1] 1- [a2] 1- [b] 0- [c] 6- Total	1- [a1] 1- [a2] 1- [b1] 1- [b2] 4- Total	0- [a1] 0- [a2] 0- [a3] 0- [a4] 0- [b] 0- Total	0- [a1] 0- [a2] 0- [a3] 0- Total	0- [a1] 0- [a2] 0- [a3] 0- [a4] 0- [b1] 0- [b2] 0- [b3] 0- [b4] 9-Total	4- [a1] 0- [a2] 0- [a3] 2- [b1] 1- [b2] 7-Total	7 [a1] 3- [a2] 2- [a3] 4- [b1] 5- [b2] 21-Total	4- [a1] 3- [a2] 4- [a3] 4- [b] 5- [c1] 3- [c2] 3- [c3] 26-Total	2- [a1] 3- [a2] 0- [a3] 0- [a4] 1- [a5] 1- [a6] 1- [b] 8- Total	2- [a1] 2- [a2] 1- [b1] 0- [b2] 0- [b3] 0- [b4] 5- Total
Fraction of Baldrige Areas Addressed by JCAHO	2/7	3/4	4/4	0/5	0/3	0/8	3/5	5/5	7/7	5/7	3/6

Categories	Process Management		Business Results					
Basic Items	6.1	6.2	7.1	7.2	7.3	7.4	7.5	7.6
Baldrige Areas and Requirements	6	6	2	1	2	3	3	4
JCAHO Requirements	Value Creation Processes	Support Processes	Customer Focus Results	Product and Service Results	Financial and Market Results	Human Resource Results	Organizational Effectiveness	Governance and Social Responsibility
Number of times JCAHO requires a Baldrige Area or Sub Area to Address	2- [a1] 12-[a2] 14-[a3] 20 [a4] 17-[a5] 0- [a6] 6- [a7] 51 Total	0- [a1] 0- [a2] 0- [a3] 1- [a4] 0- [a5] 0- [a6] 0- [a7] 1-Total	3- [a] 3-Total	0- [a1] 0- [a2] 0- Total	0- [a1] 0- [a2] 0- Total	0- [a1] 0- [a2] 0- [a3] 0-Total	0- [a1] 0- [a2] 0- [a3] 0-Total	0- [a1] 0- [a2] 0- [a3] 0- [a4] 0-Total
Fraction of Baldrige Areas Addressed by JCAHO	6/7	1/7	1/1	0/2	0/2	0/3	0/3	0/4

Figure 52 Baldrige and JCAHO gaps and similarities

Appendix E: Alignment of Baldrige With Six Sigma, Lean Thinking, and Balanced Scorecard

Prepared by Paul Grizzell and Mark Blazey

INTRODUCTION

"Baldrige? Six Sigma? Lean? Balanced Scorecard? We don't have time for all of these initiatives! Let's just pick one and go with it!" How many times have you heard (or perhaps even said) something similar? The statement suggests the initiatives are equivalent. They are not. As has been discussed earlier in this book, the Baldrige Criteria for Performance Excellence represent a comprehensive set of processes that organizations should have in place in order to optimize performance. Six Sigma, Lean, Balanced Scorecard, and other initiatives represent some of the tools, albeit powerful tools, that organizations can use to enhance performance.

The use of these tools in isolation, without regard to the needs of the entire management system, will not produce optimum benefits or optimum performance for the organization. Many times when the concept of using the Malcolm Baldrige Criteria for Performance Excellence is discussed, Six Sigma is brought up as an alternative management system. Many articles and books tout Six Sigma as the most effective management system ever. Those opinions are not supported by data. Six Sigma tools, properly implemented, do produce great results, but the tool does not cover all of the elements needed to optimize organizational performance. Six Sigma can best be viewed as a tool that helps an organization drive toward performance excellence; however, Six Sigma, Lean, Balanced Scorecard, and other tools can become more useful if they are used together within the context of a Baldrige-based integrated culture of performance excellence. The use of these tools as part of an integrated approach to maximizing performance, which Baldrige represents, is the best way to drive toward better results.

Baldrige Overview

The Malcolm Baldrige Criteria for Performance Excellence have the over-arching goal of strengthening U.S. competitiveness in an increasingly global and competitive marketplace. The Baldrige Criteria focus on helping organizations use a focused and systematic approach to performance management that results in:

- Delivery of ever-improving value to customers, contributing to marketplace success

- Improvement of overall organizational effectiveness and capabilities

- Organizational and personal learning

The Criteria are based on a set of Core Values and Concepts (Figure 53) that have been found to be integral beliefs and behaviors in high-performing organizations.

Summary of Baldrige Core Values and Concepts	
Visionary Leadership	Managing for Innovation
Customer-Driven Excellence	Management by Fact
Organizational and Personal Learning	Social Responsibility
Valuing Employees and Partners	Focus on Results and Creating Value
Agility	Systems Perspective
Focus on the Future	

Figure 53 Baldrige Core Values and concepts.

These Core Values and Concepts are the underpinnings of the systematic approach and deployment methods used to drive toward improved business results within organizations using the Baldrige Criteria as their management system. (See pages 30–38 for a complete description of Core Values and Concepts.)

The Baldrige Criteria helps an organization ensure a systematic approach to improvement by developing approach and deployment methodologies for Categories 1–6, and looking for how these approach and deployment methods are linked to improved business results. The Baldrige Criteria are non-prescriptive—they don't tell an organization how to do something; they tell what it should be doing, then leave it to the organization to determine the processes that best fit the organization, its culture, and goals.

Some managers see the Baldrige Criteria only as an award process; however, in reality, most organizations that use the Baldrige Criteria do not apply for a national or state award. Thousands of organizations use the Baldrige Criteria as a management model or assessment tool to gauge the maturity and effectiveness of their own management system. The Criteria, available in Business, Education, and Health Care versions, are very flexible. This is demonstrated by the diversity of organizations that have used the Criteria to move to performance excellence. These include a high-school classroom, churches, internal suppliers, non-profit agencies, and others that have tailored the model to their particular application.

Six Sigma Overview

Six Sigma is an extremely effective tool for systematically attacking the highest priority production and support/functional problems within an organization. A goal of Six Sigma is to reduce both defects and variation within a work process. It is not, however, the best tool to apply to every problem. Six Sigma requires a significant investment in up-front training, time and people to carry out the projects, and leadership commitment to project reviews. Some problems may not require Six Sigma's highly intensive methodology. Effective leaders separate the problems that deserve a Six Sigma approach from those requiring a different methodology.

General Electric has been recognized as a good example of a corporation that has used Six Sigma effectively. Several of the key reasons that Six Sigma has been so successful at GE have nothing to do with the Six Sigma process, but are the "enablers" that have driven that success. Several of those enablers include:

- Consistent leadership that drives the organization to quantifiable results

- A culture that is relentless in driving toward continuous improvement

- Effectiveness in committing the resources that increase the chances of a successful project outcome.

Baldrige and Six Sigma Alignment

An example of the Six Sigma Define-Measure-Analyze-Improve-Control (DMAIC) problem-solving process is provided in Figure 54. It is easy to see how this systematic improvement process can help an organization meet some of the requirements of the Baldrige Criteria in Category 6, Process Management, for improving "…value creation processes [Item 6.1] and certain support processes [Item 6.2] to achieve better performance, to reduce variability, to improve products and services, and to keep the processes current with business needs and direction." In addition, Six Sigma encourages a focus on understanding and meeting customer requirements [Baldrige Category 3], a leadership-driven initiative [Baldrige Category 1], alignment of improvement projects to the organization's strategy [Baldrige Item 2.2a(1)], effective development and training of human resources [Baldrige Item 5.2], and data-driven decision-making [Baldrige Category 4]. *Effective organizational alignment with the Baldrige Criteria can help focus the positive impact of Six Sigma improvement initiatives.*

The most effective integrated management system would be one in which an organization uses the Baldrige Criteria as a method of establishing a culture of excellence, assessing performance, and prioritizing initiatives. Six Sigma can be used to examine

Six Sigma DMAIC Problem Solving Process			
Phase	*Step*	*Primary Activities*	*Primary Output*
Define	**1. Establish the focus**	Review initial project charter	Project objective
		Form the team	
		Identify and describe the performance gap	
		Verify the performance with data	
		Complete charter	
Measure	**2. Examine the current situation**	View the process in detail	Strategies and strategy measures
		Describe the current situation in detail with data	
		Develop strategies	
Analyze	**3. Analyze the causes**	Brainstorm and prioritize root causes	Root causes
		Use data to verify the causes	
		Select root causes to address	
Improve	**4. Act on the causes**	Brainstorm possible actions	Actions
		Select actions to take	
		Develop action plans	
		Implement actions on a small scale	
	5. Study the results	Study the results and modify action plans	Revised action plans
Control	**6. Standardize the changes**	Implement actions on a large scale	Control plan
		Standardize successful actions	
		Develop a process management plan	
	7. Draw conclusions	Identify benefits, difficulties, and lessons learned	Project summary
		Discuss future plans	

Figure 54   Six Sigma DMAIC Problem Solving Process.
©Used with permission of Bluefire Partners, Minneapolis, MN

root causes to solve the organization's highest-impact problems, consistent with the requirements of Baldrige Category 6, Process Management. Visionary leaders will be able to see the value of both the systematic overview of the business that is provided by a Baldrige integrated management system and the structured problem-solving methodology provided by Six Sigma. *One is not a substitute for the other; they align well with each other and mutually help drive toward improved business results.*

Baldrige as an Aid to Six Sigma Project Selection

A key concern with the Six Sigma process is how to choose the appropriate projects on which to spend valuable time and resources. An article by Ronald D. Snee in the March, 2001 edition of *Quality Progress* (published by Quality Press, Milwaukee, WI) was titled "Dealing With the Achilles' Heel of Six Sigma Initiatives: Project Selection is Key to Success." When Six Sigma is approached from a Baldrige management system perspective, areas of focus have already been identified in a variety of ways:

1. Completion of an Organizational Profile that walks the organization through an overview of the organizational environment in which it operates, key relationships with customer groups and suppliers and partners, the competitive environment in which it operates, the strategic challenges it faces, and its performance management system. This Organizational Profile is the first step in moving forward with a Baldrige assessment; however, its greatest value may lie in its ability to move the entire organization to a common understanding of its culture, its customers, and its strategic challenges and opportunities. Key Business Factors naturally emerge from the Organizational Profile, providing a prioritization capability that can be used to align Six Sigma efforts with the highest priorities of the organization.

2. As the organization becomes more mature and assesses its management systems against the Baldrige Criteria, it is able to identify and address key strengths and opportunities for improvement that relate directly to its key success factors. The organization may decide to participate in a state- or national-level Baldrige assessment or develop a Baldrige-based in-house assessment program. The more formal state and national Baldrige assessments make use of independent, externally trained examiners to assess the organization. The resulting feedback report identifies the most critical strengths and opportunities for improvement, based on the level of development or maturity of the organization.

Other Process Improvement Initiatives

In addition to Six Sigma, there are various other initiatives that organizations see as opportunities for significant results improvement. Like Six Sigma, these are best viewed as tools for improvement whose deployment can be enhanced by effective alignment with the Baldrige criteria. Two of these tools are Lean Thinking (or Lean Manufacturing, or simply Lean) and the Balanced Scorecard.

OVERVIEW OF LEAN THINKING

Lean can best be described as the relentless pursuit, identification, and elimination of waste in all business processes. Over time, business processes tend to become fat, bloated, and inefficient, Steps are added to processes and become ingrained, after which new steps are added. Too soon, unnecessary process steps become "the way we do things" and the problems become invisible to workers and managers. Without a periodic re-evaluation of each process step's value, increased bloating and inefficiency is inevitable.

Lean Thinking starts with developing Value Stream Maps that describe and document the "current state" of the most important processes. A "future state" map is then developed to show what the process would look like if identified waste were eliminated. Various lean tools are used to help convert the current process to the future state. Lean revolves around developing teams to identify waste, and then reduce waste through processes such as workplace organization, safety, cleanliness, and visual management. In addition, there is a focus on reducing raw material, work-in-process, and finished goods inventory through Just-in-Time production (another improvement tool).

Although the concepts of Lean Thinking are most easily understood and applied in manufacturing, Lean can be a useful tool for virtually all processes within an organization. Lean can be used to eliminate waste in administrative processes (for example, reducing time to generate an invoice), human resources (reducing time to fill open positions), and sales (reducing the time of the sales cycle). Lean Thinking is one way of implementing the Baldrige requirement of evaluating and improving all management processes in all six process categories.

Overview of Balanced Scorecard

Balanced Scorecard is a tool that helps ensure a balanced look at key results measures of an organization. A fundamental belief concerning this tool is that business results are integrated—that you cannot view one measure without acknowledging the relationship to other results. A Balanced Scorecard typically looks at four key elements of the business:

- Financial: "To succeed financially, how should we appear to our shareholders?"

- Customer: "To achieve our vision, how should we appear to our customers?"

- Internal Business Processes: "To satisfy our shareholders and customers, at what business processes must we excel?"

- Learning and Growth: "To achieve our vision, how will we sustain our ability to change and improve?

Objectives, measures, targets, and initiatives are developed for each of the identified perspectives.

The scorecard balances leading and lagging performance indicators as Figure 55 indicates. The most lagging indicator is financial. For example, financial results reflect all of the errors, satisfied customers, lost customers, production efficiencies and inefficiencies, waste, employee motivation, morale, and skill (or lack thereof) that exist in the organization.

An *unbalanced* scorecard (Figure 56) typically looks extensively at financials as the driver of organizational priorities, often to the exclusion of the more predictive indicators such as internal business processes, and learning/growth. Relying too much on financial indicators to drive decisions is comparable to driving an interstate highway by only looking in the rear-view mirror. The scorecard is considered unbalanced as Figure 56 demonstrates.

A properly developed Balanced Scorecard aligns closely with the Results categories of Baldrige (See Figure 57). A well-developed Balanced Scorecard should align with the results expected in Baldrige Category 7 (which are driven by key processes in Baldrige Categories 1–6.)

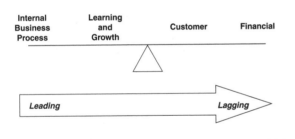

Figure 55   Balanced Scorecard or leading and lagging indicators.

Figure 56   Unbalanced scorecard emphasizing lagging indicators.

Baldrige Results Category	Balanced Scorecard Perspective
7.1 Customer-Focused Results	Customer
7.2 Product and Service Results	Customer-Valued Product and Service Features (part of customer)
7.3 Financial and Market Results	Financial
7.4 Human Resource Results	Learning and Growth
7.5 Organizational Effectiveness Results	Internal Business Processes
7.6 Governance and Social Responsibility Results	*Not specifically examined but may be a part of internal business process results*

Figure 57 Baldrige-balanced scorecard alignment.

Alignment of Baldrige, Lean, Six Sigma, and Balanced Scorecard Factors

The success of Six Sigma, Lean Thinking, and the Balanced Scorecard can be enhanced by a "Culture of Excellence" that is characterized by the Malcolm Baldrige Criteria for Performance Excellence. An integrated Baldrige management system is one of the best predictors of a successful Six Sigma initiative. (See Figure 58) The alignment of Baldrige, Six Sigma, Lean Thinking, and Balanced Scorecards is demonstrated in Figure 59. Note the systematic method by which the Baldrige-based culture of excellence is established, waste is eliminated from processes through Lean Thinking, processes are moved toward perfection using Six Sigma, and progress is measured using a Balanced Scorecard to assess results. *The Baldrige criteria require waste reduction, process improvement, and results that are aligned with business strategies and goals. Six Sigma, Lean Thinking, and Balanced Scorecard tools demonstrate how some organizations have chosen to carry out these requirements.* The goal of this effectively aligned process is to drive beyond incremental improvement to breakthrough improvement—*and breakthrough improvement is where significant competitive advantage is gained.*

Management Challenges	Six Sigma Solution	Baldrige Criteria Values and Requirements
Lack of linkage and alignment throughout the organization	Linkage and alignment of Six Sigma initiative to the business's "bottom line"	**Baldrige Core Value:** Focus on Results and Creating Value **Baldrige Alignment:** Categories 1–6 These "Approach and Deployment" categories must align with Category 7, Business Results. Approach and Deployment processes that don't drive toward improved business results contribute very little value to the organization. Baldrige Category 7, the Baldrige "Results" categories are a balanced set of measures, including Customer-Focused, Product and Service, Financial and Market, Human Resource, and Organizational Effectiveness, and Social Responsibility and Governance results.
Senior leadership delegation of leadership of TQM initiative to Quality or other department	Senior leadership responsibility for success of the Six Sigma initiative	**Baldrige Core Value:** Visionary Leadership **Baldrige Alignment:** Item 1.1a(2) requires leaders to create an environment for empowerment, innovation, organizational agility, and organizational and employee learning. Item 1.1b(3) requires leaders to translate organizational review findings into priorities for improvement and opportunities for innovation
An unclear concept, direction or focus	A leadership-driven, consistent, simple message	**Baldrige Alignment:** Item 1.1a(1) requires top leaders to set and deploy organizational values, directions, and expectations.
An unclear goal	Strong focus on ambitious, non-ambiguous goals	**Baldrige Core Value:** Focus on Results and Creating Value **Baldrige Alignment:** Item 2.1b requires the identification of key strategic objectives and timetables for accomplishing them. These objectives should address the key challenges faced by the organization. Items 6.1 and 6.2 require the improvement of value creation processes and support processes, including the focus on customer/market requirements and the use of key performance measures/indicators to control and improve performance.
One initiative deployed at the expense of others "All eggs in one improvement basket"	A set of "tools" to address problems systematically. Integrates well with other programs such as Baldrige and Lean	**Baldrige Concept:** Baldrige is non-prescriptive. It insists that an organization develop improvement methodologies based on its particular business requirements and current circumstances.
Different organizational "silos" with different improvement initiatives	Cross-functional process focus—integration across the organization	**Baldrige Core Value:** Systems Perspective **Baldrige Concept:** The Baldrige Criteria focus on the integrated business system, aligned with strategic objectives and related action plans, not functional "silos," in a way that demands alignment throughout the organization and ensures links with demonstrated business results.
Incremental versus breakthrough change	Incremental *and* breakthrough change	**Baldrige Concept:** Baldrige-aligned companies continuously compare their results to best practices, both inside and outside an organization's industry. This helps them understand world-class performance to drive to incremental *and* breakthrough process improvement.
Training as an end in itself	Systematic training aligned with business-critical processes	**Baldrige Core Values:** Organizational and Personal Learning; Valuing Employees and Partners **Baldrige Alignment:** Item 5.2 focuses on using education and training to help achieve action plans and strategic objectives, helping to ensure that the organization aligns its education and delivery methods to support key business requirements.
Quality as a product or service characteristic only	Improvement of *all* business processes	**Baldrige Core Values:** Customer-Driven Excellence, Organizational and Personal Learning and Systems Perspective **Baldrige Alignment:** Baldrige Category 6 Process Management 6.1 Product and Service Processes .6.2Business Processes 6.3 Support Processes The Baldrige Criteria go beyond reducing defects and errors, meeting specifications, and reducing complaints. They focus on continuous improvement of all processes throughout the entire organization and ensuring that all parts contribute value to customers.

Figure 58 Alignment of Baldrige, Lean, Six Sigma, and Balanced Scorecard.

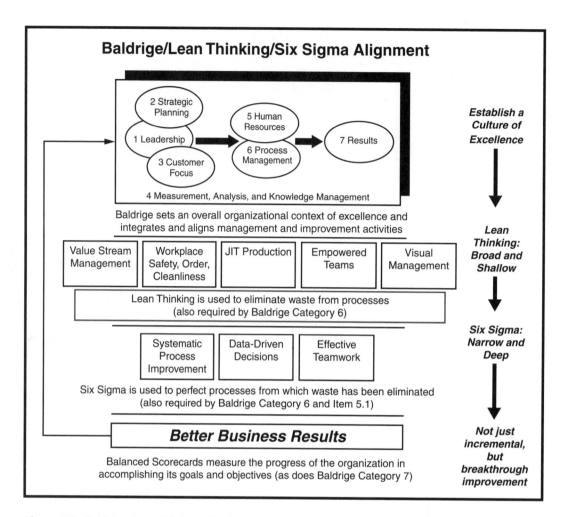

Figure 59   Baldrige, Lean Thinking, Six Sigma.

Effective alignment of the organization through use of the Baldrige Criteria for Performance Excellence can help jump-start Six Sigma initiatives by formalizing leadership commitment, ensuring appropriate resource availability based on the importance of a project to the organization, and providing an aligned management system that focuses the organization's efforts on the right improvement projects. Baldrige is a management system that focuses and aligns *performance excellence* activities. Six Sigma is a tool that focuses *performance improvement* activities.

This section was prepared by Paul Grizzell of the Performance Leadership Group with input from Mark Blazey.

About the Author

Mark L. Blazey, EdD

Mark Blazey is the president of Quantum Performance Group, a management consulting and training firm specializing in organization assessment and high-performance systems development. Dr. Blazey has an extensive background in quality systems. For five years he served as a senior examiner for the Malcolm Baldrige National Quality Award. He also served as the lead judge for the quality awards for New York State, Vermont, and Aruba, and a judge for the Wisconsin Forward Award and Delaware Quality Award. Dr. Blazey has participated on and led numerous site-visit teams for national, state, and company-private quality awards and audits over the past 15 years.

Dr. Blazey has trained thousands of quality award examiners and judges for state and national quality programs including the Alabama Quality Award, Delaware Quality Award, Illinois Lincoln Award for Business Excellence, Kentucky Quality Award, Minnesota Quality Award, New York State Quality Award, Pennsylvania Quality Leadership Award, Nebraska Quality Award, Vermont Quality Award, Wisconsin Forward Award, Aruba Quality Award, Costa Rica Quality Award, and the national Workforce Excellence Network Award, as well as managers and examiners for schools, healthcare organizations, major businesses, and government agencies. He has set up numerous Baldrige-based programs to enhance and assess performance excellence for all sectors and types of organizations, many of which have subsequently received State and Baldrige recognition.

Dr. Blazey has written many books and articles on quality, including the ASQ Quality Press bestseller *Insights to Performance Excellence*, and co-authored *Insights to Performance Excellence in Education* and *Insights to Performance Excellence in Health Care*. He is a member and a certified quality auditor of the American Society for Quality.

Dr. Blazey may be contacted via e-mail at authors @asq.org or Blazey@QuantumPerformance.com or by telephone at 315-986-9200. He encourages feedback, recommendations, and questions about this book.

Index

Note: Italicized page numbers indicate illustrations.

A

accountability, 54
action plans, 119–20
actionable information, 136
agility, 191
agility, as core value, 333
alignment, of work unit, 119–20
anecdotal, 253
application,
    2004 Application template, CD-ROM
    instructions, CD-ROM
    preparation for, 237–46
award categories, and point values, 80
award criteria
    organization of, 79
    See also Baldrige criteria; criteria
award criteria framework, 77–79
award cycle fees, 246, CD-ROM
award winners, 9–22, CD-ROM

B

Baldrige criteria
    versus certification programs, 357–48
    2004 Award criteria, CD-ROM
    worldwide use, 23
    See also award criteria; criteria
beginning implementation, 6
behaviorally anchored survey, 287–92
    sample, 293–302
benchmarking data, 55–56, 147
brain center, 78–79, 145, *78*
business results, 57–58, 77–78, *78*
Business Results, Category 7, 209–36
    7.1 Customer-Focused Results,
        211–14
        Adverse Consequences, 214
        Approach/Deployment, 211
        discussion, 211–12
        Item Linkages, 213–14
        Sample Effective Results, 214
    7.2 Product and Service Results,
        215–18
        Adverse Consequences, 218
        Approach/Deployment, 215
        discussion, 215–16
        Item Linkages, 217
        Sample Effective Results, 218
    7.3 Financial Results, 219–22
        Adverse Consequences, 222

Approach/Deployment, 219
    discussion, 219–20
    Item Linkages, 221
    Sample Effective Results, 222
7.4 Human Resource Results, 223–27
    Adverse Consequences, 227
    Approach/Deployment, 223
    discussion, 224–25
    Item Linkages, 226
    Sample Effective Results, 227
7.5 Organizational Effectiveness
        Results, 228–31
    Adverse Consequences, 231
    Approach/Deployment, 228
    discussion, 228–29
    Item Linkages, 230
    Sample Effective Results, 232
7.6 Governance and Social
        Responsibility Results, 232–35
    Adverse Consequences, 235
    Approach/Deployment, 232
    discussion, 232–333
    Item Linkages, 234
    Sample Effective Results, 235

C

calibration guidelines, 248
CEO skills, 5
CEO survey, 4–5
change management, 49, 59–60
competency gaps, 4–5
competition, 5
competitive comparison, 147
complaint information, 136–37
compliance model, versus
        maturity/excellence model,
        Appendix B, 337–40, CD-ROM
        Appendix D, 345–48, CD-ROM
contacts, state and regional awards,
        CD-ROM
contephobia, 54
continuous improvement, 81, 252–53, *82*
core training, 45
core values, 30–38
    agility, 33
    customer-driven excellence, 31
    focus on results and creating value,
        37
    focus on the future, 34
    management by fact, 35
    managing for innovation, 35
    organizational and personal learning,
        31

social responsibility, 36
    systems perspective, 37
    valuing employees and partners, 32
    visionary leadership, 30
cost reduction, 4, 191
criteria
    changes from 2003, 82
    key characteristics of, 81
    worldwide use of, 23
    See also award criteria; Baldrige
        criteria
critical skills, 45
customer and market focus, 53–54
Customer and Market Focus, Category 3,
    127–44
    3.1 Customer and Market
        Knowledge, 127, 128–34
        Adverse Consequences, 133
        Approach/Deployment, 128
        discussion, 129–31
        Item Linkages, 132
        Sample Effective Practices, 134
    3.2 Customer Relationships and
        Satisfaction, 127, 134–44
        Adverse Consequences,
            142–43–34
        Approach/Deployment, 135
        discussion, 136–39
        Item Linkages, 140–41
        Sample Effective Practices, 144
customer requirements, 24–25, *25*
customer satisfaction, 137–38
customer-driven excellence, as core
        value, 31
cycle-time reduction, 4, 191

D

dashboard, to monitor progress, 27, *27*
data alignment, 147
data analysis, 147–49
Deming Prize, 1, 343
Deming, W. Edwards, 1, 343
dot-coms, 2
DRIP, 54
driver triad, 77, *77*

E

eligibility forms, CD-ROM
eligibility guidelines, CD-ROM
employee feedback, 52
employee management, 4
employee performance management, 165

359

employee satisfaction, 56
European Quality Award (EQA), 335–36
    compared to Baldrige, *335*
expected results, 244, *320*

F

fear, 54
focus on results and creating value, as
    core value, 37
focus on the future, as core value, 34

G

global view, of quality, Appendix A,
    335–36
globalization, 3
glossary, 323–30
good citizenship, 101–2
guidelines, for criteria response, 240
    Process Items, 240–42
    data and measures, 243–45
    general, 237
    Results Items, 242–45

H

Hendricks, Kevin B., 6–7
human resource focus, 55–56
Human Resource Focus, Category 5,
    163–90
    5.1 Work Systems, 163, 164–73
        Adverse Consequences, 170–71
        Approach/Deployment, 164
        discussion, 165–67
        Item Linkages, 168–69
        Sample Effective Practices,
            172–73
    5.2 Employee Learning and
        Motivation, 163, 174–82
        Adverse Consequences, 180–81
        Approach/Deployment, 174
        discussion, 175–77
        Item Linkages, 178–79
        Sample Effective Practices, 182
    5.3 Employee Well-Being and
        Satisfaction, 163, 183–90
        Adverse Consequences, 188–89
        Approach/Deployment, 183–84
        discussion, 184–86
        Item Linkages, 187
        Sample Effective Practices, 190

I

If Japan Can, Why Can't We?, 1
implementation cycle, of quality
    management, 6
information and analysis, 49
innovation, managing for, as core value,
    30

integrated management systems, 24–28
    consequences of missing elements,
        29
integrated systems, 252
International Organization for
    Standardization (ISO), 337
ISO 9001, 337–338, *339*

J

JCAHO, 345
    comparison to Baldrige, 345–48

K

knowledge management, 3

L

leadership, 26–27, 50–52, *27*
Leadership, Category 1, 89–106
    1.1 Organizational Leadership, 90–99
        Adverse Consequences, 96–97
        Approach/Deployment, 90–91
        discussion, 91–93
        Item Linkages, 94–95
        Sample Effective Practices, 98–99
    1.2 Social Responsibility, 100–106
        Adverse Consequences, 105
        Approach/Deployment, 100
        discussion, 101–3
        Item Linkages, 104
        Sample Effective Practices, 106
leadership practices, 59–62
learning, organizational and personal, as
    core value, 26
lessons learned, 46–58
    customer and market focus, 53–54
    human resource focus, 55–56
    measurement, analysis, and
        knowledge management,
        54–55
    leadership, 50–52
    process management, 57
    results, 57–58
    strategic planning, 52–53
Likert scale survey, 287
Link, Albert N., 22

M

Malcolm Baldrige National Quality
    Award (MBNQA)
    compared to EQA, 335, *335*
    economic impact of, 17
    establishment of, 1–3
    key purpose, 1
management by fact, as core value, 35
Management Effectiveness Survey, 64,
    66–67

managing for innovation, as core value,
    35
manufacturing, 4
market size, *5*
mature implementation, 6–7
maturity/excellence model, versus
    compliance model,
        Appendix B, 337–39
        Appendix D, 345–348
measurement, analysis, and knowledge
    management , 55–56
Measurement, Analysis, and Knowledge
    Management,
    Category 145–61
    4.1 Measurement and Analysis of
        Organizational Performance,
        145, 146–54
        Adverse Consequences, 152–53
        Approach/Deployment, 146
        discussion, 147–50
        Item Linkages, 151
        Sample Effective Practices, 154
    4.2 Information and Knowledge
        Management, 145, 155–61
        Adverse Consequences, 159–60
        Approach/Deployment, 155
        discussion, 156–57
        Item Linkages, 158
        Sample Effective Practices, 161
motivated people, 25–26, *25*

N

"The Nation's CEOs Look to the
    Future," 3–5

O

optimum performance, 24
    keys to, 59–62
organizational and personal learning, as
    core value, 31
Organizational Profile, 83–87
    importance of, 83
    P.1 Organizational Description, 84
        Item Linkages, 85
    P.2 Organizational Challenges, 86
        Item Linkages, 87

P

performance excellence standards,
    70–75
performance improvement council,
    38–45
    council membership, 39
    critical skills, 45
    customer value champion, 41–42
    human resources focus champion,
        43–44
    learning and planning, 39

measurement, analysis, and
  knowledge management
  champion, 42–43
organizational leadership champion,
  39–40
process management champion,
  44–45
results champion, 45
strategic planning champion, 40–41
performance standards, for managers,
  68–72, *72–76*
plan–do–check–act (PDCA), 81, *81*
point values, and award categories, 80
potential customers, definition of, 129
prevention-based systems, 252
process management, 57
Process Management, Category 6,
  191–208
  6.1 Value Creation Processes, 191,
    192–202
    Adverse Consequences, 198–200
    Approach/Deployment, 192–93
    discussion, 193–96
    Item Linkages, 197–98
    Sample Effective Practices,
      201–2
  6.2 Support Processes, 191, 203–8
    Adverse Consequences, 207
    Approach/Deployment, 203
    discussion, 204–5
    Item Linkages, 206
    Sample Effective Practices, 208
processes, 25–26, *25*
promising practice, 2

Q

quality, use of word, 51

R

Regional Quality Award Contacts,
  CD-ROM
research study, Hendricks and Singhal,
  6–7

results, 57–58
results, focus on, as core value, 37

S

scoring, clarifications, 257–58
scoring, guidelines
  by category, 259–84
  expected observations, 259–84
scoring requirements,
  basic, 256
  multiple, 257
  overall, 256–57
scoring system, 247–54
  Approach/Deployment Items, 247
  dimensions, 247–48
  results, 247–48
Scott, John T., 22
self-assessments, 285–92
  behaviorally anchored survey,
    287–92
  full-length written narrative,
    285–86
  short written narrative, 286–87
  survey approach, 287
seven must-do practices, 59–62
Singhal, Vinod R., 6–10
site visit, 303–321
  characteristics of, 303–04
  conduct of examiners, 305
  conducting, 305
  general employee questions, 321
  generic questions, by category,
    306–20
  important issues, 304
  preceding discussions, 304–05
  purpose of, 303
social responsibility, as core value, 36
stakeholders, 5
State Quality Award contacts, CD-ROM
strategic planning, 53–54
Strategic Planning, Category 2,
  107–26
  2.1 Strategy Development, 108,
    109–17

    Adverse Consequences, 116
    Approach/Deployment,
      109–10
    discussion, 110–13
    Item Linkages, 114–15
    Sample Effective Practices, 117
  2.2 Strategy Deployment, 108,
    118–26
    Adverse Consequences, 124
    Approach/Deployment, 118
    discussion, 119–22
    Item Linkages, 123
    Sample Effective Practices,
      125–26
strategies, execution of, 5
strategy, 28
supply chains, 4
systems, 252
systems perspective, as core value, 37

T

table of expected results, 244, *320*
terms, clarification of, 331–33
training, 55–56
trends, in business environments, 3–5

U

U.S. Congress, 23
upward feedback, 64–65

V

valuing employees and partners, as core
  value, 32
visionary leadership, as core value, 30

W

winners, list of, 9–22, CD-ROM
work core, 77, *77*
work results, 24
written narratives, 285–87